CONTRIBUTORS

Letitia J. Allan Psychologist, Department of Community Welfare, Perth, Western Australia

J. J. Gayford Consultant Psychiatrist and Consultant-in-Charge of the Alcoholic Unit, Warlingham Park Hospital

Richard J. Gelles Associate Professor of Sociology, University of Rhode Island

Bill Jordan Lecturer in Social Work, University of Exeter

Peter Loizos Lecturer in Social Anthropology, London School of Economics and Political Science

F. H. McClintock Professor of Criminology, University of Edinburgh

Dennis Marsden Senior Lecturer in Sociology, University of Essex

J. P. Martin Professor of Sociology and Social Administration, University of Southampton

Margaret May Senior Lecturer in Social Policy, City of London Polytechnic

Joy Melville Assistant Editor, *New Society*

Jean Packman Senior Lecturer in Social Administration and Social Work, University of Exeter

Jacquie Roberts Research Social Worker, The Park Hospital, Oxford

North West Region of the National Women's Aid Federation has endorsed chapter 13 which was written by a practising social worker

Violence and The Family

Edited by

J. P. Martin

Department of Sociology and Social Administration
University of Southampton

JOHN WILEY & SONS

Chichester · New York · Brisbane · Toronto

Library of Congress Cataloging in Publication Data:

Main entry under title:

Violence and the Family.

Includes index.

1. Conjugal violence—Addresses, essays, lectures. 2. Wife beating—Addresses, essays, lectures. 3. Child abuse—Addresses, essays, lectures. I. Martin, John Powell.

HQ728.V55 301.42'7 77–21846

ISBN 0 471 99576 2

Typeset by Computacomp (UK) Ltd., Fort William, Scotland, and printed by Unwin Brothers Ltd., The Gresham Press, Old Woking, Surrey

CONTENTS

INTRODUCTION

J. P. Martin

The home can be a dangerous place, particularly for women and children. The family, the most intimate group to which the majority of people belong, at its best is an unrivalled source of strength and comfort, but its very closeness can also intensify the worst in human relations. Love may be corrupted to envious possession, and discipline to cruelty. Above all, the private focus of hopes and fears may foster dual standards of private and public behaviour.

There is nothing new in these observations. The English theatre would be impoverished indeed if deprived of such themes, but they have had a less central place in academic literature, so that volumes on violence in a family setting are comparatively rare. Several factors make this an appropriate time for a further survey of what has recently been given new emphasis as a social problem. In England, publicity relating to 'battered wives', together with a series of notorious cases of abuse resulting in the deaths of children, have combined to arouse public concern. In 1975 the House of Commons set up a Select Committee to consider Violence in Marriage, and in 1976 this was reconstituted with the wider brief of covering Violence in the Family.

Second, the general development of the women's movement has led to a more insistent questioning of the inequality of the partners in marriage. Naturally this includes the notion that one member has a right to inflict pain and suffering on the other if they fail to do what is expected of them. Some such rights are still accepted in respect of children, but even these are increasingly subject to scrutiny.

Third, both the increase in divorce and the continuingly high proportion of violent crime that occurs in the form of domestic disputes are powerful indicators of aspects of family relations which constitute social problems in themselves and which also raise difficult questions of interpretation in law enforcement.

For all these reasons there is, *prima facie*, a social problem deserving comprehensive analysis and discussion. But how far is it a single problem? How legitimate is it to talk about violence *and the family*. Why not just consider child abuse and wife battering separately?

Without attempting to pre-empt any of the conclusions reached in this volume it seems justified to discern a number of common threads sufficient to link the various forms in which violence may be related to family life. In the first place, in a significant proportion of cases there is an actual overlap, families where both mother and children are maltreated. Second, children of battered wives are themselves often affected by the experience and later, as adults, may evolve similar patterns of behaviour in their own marriages. Third, there seem to be some psychological factors in common, in that violence is often provoked by the failure of woman or child to respond to husband or parent in the way deemed appropriate, and reaction to this frustration is violent.

Fourth, there is also a series of more general sociological factors. The first is in the existence of cultural settings in which violence is seen to provide a 'solution', or to be an appropriate reaction, to personal problems. Violence above a certain degree may not be positively approved, but some at least may be regarded as legitimate, or perhaps merely condoned as being regrettable but understandable in the circumstances. The violent person, needing some rationalization for his or her behaviour, may be able to find it in the knowledge that such a substratum of tacit approval exists.

A second apparently widespread sociological influence is the fact that for many people, and in many societies, members of a family are in some way seen as constituting the property of its head. Undoubtedly this implies that he has responsibilities towards them, but these may be less strictly interpreted and enforced than his corresponding rights over them. In so far as such notions of a wife or child's duties hold sway then failure to perform them may be held to justify violent punishment.

Family violence also presents peculiarly testing problems of law enforcement. What happens in the home may be subject to both civil and criminal law, but even though the notion that 'an Englishman's home is his castle' has been significantly eroded (and the phrase is now rarely heard) legal intervention is far from easy. Events in a house or apartment are usually invisible, and may even be inaudible, to outsiders. If domestic violence occurs someone has to take the initiative of bringing it into the open.

The sufferings of an abused child almost certainly have to be discovered and revealed by others. An abused woman may voice her own complaint but, having done so, she faces problems of substantiating it and, above all, of sustaining it while in fear of further violence, particularly if still living in the house. It will be all too clear to her that the law may consist of no more than an occasional crisis visit from policemen reluctant to intervene, and the threat of punishment for her tormentor only as the aftermath of her renewed suffering. None of these may be of much help to her when threatened by a violent man in the early hours of the morning: as one witness told the Select Committee.

I have been to the police. I nicked my husband. He gave me ten

> stitches, and they held him in the nick over the weekend and he came out on Monday. He was bound over to keep the peace, that was all. On the Tuesday he gave me the hiding of my life. (SC 1975, Evid. Q. 99)

Even when legal intervention takes place the interpretation of what has occurred may be highly dependent on social considerations. Not only are there ambiguities about what may be legitimate in punishing children, but the seriousness with which marital violence is viewed will probably be related to actual, or supposed, local customs. Wide variations, therefore, may occur from area to area.

The last social factor to be reckoned with is the unwillingness of people to recognize the existence of violence in a family setting. This is not so much a total denial of the possibility as a tendency to maintain 'it can't happen here'. It seems that doctors can find it hard to suspect their patients, social workers dislike violent situations, while public authorities naturally do not want to draw attention to such aspects of their areas. Rather than a conspiracy of silence it is reluctance to get involved in situations fraught with tensions, and possibly danger. The memory of older more violent traditions, ostensibly buried, may nevertheless linger on, providing yet another rationalization for non-interference, on the basis that this is just a vestigial remnant of what was once widespread.

These social and psychological threads may be found running through all types of family violence, and any policy must take them into account. The manifold ways in which they do so will be shown in greater detail in the chapters that follow.

This volume is intended to make a comprehensive examination of the subject from a variety of points of view. It has three main aims: first, to give an indication of what is known about family violence, and to put this knowledge in a psychological and sociological perspective. Second, to describe and discuss policies and practices which may help to prevent or mitigate the sufferings of the victims. Third, to contribute to a longer-term process of education, both for social workers and other professionals, and for the public in general.

All the contributions have been specially commissioned, and this has resulted in a happy blend of established authorities and relative newcomers to academic publication. All, however, are able to write from a knowledge of recent research and, in some cases, direct experience. The approach is deliberately eclectic; the authors have a common concern about the suffering involved, but have been encouraged to develop their suggested topics in their own ways. In the last chapter the editor attempts to draw from this diversity certain common themes, to elicit underlying assumptions, and to suggest certain broad implications for social development and public policy.

Although a book having its roots in Britain inevitably tends to focus on the local situation it tries hard to avoid an excessive parochialism of the here and now. Hence we include studies relating to the United States, and to Mediterranean cultures, while Britain is also considered in the perspective of a social historian. On the other hand the discussion of family violence as a problem for policy and social service administration is unashamedly based on a close examination of what happens in England and Wales. Because it is so detailed and specific the reader able to compare this with his or her own situation may find this more instructive than broader and vaguer generalities. Whatever the differences in social service organization the problems themselves are likely to be formed from similar ingredients even if combined with different emphases. There may indeed be considerable advantages in presenting a fairly comprehensive review of what happens in one small country with a coherent system of law and welfare provision. The main conclusions, however, are stated as far as possible in general terms by no means restricted to Britain. The actual structure of the book is as follows:

PART I is primarily concerned to illustrate marital violence and the kind of family life which may result. This is done both by presenting individual case studies and by a clinician considering what can be learned from a sample of battered women.

PART II considers the context of family violence and demonstrates a number of perspectives. A psychologist surveys the literature on child abuse, a criminologist examines the statistical evidence, while a sociologist relates family violence to various theories of the nature of society. An important comparative view is provided by an historical consideration of family violence in Britain, and by studies of the United States and of some Mediterranean countries.

PART III focuses on family violence as a social problem in England and Wales. Chapter 9 attempts to consider, as systematically as possible, what social service organization is needed, and how it might be established. It covers the issues of law enforcement, housing, and social security, and the role of the social services in protecting children in public care.

Various practical measures are discussed. Chapter 11 describes the characteristics of some refuges for battered women, the development of which, perhaps more than any other factor, made it possible to reopen the subject of marital violence. Previously many women felt they had to put up with violence for want of any realistic way out of their difficulties; refuges, while not a solution in themselves, pointed to the possibility that alternatives might exist. Social work as such is dealt with in two chapters, a longer one discussing work on behalf of abused children, (chapter 10) and a shorter one more concerned with what might be done if social work was to concern itself seriously with the needs of battered women (chapter 13). Equally important is to know how battering men might be helped. To illustrate some possibilities a brief account is given of Men's Aid, a recently established centre for men who want to do something about their own marital violence.

Having considered fairly fully what social workers might do for the victims of family violence it was logical to ask how well they may be equipped to face what may be very traumatic situations, and how social-work education might be improved in this respect. If one thing is clear, both from the inquiries into child deaths and from our own contributions on social work, it is that young and quite inexperienced social workers are liable to find themselves facing situations of social difficulty that would tax even the most mature. We have, therefore, included a chapter by two experienced social-work teachers who have thought about the problem, and consulted present and former students in finding ways of helping students to meet it. In this way it is hoped not only to pass on knowledge about family violence, but also to add to the literature of social-work education.

It is impossible to summarize in one chapter all the evidence and comment of the the contributors, but certain broad conclusions can be drawn, and these are discussed in the editor's final chapter.

PART I

The Experience of Family Violence

1

SOME VIOLENT FAMILIES

Joy Melville

These accounts of violence in families were complied from interviews with battered women who had finally left home and gone to refuges. They are, therefore, partial accounts, but give a vivid impression of some milieux of family violence, always affecting the wife, but often the children as well. Between them they illustrate many of the points dealt with in a more systematic way in later chapters. They do not, however, cover cases where the only victims are children who suffer at the hands of their parents; first-hand accounts from such sources are obviously difficult to obtain, but a number of cases of child abuse are described in Jacquie Roberts's chapter later in this book.

All the wives were interviewed while resident in refuges, and this was done anonymously. For the purposes of these accounts it seemed better to give them names rather than numbers, and this has been done on a simple principle of working through the alphabet.

ANN BROWN

He was my second husband. I had two young kids by my first, and one by him. He came from a very bad home life, his father was the same. Basically the trouble was that he used to fly into moods over trivial things and then became violent and then be all right. He was so helpful when we were first married. He would bring up breakfast, or a cup of tea. You couldn't wish for a better man. About 3 months after we were married, he went into one of his moods.

He would sit there and not speak for days and days. I remember once, I lit my own cigarette and he went into a mood over that; or if I had dinner before him. He did not know how to treat children; he dominated and suffocated us and his word was law. 'I am the man in my home,' he'd say. Sometimes, if I spoke out of turn, he'd threaten to put my head through the window.

I was a few months off having his son, and he gave me a head butt. Once I was nearly strangled because I drew some money out of the Post Office. For a month I could hardly speak. And he was cruel to the children, mentally cruel, because he used to put us into fear. We all knew what was going to come. I can't describe the fear he put us all through, like living in a nightmare world. When he was in one of his moods, everyone suffered.

Of course he never worked, always on the dole. I had spoken to his probation officer; and then the police were called in twice because my family phoned to say he was terrorizing the family. I spoke to the social worker too. In fact one of them had to get the eldest girl a job, as he was always after her and the worst that ever happened was when I was taken into hospital (we were in caravan) and he locked all three children in the bedroom and terrorized my daughter.

One day he was so unkind; wouldn't let the youngest boy have his toy and it was freezing cold and he kept punching and smacking him until that child started to pee. I can't describe it, it was horrible. He did not know if he was coming or going. He'd make me take my make-up off, throw the lipstick on the fire. He turned to hate, just full of hate. It was the way he was brought up, you could feel sorry for him. His mother is a so-and-so to him. If they can't feel love, they can't return it. To live in fear, worse than beating. I was a prisoner, never allowed to breathe, but he could do as he liked.

I went out with my daughter once and he came in and I wasn't there. When I came in he tore the water pipe out and put his fist through the door, yelling. The children sat on the settee in terror. I carried on washing up. If I had said anything he would have turned on me, they knew it.

I had been trying to escape for 3 years—I'd only been married for 4—but if you haven't anywhere to go, how can you take four children on the streets? I grew up in a home with a lot of love, no fear, and then suddenly you get involved with a creature like him. There was nothing nice about him. Though he liked his dogs: he thought more of them than his family.

If he could be treated and probably have an operation, then I'd go back because I still think a lot of him. I am married to him, he is my husband. If men like him had help, then a lot of women and children would be spared this. But society says treatment has got to be voluntary and this type of man doesn't believe there is anything wrong with them. He was very sorry after he hit me: 'I am sorry me baby, I did not mean to do that.' Most of the time he treated me very good, it's just this hate he fills up with.

You get all that 'please come back' when you've left them. But the leopard can't change its spots. They can promise you the earth, but you know if you come back what you will let yourself and your children in for.

CAROL DAVIES

It's difficult to accept yourself as a battered wife as the term isn't right. I have had a lot of marital troubles, which have included violence. Despite all my attempts to make the marriage work, I had no choice but to get away. So I got out and was put in touch with this refuge, who accepted the problems that I had got and prepared to give me refuge while I tried to get divorce proceedings going.

My husband still can't accept that. He did not believe that I had made my mind up and wouldn't carry on. He drank a lot; some physical violence. The mental cruelty is very difficult to prove. He did not work, I didn't have enough money, and our children would go hungry, I would get knocked about and he was staying out at night; many times he would hit me but not know it, he was so drunk, and wouldn't let me go out on my own. He wanted me to be a general housewife for him, to stay at home and cook and wash.

A lot of women say 'What do I do?' I had had such feelings for a long time. When I went to social security, they said, go to a solicitor, which I did and was advised to leave my husband. My family came from time to time; they knew I had difficulties, but not the extent—because I felt embarrassed. I just tried to pacify him. So many times he would say, 'I did not mean it,' so it meant something to him to hit me. A way of releasing his feelings.

When I first met him, until I had my child, I did not have many problems; he seemed to accept me as someone with my own feelings. But when the child came along, he did not appear to take it as his responsibility, but as mine, and tried to dictate that I should stay at home and should do this and not that and be a good wife. This appeared to be where the problems started, he would pass over the responsibility of the children and then he started drinking.

He was there during the day, and hated me to go out. He would never let me go to social security or even the doctor.

To a certain extent it helps to know that other people are in a similar situation because in your own home, there's no one else to say, 'I know how you feel.'

ELLEN FRENCH

A few weeks after we were married, he started to suffocate me with a pillow. We had just had an argument about the usual thing in marriage [sex] and I left him and went back to my mother and he knew where I had gone. He got on his knees, and he cried, and like a fool I went back and he started kicking me after that. We were living in one room and he dominated me from then on. Life was a living hell, and I put up with him 26 years. If there had been a place like this refuge 20 years ago, I would have gone then. Went to my sister's, but she only wanted me so many days, and then I had to go back.

It was the drink; that was his main problem all through his married life: he was violent with drink: it made him worse than he was. He was always nasty tempered. He was nice until we were married, but things changed when I got a ring on my finger. He started getting jealous, asking who I was with at home, very possessive. I always had a bruise on me, from him knocking me around.

I have been living with him now for 26 years: how many times I have left him I have no idea. I just had to get away because of his violent temper. Then I became pregnant, and had a baby. I was breastfeeding her and he started knocking me about. I left the baby with him, went back to mother and had to have tablets to get rid of the milk because I was that frightened to go back for a while.

Each time I had a child he got worse. I went 14 years and then had a son, and he got worse then ever since having this last baby and that's what caused me to leave him for the last time. He has got his own house and there is nothing there I want. He is contesting the divorce, wants me back. Sends me really stirring letters, eight pages, pathetic they are. My daughter brings them: he doesn't know where I am. I am glad, with his violence.

I'll tell you what he used to do with my two eldest daughters. He used to make them stand in the bedroom and watch us in bed. He had a belt at the bottom of the bed. He was sexually disturbed in that way. He used to throw things at me: slippers, knives, tins, eggs, everything out of the larder—and Saturday night, all the supper pots. I never had any cups; he smashed everything I had got. Revolting the way he went on. I just made up my mind I had to get away and my sister helped me. I was losing weight: I went down to 7 stone. I went to social services and they got me away. I met him one day in town. He was kissing me all over: nearly went on his knees. He said, 'Will you come back?' I said, 'I'll consider it', just to get rid of him.

I have slept in empty houses; on seats; in a woman's toilet one night—just frightened to go home. He used to lock the door. 'You are not coming back in here tonight.' He said I'd been with other men, but I had not as I hardly ever used to go out. No one was allowed into the house when he was there: 'Lock the door when I have gone to work,' he'd say. When I went shopping, he would go on: 'Where have you been?' He was the man of the house and I had not got to forget it. He would say, 'I am going to do what I like.' He thought a woman had to be dominated. He had his friends, that was different. I would sit up and wait, even at 1 a.m.: daren't go to bed without him. He used to keep me talking in bed till about 4 a.m. I was dead beat. Next morning, I got his clothes and boots ready and he would say, 'I will have a day off today.' He only worked 3 or 4 weeks a year. When I left, he wouldn't go to work, and he hasn't worked since.

No point in going back because it would only happen again. It got worse each time I went back: still bruises on me since Christmas. I said, 'Are you going to have treatment?' and he said, 'I am not having nothing,' and I said, 'You will be sorry.' He said, 'You won't have the guts to leave me.' If the refuge had not been here, I couldn't have carried on, I had nowhere to go. The other people in the refuge help you: we talk about different things.

A neighbour called the police once. My husband said, 'This is my house, I own it, no one is coming through the door.' The police used to argue with him. But they just said to me, 'See how it goes on.' He is not going to change now, he likes the drink. I said, 'If you pack the drink up, I will stay with you.' My daughter never wants to see him again as long as he lives.

In the middle of the night, many's the time I have picked the baby out of his cot and put him in the pram and gone out of the door into the freezing cold with him and walked the streets and he has fetched us back. He'd say, 'It's my house, I pay for it. If you don't like it, do the other.' He used to pick the baby up by his ears. He used to belt the eldest two, and they had to go to school with marks. He used to tie my hands behind my back. Once he painted my body all different colours. I once went to bed and put a knife under the mattress. He would stand there with the scissors and say, 'Come and use them.' He was frightened when I put the knife there. I said, 'If you ever do that again, I will use it.' They are cowards at heart, if anyone else tries to threaten them.

It's just made me bitter, for what have I done to have to put up with this? I thought God was good. I have prayed many a time to God. No one has cried more than I have. I have tried to commit suicide. I took tablets, but it didn't work. It's made me bitter for being what I have to him. I used to go to work and give him money and cook for him. I never had a dirty house, because I was like that. I didn't deserve it and that I can't forgive him for.

GILLIAN HAYES

I had 9 very happy years with my husband. Then he became a director of a company at 29 and the managing director would take my husband off with him; and that was when the trouble started. He started gambling, drinking, getting back at 3 a.m. and 4 a.m.

He was always picking fights with me and our eldest daughter, never the boy. If he came home late, that would start an argument. Life was absolute hell. I had left him several times, but only went to my sister's and I had to go back again. I started training as a nurse at the hospital; but he would go off and leave the children on their own. He did this to get me out of nursing. He kept saying I was wearing the trousers. Once before, when I wanted a Saturday job, he went up the wall. He said, 'My mother went to work and left us.' But I wanted to go to work to get away from four walls and the baby. He had a terrible hangup over women having any sort of independence, so I had to give up my nursing. They would have given me leave of absence; but he took an overdose.

He lost his job and we lived on social security. He was still drinking. Once, in a frenzy, he smashed the car up and was in a flaming temper and demanded money. I had not got any. The children were downstairs and he threw my handbag across the floor and sloshed me. He followed me downstairs when one of the children called me and then got hold of me and started to bang my head viciously against the wall. The little boy picked up a milk bottle and smashed it and stuck it into his father's arm and that stopped him. By that time I had collapsed and the police came and then fetched the doctor. I couldn't stop wetting myself with fear. The police stayed outside patrolling and finally went and much later on he came home. By this time the doctor had put me to bed and I remember still saying, 'I haven't got any money, don't come near.' But by that time he had calmed down. Next day, I rang my sister and said, 'I have got to get out.' I planned the move. I told him I'd have dinner ready, but the moment he was out of the door, I was on the train to London, with two kids, a bike, and a dog. My sister met me, took me to a nearby room she had managed to rent for me, and he couldn't find me. My little boy wouldn't leave my side. One day he took a knife to school, to keep as protection for me in case I was attacked.

I was still in love with my husband, but I went through with a divorce, hoping the shock of it would bring him to his senses. Every Sunday he would turn up and give me the old love stuff. He gave me a new engagement ring the next Christmas, which I 'could wear when I wanted to'. He gave me the full treatment. He said he wasn't drinking, and he certainly wasn't in my presence. No tremors, or shakes. I moved back near to where he was, as my sister herself moved. The pressure was on me every weekend to remarry. He was wonderful to my daughter, whereas before he had been really horrible and knocked her about.

After a time, I went back to him again. I was typical of any stupid woman who keeps saying, 'I love him.' It wasn't long before things gradually deteriorated. He used to make us sit up in chairs and listen to him lecture us. We couldn't go to bed until he said, even though we were tired. When I did, I would get blamed for his impotency and I used to get kicked out of bed. He bought sex books to stimulate him, but drink made him impotent.

He started knocking us about again, particularly the daughter. If I got up to prevent it, I would get knocked across the room. It was always when she was going out: 2 minutes before she went, he would tell her she couldn't go. She was 15. One night he ripped the phone out of the wall because I was going to ring 999. My elder daughter got out of the French window and when she came back he threw her out. I said, if she goes, I go. We got a taxi and he followed and came into the hotel and made such a scene that we had to leave.

One evening my daughter was going out and I was outside the house when I heard these violent screams. I went flying back—no one will come to your aid—and he had smashed her glasses into her face. She was in a terrible state. I am sure the man was insane. After that, my daughter left home. He wouldn't allow her to take her A levels—she got eight O levels—he can't stand brilliant women. His hatred was getting worse. He threw beer all over me in a pub when I had gone to find him, and once hit me on the head with a frying pan. One night he viciously bit me when he was impotent.

He thought I was trapped and started in on the boys. We were still getting lectures at 3 a.m. One night he came in and kept making one boy stand up on a chair. Each time he did, he pushed him down again. I called the police, but my husband became nice and plausible and said the boy was a hysterical child that needed a hiding. The policeman said if I needed help, to give him the word. I phoned my sister next day and she phoned this policeman and got the address of the refuge. I acted as if everything was all right. Everything my husband said, I did. I packed a suitcase and met the boys from school and explained that Mummy was taking them away. I arranged through solicitors that he could see the children but that I would never return. He tried his 'weak' stuff, but it doesn't work any more.

For me, the end came when he started beating my daughter: a mother never forgives her children being hurt. And also when he started demanding I did all those horrible things in sex.

But that fear—I have never been so frightened. For one whole year after that dreadful attack on me, I used to wake up in the night. The mental anguish and torture you put yourself through is ridiculous. He will never get at me again: they are not worth killing yourself for. You don't know where love ends and hate begins. But I had to divorce him and go back before I found out.

IRENE JONES

People often think that battering is exclusively physical, but it's not: it is a mixture of mental and physical. All the women in this refuge have had mental cruelty as well as the physical kind. It's not just the occasional row, it's definitely a chronic habit which progresses from being rude, insolent, and abusive to getting into absolute fits of rages which they can't control. They don't even seem to be in touch with themselves, and it's impossible to communicate with them when they are in these states. They just scream abuse.

They are often very charming socially, but have two different personalities: they save up all their anger for the domestic situation, when suddenly a completely different person appears. The amount of anger, abuse, and screaming is totally inappropriate to what has caused it. After it, they seem quite all right until the next time. But they know how to manipulate the isolation which women are in, because they wouldn't dream of behaving this way to a social worker or a neighbour. They are very careful how they appear to other people and just show this side in private. So people can't believe it, since the man looks such a nice person.

In my case, I only had one indication of what was to come, which was an outburst—a very minor outburst—on the telephone when I was going out with my boyfriend before I married him. I just couldn't understand what had happened and why he was so totally angry and abusive for a totally irrelevant cause. I was very shocked.

My husband is very articulate. He is a university lecturer and all his aggression is verbal: it was only physical about twice. He'd have long outbursts, which went on for 4 hours and got worse and worse and worse. He started blaming me for things I had never done, saying how everybody hated me, and turned completely paranoiac, screaming about what people were saying about me. He attempted to enclose me in a world of fear.

In the end I learned the only escape was to go out. By the time I'd returned he would have calmed down, but I'd still be distraught, crying and that. He'd say, 'What's the matter with you, what have you got that sort of face for?'

And I'd say, 'Don't you know what you've just been saying?' And he'd say, 'There you go again, you're starting up all over again.' He wouldn't let me speak, I couldn't communicate with him. I realized in the end he wasn't making any attempt to get through to me. As a man, he didn't need to bother. He had a good career, nobody questioned what he was doing, nobody really knew. He used me as a convenient way of unleashing work stress.

Another couple near us had terrible rows, but they could communicate after them, they weren't destructive. My husband would say, 'How could this other man be such a bastard.' He could never relate anything to himself.

He did have a difficult childhood. His father drank a lot and got quite violent with him. He was sent away to public school at 7, where he got a very typical male culture: stiff upper lip, no emotions. The boys were caned, and it was very authoritarian and repressive. That was the model of male behaviour which he had. He threw himself into the world of books. He was never allowed to be angry with his father, although he was, murderously so. He had to show respect, so his anger was totally repressed. He got a first at university and became institutionalized. He doesn't function emotionally—he's split between repression and a desire to have deeper personal relationships.

He's charming socially. He never shouts at anyone; and if anybody was rude to him in the street, he would never say anything back. He can't use anger positively. He shows respect to every social or authoritarian figure: but with me, it all came out. He's angry at himself at not being able to be angry at them, so took it out on me. He's totally controlled, but full of aggression, and when he is finally in a socially permitted situation to be angry, without losing face, he goes berserk.

He told me once to get out—screamed that I was getting too dependent on him, and was getting in the way of his work. I did leave, too, and stayed with a relative. I wrote him several letters, and tried to broach the subject of his aggression. After 6 weeks, he came over and he was drunk and started screaming at me about his rights, that he was going to take the baby away and call the police, and that they'd take me back to the matrimonial home which I'd deserted. I sat immobile, didn't say a word, and after a few hourse I made him sit down. He was exhausted by then and broke down and cried. I thought this was a major breakthrough, that he actually cried, and I went back. Two weeks later he'd forgotten all about it. I asked him if he didn't remember why I'd come back, and he said, 'What? When?' Then he started screaming abuse again.

I tried everything I could think of: total silence; showing how upset I was: not showing how upset I was; shouting back saying I wasn't standing for any more. But I used to get exhausted. He would start off again the next day and I couldn't keep up. He would scream that I wasn't fit to be a mother, that I was repressing the child, neglecting him. When he got into one of his screaming fits, he was totally oblivious of the child. Once I was reduced to a catatonic state, just crying and crying, and I tried to leave the room so the child wouldn't get too upset, but he tore my skirt and flung me on the sofa. He would show off the baby in front of relatives: that was important to his image. But he never questioned his own role. When he was a boy, his mother did all the chores and worked hard, and boys were expected to be boys and ride bikes. He was never made conscious of a man's role *in the family*.

When I told him first that I was pregnant, he was thrilled, and then the reality of it hit him, and his aggressive, insolent behaviour started. Before that, we had a lot in common, like a love of studying, and books. Once I told him I loved him, and he went very white and said, 'I know, but I can't.' He put tremendous pressure on me to get married, but this was to appease his relations, because I was expecting his child. He was very frightened of his father. On the phone to him he was so obsequious, unable to have a relaxed conversation.

He doesn't have any male friendships, doesn't share his emotions with anybody. Friends invited him over to dinner recently and apparently he told them that I had left because I had never been committed to him in the first place: and secondly was very involved in women's liberation and had attitudes that made him angry; and thirdly, because my mother persuaded me to.

He dissociated everything from himself. It's easy for a man to escape into a male social world, in which the private side of them is never exposed. He was married before, and was very oppressive in his relationship with his first wife, who was only in her late teens. He tried to mould me, too. I used to have my own books on shelves above my desk, but he kept taking them down and slipping them in between his own books which were all round the rest of the room. When I said I wanted mine all together, he wouldn't have it; he said they were in the room and why did it matter where they were? I kept putting them back, and coming home and finding he'd moved them again. I was writing articles at the time and I think he looked on this as a challenge to him.

His anger and aggression were incredible: he was totally unaware of how much tension he was carrying. He would get very white in an ordinary social situation. I couldn't reach him. He would talk about work as if nothing else mattered. Even if men have had quite fraught childhoods, that doesn't really explain this type of behaviour: one doesn't have to abuse a person constantly. Men exploit the social situation: their attitude is that it's a man's right to treat the woman as he wants. They assume the woman is not going to tell anyone, having nowhere to go. It's the traditional thing that the woman's place is in the home, looking after kids. The conditioning is so deep-seated. I tried to leave and find a place to rent. I traipsed miles trying to find somewhere to go. But there were only rooms for professional people. It was always, 'No children, no pets.' I tried the council, social services, church organizations. The whole of society is just geared to the family: the commitment to your house, baby, and husband. By the time you leave, you've really been driven out.

Even the baby, who was only 1¾ years when we left, knows why we're at this refuge. I was tired of explaining one day that we were in one house, and

Daddy was in another, and I said to him, 'Do you know why we're here?' He said, 'Yes. Daddy naughty, Daddy scream, scream till Mummy cry.' Yet all the social pressure is on you to stay married and 'be a good wife'.

2

BATTERED WIVES

J.J. Gayford

It was only in 1971 that Chiswick Women's Aid first gave sanctuary to a woman who was seeking refuge from her husband's violence. The emotive term 'battered wife' was used following the example of Kempe *et al.* (1962) who had first described a battered-child syndrome. It is difficult to think of a less emotive term which still desribes what has happened. Information available on battered wives does not yet allow a classical, dogmatic, textbook account. We are still at the stage of collecting information, so that an account has to take the form of presenting evidence and formulating hypotheses which will later be proved right or wrong.

DEFINITION OF A BATTERED WIFE

A battered wife may be defined as any woman who has received deliberate, severe, and repeated demonstrable physical injury from her marital partner (Gayford, 1975b). The term 'marital partner' means either the spouse or the cohabitee. By using the term 'demonstrable physical injury' the battered wife is limited to women who have been physically assaulted. This does not mean that psychological cruelty is considered of no consequence. In almost every divorce petition there is a claim which amounts to psychological cruelty, either by one partner or the other. Battered husbands in the full sense of the term do exist, but are extremely rare; first, because the male when he loses control is physically stronger than the female in most marital partnerships; and second, the man can always leave the marital home without the children, whereas the woman finds this very difficult.

REVIEW OF THE LITERATURE

Faulk (1974) reports on 23 men remanded for assaulting their wives, and concludes that the younger men are more psychopathic and the older men more likely to suffer from a psychiatric disorder. Fonseka (1974) concluded from diagnostic X-rays of women over 16 years of age who were treated at a casualty department for non-accidental injuries, that most of the trauma was to the face. Levine (1975) reports on 50 cases of battered wives seen in general practice. From the family records he states that 37 of the men had violent backgrounds. He is also able to report on the disturbance in the children. Marsden and Owens (1975) collected 19 cases by advertising and showed that there are two sides to the characters of these men. The ostensibly affable nature can suddenly change to rage and violence.

Other surveys not primarily concerned with battered wives have nevertheless found them and commented on their existence. Wilson (1974) reports that of the first 300 women referred to the domiciliary family-planning service 69 were seen to bear marks of domestic violence. The Royal Scottish Society for the Prevention of Cruelty to Children (1974) recorded 74 cases of battered wives in a 3-month survey of child abuse. The National Citizens' Advice Bureaux Council (1973) claimed they had handled 3150 cases in the preceding year with about 50% of them presenting signs of physical violence. The Leeds Samaritans are cited as claiming that 30% of their cases are battered wives (P. D. Scott, 1974). In a small survey at Holloway Prison 17·3% of the women committed had been battered by their husbands or cohabitees (P. D. Scott, 1974). Orford *et al.* (1976), reviewing the hardships of 100 wives of alcoholics, found that 45 had been subjected to physical violence.

There is some controversy as to whether women who are repeatedly assaulted by their husbands are of the same type as those who are murdered by their husbands. Perdue (1966) reported on 30 men imprisoned for murdering their wives and found difficulty in establishing a motive as the true facts were covered by rationalizations. It was estimated that about half these men had long histories of violence and half suddenly gave way to an act of violence which was out of character. Schultz (1960) reported on 14 men who attempted to kill their wives and concluded that most had a long history of violence. P. D. Scott (1974) quotes from his own experience of interviewing men charged with murdering their wives and claims that most were controlled until the final outburst. Gillies (1976) reports on 400 persons charged with 307 murders where 14% of the victims were wives, cohabitees or girlfriends. About half these men had a record of previous violent offences. He described the common personality trait as 'a fiery disposition reacting with physical violence to insults'. It would appear that about half the women murdered by their husbands or cohabitees would also have been battered wives.

There is a considerable literature of speculative accounts of why men beat their wives. Most set out with the objective of putting the blame on the woman, in much the same way as Price (1945) and Whalen (1953) have tried to lay the blame for a man's alcoholism on to his wife. Snell *et al.* (1964) make the sweeping statement that women who are beaten are aggressive, efficient, masculine, and sexually frigid. This idea is very convenient, as it allows the dismissal of cases, as described, with the wildly inaccurate implication that the women enjoy their battering. It is hard to see how any human being can enjoy having her eyes blacked, her teeth or nose broken, and her ribs or her abdomen kicked. P. D. Scott (1974) would agree that battered wives do not enjoy their sufferings—in fact very much the reverse. The term 'masochist' is over-used and really only applies to the fantasy concepts of assault and domination. The first taste of reality will kill the fantasy and all the supposed enjoyment.

The work among battered wives is described from the grass roots by Pizzey (1974) in her book about Chiswick Women's Aid. Harrison (1975) discusses some of the problems related to open-door hostels and restricted-admission hostels. Evidence puts before the Select Committee of the House of Commons (1975) presented many different points of view, from police statistics to anecdotal accounts from women who had suffered. The report concluded that there is a need for family crisis centres to be set up in all areas where the population is in excess of 50 000 and that these need to be staffed for 24 hours a day. Refuges were also recommended on the basis of one place for a woman and her children per 10 000 of the population.

A SURVEY OF 100 BATTERED WIVES

At the beginning of 1974 the author of this paper undertook a survey of battered wives, drawing cases from psychiatric practice (11%) and from Chiswick Women's Aid (89%). A questionnaire was devised which was put through both a pilot and a trial run before a working form was settled. In some cases women were invited to complete their own questionnaire, others were helped by one of five interviewers selected from volunteers at Chiswick Women's Aid. All cases were seen personally by the author to clarify information. Where other information was available, for example from social workers or general practitioners, this was included. Forty-eight cases were rejected where there was difficulty in obtaining information either because of conflicting accounts from other sources or because the woman was a poor informant herself. The results from the 100 selected cases were analysed with the aid of the London University computer.

The ages of battered wives and their husbands or cohabitees, together with nationalities, the length of their relationships, and the number of years of that relationship in which violence occurred are shown in Tables 2·1 and 2·2.

Although there was a wide age range most women were still within the child-bearing age group. Men were, in the main, marginally older but the majority were under 40 years of age. It is interesting to note that three women did not know the age of their husband or cohabitee. There was a high incidence of immigrants among both the men and women, especially from the Republic of Ireland and the West Indies.

In 25% of cases violence started before marriage and in the remainder it started soon after. The arrival of the first child or even the pregnancy was in many cases the factor which precipitated violence. It was rare for a relationship to be trouble-free for a long period and then suddenly to erupt into violence.

Table 2.1 Age of battered wives and their husbands or co-habitees together with the length of relationships and years of violence in that relationship

	N =	Range (years)	Mean	Standard deviation
Age of battered wife	100	19–59	30·66	7·23
Length of relationship	99	1–25	8·76	6·50
Length of above relationship in which violence occurred	100	1–25	6·77	5·95
Age of husbands or co-habitees	97*	20–61	33·90	8·92

* In three cases the man's age was not known.

Table 2.2 Nationality of battered wives and their husbands, or co-habitees, as compared with the incidence of immigrants within the general population of Great Britain (corrected for age and sex)

Nationality	Percent of women in survey	Percent of women in population	Percent of men in survey	Percent of men in population
British	66	92	55	91
Republic of Ireland	17	1	21	2
West Indian	9	1	14	1
Other nationalities	8	6	10	6
Total	100	100	100	100

The fact that 20 women tolerated over 10 years of violence at first seems surprising. However, some of these women had been persuaded that the violence was their fault. Certainly nearly all the older battered wives were under the impression that their situation was unique. Before the days of refuges for battered wives there was little chance of escape especially while the children were young. By the time the children had left home violence had become a way of life, and one gained the impression that the psychological effects of the repeated crises, to say nothing of the physical damage, had robbed these women of the ability to make lives of their own, always presuming they had this ability in the first place. It is difficult to imagine the fear that some women live under from their husbands; they know he will always find them wherever they go, and they see their only safety in staying at home and appeasing him. There is no doubt in my mind that this is a type of brainwashing or constant indoctrination. Only when one has seen the lengths to which men will go to find their wives, and even when divorced to keep watch on them, can one appreciate the grip that the possessive husband can have on his wife.

A variety of injuries had been sustained by women in their relationships; all had received the minimum of bruises, but 44 had also received lacerations, of which 17 were due to attack with a sharp instrument, such as a broken bottle, knife or razor. Twenty-six had received fractures of nose, teeth or ribs and eight had fractures of other bones, ranging from fingers and arms, to jaws and skull. Two had their jaws dislocated and two others had similar injuries to the shoulder. There was evidence of retinal damage in two women and one had epilepsy as a result of her injuries. In 19 cases there were allegations that strangulation attempts had been made. Burns and scalds occurred in eleven and bites in seven cases.

All women were attacked with the minimum of a clenched fist, but 59 claimed that kicking was a regular feature. In 42 cases, a weapon was used, usually the first available object, but in 15 cases this was the same object each time, eight being a belt with a buckle.

The picture presented was a man losing control completely, punching and kicking in a vicious and indiscriminate way. Women were often pushed and thrown about the room; some were held by the hair and their heads banged against the wall or floor. Where violence took place in the kitchen, even cooking utensils were used as weapons, resulting in greater injury if they happened to contain hot liquids. Most women claimed that the abdomen, even a pregnant abdomen, was the target of attack. There were a number of claims that this precipitated an abortion. Horrific though this loss-of-control attack may be, it does not compare with the premeditated attack, where cunning is used to inflict painful injuries that will leave little mark. In this category are women who were hit about the hair line or received injury to the ears. Others were punched or beaten in the lumbar-sacral region of the back. Arms were twisted and fingers bent back. Cigarette burns were deliberately inflicted, and one woman was attacked with a red-hot poker which had been heated up for the purpose. Where there is an element of premeditation the character of a sinister and cruel man is projected.

Some examples perhaps need to be quoted:

Case 1

A 22-year-old woman cohabiting with a 31-year-old man. They have a baby of 5 months and have lived together for 2½ years. Violence has only occurred for 2 years of their relationship and generally follows the husband's drinking. Most of her injuries have been caused by his fists, but items of furniture have been thrown at her. On many occasions she has received bruises to her face and head. Her front teeth have been fractured and one has had to be extracted. The malar bone of her face has also been fractured. Early in the relationship she was kicked in the abdomen when pregnant and aborted soon afterwards. She left her husband and went back to her mother, where he arrived drunk and did considerable damage. Her mother asked her to leave as she claimed she could not tolerate such violence.

Case 2

A 23-year-old woman cohabiting with a man of 31 who has a child of 7 weeks by her cohabitee and two older children by a previous marriage which ended due to her husband's violence. As in the first case, her cohabitee attacked her when drunk. Usually he punched her and pulled her hair, but when really enraged he would kick her and throw her around the room, using anything that came to hand as a weapon. This had resulted in a radio being thrown at her and a milk bottle being used as a weapon. Violence became worse when she was pregnant, but there had been violence throughout the whole of their 3-year relationship.

Case 3

A 43-year-old woman who had been subjected to intermittent violence for the 6 years of her second marriage. Her first marriage ended due to the death of her husband. The second husband was the same age as her, had a good job, and did not have a drinking problem. She had been pushed downstairs, kicked, and punched. When violence was completely out of control she would leave her husband, but returned in response to his pleading and promises. Violence would soon recommence; on one occasion on the same day as she returned. There were two children of this marriage, aged 4 and 2½ years.

FACTORS WHICH PRECIPITATED VIOLENCE

In 44 cases the violence only occurred after the husband had been drinking. Alcohol appeared to be a problem for most of the men, with 52 becoming drunk on a weekly basis and 22 on a monthly, or at least 3-monthly, basis. It was quite common for a row to start with the man starting to drink in an aggressive state of mind. He would then return home under the influence of alcohol and a row would escalate. In his drunken state he might demand sexual relations either to test or to repair the relationship; refusal would lead to further violence, which could be interpreted as having sexual connotations.

Jealousy was a common factor among the men, with 66 of the women claiming that their husband was either constantly accusing them of flirting with other men or of having extra-marital affairs. Some men went as far as to check their wives' movements by spying on them, or using other people to do this, and some would cross-question wife and children. Four men even claimed they had not sired their wives' children during the marital relationship. The connection between jealousy and heavy drinking just failed to reach significance at the 5% level (chi squared = 2·31, d.f. = 1·0, $p > \cdot 1$) but showed an interesting trend. In 20 of the 66 jealousy cases there appeared to be evidence of some provoking factors, such as extra-marital affairs by the women or previous pregnancies by another man without marriage.

THE EFFECT OF VIOLENCE

Most of the women could not find a method of dealing with the violence. Only eight repeatedly tried to fight back, and even those admitted that this made matters worse. Some tried to reason with their husbands and others tried passive methods of submission, but neither met with much success. A few tried to flee when they saw violence was about to erupt, but were hampered by the fact that they had nowhere to go and had children they could not leave. Few lived in the type of accommodation that made avoidance possible; those who tried it found that this met with no more success than other methods.

Only five women were living with their husbands at the time of interview. All but 19 women had left their husbands more than once; some had left so many times that it was impossible for them to make an accurate estimate. Usually they went to stay with relatives or friends, but a quarter had stayed in hostels, hotels, boarding-houses or convents prior to Chiswick Women's Aid. Nine had actually wandered the streets with their children. Only eleven had been admitted to hospital for more than 48 hours and then for psychiatric reasons.

Usually a woman returned to her husband because of his promise to reform. Seventeen returned because of threats or demonstrations of further violence, and 14 returned home because there was nowhere else to go. The fact that the children were still in the marital home was the deciding factor for 13 women.

Violence extended to the children in some cases. Thirty-seven women admitted they were violent to their children. In 54 cases there was a claim that the husband had extended his violence to the children. Women who said they were subjected to violence in their childhood were more likely to be violent to their children (chi squared = 7·6, d.f. = 1, $p < \cdot 01$ significant at the 1% level).

Suicidal attempts were common in battered wives, with 34 women taking a drug overdose and often repeating the attempt. Seven women made at least one self-mutilation attempt and nine women used other methods. Few really wanted to kill themselves, but most wanted to draw attention to their plight. Women with unhappy home backgrounds in their childhood were more likely to make suicidal attempts (chi squared 7·0, d.f. = 1, $p < \cdot 01$ significant at the 1% level).

Seventy-one women had been treated with anti-depressants and tranquillizers by their general medical practitioners. There was no statistical significance in the relationship between these prescriptions and suicidal attempts (chi squared = 0·02, d.f. = 1, $p > \cdot 9$). Many women hid the real disorder from their doctor and those who confided found sympathy, but no real practical help.

Forty-six women were referred for psychiatric consultation and, as would be expected, there was significance between this and suicidal attempts (chi squared = 7·28, d.f. = 1, $p < \cdot 01$ significant at the 1% level). According to the women, a variety of psychiatric diagnoses were made, with 21 receiving further treatment for depression, either with ECT. or more anti-depressants. One woman had been subjected to a leucotomy. It would be impossible to speculate which came first, or which was cause and which effect, out of psychiatric illness and the marital violence.

FAMILY BACKGROUND OF BATTERED WIVES

Twelve women had been brought up by one or two step-parents. Seven were brought up by other relatives and eleven grew up in one-parent families. For six, their upbringing was mainly in an institution. Only 65 women claimed to have regular contact with their parents to the age of 15. Nineteen of the parents were divorced.

Twenty-three women witnessed violence by their fathers towards their mothers and 19 claimed that the violence extended to themselves. After all this it may seem surprising that 48 women described their fathers as long-suffering or placid.

Only 93 of the 100 women were able to give any information about their fathers. Of these, 27 witnessed heavy drinking in their father and 13 described him as having employment problems. Nine women knew that their fathers had been to prison. It might be suspected that the women came from a deprived lower social class, but this was certainly not always true, with two fathers from professions and 32 described as being skilled tradesmen. Only 56% of fathers were from the United Kingdom, with 23% from the Republic of Ireland and 10% from the West Indies.

Only 14 women claimed they were subjected to violence from their mothers or step-mothers. Forty women described their mothers as long-suffering or placid. Six admitted seeing their mother drunk during childhood but only two claimed this was a regular occurrence. Three mothers were said to have a prison record for shoplifting or theft. Two mothers were described by their daughters as prostitutes. These tended to be large families with a mean of 3·33 siblings to each battered wife, and this takes no account of half-siblings of women—of these it was impossible to make an accurate estimate. Some of the families were large with one woman being one of 16 children and 27 being one of six or more children. Only 14 were only children and the same number had one other sibling.

Women were invited to describe their childhood, the replies being fitted into a five-point scale. From 97 replies, 47 saw their childhood as happy and eleven claimed that in the main it was happy. Twelve had mixed feelings, but eight claimed that it was mostly miserable and 19 described unhappiness.

EDUCATION AND WORK RECORDS

Seventeen women said that at least part of their education was at a grammar school and nine claimed either private or convent school experience.

Seventeen passed some GCE O level examinations and four others advanced to A levels. Seven passed some CSE subjects and four passed the eleven-plus, but were not able to take up their grammar school place. After leaving school none of the women went on to university, but eight started a nursing training and six, teacher training. In all 30 went on with their education after school, the majority with secretarial courses.

Seven of the women were never employed after leaving school, but 32 were employed in one job for longer than 3 years. There were an overlapping 36 who claimed they had received some work satisfaction, but another 28 claimed it was only the financial reward that encouraged them to work.

ALCOHOL, DRUG ABUSE, AND CRIMINAL RECORD

Twenty women said they liked the effects of alcohol, and 14 admitted they had been drunk on a number of occasions. Twelve admitted to experiencing the effects of cannabis. Eight women admitted they had taken drugs with the express purpose of experiencing the 'stimulant' effects; in two cases this involved opium alkaloids and neither of these became addicted. Drug addicts can easily become battered wives, but none were seen in the survey as Chiswick Women's Aid does not usually admit drug addicts because of the disruption they cause.

Sixteen women admitted to a criminal record, twelve of these were for theft or shoplifting. Only one woman admitted to a prison sentence and one had been to Borstal.

COURTSHIP AND MARRIAGE

Only 22 women went through a period of engagement to the man who subsequently became their violent marital partner. Eighteen women, including some of the above, had other engagements which did not end in a marital relationship. One woman had four engagements before her violent marriage. A quarter of the total number were subjected to violence before marriage or cohabitation. The mean age of marriage or cohabitation was 20·3 years, with a standard deviation of ± 3·2 years.

Eight-five women had sexual relations without the use of contraceptives before marriage or cohabitation. This needs to be considered with the fact that 60 of the women were pregnant before they started their marriage or cohabitation. Only two women regularly used some form of contraception before marriage or cohabitation. A quarter of the women who became pregnant before their marital relationship were pregnant by another man, not the man they subsequently lived with in their violent marital relationship. The mean age of first sexual intercourse was, according to the information given by the women, 18·2 years, with a standard deviation of ± 2·9 years. Again according to the information given, this came after their first serious emotional relationship with the opposite sex in the majority of cases.

This was given as happening at a mean between 16 and 17 years, with a standard deviation between 2 to 3 years.

For 23 women their current marriage was their second, of which 16 claimed their first had ended due to violence. For four this was their third, and for one her fourth marital relationship. All but one of these had experienced violence in a previous relationship.

SEXUAL RELATIONS DURING MARRIAGE

Half the women agreed that there was no problem in their sexual relationship, in spite of the violence. Just under a quarter claimed that sexual relations had never been good and about 20% claimed that there had been a good sexual relationship, but with violence this had deteriorated. Seventeen women admitted that they had indulged in extra-marital sexual activity.

Some effort was made to discover if there was any sexual association with violence. Information had to be handled with great care, and interpretations, if they are to be made at all, can only be made in the light of the total relationship.

Almost a third of women had clothes torn off them in the course of violence. In most cases this was because clothes were grabbed, often to prevent a woman from escaping. As much of the violence occurred late at night, even when women had retired to bed, there was little in the way of clothing to be removed. Only one women insisted that there was a sexual motive in this part of the attack.

It appeared that men quite commonly wanted sexual relations after the violence, but this does not prove that violence increased their sexual desire. There was evidence that in most cases this was either an attempt to improve the relationship after the violence, or, at its worst, an attempt to take what was considered to be a right of marriage. In the five cases where sexual intercourse was sometimes attempted while the woman was allegedly tied up, a sadistic element cannot be excluded.

Seven men are alleged to have asked their wives to hit them back, promising not to retaliate, but even then only one case was associated with sexual excitement. None of the women admitted to experiencing any sexual pleasure from the violence they received and only about 10% could distinguish between fantasy token violence and the real event.

THE MEN WHO BATTER THEIR WIVES

In the survey of the 100 women none of the men was interviewed; information about them was obtained from other sources, such as social workers and general practitioners. Most of the information came from the women. It would be more accurate to head this section 'the way the battered wives projected the men who beat them'. However, it has been possible in other work to interview men who batter their wives and the general impression is that where all the evidence is taken together the overall picture is fairly accurate.

Five of the men were from the professional or executive class (Social Class I) and 29 were skilled in some trade, most of whom would be classed as Social Class III. The remaining 65 were unskilled, the majority from Social Class V, which includes those who were rarely employed.

Eleven of the men were said to be mostly unemployed and 18 experienced frequent unemployment. About half the men had no employment problems. It appeared that gambling was a real problem for a quarter of the men. Just over half were alleged to have a prison or Borstal record. For a third, this was for violent offences ranging from bodily harm to armed robbery or attempted murder.

Just under half the men were accused of extra-marital sexual relationships, and the majority of these accusations included more than one affair. Thirty-seven of the men were also said to have had previous marital-type relationships before they associated with the battered wife.

Three-quarters of the men whose domicile was known were still living in the marital home and another 10% had gone back to their parents or were staying with other relatives. In four cases, women claimed that the men were sleeping rough, two were alleged to be in prison, and one in a psychiatric hospital. Surprisingly, only one was accused of currently living with another woman. In 16 cases the domicile of the man was unknown to the women at the time.

About a quarter of the men were alleged to have received psychiatric treatment, but many more were stated to be in need of this in the opinion of the battered women.

Seventeen of the men were accused of being illiterate, or near illiterate, and only five were said to have achieved a diploma or degree. Just under three-quarters of the women claimed they had discussed childhood experiences with their husbands and this resulted in 40% of them being convinced that their husbands had been subjected to parental violence, or had seen their parents' violence towards each other.

FEELINGS OF THE WOMEN TOWARDS THE MEN WHO BATTERED THEM

Slightly over a third of the women just wanted the violent man out of their lives and about another third simply felt indifferent towards him. About 10% still had some feeling left and some of these would willingly have gone back to him provided the violence would cease. A further 10% felt sorry for the man and would have liked to have helped him in some way. Few of the women felt vindictive, although some saw the only way of keeping him out of their lives was for him to be held in some form of custodial care.

Seventeen of the women still saw the violent men, and 10 of them were still living with them.

CHILDREN OF BATTERED WIVES

Only three women had no children at the time of the survey, and two of these were pregnant. In all, the 100 women had 315 living children, of whom 254 were sired by the men who battered them. Only 201 of the children were dependent and still in their mothers' care at the time of the interview. Even so, ten women had five or more dependent children. From the 1971 Census it would be predicted that only 2% of women would have five or more dependent children.

Many of these children were very disturbed and were attending child guidance clinics. Temper tantrums, bed wetting, stealing, and acts of vandalism were common among new-entry children at Chiswick Women's Aid. Reports of school difficulty were common, with children refusing to attend school, fighting in a vicious way with other children and even with their teachers.

HELP SOUGHT BY WOMEN PRIOR TO THEIR APPEAL TO CHISWICK WOMEN'S AID

Of the 89 women seen at Chiswick Women's Aid, 57 had previously asked for help from the social services. Although most of them had received some sympathy, they claimed that no practical help had been given. Many had actually presented at the social services building after an episode of violence, fleeing from their husbands. It appeared that the usual help they were offered at this stage was a visit of a social worker to their home. The women were quite clear that the help they were seeking was alternative accommodation away from their violent husbands. Generally it had been pointed out to them that they were not homeless and therefore did not qualify for emergency accommodation. Occasionally bed and breakfast was offered, but with their disturbed children this could not be prolonged.

The police or probation service had been approached by 32 women, 25 of whom had also visited the social services. Usually the police were called during violence. Again many received sympathy, but found the police impotent in helping them. There was reluctance on the part of the police to intervene in a domestic dispute. Often by the time they arrived the violence had subsided and the husband was able to give the impression that it had just been a minor domestic dispute. Women prepared to deny this were invited to bring charges against their husbands themselves—but few dared to do this. Most women admitted that there were no witnesses to the violence, and those who did try to proceed with charges found that they had to fight battles in two courts, for separation and assault. The proceedings of both courts still left them living with a violent man who was likely to be provoked to still further violence by the court action. It was a brave woman who proceeded in these circumstances.

Six of the women had visited a Citizens' Advice Bureau. More women would have attended if they had reason to expect practical help. Those who did attend spoke well of the bureaux, but said that, true to their name, they only gave advice, and this was to seek help at a Woman's Aid Centre.

Ten women had consulted solicitors, but found few solicitors wanted to handle their type of case. Even those who appeared willing were not prepared to move with the speed that the women considered their emergency circumstances warranted.

Fourteen of the women at Chiswick Women's Aid had approached other organizations before making their escape through Chiswick. Very rarely were other organizations able to give them the sanctuary they were seeking. If they had been on their own without children, it would have been a very different matter.

THE ROLE OF THE GENERAL MEDICAL PRACTITIONER

Levine (1975) has shown what an excellent chance the general medical practitioner has in observing signs of marital violence, once he has been alerted to the tell-tale signs and symptoms. Gayford (1975a,b) has shown that battered wives frequently visit their general practitioner, not always as a result of the trauma. In 71 cases of the present survey, women presented with signs or symptoms which caused their general practitioner to prescribe anti-depressants or tranquillizers. We shall never know how many of these practitioners suspected marital violence as a cause of the symptoms. Few women confided, some because the husband always insisted on being present when his wife was interviewed. Those doctors who did make the correct diagnosis were projected as sympathetic but impotent to do anything constructive to prevent recurrence.

Clearly there needs to be a route of referral that can be used in cases where marital violence is suspected. Most doctors would like to be able to refer cases to a social worker with special training in dealing with marital violence. It would be imperative that such a social worker had access to a hostel where women and children could seek safety.

ROLE OF THE ACCIDENT AND EMERGENCY DEPARTMENT OF THE HOSPITAL

Fonseka (1974) has shown how commonly women over the age of 16 with non-accidental injuries present to hospital accident and emergency departments. Gayford (1975a) has shown how commonly battered wives make suicidal attempts and even repeat these again and again, although not all cases are admitted to hospital. Even so there is clear evidence that a large number of battered wives are presenting themselves at casulty departments. The pressure of work in these centres means that the true diagnosis is often missed, but also patients are removed from hospital against medical advice by husbands or the patient discharges herself because she is afraid of what is happening to the children in her absence. Many women spoke highly of the staff at the local hospital who had tended their wounds on a number of occasions with sympathy, but with a feeling of impotence. Again there needs to be a referral agency for such cases.

THE ROLE OF THE PSYCHIATRIST

Gayford (1975a) showed that 46% of women had been referred for psychiatric opinion. Again there were cases where the diagnosis was obscured or missed. Psychiatrists were not projected in a good light by the majority of battered wives. Twenty-one per cent had been rightly or wrongly diagnosed as depressed and subjected to further chemical treatment and some to physical treatment. No doubt the women appeared to need this at the time. Some women knew that they were regarded as having personality disorders and being a nuisance to the psychiatric service. Attempts to untangle the problem met with frustration as there appeared to be no solution.

There is a tendancy for those who follow certain types of analytical theory to project the blame on to the women, and many women claimed that the psychiatrist had made them feel guilty for their own plight. Most psychiatrists do not like treating cases where there is an element of marital violence, as the case can be very time consuming and the results poor. Many psychiatrists would claim that wife battering is not a psychiatric disorder and the psychiatrist is not the person to be treating the problem.

Once again there is the professional frustration of being lumbered with a case that is untreatable with the facilties available. Few psychiatrists would deny the need for a specialized team and facilities to deal with the problem.

THE PSYCHO-DYNAMICS OF MARITAL VIOLENCE

The behaviourist would say that violence is a learned pattern of behaviour (J. P. Scott, 1958) and, in terms of marital violence, the men must have experienced violence to bring violence into their marital relationship. Women who have been subjected to marital violence tell us that, as far as they know, 40% of their husbands and cohabitees had seen violence in their parental relationships, and 23% of the women themselves witnessed violence in their own parents. A third of the men are reported to have served prison sentences for violent crimes and 52% had been to prison, to say nothing of those who had committed acts of violence but were not caught and sent to prison.

Analytical theory would have us believe that all acts of violence are due to frustration or provocation (Dollard *et al.*, 1944). Different levels of frustration could be tolerated by each man. This might vary from time to time and in different external and emotional circumstances. It would be possible to place men on a continuum from high frustration tolerance to low frustration tolerance. The men with low frustration tolerance are more likely to be provoked to violence in the marital relationship. Women could be placed on a scale according to their provocation, which again could vary according to the external and emotional circumstances. There would be women of low to high provocation. If men with high frustration tolerance were paired with women of high provocation, violence could not be likely to arise, but women of high provocation with men of low frustration tolerance would produce a combination where violence could be predicted.

Closer examination of the man of low frustration tolerance and the woman of high provocation seems to be required. This type of man has an aggressive personality which may be masked in many ways. It may give rise to many useful qualities, or simply result in a man who expects always to be quickly gratified. Some of these men may have a highly sophisticated veneer, while others are crude; some are useful citizens, while others are idle layabouts. In all cases they have great difficulty in dealing with frustration. The danger comes when this type of man learns the effectiveness of violence. Provided he is physically stronger than those around him he can achieve his aims and avoid frustration by violence. Usually some degree of control is exercised, but if the frustration becomes too great, or the control is removed, violence can erupt. There may be imposed on this a complex learning pattern of how and when to use violence. A common factor in loss of control is alcohol, and we have frequent accounts of women claiming that their husbands can be two different people, with and without the effects of alcohol. There is often considerable remorse when the results of the violence and its consequences can be seen. Elaborate attempts may be made to cover up the damage and prevent others seeing the woman or exploring the situation while there are visible signs.

A woman who is highly provocative may be equally complex. Her provocation may be active or passive and may be the result of repeated exposure to violence. Various types of battered wives have been described (Gayford, 1976); each in her way can be provoking as, it is probably fair to say, can any human being.

The dowdy woman who is overcome by the task of looking after family and home, both of which require qualities of management she does not possess, has passive provocative qualities to a man who cannot understand her limitations. Repeated crises brought about by violence undermine her already poor coping abilities and a spiral of violence and increasing inadequacy begins.

Ironically, other women are attacked physically not because of their inabilities, but because of their superiority to their male partner. These women are often intelligent and good home managers. It is their over-controlling qualities which give them the ability to win every verbal argument and leads to their downfall. The only way the man can win the day is by using physical force. Often there will be a period of build-up of tension with a final explosion which may need alcohol to release the violence. In this type of relationship there is a limit to the amount of violence which will be tolerated by a woman who will eventually use her abilities to break out of the violent relationship.

It would appear that for some women suffering becomes a way of life. Their mothers often tolerated a long and stormy marriage; they themselves have tolerated 15 years or more of violence. In many cases their children have given up and left home. Over the years they have learned some ways of managing the violence, generally by total submission to their husband's domination. Eventually they lose the ability, and even the desire, to break free. They develop pity for their tormentor, realizing that he is unable to cope without them. As they watch him grow older they appear to know that his attacks will become more feeble and it would also appear that they seem to sense that they will out-live him.

Where the woman is highly flirtatious, and even promiscuous, it may at first seem easy to understand what motivates the male to violence, but almost invariably in these cases he himself has indulged in the same practices with the opposite sex. It must be rare to find a promiscuous man who will tolerate promiscuity in his own wife. There is a certain type of female alcoholic who is really an extension of this pattern, with frequent substitution of alcohol for extra-marital sexual activity.

With such a high percentage of battered women presenting with psychiatric histories it is difficult to say which came first, the violence or the psychiatric disorder. It is not easy in marital relationships to understand the partner's mood swings, especially if there is no clear evidence of a precipitating cause. The sullen silence and anergia of depressive reaction can be cited as a provocative factor which tests the frustration tolerance of the partner. Anxiety features can be equally annoying and may be seen as nagging. The woman with shallow affect who can appear vivacious and exciting may turn out to be a frigid lover, apparently incapable of emotional warmth. It is possible to understand the frustration which would be experienced by a man who is desperately trying to find a deeper relationship than this type of woman is capable of giving.

As the case of the battered wife becomes more widely known and facilties for dealing with the victims improve, abuse of the facilities is to be expected. If to claim that a husband has been violent becomes a quick and effective way of bringing a man to heel, or of ending an otherwise unsatisfactory relationship, there will be women who will not hesitate to make false claims. At present these are few in number and, when confronted with overcrowded hostels of refuge, they generally realize that there are better methods of achieving their aim.

Bach-Y-Rita *et al.* (1971) have described an episodic dyscontrol syndrome with outbursts of violence. In some cases there was an almost seizure-like outburst of violence with diminished awareness of the events during that period of time. Others were very anxious individuals, with a build-up of anxiety being released by violence. In another group there was always intoxication. It would appear from listening to the women's accounts of the attacks of violence, that all three types were represented. Even without intoxication, many of the men had claimed amnesia of the events. There is no way of telling what type of amnesia this is and we know that the human mind has a very convenient mechanism for blocking the memory recall of unpleasant events. In interviews with violent men one soon becomes aware of the high level of anxiety. Toch (1969) even goes as far as to claim that violent men, and even women, for that matter, can deliberately provoke a situation until there is in their mind some justification for violence.

Women commonly described this build-up of tension; in some cases it only took minutes or hours, but in others it took days. They could feel that their partner was spoiling for a row. Some claimed they had tried to pacify him or had tried to keep out of the way, but eventually some excuse would be found and the violence would erupt. After this there would be a period of calm, until once again they would feel the tension rising. Some men appeared to have no remorse for what had happened; others were full of remorse and tried to make material restitution, either by gifts or by helping about the house.

It was quite rare to hear of a husband who did not care in some way about his wife and family. Perhaps if such men cared less, they would just desert their wives and children. When women have fled they have been relentlessly tracked down; often this is because the husband cannot manage without a wife and left on his own changes from a wild, violent man to a pathetic creature who makes suicidal gestures, which can even result in his death. There are cases where the wife has succeeded in obtaining a divorce, but still the ex-husband continues to pester her. On the one hand he appears to have a vendetta against her, and on the other he seems to want her more than anything else in the world. This type of jealousy is particularly sinister when it is accompanied by the sentiment 'If I cannot have her, then nobody else will.' It is not unknown for a woman who has been divorced for some years to find that her ex-husband keeps watch on her house to see if she has any boyfriends.

THE BATTERED WIFE AND ALCOHOL

The survey shows pointers of correlation between alcoholism and wife battering. As many as 52% of women claimed that their husband or cohabitee was drunk at least once a week, and a further 22% claimed that drunkeness occurred at least monthly. For 44·1% of women violence only occurred when their man was under the influence of alcohol. Some women could even predict the events, with tension rising, perhaps with a row over a trivial matter, followed by their husband's drinking heavily to the point of intoxication, and then violence erupted.

Orford *et al.* (1976) presented hardship questionnaires to wives of alcoholics and found that 72% had been threatened, 45% beaten, 49% had witnessed the man breaking up furniture, windows, and china. It is also interesting to see Orford finding 49% of the men as possessive and jealous.

About 10% of the women admitted that alcohol had been a problem to them personally. Even some of the women who were not heavy drinkers at the time of the survey, admitted they had passed through a phase of very heavy drinking.

It was alarming to see how many women only knew of one social outlet, and that was to go drinking in male company. Even when the battered wife has finally broken the relationship with her husband she has the problem of finding a new male partner. If the only social outlet she can find is with heavy-drinking men who often themselves have broken marital relationships, it will be obvious that she is associating with men of a similar type to her husband. Tragically, the whole cycle of events is likely to repeat itself and she will once again be precipitated into a violent marital relationship.

CONCLUSIONS

The problem of the battered wife is nothing new, but only now is the climate right for bringing it to public notice and seeking a remedy. It must be seen as a step towards greater civilization that a country can recognize this problem and try to come to terms with it. The fact that wife abuse was first described in Great Britain does not mean that there is a greater prevalence in this country. It is probably true to say that men batter their wives in every country in the world.

When wife battering was first described there was great reluctance to accept that this actually happened in all social classes. Attempts were made to dismiss the subject by claiming that women deserved the violence directed at them and usually enjoyed it as a sign of affection. Fortunately this view is beginning to fade as the full seriousness of the situation is made known. It is quite true that many women provoke men to violence and need protection from their own provocation. Gradually public opinion is swinging against the man who holds his wife and children in subjection by violence. From a man to be feared and even respected, he is becoming an object of scorn and even pity.

It is to be hoped that young children at school will learn more about relationships and how destructive violence can be. If as a result the violent young man loses his appeal for the opposite sex, then he will be subjected to a passive changing influence. The exciting lover will not always make the good husband. Most young women exposed to violence in courtship would seek to end the relationship. Those who, for a variety of reasons, would tolerate this, are vulnerable and need protective guidance, provided a form can be found which would be acceptable to them. Adequate use of contraception would prevent women being forced into a marital relationship as a result of pregnancy. This would also allow them time to test, and even reject the partnership, as being unsuitable.

Where violence is occurring in marriage, the sooner it is stopped the less damage will be done, both physically and psychologically. If a man knows his wife will leave him if he is violent he is less likely to repeat the act. On the other hand, if he finds it brings him some reward he will almost certainly repeat it. Social support can remove some of the frustrating and provoking factors, but in the last analysis there has to be a genuine desire to change. Crises refuges for battered wives have revolutionized the situation and have made it possible for a women to escape to sanctuary. Here she can make her own decision about the future of the relationship, free from the influence of further threats of violence. Most women will consider returning, provided the violence has not been too prolonged and there is some reasonable chance of it ceasing. Where the relationship has become too damaged she has the chance to leave without impossible obstacles to surmount and, again, without the influence of threats and violence. It was as a result of experience with the first refuges that the Select Committee of the House of Commons in 1975 recommended that there should be shelter for women and children on the basis of one family place per 10 000 of the population.

Women who have escaped from a violent marriage with disturbed children will need support for some time before they can fend for themselves. Secondary refuges will be needed where they can live in a supportive environment. For some, this will just mean a house with a chance to support themselves and their children, but the majority will need more than this in the form of a group home with other women for support. In some cases professional supervision will be needed.

Children of battered wives are very vulnerable and there is increasing evidence that they have an above-average chance of becoming the battered wives and violent husbands of the next generation. Special facilties are needed to support them. When they are young the care that their mothers are able to give them may need to be supplemented. As they get older, so the type of help they need will change, from supplemental mothering they will need surrogate fathering and an introduction to constructive excitement.

It would be a one-sided account that made no recommendation for the men who batter their wives. Unfortunately, few would accept constructive help, but there is an ever-increasing number of men who recognize that they have a problem in this direction and need help. Just to turn a man out of his house because he is violent only invites him to find another partner and to repeat the whole process all over again—or forces him to continue pestering his wife.

Where alcoholism is a problem, some possible help in overcoming this will make a difference to his way of life. When deprived of their wives' support some men appear pathetic and inadequate and could easily become itinerant. Hostels for men who have battered their wives may be something we shall hear more of in the future.

REFERENCES

Bach-Y-Rita, G., Lion J. R., Climent, C. E., and Ervin, F. R. (1971) 'Episodic dyscontrol: a study of 130 violent patients', *American Journal of Psychiatry*, **127**, 1473–1478

Dollard, J., Miller, N. E., Doob, L. W., Mowrer, O. H., and Sears, R. R. (1944) *Frustration and Aggression*, Institute of Human Relationships, Yale University.

Faulk, M. (1974) 'Men who assault their wives', *Medicine Science and the Law*, **14**, 180–183.

Fonseka, S. (1974) 'A study of wife-beating in the Camberwell area', *British Journal of Clinical Practice*, **28**, 400–402.

Gayford, J. J. (1975a) 'Wife battering: a preliminary survey of 100 cases', *British Medical Journal*, **1**, 194–197.

Gayford, J. J. (1975b) 'Battered wives', *Medicine Science and the Law*, **15**, 237–245.

Gayford, J. J. (1976) 'Ten types of battered wives', *Welfare Officer*, **25**, 5–9.

Gillies, H. (1976) 'Homicide in the west of Scotland', *British Journal of Psychiatry*, **128**, 105–27.

Harrison, P. (1975) 'Refuge for wives', *New Society*, **34**, 361–364.

Kempe, C. H., Silverman, F. N., Steele, B. S., Droegemuller, W., and Silver, H. K. (1962) 'The battered child syndrome', *Journal of American Medical Association*, **181**, 17–24.

Levine, M. B. (1975) 'Interparental violence and its effect on the children: a study of 50 families in general practice', *Medicine Science and the Law*, **15**, 172–176.

Marsden, D., and Owens, D. (1975) 'The Jekyll and Hyde marriages', *New Society*, **32**, 333–335.

National Citizens' Advice Bureaux Council (1973) 'Citizens' Advice Bureaux' experience of the problem of battered women' a memorandum for the Department of Health and Social Security.

Office of Population, Censuses and Surveys (1973), 'Census 1971. Great Britain Summary Table (1 % Sample)', HMSO.

Orford, J., Oppenheimer, E., Egert, S., Hensman, C., and Cuthrie, S. (1976) 'The cohesiveness of alcoholism-complicated marriages and its influence on treatment outcome', *British Journal of Psychiatry*, **128**, 318–339.

Perdue, W. C. (1966) 'A preliminary investigation into uxoricide', *Diseases of the Nervous System*, **27**, 808–811.

Pizzey, E. (1974) *Scream quietly or the Neighbours will hear*, Harmondsworth: Penguin Books.

Price, G. M. (1945) 'A study of the wives of twenty alcoholics', *Quarterly Journal of Studies in Alcoholism*, **5**, 620–627.

Royal Scottish Society for Prevention of Cruelty to Children (1974) *Battered Wives' Survey*.

Schultz, L. G. (1960) 'The wife assaulter', *Journal of Social Therapy*, **6**, 103–112.

Scott, J. P. (1958) *Aggression*, University of Chicago Press.

Scott, P. D. (1974) 'Battered wives', *British Journal of Psychiatry*, **125**, 433–441.

Select Committee of the House of Commons on Violence in Marriage (1975) *Report, Minutes of Evidence*, and *Appendices*, session 1974–1975 (HC 553–II).

Snell, J. E., Rosenwald, R. J., and Robey, A. (1964) The wifebeater's wife: a study of family interaction', *Archives General Psychiatry*, **11**, pp.107–112.

Toch, H. (1969) *Violent Men*, Harmondsworth: Penguin Books.
Whalen, T. (1953) 'Wives of alcoholics: four types observed in a family service agency', *Quarterly Journal of Studies in Alcoholism*, **14**, 632–641.
Wilson, E. (1974) 'Battered wives: why they are born victims of domestic violence', *The Times*, 4 September, 13.

PART II

THE CONTEXT OF FAMILY VIOLENCE

3

CHILD ABUSE: A CRITICAL REVIEW OF THE RESEARCH AND THE THEORY

Letitia J. Allan

INTRODUCTION

Violence and aggression are aspects of human behaviour which have always interested psychologists and psychiatrists, but today, with the apparent increase in violent crime suggested by the official statistics and the wide coverage given to such problems as football hooliganism, vandalism, and muggings by all the media, we are perhaps more aware of violence and more concerned about it than ever before. This increased public awareness has naturally led to more persistent demands for explanations and answers to these worrying problems, and the output of research papers, discussion documents, and theoretical formulations of one kind or another by various groups of professionals and academics is testimony to their efforts to meet these demands. It is also a testimony, however, of the degree of disagreement which exists between them. Their debate starts at the point of defining violence, continues over the question of causation and ends with an argument about the most effective and appropriate ways of diminishing violent behaviour in the individual and in society as a whole. Obviously we are still a long way from fully understanding this complex phenomenon.

It is proposed in this chapter to look at only one area of violence, and to examine critically the progress which has been made there. Three major questions will guide the development of the discussion; first, what are the difficulties associated with defining the area, second, what is the quality of the research like and how reliable and valid are its results, and third, what help can existing theories provide in furthering our understanding of the behaviour under investigation?

The major focus of attention will be violence in the family. Although it has been argued that there is no necessity to make this a separate issue, that violence in the family may be treated as part of a more general study of violent behaviour (Goldstein 1975), there are good reasons for being so specific. First, it is rather ironical that despite all the publicity given to certain kinds of violent people such as vandals or teenage gangs we do not in fact have to look further than the home to discover where the largest percentage of offences occur. More violence occurs within the nuclear family than within any other social group (Gelles, 1972) and this remarkable fact needs to be explained. What is it about the composition, structure, and dynamics of this group which make it so vulnerable? Second, there is the reason that general theories need to be tested against specific examples and we need to know how well our current theories can explain the occurrence of violence in the family. Finally there is the problem of reducing violence in the family, and since most studies have concentrated on treatment at the level of individuals or small groups, evaluation needs to proceed from this perspective first.

The description 'family violence' covers a wide range of phenomena. It includes violence against children, violence between children, and violence between spouses, and yet our knowledge in these three areas is very uneven. Certainly there are overlaps in these categories; some husbands batter their wives *and* their children, some husbands batter their wives and their wives are then provoked to batter their children, but these groups, at present, seem to represent a fairly small proportion of the total violent population and there is almost no research on them. The research into battered spouses has just begun to gain some momentum but it is still very limited, and so for the purposes of this discussion the focus must be largely on child abuse since this is the area in which the research is most extensive and the explanations most developed. Occasional reference will be made to violence between spouses where it seems appropriate to draw analogies but such references will be kept to a minimum. Of more importance are the methodological lessons which can be learned from the child-abuse studies and which have relevance to all the research into family violence.

PROBLEMS OF DEFINITION

The difficulties in reaching an agreed definition of child abuse are clearly illustrated in the writings of those working in the field. Different theoretical perspectives have resulted in a proliferation of different definitions, some conceptualizing the problem in terms of a spectrum of abuse (Steele, 1968) while others take a much narrower medical view (Oppé, 1968). The crux of the matter, as the NSPCC (1976b) have pointed out in their report, is that non-accidental injury is a socially defined phenomenon and therefore its boundaries cannot be stated as if they were fixed and permanent. Consequently, there are problems both in producing accurate statistical estimates of the extent of abuse and in establishing appropriate limits to the scope of research proposals.

The most common way of defining abuse has been in terms of the physical injuries to the child. A typical definition of this kind is given by Oppé (1968):

> a battered baby is an infant who shows clinical or radiological evidence of injuries which are frequently multiple and involve mainly head, soft tissues, or the long bones and thoracic cage and which cannot be explained unequivocally by natural disease or simple accident.

The list of injuries has been steadily expanded and made more explicit so that it now includes bleeding into and around the skull (Birrell and Birrell, 1968), severe bruising (Silverman, 1968; Caffey, 1972), mutilation (Cameron, 1972), skull or facial bone fractures (O'Neill, *et al.*, 1973) bites (Sims *et al.*, 1973), cigarette burns and scalds (Smith and Hanson, 1974), and even then the list is not exhaustive.

Such medical descriptions of abuse cannot in themselves constitute a definition—they are examples of the phenomenon only, and their continued elaboration brings one no nearer to a general statement of what, in essence, constitutes abuse. Furthermore, if the purpose is to aid identification of abuse, then factors other than purely medical ones must be acknowledged as important. These include changes in explanation given by the parents, delays in reporting the injury, parents' lack of curiosity and expressed anxiety about the cause of the accident, and the quality of the parent–child interaction. The NSPCC (1976b) have tried to incorporate these additional indicators into their definition:

> All children under 4 years of age, where the nature of the injury is not consistent with the account of how it has occurred, or other factors indicate that it was probably caused non accidentally.

The imposition of an age limit reflects a more recent trend based on research which indicates that it is children under 4 years of age who are most at risk from abuse (Skinner and Castle, 1969; Castle and Kerr, 1972) and this complicates data analysis from the older studies since they frequently encompass a much greater age range (Young, 1964; Gil, 1970; Terr, 1970).

It has been argued that any definition which does not acknowledge the motivation of the perpetrator as a very important element is inadequate. Gil (1970) has recognized this aspect and included it in the following manner:

> Abuse of children is the *intentional*, non-accidental use of force or *intentional*, non-accidental acts of omission on the part of the parent or caretaker interacting with the child in his care, aimed at hurting or destroying the child.

Although from a theoretical point of view this definition is better it raises new difficulties of an even more complex nature. First, there is the problem of the ambiguous case where 'deliberate intent' cannot be confidently inferred or where unconscious motives may be operation. Second, Gil has broadened the definition to include acts of 'omission' or neglect.

Giovannoni (1971) argues that neglect and abuse may be usefully distinguished for the purpose of explanation but that the distinction has no practical value at the level of intervention. Young (1964) disagrees and considers that physical abuse and neglect can be distinguished at both a causal and a treatment level and she treats the two groups separately. Such a clear distinction is misleading, however, since it often happens that severe abuse cases also include elements of neglect. Renvoize (1974) tried to distinguish three categories—neglect, abuse, and battering. Neglect involves insufficient care, abuse is non-accidental physical attack (including both minimal and fatal injuries), and battering is physical abuse by a caretaker who loves the child but is over-fussy and over-possessive. No attempts have been made to validate this typology and so it is impossible to say whether the extra category is particularly useful.

Psychological stress and mental abuse have also been mentioned in the literature (Cherry and Kuby, 1971; Clegg and Megson, 1968) but they present difficult problems for the researcher. It is true that emotional damage deliberately inflicted on a child may have just as serious consequences as any physical battering but in practice the difficulty of establishing such parental practices where there are no visible physical scars makes detection practically impossible, and for this reason although references to it occasionally appear in the literature, psychological abuse is generally omitted, both from definitions and from research studies.

The question of severity and frequency of physical injury has been discussed with a view to defining the limits of the spectrum of abuse but here again there are difficulties. At the extreme-violence end of the spectrum are the cases of infanticide and child murder. The category of fatal injuries may belong to this group or not depending on the discretion of the particular author. Steele and Pollock (1968) argue that infanticide and child murder should be kept distinct because their motivation is quite different. However, as Gibbens (1972) has pointed out, whether a child dies or survives an attack may be entirely fortuitous, and in fact Bakan (1971) includes both infanticide and abuse in his discussion of violence towards children.

At the other end of the spectrum are the difficulties involved in trying to distinguish punishment—which is considered to be legitimate violence towards children—and abuse which is considered to be excessive, inappropriate, and illegitimate. What is thought to be an acceptable level of violence depends on the parents' conception of their role, their own experience as children, their religious or moral beliefs, and the cultural environment of which they are a part. The Newsons' survey (1968) of the child-rearing practices of parents in Nottingham illustrates the difficulty sometimes found in trying to distinguish between the disciplinarian, and the child abuser. Although a few of the parents in their sample seemed to be excessively harsh and intolerant towards their children, these parents would no doubt have been astonished and indignant had they heard themselves described as abusers. For example, in one extract from an interview with a manager's wife:

> —About how often does he in fact get smacked? 'Well he's had two really good hidings today; and if it wasn't for the fact that we went out he'd have had another one.' —And is that about average? 'That's about average I'm afraid.' —And you mentioned a wooden spoon just now—do you use that? 'Yes it's quite serious. I use that on Eric [8 years] .... '

Whether two 'good hidings' a day with the occasional use of an implement could be described as abusive is clearly a matter of opinion, but to the mother concerned such a suggestion would probably be ludicrous. Thus the line between discipline and abuse is not always an easy one to draw.

A similar situation arises in trying to define a battered or abused wife. The occasional blow may be regarded as quite innocuous or even an exercise of a husband's legitimate rights. Current definitions tend to push the limits much beyond what would be tolerated for a child. Gayford's criterion (1975) is:

> A woman who received deliberate, severe and repeated demonstrable physical injury from her husband.

The purpose of discussing definitions and the problems associated with them is twofold. First, it highlights the complex nature of the phenomenon of violence towards children and the effect which different definitions will have on the scope and the results of any piece of research; and, second, it illustrates the difficulties which one faces in trying to draw general conclusions from studies which have taken different definitions as their starting points.

In the review of the research which follows some of the studies discussed include neglect cases. Although neglect may be described as a form of passive violence towards children it is not intended to be a major focus of interest here, as it is likely to complicate the picture unnecessarily by its different motivation. Sexual abuse of children has also been omitted from the review on similar grounds.

PSYCHOPATHOLOGY OF PARENTS

A great deal of research has been concerned with individual factors and a number of attempts have been made to build a psychopathologic model based on the various personality and psychiatric abnormalities discovered in abusing parents. A survey of the literature in this area has revealed a perfect 'goldmine of psychopathology' (Steele and Pollock, 1968) but there are no psychiatric labels which are significantly and specifically associated with child abusers.

Schizophrenia and psychopathy have been diagnosed (Gibbens and Walker, 1956; Nurse, 1966; Court and Okell, 1970; Terr, 1970; Smith, Hanson and Noble, 1973; Ounsted, Oppenheimer, and Lindsay, 1975) but are present in only a small minority of battering parents. More frequently they are described as having a character or personality disorder (Cameron, Johnson, and Camps, 1966; Bennie and Sclare, 1969; Terr, 1970; Oliver *et al.*, 1974) which allows for the uncontrolled expression of aggression (Holter and Friedman, 1968). Impaired impulse control (Bennie and Sclare, 1969; Green, Gaines, and Sandgrund, 1974), grossly immature personalities (Johnson and Morse, 1968; Fontana, 1973; Ounsted, Oppenheimer, and Lindsay, 1975), violent impulses (Feinstein *et al.*, 1963), and chronic aggression (Merrill, 1962; Bryant, 1963; Nurse, 1966) are all diagnoses thought to be indicative of this kind of disorder.

Some parents, however, have been described as rigid, cold, and detached (Merrill, 1962; Bryant, 1963; Young, 1964; Skinner and Castle, 1969; NSPCC, 1976a), and Feinstein *et al.*, (1963) found intermittent periods of chronic frigidity in his sample of women. In contrast to this, excessive anxiety (Lynch, Steinberg, and Ounsted, 1975), chronic depression (Court and Okell, 1970), and excessive guilt (Holter and Friedman, 1968) have also been found.

Fantasies which relate to the children who are abused have been observed by Terr (1970). Although there was no predominating theme which might be linked specifically with child abuse, Terr suggests that the fantasies do have a significant influence on the attitudes and behaviour of the parent towards the child. For example, in one case, a mother who perceived her child as a dangerous rival to her husband's affections attributed extraordinary and completely unrealistic sexual powers to her. This then provided both a motive and a rationalization for the abusive behaviour which followed. Terr emphasizes the necessity for studying each fantasy separately in view of it's highly individual character, but the small size of his sample is a severe limitation on the conclusions which can be drawn and it is likely also that the incidence of such fantasies is exaggerated as a result of his sample-selection procedures.

The evidence on intelligence levels in abusing parents is conflicting. Smith (1975) found that half his sample of battering mothers were on the borderline of subnormality or below and this represents a highly significant result when compared with his control sample. However Hyman (1973) has criticized this conclusion on the grounds that the test scores have been averaged in a way which is particularly misleading when the shortened form of the Wechsler test is used. Differences between verbal and non-verbal abilities are obliterated, and there is evidence to suggest that they might differ. In the most recent NSPCC study (1976a) parents had quite normal levels of intelligence although they scored lower on the verbal than on the performance tests. Such a pattern was seen as being consistent with a personality pattern which emphasizes withdrawal and depression as prominent features. In contrast to this Young (1964) found that 58 from an available sample of 110 were mentally retarded, and Cameron, Johnson, and Camps (1966) state that 93% of their men and 70% of their women ranged from 'low average' to 'very low' IQ. Fontana (1973) believes that such low intelligence prevents parents from being able to reason through a crisis and so they become overwhelmed and are unable to cope. Steele and Pollock (1968), however, state that their parents' IQs range from 70 to 130 and therefore spread across the entire spectrum. Since they do not mention in what proportions high and low IQs are represented it is difficult to interpret what these results imply about child abusers. In summary, then, the evidence of mental illness and the various assessments of intelligence which research has revealed do not suggest any consistent pattern among violent parents.

THE DEVELOPMENT OF TYPOLOGIES

The appearance of various characteristics in small groups of battering parents has led some authors to try and develop typologies in which clusters of personality characteristics are associated together, each cluster having its own underlying psycho-dynamic pattern. Merrill (1962) was the first to attempt this, and he described three clusters of personality characteristics which applied to both parents, and a fourth one which was only applicable to fathers. They can briefly be summarized as:

(1) The habitually aggressive and hostile type.
(2) The cold, rigid, compulsive type.
(3) The strongly dependent and passive type.
(4). The physically-disabled and unemployed type.

An almost identical typology was described by Bryant (1963) and a further attempt to validate these clusters was made by Boisvert (1972). He began by dividing his sample into two categories—uncontrollables and controllables. The uncontrollable group were then divided into four subgroups:

(1) The psychotic personality for whom the child plays some idiosyncratic role in the fantasies of the parent.
(2) The inadequate personality who is impulsive, immature, and typically responds to conflict with aggression.
(3) The passive–aggressive personality who sees the child as a competitor for the affections of the spouse.
(4) The sadistic personality.

The controllable group were then subdivided into two subgroups:

(1) The cold, compulsive personality who severely disciplines the child while maintaining a moral attitude.
(2) The displacement-of-aggression type who is usually an adequate

> personality but cannot cope with marital difficulties. This results in an impulsive displacement of aggression onto the child which is immediately regretted.

Although there are similarities between the typologies they are by no means identical, and the small size of Boisvert's sample does not make his study a very strong test of the original grouping.

Much clearer confirmation of Merrill's personality clusters comes from Skinner and Castle (1969) who identified three groups in their sample of parents of 78 battered children. These were:

(1) The habitually aggressive type.
(2) The rigid controlling type.
(3) The emotionally impoverished type.

In contrast to this, however, is the conclusion of the latest NSPCC study (1976a) which states that the parents observed could not be fitted easily into any personality category.

Weston (1968) has suggested that a distinction could be made between parents who have never abused their children before and those who are consistent abusers. The first group of parents are concerned and generally loving towards their children and have responded violently only under extreme exasperation or stress. They seem similar to the second personality type in Boisvert's 'controllable' group. The consistent abusers are more likely to be responding to stresses which have originated in their own childhood. Gibbens and Walker (1956) make a similar distinction in their discussion of cruel parents. They claim that the most marked clinical division of parents, other than into normal or mentally abnormal categories, was a division into persistent or sudden aggressors. The description by Megargee (1970) of undercontrolled and overcontrolled aggressive types seems to fit into both sets of observations quite well, but the main difficulty arises over recognition of the overcontrolled group. As Megargee (1970) has pointed out, because they are so consistently and outwardly normal most of the time these people are unlikely to be recognized until they have committed acts of violence and so their categorization will almost always be retrospective.

Scott (1974) emphasizes the importance of developing a reliable and valid classification system if violent parents are to be successfully treated, but as the preceding studies have illustrated this is not an easy task. Walters (1975), who has produced a list of ten different categories based upon his own clinical experiences, admits that there are problems with overlaps and that examiners do not always agree about where to place a parent. This is a common problem today in certain areas of psychiatric diagnoses and it would be most undesirable to increase the problem by creating further areas of uncertainty, particularly when the consequences in terms of treatment or legal action may be quite serious. Thus any new classification system must have its categories well founded on evidence, and clearly defined and validated before they can be considered for general use.

Finally it needs to be stated that although typologies may be a helpful guide to treatment of battering parents there is also a positive danger in their use. If such parents are labelled in psychiatric terms then it may encourage people to think of them as 'mentally ill' or abnormal when such a conclusion is by no means completely justified. In fact it is strongly argued by some authors that we all carry within us the potential for abuse and that it only requires a sufficient number of stressful circumstances or poor controls to spark off similar violent responses.

THE CHILDHOOD HISTORY OF ABUSING PARENTS

The most commonly revealed factor in the history of abusing parents, and one which is regarded by many authors as fundamental to the whole problem, is that these parents were themselves abused and rejected as children (Feinstein *et al.*, 1963; Nurse, 1966; Johnson and Morse, 1968; Steele and Pollock, 1968; Silver, Dublin, and Lourie, 1969; NSPCC, 1976a). Ounsted describes this chain of rejection and violence from generation to generation as 'the hostile pedigree', and Oliver and Taylor (1971) in their study of one family traced it through five generations of social-work records. The low self-esteem and chronic depression which characterizes many of these parents (Court and Okell, 1970) have been related to these unhappy childhood experiences.

A small in-depth study by the NSPCC (1976a) draws attention to the mixed patterns of care which many parents suffered as a result of severely disrupted relationships in early life. Drawing upon the observations of Rutter (1974) that it is the quality of care which a child experiences that is the most important influence on subsequent development, they suggest that the record of inadequate substitutes and several changes of caretaker which these parents experienced may be an important influence on their relationships with their own children. It would appear, in fact, that many of these mothers are repeating the patterns of inadequate caring which they themselves experienced. Mothers' lack of concern for their own child's safety and whereabouts has been found by Smith (1975) and NSPCC (1976a), and it is interesting that Farrington and West (1971) found undervigilance in parents to be an even more important predictor of violent delinquency, than of delinquency in general.

Not all parents recalled having a particularly unhappy childhood (Lukianowicz, 1971). Scott (1973b) in his study of fatal battered-baby cases found that ten men claimed 'normal' homes and this was confirmed in six cases. On the basis of this he concludes that mental immaturity may sometimes exist as a clinical entity independent of mishandling and that such cases need to be contrasted with the more common ones in which aggression has its roots in childhood experiences.

THE PARENTS' ATTITUDES TOWARDS THEIR CHILDREN

Workers in the field of child abuse have frequently commented on the inappropriate attitudes which many parents hold regarding their children. Often it seems these parents have quite unreal expectations of their children, wanting them to be a source of love and comfort and to respond to their emotional needs in an adult fashion. Morris and Gould (1963) have called this the 'role reversal' phenomenon and suggest that the parent views the child as his own absent parent who made excessive demands upon him and continually frustrated his dependency needs. The aggression which is intended for the parent is displaced onto the child when it fails to provide the hoped-for emotional comfort. This role reversal has also been observed by Johnson and Morse (1968), Steele and Pollock (1968), Green, Gaines, and Sandgrund (1974), and the NSPCC (1967a).

Distorted perceptions of the child's behaviour and intentions have been commented upon by other authors (Fontana, 1973; Scott, 1973b; NSPCC, 1976a). Scott (1973b) found evidence not only of the role reversal but also of a 'reversed Medea' situation in which the child made the father feel left out because it seemed to prefer the mother. Gregg and Elmer (1969) comparing abused with accidentally-injured children found that the mothers' perceptions of their infants differed in the two groups: the former ascribing more irritability and difficult behaviour to their children than the latter group, while the NSPCC team found mothers who had both distorted perceptions of their children and high expectations of their behaviour. They observed:

> these mothers were frequently noted to ascribe behaviour to their children unjustifiably, and to misconstrue their children's moods, particularly misery, which they often interpreted as temper.

Unrealistic demands for obedience have also been commented upon by Court (1974) and Ounsted *et al.* (1975).

Highly punitive attitudes frequently seem to accompany the demands for perfect behaviour, and these parents often regard their harsh discipline as justified and morally defensible (Johnson and Morse, 1968; Fontana, 1973). In terms of their personality structure, at least a few seem to belong to the type described as cold, rigid, sadistic, and compulsive (Merrill, 1962; Bryant, 1963).

However, such extreme behaviour may not always be the manifestation of some character disorder in a parent. Parents who have been raised themselves on a 'spare the rod and spoil the child' philosophy may be repeating their own child-rearing patterns without any malicious intent (Paulson *et al.*, 1972). One parent justified his punitive behaviour by saying:

> It may seem cruel to you, but as children this is the type of

> punishment we received, my wife and I, and we were just using the same type of punishment ....

Similarly, the lack of understanding of children's developmental capacities, demonstrated by the high expectations of abusing parents, may be partly due to ignorance. De Lissovey (1973) interviewed 48 ordinary adolescent couples with young babies and found that they possessed little knowledge of basic developmental norms (e.g. when to expect the first words, the first step alone, when the infant should be toilet trained) and that such unrealistic estimates contributed to their impatience and cruel treatment. At least part of their behaviour was attributed to the lack of information and guidance which they received from parents and doctors. Another contributing factor was their emotional immaturity. When so many battering parents are also youthful, it becomes easier to understand how a few additional stresses may make all the difference to the safety of a young child.

MARITAL DIFFICULTIES

The quality of marital relations between battering parents has been of interest to a number of authors, and the majority of studies seem to indicate that chronic difficulties and disharmony are extremely common (Young, 1964; Elmer, 1967; Holter and Friedman, 1968; Johnson and Morse, 1968; Terr, 1970; Lukianowicz, 1971; Smith, 1975). They have been regarded both as an overt sympton of an underlying disorder (Court, 1974) or as central to the problem of abuse (Smith, 1975). Lukianowicz (1971) found that 50% of his abusing mothers had negative attitudes towards their husbands—although in general the husbands expressed positive feelings towards their wives—and Feinstein *et al.* (1963) on the basis of group-therapy data state that the majority of their sample displayed an intense hatred of men partly on the basis of their early experiences of unwanted pregnancies and desertion by the father, and partly because the husbands failed to meet their wives' dependency needs. Both authors suggest that the frustrations engendered by unsatisfactory marital relationships are displaced onto the child. Displacement has also been the mechanism proposed to account for maternal violence in cases where wives who are battered by their husbands (Weston, 1968; Smith, 1975) go on to batter their children.

Gibbens (1972) did not find discord between parents in cases of joint cruelty. Instead, he noted that the parents had an unusually strong emotional bond between them and he suggested that in such cases the child becomes a scapegoat for those aspects of the relationship which must be eliminated. Ounsted has suggested that the dependency needs of both parents binds them together in an extremely close yet often hostile relationship in which neither partner can achieve satisfaction, and the pattern of continued separation and reunion which Young (1964) and Elmer (1967) found among their parents lends support to this description of an ambivalent relationship. Young (1964), however, also found a dominant–submissive pattern among some of her parents and this has also been described by Terr (1970) and Scott (1973b). In such cases it appears that the passive partner colludes in the abuse of the child by remaining unprotesting.

The role of the child as a competitor for the affections of the spouse has been discussed by Wasserman (1967) and Court (1970). Some support for this hypothesis comes from Lynch, Steinberg, and Ounsted (1975) who describe the presence of pathologically jealous parents, particularly fathers, among their families receiving treatment, and it is interesting to note that a similar group has been identified among wife batterers (Scott, 1974; Marsden and Owens, 1975). That this may be an important factor in accounting for violence among fathers is also suggested by Johnson and Morse (1968) who found that marital conflict was particularly associated with the husband inflicting injuries on the child.

The concept of stress has featured prominently in discussions of the motivating forces behind abuse and a number of stresses associated with marital problems to be very common among mothers who batter their children. Premarital conception, unwanted pregnancies, and youthful parenthood are all frequent features of the life history of these parents (Skinner and Castle, 1969; Gil, 1970; Oliver *et al.*, 1974; Lynch, 1975; Smith, 1975). In Smith's sample, 54% of the mothers gave birth to their first child before they were 20 and in a study by Lynch (1975) 40% of the mothers were under 20 when they had their first child. All these authors stress the hazards of taking on the responsibilities of parenthood at an early age particularly in view of the emotional immaturity which many of these couples show themselves to have.

Studies by Cameron *et al.* (1966), Johnson and Morse (1968), Lukianowicz (1971), and the NSPCC (1976a) showed that at least 50% of the mothers stated that their pregnancies were unplanned, unwanted or resented. Although maternal attitudes may change between pregnancy and birth (Pohlman, 1969) the NSPCC follow-up during the first 3 months of treatment showed that slightly over 50% of the mothers still had strongly ambivalent feelings, acceptance of their child being conditional on its providing rewarding interactions for them. Other mothers have tried to obtain sterilization or abortion but have had their requests refused (Oliver *et al.*, 1974).

In contrast to these predominantly negative feelings about pregnancy Smith (1975) found that his index and control samples did not differ significantly on the reservations they had about pregnancy or on their considering the possibilities of an abortion, but significantly more index mothers expressed negative attitudes towards the taking of contraceptives.

The burdens of early and frequent pregnancy have been suggested as important factors in precipitating abuse. Elmer (1967) looked for additional stresses at the time of battering and found that the single most significant factor was the birth of a sibling less than a year before or after the abuse of the child. Skinner and Castle (1969) reported that 17 of their mothers were pregnant at the time of abuse and the NSPCC registers for Manchester and Leeds (1976b) show that injured children come proportionally more frequently from large families when the youth of the parents is taken into account. These findings agree with Bibring (1961) who suggests that pregnancy is a biologically determined maturational crisis which is not resolved with birth but may carry on for a period afterwards. The mother with several children close together may never have time to recover fully from one crisis before entering the next. In this context, the increased marital stress during pregnancy, reported by the NSPCC mothers (1976a), and the impatience, lack of understanding, and generally unhelpful attitudes of fathers complained about in an Oxford study (Ounsted *et al.*, 1975) seem to indicate that many mothers are not receiving the extra support they may need during this particularly difficult time. Where tranquillizers and anti-depressants are prescribed to combat the resulting depression their 'disinhibiting' effects (Lynch, Lindsay, and Ounsted, 1975) may increase rather than decrease the dangers to the child.

Finally, a number of authors have suggested that the loneliness and isolation which are frequent features of the abusing mother's environment may exacerbate an already stressful situation (Nurse, 1966; Skinner and Castle, 1969; Giovannoni, 1971). The Birmingham study (Smith, 1975) showed that few fathers complained of having no social activities, thus confirming the notion that often it is the young wife who is left to cope with most of the burdens of caretaking, and when there are few contacts with parents and relations (Young, 1964; Holter and Friedman, 1968) the continued long periods loneliness with a young child may become too much. Elmer (1967), however, has commented that this isolation seems to be the result of active resistance on the part of the parents rather than an imposed state brought about by the family circumstances, and social workers have also commented on the difficulties of making and sustaining contact (Young, 1964; Foresman, 1965; Davoren, 1968; NSPCC, 1976a). This negative response has been regarded as an indication of the parents' lack of trust in their relationships with others—a lack of trust based upon their own experience of rejection in childhood.

THE CHILD

When violence occurs there is a strong temptation to concentrate all the attention on the attacker, and the much more limited amount of research data available on the child is evidence of this. The majority of studies indicate that a child is most vulnerable between the ages of 3 months and 3 years. Gelles (1973) has argued that this is because the infant is not yet capable of much meaningful social interaction and is therefore likely to frustrate the parent who has unrealistically high expectations of a rewarding relationship. A child at this age is also at its most demanding and helpless and the restrictions on freedom and economic hardships which may result are added stresses for young parents to bear. Gil (1970), however, accounts for these statistics by suggesting that younger children are more likely to be severely injured when hit.

Some authors believe that only one child in the family is likely to suffer abuse and they have looked at the ordinal position of the child and its characteristics in order to discover why it should be singled out. Other authors have not found any distinctive pattern and have stressed the dangers to subsequent children if one is abused.

Nurse (1966) found that usually only one child in a family was the victim and that parents did not customarily use physical punishment on their other children. The most vulnerable children in her sample were whose who were illegitimate or premaritally conceived. Feinstein *et al.*'s (1963) sample of women nearly all displayed an intense hatred of men and their victim was generally a male child, while Terr (1970) emphasized the importance of the child in the individual fantasies of parents. Lukianowicz (1971) found that 80% of his abused children were the only children of very young mothers, and Bennie and Sclare (1969) have suggested that youngest children are more at risk than their older siblings. In contrast to these findings Elmer (1967) states that there was no association between abuse and sex or abuse and ordinal position in her study and the NSPCC (1976b) agree with this on the basis of their epidemiological survey. Skinner and Castle (1969) found that 68% of their injured children were first-born and they emphasize the subsequent high risk to other children in the family, and Oliver *et al.* (1974) reiterate this warning.

Feeding problems, crying, whining, and excessive clinging have all been complained of by abusing parents (Green *et al.*, 1974; Smith, 1975; NSPCC, 1976a) and the colicky-child syndrome has been identified in a number of cases (Ounsted *et al.*, 1975). In this latter study two-thirds of the mothers also said that their children could not be cuddled. Evidence of innate differences in infants comes from other sources and may lend some weight to these claims. Schaffer and Emerson (1964) in a study of ordinary non-abused infants found variations in social responsiveness and avoidance of physical contact. Birns, Barden, and Bridger (1969) found individual differences in irritability, sensitivity, and soothability which were recorded from 3 days after birth to 4 months later, and Bernal (1973) found a distinctive group of night wakers in a sample of full-term infants which he studied.

Lynch (1975) compared 25 abused children with their sibs and found statistically significant differences on a number of health factors. In summary, it appeared that while the sibs were outstandingly healthy as infants, the abused group and their mothers were exceptionally ill during the first year of life. The results can only be suggestive because of the small sample size, but taken together with some of the other research findings, it would appear that at least some mothers do experience genuine problems which are caused by an unusually ill or difficult child.

Premature and difficult births are over-represented among cases of abuse

(Elmer and Gregg, 1967; Elmer, 1967; Skinner and Castle, 1969; Oliver *et al.*, 1974; Lynch, 1975) as are low-birth-weight babies. The NSPCC registers in Manchester and Leeds (1976b) reported that weights below 2 500 gm were four times the national average for families of the same social class background, and that weights below 2 000 gm were seven times that of the national average. These findings have given rise to the hypothesis that one of the factors in non-accidental injury is a bonding failure between mother and infant, due to their immediate separation at the time of birth (Klein and Stern, 1971). If there is a crucial attachment period, and premature or problem babies are immediately removed from their mothers for more intensive care, then the period at which a mother is most sensitized to be responsive to her child may pass.

This kind of attachment hypothesis has been criticized as too simplistic. Richards (1974) and Klaus *et al.* (1972) reported no difference in attachment behaviour between groups of mothers with extended contact and those with normal separation, after 4 weeks and Rutter (1974) has pointed out the necessity for regarding the parent–child interaction as a continuing developmental process rather than something which can be studied at one short period in time. Ounsted has suggested that instead of an immediate attachment taking place in the neonatal period there is a 'period of courtship' between mother and child in which communication gradually develops. Finally, the NSPCC studies (1976b) have shown that the first known injury to low-birth-weight babies does not occur earlier than for normal babies as might be predicted if there was a bonding failure soon after birth.

ADDITIONAL SOCIAL STRESSES

The concept of stress is protean, and as is so frequently the case with other kinds of deviant behaviour many abusing parents seem to be handicapped in numerous different ways simultaneously. Poor housing (Skinner and Castle, 1967; Ounsted *et al.*, 1974; Smith, 1975; NSPCC, 1976a), financial difficulties (Young, 1964; Skinner and Castle, 1969; Gil, 1970), unemployment (Merrill, 1962; Skinner and Castle, 1969; Ounsted *et al.*, 1974; NSPCC, 1976b), physical illness (Lynch *et al.*, 1975; Court, 1974), mental illness (Smith, 1975; Ounsted and Lynch, 1976), and dependency on welfare agencies (Giovannoni, 1971; Oliver and Cox, 1973; Oliver *et al.*, 1974) have all been mentioned. Whether in fact these stresses are directly related to child abuse or are merely a function of the social class bias inherent in many samples is a crucial question. Smith (1975) weighted for social class differences in his statistical tests and found that income, unemployment, and household worries became insignificant. Lynch, Roberts, and Gordon (1976), however, do not attempt to sort out which stresses are particularly associated with abusing parents. They have found it more useful to distinguish between the 'diffuse problems' of these families—which are described as a series of interlocking difficulties from which there appears to be no escape (Ounsted and Lynch, 1976) and the more clearly-defined problems of other families requiring social-work help.

PROBLEMS OF INTERPRETATION

It would appear from these complex and often contradictory results that child abuse is not readily explained by any single easily-identified factor or group of factors. So many variables appear to be inextricably mixed that to establish which ones are causally prior or independently related to abuse seems almost impossible.

Retrospective studies which look to childhood experiences of physical punishment and rejection as the fundamental link behind all abuse are not easily interpreted. High correlations between the aggressive behaviour of parents and their children are not amenable to simplistic explanations and in fact may be accounted for in a variety of different ways. Anyone wishing to sort out the mediating mechanisms must disentangle a great many uncontrolled variables, and yet to do this satisfactorily under experimental conditions is almost impossible. In fact, determining the effects of parental influences is so complex that it is highly unlikely that any etiological relationship can be established either by studying correlations or by simple experiments and they may at best be used to support clearly stated hypotheses.

Studies which have emphasized the various environmental stresses impinging upon abusing parents are equally difficult to interpret. In general, they have based their sample selection on hospital admissions registries or welfare-agency records and these consistently show that abusing parents come from the lower end of the socio-economic scale. This is hardly surprising in view of the reporting procedures. Rarely do cases come to the notice of agencies through GPs or other sources likely to have contact with the upper or middle classes. It therefore becomes difficult to decide which sample population is more likely to be representative of abusing parents and how stress factors such as bad housing, poverty and low birth weight relate to abuse. Whether environmental stresses are independently related to abuse or whether they are artefactually related by way of the social-class characteristics of the abusing parents is impossible to tell from most of the studies discussed. Similar problems are encountered when one looks at the research on the characteristics of the abused child. Most studies have had to depend on the mother's description of her child's characteristics, and in such cases it is extremely difficult to know what is a congenital problem and what is the sensitive response of an infant to its mother's handling. The extremely subtle influences which are continually at work in the mother–infant interaction may begin to operate even before birth (Ottinger and Simmons, 1964).

Finally, it has been pointed out, that for all the cases of economic hardship, unemployment, social isolation, and the rest, there are many families in which such problems exist but the parents never resort to violence.

The long list of factors associated with abuse suggests that many families are living under highly stressful and disadvantageous conditions. Many appear to suffer from physical and mental illness, they may have a particularly difficult child, or they may just have too many too quickly to cope with. Some parents appear to have come from violent and abnormal home backgrounds and to be repeating these patterns with their own children. Whatever the problems, however, without any attempt to weight or order the factors so that their relative contribution can be assessed this information does little to further our understanding and all we can do is speculate about the significance of the interrelated variables. What is needed more than anything else at present is an improvement in the quality of the empirical research.

METHODOLOGICAL PROBLEMS AND CRITICISMS

In order to provide more detailed information on some of the studies referred to throughout the chapter, Table 3·1 has been compiled and included at the end. Only studies which have used a control group have been selected, and, because of their small number, epidemiological studies have been omitted. It will be obvious from a brief study of this table that, since the earliest publications on child abuse, only a few British and American authors have attempted to improve the quality of their research by the use of any control group, and even with this slight refinement there are other obvious weaknesses inherent in much of the work.

The problems of definition discussed earlier have been responsible for wide variations in the characteristics of research samples used, and of course this has led to great difficulties in interpreting results. Several studies include cases of neglect—although it has been suggested they have a different aetiology (Giovannoni, 1971), and several include fatalities or child murders, although Court (1974) has reservations about the inclusion of this latter group on the grounds that it may artificially increase the estimated proportion of aggressive psychopaths present in battering parents. What is needed is clearer thinking in the selection of samples for research purposes. Authors should be able to justify their decisions for including or excluding certain groups in the population, and they should avoid adding to the complications of interpreting results by choosing groups of parents who represent a much narrower range of the total violent population. Without placing such restrictions we can hardly hope for consistency in results and clarity of thinking.

As has already been pointed out, research into child abuse is almost continually haunted by the possibility of sample bias. Welfare cases and people requiring social-work assistance are generally more visible, and the skew towards the lower socio-economic levels in most research samples which have used hospitals and agencies as their source of referral clearly reflect this. Bias, of course, may occur in other ways; some parents may refuse to participate in a study (Elmer, 1967; Smith, 1975) and hospital samples may represent only the most serious cases of injury. Whatever is the case, a great deal could be done to improve the situation by using control groups and yet this has seldom been done. Even in cases where a control group has been used the actual sample sizes are generally too small to make meaningful generalizations. Frequently the research and control samples are of different sizes so that the claim to have 'matched' or 'held constant' several variables is inaccurate and misleading. Furthermore the reliability and validity of the information and results obtained generally remain unmentioned, probably because in a large number of retrospective studies, at least, these are difficult measures to obtain. Studies the purpose of which has been to produce typologies of personalities are not so hampered, however, and yet there seem to be few if any which attempt blind diagnosis and validation of results either by follow-up studies or by cross-validation with other research.

The problems of data collection are numerous, particularly in retrospective studies where records may be incomplete and inaccurate (Oliver *et al.*, 1974). Authors who are searching for significant factors in early childhood rarely stop to define such terms as 'harsh upbringing' or 'rejecting parents' and so it is impossible to discover what degree of punishment or rejection is likely to result in serious damage to the personality.

Research which tries to collect a lot of personal information quickly is also likely to have to sacrifice a certain amount of reliability. For example, interviewing parents on the topic of child abuse before any real relationship has been established with them, is not likely to encourage openness. Similarly, it has been argued that psychiatric diagnosis needs to be a 'progressive process' (Ounsted *et al.*, 1975) rather than based on a single interview.

As an illustration of some of the methodological weaknesses and problems discussed above a more detailed critique of a single set of studies will be undertaken. The extensive work of Smith in Birmingham is an interesting example to choose, not because it is more vulnerable to criticism than other studies but because it still suffers problems despite its more apparently sophisticated approach.

Over a 2-year period the Birmingham group collected information on an index sample of 134 battered children and 214 parents. A child was identified as battered if the parents admitted their guilt or if no adequate explanation of the injuries could be given. All the children were under 5 years old and most of them had been admitted to hospital. Of the 134 children, 20 had subsequently died from their injuries. The control sample comprised 53 children admitted to hospital as emergencies, excluding accident and trauma cases. Parents were matched on the basis of the mothers' age, and the age of the child, and the following variables were held constant: area of residence, consultants referring the case, and the particular circumstances in which the child became suddenly and inexplicably ill. All parents were seen both at the hospital, as soon as possible after the child's admission, and at home, and were given standardized psychiatric, psychological, and social interviews. The index and the control samples were equated for social class by the use of a statistical weighting technique. The total volume of information accumulated on a wide range of topics is impressive and the fact that Smith obtains some significant results which conflict with many of the previous research findings is particularly interesting.

On the issue of sampling procedures, the selection of the index group largely from hospitals results in the predictable low socio-economic bias. While an attempt is made to control for this in the statistical analyses of results, the inclusion of 20 fatal cases may over-represent the number of serious cases of injury in the population, and Court (1974) has already voiced concern at the implications of this on the diagnosis of parent pathology. Still on the issue of sampling, the author has used confession or inadequate explanation of the child's injuries as the selection criteria for his index sample. Additional factors such as lack of concern by the parents and delay in reporting the injury could have provided useful indicators to decide ambiguous cases, but there is no mention of these being used.

The control group is also weak on three points; its relationship to the general population is not known, the control children have not been balanced by a second control group of healthy children, and the control group of parents is considerably smaller than the index group so that claims to have 'matched' them on two variables is not strictly true.

Concern has been voiced over the length and timing of the interviews with the parents (Franklin, 1975). Parents seen just 24 hours after the trauma of the hospital admission and probably feeling highly anxious about the consequences of their child's injury are not likely to give highly reliable answers to a host of personal questions, and the fact that 38% of the index mothers and 20% of the control mothers scored over four on Eysenck's Lie Scale may be an indication of this.

In order to obtain a maximum amount of information as quickly as possible the author relies on the verbal responses of parents to build up a picture of their home life, domestic problems, and child-rearing practices. But the discrepancy between what people say they do and how they behave in reality is often quite marked, even where no deception is intended. In certain situations observation may be the more reliable technique. When the Birmingham study parents were asked about their child-rearing practices and problems many of the habits previously associated with abusers were found to be non-significant. Such discrepancies in the results are not really surprising, however. Parents are less likely to admit their difficulties or portray themselves as over-anxious, harsh or intolerant when they are uncertain about the repercussions of their child's injury on themselves. For example, one of the items which significantly differentiated the two groups was whether wives were glad to get away from their children at times. Smith suggests that the index parents are shown to be deficient in realistic attitudes towards their children because they do not admit to 'finding a break' welcome, but an alternative hypothesis is that they are responding in what they perceive to be the socially desired way.

It can be argued that to collect data over a long period so that the workers and their families become better acquainted and more relaxed in their relationship is likely to introduce new forms of bias. Objective tests ate replaced by subjective judgements. This is true, but some checks can be made by having several people—clinicians, social workers, paediatricians, health visitors, and psychiatrists—collect their various opinions independently over a period of time and then discuss the results together. The difficulty with the Birmingham study and others like it is that although their design allows for a rapid collection of data on a large number of parents there is always a lurking danger of being superficial. The defensiveness, hostility, and lack of willingness to communicate which many abusing parents have shown in response to efforts to make contact, suggests that their response to intensive testing immediately after an abusing incident could well be unreliable.

In conclusion it may be said that the quality of research in the area of child abuse still leaves much to be desired. There has been little attempt to review previous research with a view to formulating and testing specific hypotheses. Spinetta and Rigler (1972) concluded after their survey of the literature that frequently studies 'seem to start and finish with relatively untested common-sense assumptions'. Much of our existing knowledge has been gathered from descriptive studies which lack controls and proper sampling procedures. This has enabled authors to make claims and counter-claims about the importance of different variables, in the absence of any sustained efforts to discover which are directly and which are artefactually related to abuse and consequently theory building becomes more problematic.

From our current state of knowledge, it appears that child abuse is the end product of a highly complex set of interacting factors, both psychological and social. In some cases external environmental stresses seem to predominate and in other cases individual factors take precedence. In the light of these facts how can our present psychological theories contribute to understanding child abuse?

THE RELEVANCE OF THEORIES OF AGGRESSION

There have been very few attempts to fit the available research results to existing theories of aggression and at present it appears that no single psychological theory is adequate either in its explanation or its predictive capacities. Consequently the most recent attempts to construct models of violence have taken an eclectic approach and have borrowed from several different psychological theories (e.g. Gelles, 1972; Kaplan, 1972).

Although individually these theories can help us to understand a little better the dynamics of behaviour they have very definite limitations. As Megargee (1970) has pointed out, for obvious ethical reasons most experimental data is concerned with the relatively mild forms of aggression, and psychologists have been forced to extrapolate to account for the more extreme forms despite the fact that there is little empirical evidence to suggest that moderate and extreme aggression are characterized by the same dynamics. Another problem is that some theories are more amenable to scientific testing than others. Despite the very great influence which psychoanalytic thinking has had on theories of aggression, and more specifically on understanding the personality dynamics of the child abuser, most of the explanations have developed from retrospective analysis, and there has been little attempt to formulate specific hypotheses which can be put to the test.

Having said all this, however, it is still important to be aware of the different perspectives adopted in seeking to understand violent behaviour and to see how successfully these can relate to the specific phenomenon of child abuse.

Most theories of aggression have something to say about the origins of aggressive motivation, and the frustration–aggression hypothesis of Dollard *et al.* (1939) has been one of the most popular theoretical statements on the subject, partly because of its simplicity and apparent generality and partly because it is more amenable to empirical testing than other theories. Much time has been spent in demonstrating that frustration can lead to aggression under carefully controlled laboratory conditions but unfortunately little work has been directed towards testing the hypothesis against situations in the 'real' world, and the more difficult tasks of defining frustration and elaborating the conditions in which a specifically aggressive response is likely to occur, have generally been avoided. In fact the inability of the hypothesis to give an operational definition of frustration has been one of its major weaknesses and has encouraged the proliferation of suggested 'frustrations' without their having any firm empirical basis. One cannot read the child-abuse literature without being aware of how often frustration is invoked as an explanation for violent outbursts and of course the 'frustrations' are numerous. Battering parents may have experienced harsh weaning, severe potty training, lack of mothering, constant physical punishment, poverty, poor marital relations, inability to escape domestic problems, etc., but taken in isolation such stresses cannot predict aggressive responses. This is because neither frustration nor aggression can be examined as if they existed as independent entities. What an individual regards as frustrating and how he responds to the experience will depend on cognitive and emotional variables which are related to his past experience, and these are just the variables the hypothesis has difficulty in dealing with.

Even so frustration has proved to be a useful theoretical construct in helping us understand some of the effects of childhood experiences and for this reason it has some relevance to thinking on child abuse. Sears, Maccoby, and Levin (1957), in their study of child-rearing practices in the United States, obtained a high correlation between parental use of physical punishment and aggression levels in children. Eron *et al.* (1963) also found that the more intense the punishment used by parents in disciplining their children, the higher the aggression rating the punished children received from their peers. The explanation put forward to account for this correlation is based upon the assumption that punishment is a frustrating experience which increases the likelihood of an aggressive response. Therefore when children who have experienced the satisfaction of behaving aggressively are punished by their parents this merely raises the children's frustration level and incites them to further aggression. Returning to the phenomenon of child abuse and remembering that a common feature in many abusive parents' history is their experience of harsh physical punishment, it is easier to understand one of the possible consequences in later life. Adults who have been frequently beaten as children are more likely to be violent in later life because of the peculiar relationship between punishment and aggression which simultaneously reinforces the behaviour and increases the motivation to behave in the punished fashion.

This hypothesized relationship can also help us understand how it is that some parents who physically discipline their children may sometimes eventually injure them. If physical punishment is used as a method of control from an early age then its major effect may be to increase the aggressive behaviour of the child. If the parental response to this is to then increase the intensity of the punishment then a spiral of violence may begin whose tragic end is the serious injury of the child. Carter (1974) has suggested that harsh discipline may be understood as part of a power game in which an insecure parent reacts to the uncontrollable demands of an apparently powerful baby like an unstable totalitarian ruler faced with a rebellion.The parent retrieves his shaky power by subduing the child in a power game which goes too far.

The effects of punishment on behaviour are extremely complex, however, partly because there may be several different consequences rather than just one. Disregarding the motivational aspects of aggressive behaviour, social-learning theorists have concentrated on the modelling effect of the punitive adult on the observer's subsequent behaviour. Experiments have shown the immediate effects of models on the behaviour of young children (Bandura *et al.* 1961, 1963) and also their persistence through time (Hicks 1965). Moreover, the quality of the adult relationship does not seem to be an essential factor in eliciting imitative behaviour as both nurturant and non-nurturant models have been used successfully (Bandura and Huston, 1961). Applying these principles to the models available in a violent home it is possible to hypothesize how generations of abusive parents are produced. To quote Bandura:

> Individuals not only imitate in later life the behaviour they witnessed as children, they also learn how to hit, what to hit with, what the impact should be, and what the appropriate circumstances are for violence.

Thus, children who are exposed to aggressive models in their formative years and who see violence being used as a method of problem solving and as a major means of communication between people, are likely to internalize such patterns of behaviour and imitate them under similar conditions in later life.

Scott (1973b) has suggested that parents who persistently batter their children are those who have learned by positive reinforcement and imitation that aggression is rewarding. By similar mechanisms they have also learned when to stop.

Another aspect of physical punishment which has been studied is its inhibitory effects on the expression of aggression. Learning theorists would argue that punishment for aggressive behaviour should inhibit violent reponses but, as we have already seen, this does not always happen—what really matters, it is agreed, is the strength of the reinforcement against the fear of punishment. If the immediate reward for aggression is sufficiently great then it will overcome the avoidance response, and aggressive acts will continue. On the other hand Scott (1973b) has argued that parents who occasionally erupt with extreme violence are not over-inhibited because they have *learned* to inhibit their responses but more often because they have no confidence in assertive responses. Clearly, learning-theory models of aggressive behaviour have their difficulties.

Despite what has been said about the effects of physical punishment on the development of the child it is quite obvious that the majority of children who are disciplined in this way by their parents do not become violent people in later life, because what really matters is the background parent–child relationship against which the child perceives these training practices. It is this vital relationship which psychoanalytic theory regards as the foundation of all healthy personality growth and consequently it has been given much emphasis by those who feel that violent impulses stem from early childhood experiences.

According to psycho-analytic theory, if a child is to develop into an emotionally mature person then he needs the experience of a satisfying mothering relationship. If this need is not met, if the child is rejected and criticized instead of being loved and valued, then as an adult he will be less able to form satisfying relationships either because of his frustrated dependency needs or because he has not learned to develop 'basic trust' (Erikson, 1963) in his relations with others.

Steele and Pollock have tried to show how this kind of analysis is invaluable to an understanding of the behaviour of abusive parents. Rather than emphasize the wide variety of personality disturbances which characterize so many abusing parents, they consider that the basic problem is a breakdown in 'mothering'. The parents' early experiences of rejection—physical or psychological—leave them unable to respond to their own children appropriately and sensitively. Instead they combine unreal expectations of emotional support with excessively high demands for mature behaviour from very small children. When these standards are not met the children are in grave danger of abuse and any additional stresses on the parent may provoke attack. A little support for this interpretation comes from Melnick and Hurley (1969). They gave a TAT test to a sample of abusing mothers and found them to be significantly higher on 'inability to empathize' and 'frustrated dependency', and significantly lower on 'need to give nurturance', than a group of controls matched for age, social class, and education. Although the experimental group were predominantly lower-class negro mothers and may therefore represent a biased sample, Steele and Pollock claim to have found similar features across all socio-economic levels and Galdston (1965) and Nurse (1966) have lent support to this finding.

Frustrated dependency needs are one possible consequence of rejection and punishment, but impotent rage (Storr, 1972) and feelings of powerlessness (Horney, 1945) have also been described as basic reactions to the same experiences. An infant cannot respond to abuse with either fight or flight—in fact there are indications that punishment tends to *increase* rather than decrease dependency (Maccoby and Masters 1970)—but it may carry its repressed anger into adult life. In a controlled study of 42 infants suffering from abuse, failure to thrive, and a variety of severe developmental problems, maternal attitudes, and personality were assessed and mother–infant interactions observed. Although not all of these cases were non-accidental injuries, the characteristics of the mothers had much in common with clinical descriptions given by professionals treating abusive mothers. Greenberg (1970) comments

> These mothers impressed us as being severely hostile ... and were amazingly unaware that this was a pervasive feature of their personality and mood.

According to this interpretation the origins of aggressive motivation are laid down by our earliest childhood experiences and when these have been particularly harsh it may need much less additional stress to precipitate a violent reponse.

The emphasis on childhood experiences of one kind or another as the fundamental factor in the aetiology of violence has been discussed at length because it represents a fairly large body of opinion in the field of child abuse. Not everyone shares this perspective, however. Goldstein (1975) takes the view that early experiences only play a minor role in the causation of violent acts and that situational variables are much more important. Gil (1971) has argued that the extreme stresses of poverty combined with our acceptance of physical force in the socialization of children are the keys to understanding. Several of the authors who have attempted to develop typologies of abusing parents include a category for parents who seem to be reacting to environmental stresses rather than to internal stimuli (Weston, 1968; Boisvert, 1972; Scott, 1973b) and there are those unaccounted for cases of abuse in which parents appear to have come from relatively happy family backgrounds (Scott, 1973a). Moreover, since it is common to find harsh and rejecting childhood experiences quoted as a significant factor in the aetiology of other kinds of criminal behaviour ranging from juvenile delinquency (Glueck and Glueck, 1950) to murder (Palmer, 1974), then any theory which attempts to explain all child abuse on the basis of early life history must be incomplete.

Not all personality theories look backward to discover the sources of aggressive motivation, however. Those who regard the maintenance of positive self-attitudes as the primary goal of behaviour can explain aggression in terms of certain situational stresses. Kaplan (1972) has suggested that when an individual cannot perceive alternative means of coping with threats to his ego then violent responses may be resorted to. For example, if it is assumed that in adult life occupational roles are a primary means of gaining self-esteem, then failure in these roles may provoke aggression. McKinley (1964) found that the lower the job satisfaction among a group of working men, the higher the percentage who used physical punishment on their children, and this relation held even when social class was controlled for. Similarly, it could be hypothesized that if a wife gains most of her satisfaction and feelings of achievement from her occupational role as wife and mother, then failure to be seen as effective may drive her to assert her superiority in a more punitive fashion. Blumberg (1974) comments that from the Newsons' studies in Nottingham of smacking, one of the most important variables involved was self-esteem. The mother decides she must show who is boss and in the end brute force settles the issue.

The hypothesis that threats to one's self-image are a primary source of aggressive motivation could also be extended into the area of wife battering. O'Brien (1971) in his study of spouses involved in divorce proceedings was able to compare a violent with a non-violent group. The two most significant differences which emerged were the higher educational achievement of the wife and conflict over income. O'Brien suggests that if frustration in the husband is engendered because attempts to be socially effective are unsuccessful and an attempt to assert dominance in more private and aggressive ways may be one alternative response. Marsden and Owens (1975), in their study of 19 battered women who volunteered information in response to an advertisement, found that several wives complained of their husbands' 'unreasonable desire to dominate' and of their resentment if the wife was educationally superior or more successful in making friends. Certainly the home is the one place where personal weaknesses and failings are most likely to be revealed—and accepted—but it is also the place where one is most vulnerable to attack, and a marital quarrel which deteriorates into a personal attack may provoke the spouse with an unstable self-image to defend himself in the only way he was left open.

Self-attitude theory has many similarities to the frustration–aggression hypothesis and it has been suggested that attacks to the ego may be a very potent form of frustration and one highly likely to encourage aggressive responses (Feshbach, 1970). In spite of its appealing plausibility, however, it only explains behaviour in a tautologous way, i.e. circumstances are threatening to the ego which produce an aggressive response and vice versa. It says nothing about why some people have a more vulnerable ego than others, or why some situations are more ego devaluing than others. In fact it is a generally plausible idea which needs much more elaboration and experimental testing to see how useful it can actually be.

In summary, then, it is possible to see how various theories of personality development and of aggression can be used to aid our understanding of the data which has emerged from the research on child abuse. That no single theory can account for all instances of parental violence is perhaps not so surprising since it appears that there is no such thing as a 'typical example of abuse' which represents the majority of cases, nor is there one factor conclusively present and relevant to all cases. Instead the research picture suggests that violence is the end product of a complex interaction of individual, environmental, and interpsychic factors in which the balance between all these influences varies with each individual. Thus theories of aggression which emphasize the importance of one factor over all others in determining behaviour are misleadingly simple. Moreover, the almost complete absence of attempts to test these theories against specific situations in real life to see how appropriate they are, is a serious limitation on their relevance. Clearly there is a need for closer association between research and the development of theoretical perspectives in the field of child abuse.

It does not follow from this, however, that the research results so far obtained have no value. Despite their methodological weaknesses these studies do seem to indicate that certain kinds of influences are quite frequently present and associated with violent behaviour in parents. In a large majority of cases it appears that the abusing parent has suffered physical maltreatment as a child or has lacked a caring and dependable adult figure with whom stable emotional ties could be established. There are the frequently quoted characteristics of youthful marriages and early parenthood often combined with economic hardship and social isolation. Then there are additional stresses such as physical and mental ill-health caused or exacerbated by such factors as marital disharmony and difficult and sickly infants. Finally, there are the problems of emotional immaturity and ignorance concerning proper child care which may result in a parent becoming over-impatient, and too demanding of a child at an early age, or excessively harsh in matters of discipline.

This is the information we have available and clearly it should be utilized in the development of long-term social policies aimed at prevention, and in the planning of treatment programmes. For example, there are certain characteristics of abusing families which maternity hospitals and antenatal clinics could be made aware of. With their access to information concerning the social conditions of families, and their opportunities for observing the earliest parent–child interactions they would be in an excellent position to recognize at an early stage some of the most vulnerable families. For those involved in the treatment process, the research data are less easy to interpret. In view of the importance attributed to the early social and emotional growth of the child their task is to try and ensure that today's abused children do not become tomorrow's battering parents. This often involves attemtping to balance the harm of separating a child from its parents against the other harm of keeping the child with its parents while attempts are made to salvage the family unit. Difficult assessments concerning the potential dangerousness of the parents, their amenability to particular forms of help, and the physical and psychological resilience of the child are all necessary, and the lack of agreement between professionals on these issues testifies to the inadequacy of our knowledge. In this situation the very limited research into the classification of violent parents merits further attention. If it is possible to group people on the basis of what has made them behave violently, then a refinement of this approach may provide a basis for more positive treatment programmes geared specifically to the needs of the individual parents at the same time as allowing difficult legal decisions to be made with more confidence.

NEW DIRECTIONS

In view of these comments, it is necessary to stop and consider in what directions we should move next.

First, and specifically in relation to child abuse, we need better-quality research which goes beyond description to the setting up and testing of hypotheses in properly controlled conditions. Second, we must try and investigate the role of the husband and the father in family violence. This has been a very neglected area of investigation, largely because of the husband being unco-operative or unavailable at the time of research. However, several authors have suggested that men and women are violent for different reasons (Elmer, 1967; Scott, 1973b) and this suggestion needs to be followed up. In particular, the husband's role in relation to the family may be of renewed interest if, with the growing equality of the sexes, fundamental changes within the family begin to take place. Finally, we need to continue the development of typologies of parents. As long as such categories are not regarded as clearly defined entities into which parents can be easily slotted without overlap, then they may have real value in sorting out the important aetiological factors in different cases. Existing typologies should be tested again and their validity and reliability thoroughly checked before they are discarded for new ones.

As regards understanding child abuse and developing a theoretical framework into which this particular manifestation of violence can be fitted, it may perhaps be helpful to think in terms of several causes and several explanations, and to start modestly by looking at small groups of violent parents or at a particular aspect of violent behaviour. By a process of careful and thorough observation it may then be possible to develop a more adequate model of violence in the family, which acknowledges not just the role of individual factors, but also the role of environmental factors and their inevitable interaction.

A final word on the various classification attempts made by researchers may serve as a starting point for this task. Although in general, authors have made their distinctions on the basis of personality differences this need not be the only way of looking at the problem. An alternative approach would be to develop a system in which weight was given to the factors thought to be most influential in producing violent behaviour in different individuals. On this basis at least four categories could be distinguished initially. First, a group of parents whose violence seems to stem largely from some extreme or persistent external pressure(s) to which they can perceive no alternative means of immediate relief. Second, a group whose early learning experiences are likely to give them a certain predisposition to behave violently because they have been surrounded by violence all their lives and have come to regard it as a normal way of reacting to many situations, or because they are not aware that there are alternatives to harsh discipline in rearing a family. Third, a group whose violence seems to stem largely from emotional deficits manifested by such characteristics as extreme egocentricity, excessive or misplaced jealousy, lack of empathy, and poor impulse control. Childhood experiences would probably play an important part in this impaired development but so also might youth and general immaturity. And finally a fourth group for whom violence is but a symptom of serious mental illness.

Although using such broad categories may seem to oversimplify a highly complex phenomenon, it is not being suggested that parents who fall into a particular category cannot share some of the characteristics and problems of parents in other groups, and obviously such categories would be subject to elaboration and refinement as the research data increase. What they do attempt to suggest is that the major source of influence on violent behaviour may be identifiable for different groups of people and these are probably the groups which in view of their nature may require different techniques of treatment.

Table 3.1 Summary tabulation of control-group studies

All the studies contained in this table have been concerned with investigating the characteristics of battering parents and/or their children. They have been selected for inclusion on the criterion that a control group of some description has been used. The studies are listed alphabetically and whenever possible levels of significance have been quoted. The following abbreviations have been used

H—Hospital C—Clinic SSD—Social Services Department P—Prison AB—Abused NS—Not significant

Author (Nationality)	Abuse group (characteristics)	Source of sample	Control group (characteristics)	Source of sample	Data	Results: Children	Results: Parents	Results: Stresses
Elmer (1967) (American)	20 families (low socio-economic)	H	11 families A mixture of 'non-abuse' and 'unclassified'	H	Hospital records	(1) Sex and ordinal position of AB children—NS (2) 31 % AB children premature. No 'non-AB', children premature		Birth of sibling less than 1 year before or after AB child's admission to hospital $p = \cdot 02$
Elmer (1967)	9 families	H	11 non-abuse families	H			(1) Abusive mothers' more negative attitude to child (2) Abusive mothers' more emotional difficulties (3) Abusive mothers socially isolated by active resistance	(1) More marital conflict (2) More household disorganization

Author (nationality)	Abuse group (characteristics)	Source of sample	Control group (characteristics)	Source of sample	Data	Results: Children	Results: Parents	Results: Stresses
Gregg and Elmer (1969) (American)	30 children	H	83 accident children	H		Ordinal position important. Many more accident cases only child	(1) Abusive mothers' more negative interpretation of child's behaviour (2) Abusive mothers' child care ability less	
Lynch (1975) (British)	25 children	H	35 siblings			(1) Sex and ordinal position of AB children—NS (2) Abnormalities during pregnancy and delivery of AB children $p < \cdot 01$ (3) Neonatal/other separations in first 6 months of AB child's life $p < \cdot 01$ (4) AB infant illness in first year $p < \cdot 001$		Abusive mothers ill during first year of AB child's life $p < \cdot 001$

Author (nationality)	Abuse group (characteristics)	Source of sample	Control group (characteristics)	Source of sample	Data	Results		
						Children	Parents	Stresses
Lynch, Roberts and Gordon (1976) (British)	29 children (11 abuse 5 neglect 1 suspected abuse 12 at risk) referred to hospital social worker during preg./neonatal period	H	55 children referred to hospital social worker during preg./neonatal period	H	Hospital records	AB children more often transferred to special care nursery for neonatal illness $p < \cdot 01$	Concern for abusive mothers' ability to cope with needs of child recorded in hospital records $p < \cdot 001$	(1) Abusive mothers admitted to hospital during pregnancy $p < \cdot 05$ (2) Diffuse social problems of abusive parents $p \cdot 001$
Melnick and Hurley (1969) (American)	10 mothers (low socio-economic)	C	10 mothers matched for age, education, socio-economic status		TAT tests	Abusive mothers' (1) inability to empathize $p \cdot 002$ (2) Low need to give nurturance $p \cdot 05$ (3) Low self-esteem $p < \cdot 05$ (4) Highly frustrated dependency needs $p < \cdot 05$		

Author (nationality)	Abuse sample (characteristics)	Source of sample	Control sample (characteristics)	Source of sample	Data	Results: Children	Results: Parents	Stresses
NSPCC psychological study (1976a) (British)	20 parents	H SSD Health visitors	20 parents matched for: age of child, age of parent, ordinal position of child, nationality, type living accommodation		Wechsler and Cattell's 16 P.F.		Abusive fathers: (1) Reserved and detached p ·001 (2) Less Spontaneous p ·001 (3) Less realistic p ·01 (4) Poor emotional control and less integration p ·001 (5) Aggressive p ·05 (6) Lower on extrov. Abusive mothers: (as above) (1) p ·001 (3) p ·05 (4) p ·001 (5) p ·02	
	15 suspected AB children and parents	Register of accidents	15 accident children and parents	Question-naire by health visitor	AB child less likely to be natural child of both parents	(1) Younger p ·01 (2) Difficult to get to know p ·01	(1) Marital stress p ·01 (2) Housing poorer p ·01 (3) Recency last pregnancy p ·01 and advice sought to	

Author (nationality)	Abuse sample (characteristics)	Source of sample	Control sample (characteristics)	Source of sample	Data	Results: Children	Results: Parents	Results: Stresses
Smith (1975) Incorporates all the studies of Smith *et al.*, 1973–1974* (British) * As it is impossible to reproduce these in their entirety, a selection has been made which attempts to summarize the major research findings relevant to the preceding discussion	134 children: AB and suspected AB 214 parents	91 H 18 P 25 SSD GPs and health visitors	53 Emergency admission children Parents matched for: age of mother and age of child Statistically controlled for social class	H	Interview Wechsler Eysenck Personality Inventory EEG Gibson Spiral Maze Foulds hostility quest Vineland social maturity scale Griffiths developmental scale	AB group: (1) Less wakeful at night p ·05 (2) Less excitable or lively p ·05 (3) Crying a problem p ·001 (4) Crying, clinging, whining, severe problem p ·001	Abusive parents: (1) Abnormal personality p ·001 (2) Mothers neurotic with ill health p ·001 (3) Lower IQ p ·001 (4) Unhappy childhood and 2 or more neurotic symptoms p ·001 (5) Mothers' impaired relations with own parents: now p ·001; in past p ·01	Abusive parents: (1) Biological father absent p ·001 (2) Illegitimate babies p ·001 (3) Premarital conceptions p ·001 (4) Mothers no breaks away from children p ·01 (5) Admit fewer marriage problems p ·05 (6) Reservations about pregnancy p—NS (7) Income worries, unemployment p—NS

REFERENCES

Bakan, D. (1971) *Slaughter of the Innocents*, San Francisco: Jossey-Bass.

Bandura, A., and Huston, A. C. (1961) 'Identification as a process of incidental learning' *J. abnorm. soc. Psychol.*, **63**, 311–318.

Bandura, A., Ross, D., and Ross, S. (1961) 'Transmission of aggression through imitation of aggressive models', *J. abnorm. soc. Psychol.*, **63**, 575–582.

Bandura, A., Ross, D., and Ross, S. (1963) 'Imitation of film mediated aggressive models', *J. abnorm. soc. Psychol.*, **66** 3–11.

Bennie, E. H., and Sclare, A. B. (1969) 'The battered child syndrome', *Am. J. Psychiat.*, **125**, 975–979.

Bernal, J. F. (1973) 'Night waking in infants during the first fourteen months', *Develop. Med. Child Neurol.*, **15**, 760–769.

Bibring, G. L. (1961) 'A study of the psychological processes in pregnancy and the earliest mother–child relationship'. In *The Psychoanalytic Study of the Child*, ed. R. S. Eisler, New York: International University Press.

Birns, B., Barsden, S., and Bridger, W. H. (1969) 'Individual difference in temperamental characteristics of infants', *Transactions of the New York Academy of Sciences.*

Birrell, R. G., and Birrell, J. W. H. (1968) 'Maltreatment syndrome in children; a hospital survey', *Med. J. Aust.*, **2**, 1 023–1 029.

Blumberg, M. (1974) 'When parents hit out', In *Violence in the Family* ed S. K. Steinmetz and M. A. Strauss.

Boisvert, M. J. (1972) 'The battered child syndrome', *Soc. Casework*, **53**, 475–478.

Bryant, H. D. (1963) 'Physical abuse of children: an agency study', *Child Welfare*, **42**, 125–130.

Caffey, J. (1972) 'The parent–infant traumatic stress syndrome', *Am. J. Roentgen. rad. Ther. nucl. Med.*, **114**, 218–229.

Cameron, J. M. (1972) 'The battered baby syndrome', *Practitioner*, **209**, 302–310.

Cameron, J. M., Johnson, H. R. M. and Camps, F. E. (1966) 'The battered child syndrome', *Med. Sci. Law*, **6**, 2–21.

Carter, J. (1974) *The Maltreated Child*, London: Priory Press.

Castle, R. L., and Kerr, L. M. (1972) *A Study of Suspected Child Abuse*, NSPCC.

Cherry, B. J., and Kuby, A. M. (1971) 'Obstacles to the delivery of medical care to children of neglecting parents', *Am. J. Pub. Health*, **61**, 568–873.

Clegg, A., and Megson, B. (1968) *Children in Distress*, Harmondsworth: Penguin Books.

Court, J. (1970) 'Psycho-social factors in child battering', *J. Med. Wom. Fed.*, **52**, 99–106.

Court, J. (1974) 'Characteristics of parents and children'. In *The Maltreated Child*, ed. J. Carter, London: Priory Press.

Court, J., and Okell, C. (1970) 'An emergent programme to protect the battered child and his family', *Intervention*, **52**, 99–104.

Davoren, E. (1968) 'The role of the social sorker'. In *The Battered Child*, ed. R. E. Helfer and C. H. Kempe, Chicago: University of Chicago Press.

Dollard, J., Doob, L. W., Miller, N. E., Mowrer, O. H., and Sears, R. R. (1939) *Frustration and Aggression*, New Haven, Conn: Yale University Press.

Elmer, E. (1967) *Children in Jeopardy*, University of Pittsburg Press.

Elmer, E. and Gregg, G. (1967) 'Developmental characteristics of abused children', *Pediatrics*, **40**, 4 Ptl, 596–602.

Erikson, E. H. (1963) *Childhood and Society*, New York: Norton.

Eron, L. D., Walder, L. O., Taigo, R., and Lefkowitcz, M. M. (1963) 'Social class, parental punishment for aggression and child aggression', *Child Dev.*, **34**, 849–867.

Farrington, D. P., and West, D. J. (1971) 'A comparison between early delinquents and young aggressives', *Br. J. Crim.*, **11**, 341–358.

Feinstein, H. M., Paul, N., and Esmiol, P. (1963) 'Group therapy for mothers with infanticidal impulses', *Am. J. Psychiat.*, **120**, 882–886.

Feshbach, S. (1970) 'Aggression'. In *Carmichael's Manual of Child Psychology*, Vol. 2, ed. P. H. Mussen, Wiley, 3rd ed.

Fontana, V. J. (1973) *Somewhere a child is crying*, New York: Macmillan.

Foresman, L. (1965) 'Homemaker service in neglect and abuse', *Children*, **12**, 23–26.

Galdston, R. (1965) 'Observations on children who have been physically abused by their parents', *Am. J. Psychiat.*, **122**, 440–443.

Gayford, J. J. (1975) 'Wife battering: a preliminary study of 100 cases', *Brit. Med. J.*, **1**, 194–197.

Gelles, R. J. (1972) *The Violent Home: a Study of Physical Aggression Between Husbands and Wives*, London: Sage Publications.

Gelles R. J. (1973) 'Child abuse as psychopathology: a sociological critique and reformulation', *Am. J. Orthopsychiat.*, **43**, 611–621.

Gibbens, T. C. N. (1972) 'Violence to children', *Howard Journal*, **13**, 212–220.

Gibbens, T. C. N., and Walker, A. (1956) *Cruel Parents*, London: Institute for the Study and Treatment of Delinquency.

Gil, D. G. (1970) *Violence against Children*, Harvard University Press.

Gil, D. G. (1971) 'Violence to Children', *J. marriage Fam.*, **33**, 639–648.

Giovannoni, J. M. (1971) 'Parental mistreatment: perpetrators and victims', *J. marriage Fam.*, **33**, 649–657.

Glueck, S., and Glueck, E. (1950) *Unravelling Juvenile Delinquency*, Cambridge Mass.: Harvard University Press.

Goldstein, J. H. (1975) *Aggression and Crimes of Violence*, New York: Oxford University Press.

Green, A. H., Gaines, R. W., and Sandgrund, A. (1974) 'Child abuse: pathological syndrome of family interaction', *Amer. J. Psychiat.*, **131**, 882–886.

Greenberg, N. G. (1970) 'Atypical behaviour during infancy: infant developments in relation to the behaviour and personality of the mother'. In *The Child and his Family*, ed. E. J. Anthony and C. Koupernick, Wiley.

Gregg, G. S., and Elmer, E. (1969) 'Infant injuries: accident or abuse?', *Pediatrics*, **44**, 443–449.

Hicks, D. J. (1965) 'Imitation and retention of film mediated aggressive peer and adult models', *J. Pers. soc. Psychol.*, **2**, 97–100.

Holter, J., and Friedman, S. B. (1968) 'Child abuse: early case finding in the emergency department', *Pediatrics*, **42**, 128–138.

Horney, K. (1945) *Our Inner Conflicts*, New York: Norton.

Hyman, C. A. (1973) 'I.Q. of parents of battered babies', *Brit. Med. J.*, **4**, 739.

Johnson, B., and Morse, H. A. (1968) 'Injured children and their parents', *Children*, **15**, 147–152.

Kaplan, H. B. (1972) 'Towards a general theory of psychsocial deviance', *Soc. Sci. and Med.*, **6**, 593–617.

Klaus, M. H., Jerwauld, R., Kreger, N. C., Kreger, N. C., McAlpine, W., Steffa, M., and Kennell, J. H. (1972) 'Maternal attachment: importance of the first post-partum days', *New Eng. J. Med.*, **286**, 460–463.

Klein, M., and Stern, L. (1971) 'Low birth weight and the battered child syndrome', *Am. J. Dis. Child*, **122**, 15–18.

Lissovey, V. de (1973) 'High School marriages; a longitudinal study', *J. marriage Fam.*, **35**, 245–255.

Lukianowicz, N. (1971) 'Battered children', *Psychiatria Clinica*, **4**, 257–280.

Lynch, M. (1975) 'Ill health and child abuse', *The Lancet*, 16 August, 317.

Lynch, M., Lindsay, J., and Ounsted, C. (1975) 'Tranquillisers causing aggression', *Brit. Med. J.*, **1**, 266.

Lynch, M., Roberts, J., and Gordon, M. (1976) 'Early warning of child abuse', *Dev. Medicine and Child Neurology,* December.

Lynch, M., Steinberg, D., and Ounsted, C. (1975) 'Family unit in a children's hospital', *Brit. Med. J.*, 2, 127–129.

Maccoby, E. E., and Masters, J. C. (1970) 'Attachment and dependency'. In *Carmichael's Manual of Child Psychology*, ed. P. H. Mussen, Wiley, 3rd ed.

McKinley, D. G. (1964) 'Work and the family'. In *Social Class and family life*, New York, Free Press.

Marsden, D., and Owens, D. (1975) 'The Jekyll and Hyde marriages', *New Society*, 32, (333).

Megargee, E. I. (1970) 'Undercontrolled and overcontrolled personality types in extreme antisocial aggression'. In *The Dynamics of Aggression*, ed. E. I. Megargee and J. E. Hokanson, London, Harper & Row.

Melnick, B., and Hurley, J. R. (1969) 'Distictive personality attributes of child abusing mothers', *J. of consult. clin. Psychol.*, 33, 746–749.

Merrill, E. J. (1962) 'Physical abuse of children: an agency study'. In *Protecting the Battered Child*, ed. V. de Francis, Denver, Colorado: Children's Division, American Humane Association.

Morris, M. G., and Gould, R. W. (1963) 'Role-reversal: A necessary concept in dealing with the battered child syndrome', *Am. J. Orthopsychiat.*, 33, 298–299.

Newson, J., and Newson, E. (1968) *Four Years Old in an Urban Community*, London: Allen & Unwin.

NSPCC (1976a) *At Risk: an Account of the Work of the Battered Child Research Department*, London: Routledge & Kegan Paul.

NSPCC (1976b) *Registers of Suspected Non-Accidental Injury. Battered Child Research Department*, London: Routledge & Kegan Paul.

Nurse, S. M. (1966) 'Familial patterns of parents who abuse their children', *Smith College Studies in Social Work*, 35, 11–25.

O'Brien, J. E. (1971) 'Violence in divorce prone families', *J. marriage Fam.*, 33, 692–697.

Oliver, J. E., and Cox, J. (1973) 'A family kindred with ill used children in one family pedigree', *Brit. J. Psychiat.*, 123, 81–90.

Oliver, J. E., Cox, J., Taylor, A., and Baldwin, J. A. (1974) 'Severely ill-treated children in North East Wiltshire', Research Report No. 4, Oxford Record Linkage Study, Oxford Regional Health Authority.

Oliver, J. E., and Taylor, A. (1971) 'Five generations of ill-treated children in one family. Pedigree', *Brit. J. Psychiat.*, 119, 473–480.

O'Neill, J. A., Meacham, W. F., Griffin, D. P., and Sawyers, J. L. (1973) 'Patterns of injury in the battered child syndrome', *J. of Trauma*, 13, 332–339.

Oppé, T. E. (1968) 'The battered child, a pediatrician's and a psychiatrist's views', address given at the 1968 Annual Council Meeting of NSPCC.

Ottinger, D. R., and Simmons, J. E. (1964) 'Behaviour of human neonates and prenatal maternal anxiety', *Psychol. Rep.*, 14, 391–394.

Ounsted, C., and Lynch, M. A. (1976) 'Family pathology as seen in England', in *Child Abuse and Neglect, The Family and the Community*, Ed. R. E. Helfer and C. H. Kempe, Cambridge, Mass.: Ballinger.

Ounsted, C., Oppenheimer, R., and Lindsay, J. (1975) 'The psychopathology and psychotherapy of the families: aspects of bonding failure'. In *Concerning Child Abuse*, ed. A. W. Franklin, Edinburgh, London, and New York: Churchill Livingstone.

Palmer, S. (1974) Physical frustration and murder'. In *Violence in the Family*, ed. S. K. Steinmetz and M. A. Strauss, New York: Harper & Row.

Paulson, M. J., Savino, A. B., Chaleff, A. B., Saunders, R. W., Frisch, F., and Dunn, R. (1972) 'Parents of the battered child', *Lifethreatening Behaviour*, 4, 27.

Pohlman, E. H. (1969) *Psychology of Birth Planning*, Cambridge, Mass.: Schenkman.

Renvoize, J. (1974) *Children in Danger*, London: Routledge & Kegan Paul.

Richards, M. P. M. (1974) 'Non-accidental injury to children in an ecological perspective', paper presented at a conference organized by the DHSS, June 1974.

Rutter, M. (1974) 'A child's life', *New Scientist*, **62**, 763–766.

Schaffer, H. R., and Emerson, P. E. (1964) 'Patterns of response to physical contact in early human development', *J. Child Psychol. and Psychiat.*, **5**, 1–13.

Scott, P. D. (1973a) 'Parents who kill their children', *Med. Sci. Law*, **13**, 120–126.

Scott, P. D. (1973b) 'Fatal battered baby cases', *Med. Sci. Law.*, **13**, 197–206.

Scott, P. D. (1974) 'Battered wives', *Brit. J. Psychiat.*, **125**, 433–441.

Sears, R. R., Maccoby, E. E., and Levin, H. H. (1957) *Patterns of Child Rearing*, New York, Evanston, and London: Harper & Row.

Selig, A. L. (1974) 'The myth of the multi problem family', *Am. J. Orthopsychiat.*, **46**, 526–531.

Silver, L. B., Dublin, C. C., and Lourie, R. S. (1969) 'Does violence breed violence?', *Am. J. Psychiat.*, **126**, 404–407.

Silverman, F. C. (1968) 'Radiological aspects of the battered child syndrome'. In *The Battered Child Syndrome*, ed. R. E. Kempe and V. H. Helfer, University of Chicago Press.

Sims, B. G., Grant, J. H., and Cameron, J. M. (1973) 'Bite-marks in the Battered Baby Syndrome', *Med. Sci. Law*, **13**, 207–210.

Skinner, A. E., and Castle, R. L. (1969) *'78 Battered Children*: a Retrospective Study, NSPCC.

Smith, S. M. (1975) *The Battered Child Syndrome*, London and Boston: Butterworth.

Smith, S. M., and Hanson, R. (1974) '134 battered children: a medical and psychological study', *Brit. Med. J.*, **3**, 666–670.

Smith, S. M., Hanson, R., and Noble, S. (1973) 'Parents of battered babies: a controlled study', *Brit. Med. J.*, **4**, 388–391.

Smith, S. M., Hanson, R., and Noble, S. (1974) 'Social aspects of the battered baby syndrome', *Brit. J. Psychiat.*, **125**, 568–582.

Spinetta, J. J., and Rigler, D. (1972) 'The child abusing parent; a psychological review', *Psychol. Bull.*, **77**, 296–304.

Steele, B. F. (1968) 'The battered child', *Child's Guardian*, Sept. 1968 pp.16–18.

Steele, B. F., and Pollock, C. B. (1968) 'A psychiatric study of parents who abuse their small children'. In *The Battered Child Syndrome*, ed. R. E. Helfer and V. H. Kempe, University of Chicago Press.

Storr, A. (1972) *Human Aggression*, London: Heinemann.

Terr, L. C. (1970) 'A family study of child abuse', *Am. J. Psychiat.*, **127**, 665–671.

Walters, D. R. (1975) *The Physical and Sexual Abuse of Children*, Indiana University Press.

Wasserman, S. (1967) 'The abused parent of the abused child', *Children*, **14**, 175–179.

Weston, J. T. (1968) 'The pathology of child abuse'. In *The Battered Child Syndrome*, ed. R. E. Helfer and C. H. Kempe, University of Chicago Press.

White Franklin, A. (1975) *Concerning Child Abuse*. Papers presented by the Tunbridge Wells Study Group on Non-Accidental Injury to Children. Edinburgh: Churchill Livingstone.

Young, L. (1964) *Wednesday's Children*: A Study of Child Neglect and Abuse, New York: McGraw-Hill.

4

CRIMINOLOGICAL ASPECTS OF FAMILY VIOLENCE

F.H. McClintock

Introduction

There is clearly a great deal of concern over the known incidence of criminal violence within the family today. Attention has been directed towards the apparent increase in this kind of violence by those concerned with law enforcement and criminal justice as well as by social-welfare administrators and members of the medical and teaching professions. During the last decade or so research into various aspects of the subject has been intensified and a considerable amount of interdisciplinary discussion has been concentrated upon the phenomenon of the battered baby and the battered spouse.[1]

Criminological studies of a systematic nature, however, have rarely been undertaken and as a result of the dearth of the data most of the discussions of the issues involved have been based upon personal impressions, assumptions or even speculations as to the true nature of the phenomenon of criminal violence in the home.[2] And even on the strength of several recent surveys on violence in Great Britain, together with collaborative work sponsored by the Council of Europe, and contributions from North America, we have to admit that we are still far from a clear appreciation and understanding of the criminal incidents in family conflict.[3]

In order to avoid confusion, it is important at the outset to be clear and precise about two matters: (1) the definition of that which is being discussed, and (2) the relationship between such a defined area and what is being excluded from the discussion. For example, from a strictly criminological and criminal justice perspective, one is concerned with social behaviour that is defined as *criminal* violence, and not with all forms of aggressive behaviour within the home. This, of course, is not to suggest that it is desirable or even possible to discuss the one without considering the other, since clearly an understanding of the nature of criminal violence in the family, as well as measures for its effective prevention and control, cannot be attained without reference to the wider context of aggressiveness in the home or indeed in society generally (McClintock, 1974b).

CRIMINALLY VIOLENT CONDUCT IN THE FAMILY

First of all, it has to be accepted that the concept of *violence* is an extremely complex one, and merely to discuss the subject on the basis that we all know what violence means can be both confusing and unproductive. Second, even after distinguishing the *criminal* aspects of violent conduct in the home, it has to be recognized that the criminal justice process is only one of the control systems within society and that the extent and nature of its operation will depend on the other systems which directly or indirectly control aggressiveness or violence in the home, e.g. medical, educational, economic, religious, and social-welfare control systems as well as the civil law. Third, the process of labelling violence in the family as *criminal* involves the appreciation of the circumstances of the parties involved—their social milieu and social class—as well as the attitude to aggressive conduct adopted by the onlooker, the police, and agencies of other systems of social control. In this context therefore the so-called 'dark figure' of criminal violence in the home—that which is not reported to or recorded as such by the police—should be seen not just as an actuarial question of the number of *known* and *unknown* acts of violence but rather in terms of the degree of perceived social deviance within different reference groups, and according to the norms of those operating the various legal and social control systems. In one sense *criminal* violence has to be both *socially* and *legally* defined (Hadden and McClintock, 1970).

Illegal violent conduct

It has been argued by some writers that the concept of violent conduct is so imprecise that it is of little use in any attempt to treat the subject in an empirical or scientific way (West and Wiles, 1973). There is much in favour of such a viewpoint, but on the other side it has to be recognized that in most societies 'violence' is a concept used in public discussion—around which are clustered a number of ideas and images—and may be regarded at least as a convenient starting point for a more systematic and serious consideration of the phenomenon.

The ideal home is often portrayed as free from aggressiveness, one in which there is a continuing mutual understanding and affection between the spouses, and between them and their offspring. On the other hand a number of psychiatrists and sociologists who label themselves as radical regard the family in its present form as a repressive and damaging social institution. How far either view should be accepted will not be discussed here, but it is clear from the literature and from direct studies of family life that in fact conflict and aggressiveness are very often a general or spasmodic feature in home life. Violence and aggressiveness in the home may take many different forms. They may be manifested in verbal attacks, such as cutting or sarcastic remarks, or outbursts of temper; in the destruction of property; in bullying and what in other contexts might be regarded as blackmail; in repressive control or restriction of freedom; as well as physical assault inflicted with the intention of causing pain and suffering in the name of the disciplining of children. On the other side there is violent or aggressive behaviour which is accepted and even sometimes encouraged, such as friendly wrestling and horseplay between siblings and with their parents; even love making may on occasion be accompanied by physical aggressiveness. In all these forms, what would be acceptable in, say, certain working-class environments could be considered a serious assault in a middle-class community. This is not to suggest that criminal violence in the family does not occur in middle-class homes. In fact, it was clear from our survey (see p. 95 below) that physical violence in middle-class homes was more likely to lead to civil court proceedings of a matrimonial sort, whereas in working-class homes the probation department or the police were generally brought in to deal with the situation.

In the family, as in other social contexts, the criminal law is only concerned with distinguishing that social behaviour which is in a formal sense *illegal* and which carries with it the possibility of a penal sanction for those found guilty; its authority is not invoked for all forms of conduct that are regarded as either socially unacceptable or morally undesirable. Accordingly, mental cruelty practised in the home, although often more harmful to the victim than physical assault, will if taken to court usually be a matter of civil and not criminal proceedings. Indeed many offensive acts which adversely affect the quality of life in the home breach neither the civil nor the criminal law.

When one makes a closer examination of the problem it is found that there is no general definition of violence in the criminal law; there is only the definition of specific offences which have been conventionally grouped together as 'crimes of violence against the person'. These include homicides, assaults, woundings, robbery, rape, and certain other sexual offences. They have in common a willingness to inflict physical injury on the person. As such they contain the two elements of *intention* and *personal injury actually inflicted*, complicated in practice by changes in the emphasis through the law on diminished responsibility, by the law of provocation, the plea of justifiable defence, and circumstances of drunkenness. The criminologist recognizes that the professional lawyer is rightly concerned with a rather restricted range of issues and usually ignores the social phenomenon of violence in the home as such; that the law is not entirely firm and rigid but is undergoing change, slowly but sometimes dramatically; and that in the enforcement of the law and judicial process there is considerable discretion exercised by the police, the prosecuting authorities, and the judiciary.[4] Such flexibility and fluidity in the legal process has to be taken into account in any systematic study of criminal violence in the family.

Criminal process and other control systems

In an earlier article on law in social control systems it has been emphasized that the way in which problems are defined and formulated is related to the structure and availability of different systems of social control (McClintock and Hadden 1970b). Violence in the home may be seen as primarily a mental-health problem and dealt with through the medical services, as in the case of the man who, seeing his doctor about depressions and anxieties, admits to violent conduct to his wife and children. It may be dealt with as a social-welfare question when the home situation reveals severe economic deprivation and overcrowding, or as an educational problem where one or both parents are found to be mentally dull and educationally backward. Again ministers of religion not infrequently have to deal with pastoral matters relating to the family where physical violence has occurred. Furthermore, one can ask whether, within the legal system, events are dealt with through the criminal or civil law process, as in the case of persistent physical violence by a husband against his wife.

It should further be noted that the *indirect* preventive aspects of criminal violence in the home are also related to the various systems of control, in measures to deal with other problems, such as alcoholism, overcrowding, and poverty, all of which have been shown to be significantly associated with known criminal violence.

Wolfgang Friedmann stated this succinctly some years ago (1972, p.234).

> It is ... no longer sufficient to concentrate on the alternative purposes and sanctions of criminal law as such .... A criminal sanction—even with the greater variety and flexibility of methods of punishment used today—is but one of a number of devices by which the modern state seeks to exercise authority over private conduct.

Social attitudes and 'hidden violence' in the family

As noted elsewhere, 'hidden violence' can be defined as those acts of criminal violence which are not reported to, or recorded in, the criminal justice system (McClintock, 1970; Hood and Sparks, 1970). The reasons why crimes of violence are not reported or recorded are varied and numerous and have been discussed in the context of the findings of hidden delinquency studies and victim studies. Such studies should not be seen mainly as an accountancy question of totalling the number of crimes of violence committed in the home, but should be seen as adding a new dimension when studying questions of law enforcement, criminal justice process, and penology. Their significance is related to the difference in social attitudes towards criminal violence that prevail within various sections of the community and among those responsible for social and legal controls.

CRIME TRENDS AND CRIMINAL VIOLENCE IN THE FAMILY

A general increase in crimes recorded by the police during the last 25 years has been manifested in most industrial countries and is fairly well documented from official crime statistics. It is also found that similar trends are now affecting the Third World countries. In most Western countries there has been an increase in recorded criminal violence against the person as well. Mostly such increases have been at a greater rate than those of offences against property, although even with such an acceleration criminal violence still accounts for only a small proportion of the total volume of crimes that are recorded by the police. For example, in England and Wales, over the last 25 years, indictable crimes of violence recorded by the police went up from under half a million in 1950 to over 2 million in 1975, which represents a more than four-fold increase.[5] During the same period indictable crimes of violence and robberies soared from 7000 to 74 000 offences recorded by the police: a more than ten-fold increase. In England and Wales crimes of violence and robbery, accounting for 1·5% of all crimes recorded by the police in 1950, by 1975 reached 4%. Thus, although Table 4.1 indicates the very substantial increase in recorded crimes of violence, the proportion of such crimes in relation to the total volume is low since the bulk of offences are committed against property. It can be seen from Table 4.1 that, for the last 5-year period for which official crime data are available, there have been substantial increases in crimes recorded in each of the main legal categories; woundings and robbery showed the main increases, amounting in that short span of years to a figure equivalent to approximately 80%. International comparisons of criminal statistics are known to be fraught with ambiguities and inequivalences. Where data are available it would appear that recorded criminal violence has been mounting in most Western European countries, but the trend has not on the whole been as accentuated as in England and Wales; while the increases and the incidence in relation to the size of the population in North America (both USA and

Table 4.1 Indictable crimes of violence and robberies known to the police in England and Wales for selected years, 1950–1975

Class of offences	1950	1960	1970	1975	25-year increase (1950–75)	5-year increase (1970–75)
Homicides and attempts	531	534	797	1014	483 (91·0%)	217 (27·2%)
Woundings	5258	14 391	39 266	67 919	62 661 (1191·7%)	28 653 (73·0%)
Rape	314	515	884	1040	726 (231·2%)	156 (17·6%)
Robbery	1021	2014	6273	11 311	10 290 (1007·8%)	5038 (80·3%)
Total	7124	17 454	47 220	81 284	74 160 (1041·0%)	34 064 (72·1%)

Canada) would appear to be very much greater. In Scotland the increase in recorded violence during the recent 25-year period has not been so great as in England and Wales, i.e. a less than eight-fold as contrasted with a ten-fold increase. Details are given in Table 4.2.

Table 4.2 Crimes of violence and robberies known to the police in Scotland shown for selected years, 1950–1975

Class of offence	1950	1960	1970	1975	25-year increase (1950–1975)	5-year increase (1970–1975)
Homicides and attempts	45	45	176	220	175 (388·9%)	44 (25·0%)
Assaults	395	1029	2236	3174	2779 (703·5%)	938 (41·9%)
Rape	30	73	187	287	257 (856·7%)	100 (53·5%)
Robberies	346	606	2138	3452	3106 (897·7%)	1314 (61·5%)
Total	816	1753	4737	7133	6317 (774·1%)	2396 (50·6%)

In making comparisons between Scotland, and England and Wales, it has to be remembered, of course, that the population in the latter combination is approximately ten times greater; and from the data available in Tables 4.1 and 4.2 it can be calculated that in 1975 the homicide and rape rates per 1000 of the population in Scotland were twice as high as in England and Wales; that of robbery was three times, while that of indictable conflict violence only half that of England and Wales. The low recorded rate of non-fatal conflict crimes of violence in Scotland is likely to be related to attitudes in reporting and recording such offences and there is some evidence to suggest that deeds of violence that would be recorded as 'other woundings' by the police in England and Wales, are not infrequently recorded as 'breaches of the peace' in Scotland and would not therefore appear at all in the serious assaults category in the official statistics for Scotland.

No direct and systematic information is available as to the number of crimes of violence directly involving members of the same family. However, in several research studies of violence attempts have been made to classify recorded crimes of violence according to the social context in which they occurred (McClintock and Avison, 1968; McClintock, 1963; McClintock, 1974a). In such studies we found that between a quarter and a third of recorded crimes of conflict violence related to domestic disputes (a category that includes quarrels between landlord and tenant, between lodgers, persons sharing flats, persons working together, etc., as well as intra-family affrays). If all but intra-family disputes are subtracted, then an approximate estimate is reached of 1 in 5 of all reported crimes of conflict violence, in

England and Wales, and 1 in 7 in Scotland as involving members of the same family. This proportion seems to have remained much the same over recent years, which can perhaps be taken as one of the indicators that criminal violence within the family should be viewed in the context of increases in criminal violence in a whole range of other social circumstances. Figure 4.1 illustrates, for the London area, the increases from 1957 to 1970 of violence occurring in different circumstances and with differing motives. It is clear that the increase in domestic disputes resulting in criminal violence follows the general pattern of other forms of criminal violence.

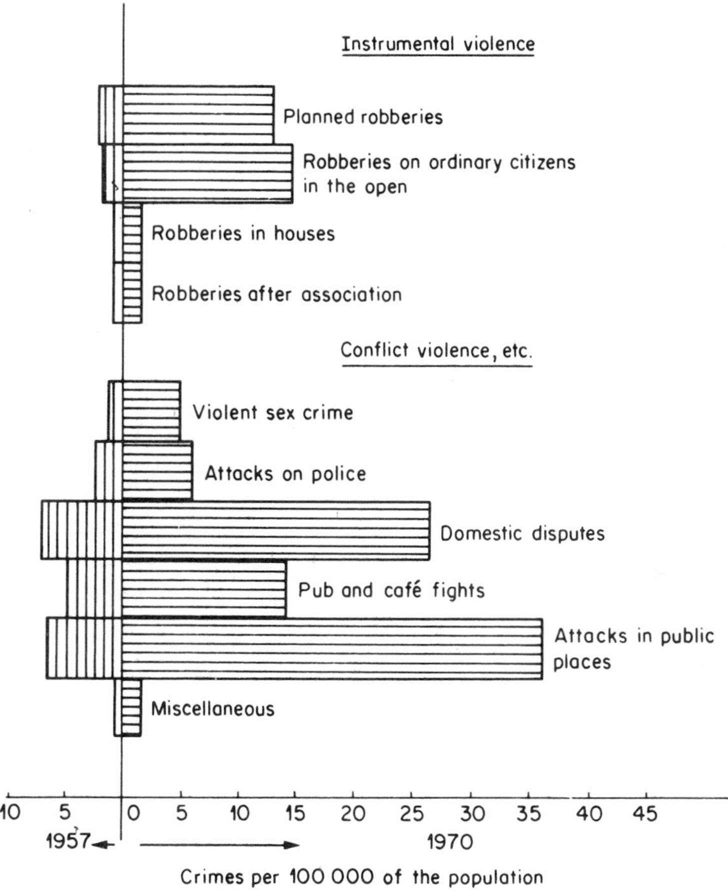

Figure 4.1 Diagram showing the situational classification of crimes of violence and of robberies known to the police in London (MPD and City) per 100 000 population, 1957 and 1970

While it is important to study family violence as a distinct subclass of conflict violence, it should not be overlooked that the resort to criminal violence in other situations of conflict—e.g. among friends, fellow-workers, associates and neighbours in places of entertainment, youths congregating in public places and at sporting events—may be directly related to any experience of violence within the home. Alternatively it can be argued that the increase of violence and aggressive behaviour in its various social manifestations results from a general breakdown in the respect for the authority throughout society and the confusions that have arisen in matured or fast-maturing industrial societies where the previous emphasis upon tradition, social hierarchy, and continuity has given way to rapid technological and social change, with its consequential accompaniment of disruptive class attitudes and pluralistic value systems (Council of Europe, 1974).

In the following section information obtained from an English survey of some 15 000 cases of violence known to the police is examined in so far as it relates to family violence. Such crimes can be divided into two broad categories, namely (1) offences against the person arising out of conflict, and (2) instrumental violence, or violence against the person in the course or furtherance of theft. Family violence is clearly predominantly in the former division, although occasionally robberies involve members of the same family as offender and victim (McClintock and Gibson, 1961).

THE MORPHOLOGY OF FAMILY VIOLENCE IN ENGLAND AND WALES

In the English survey of violence in urban areas it was found that some 15% of all indictable crimes of violence against the person were committed within the family, amounting to 1527 crimes recorded as being known to the police in 1970. The cases of family violence exclude common assaults which are dealt with as non-indictable offences in the magistrates' courts; this procedure is also discussed in McClintock (1963, chapter 1) and McClintock (forthcoming). The family unit in the 1970 survey was defined as the primary domestic group, comprising basically husband and wife and offspring and other relatives by blood or marriage domiciled with them. The definition was extended to include couples with ties of cohabitation of not less than 6 months' duration, where the association could be described as a 'common-law marriage'. The definition of the family for this survey did not include lodgers or persons sharing flats or other premises on a non-familial basis. The non-familial domestic disputes, neighbourhood quarrels, and altercations between people at work together—some of whom were related—accounted for a further 1887 crimes, but these are excluded from consideration under the definition of family violence.

The distribution of the crimes of 'family violence' recorded by the police is shown in Table 4.3. Although these districts do not constitute a truly representative sample of the whole country or even of its urban areas, it is of some interest to note that they contain approximately a quarter of the population and, where information is available on the situational

Table 4.3 Distribution of crimes of 'family violence' recorded by the police

London (MPO and City)	822 (53·8%)
Greater Manchester	339 (22·2%)
Nottingham City area	284 (18·6%)
Mid-Anglia & Hertfordshire	82 (5·4%)
	1527 (100·0%)

classifications of violence elsewhere, they appear to project much the same pattern as that ascertained for the total survey.[6]

From an examination of the basic information recorded by the police on the 1527 recorded cases of family violence a number of salient characteristics of the group can be established.

(1) Almost three-quarters of the victims were females (1128 or 74%), the remaining male victims numbering 399 (26%). Thus, while the prevalence of the battered female, or more particularly the battered wife, is confirmed, it should not be overlooked that there is a substantial proportion of battered husbands in the group as well as fathers battered by their sons. Comparisons drawn in the course of an earlier survey in the London area would indicate a greater increase in cases involving male victims over those involving female victims. There is, too, an increase in cases involving females as offenders against female victims, mainly mothers and daughters but also in those involving 'in-laws'. In the English survey there were 42 cases of criminal violence in which both parties were female, mostly mothers and daughters. As might be expected, the majority of cases involved only one offender and one victim. In only 156 incidents, or 10% of the cases, were there either two or more offenders or two or more victims. These multiple incidents fell into three categories: (a) those cases in which a parent battered more than one child, (b) those cases in which the husband attacked the wife and children, and (c) those attacks resulting from family quarrels involving adults, usually including a relation through marriage or a blood relative.

(2) In more than two-thirds of the cases of family violence the conflict or dispute was between spouses or cohabitees. The second largest group involved attcks by a parent upon a child. Two other smaller groups involved an offspring attacking a parent, and conflicts, resulting in criminal violence, between brothers and sisters. Details are given in Table 4.4.

(3) The majority of crimes of violence within the family occurred in what have been described as the slums, the transitional, or socio-economically deprived areas of urban society where there was widespread unemployment. At the time of the offence of violence, when the general level of unemployment in England and Wales was relatively low, almost a quarter of the families concerned were experiencing unemployment. More than 85% of the families were in the lower socio-economic groups of the Registrar General's classification, with the breadwinner among the manual, casual, or

Table 4.4 Members of family involved in acts of violence

Spouses	759 (49·7%)		
Cohabitees	287 (18·8%)	1046	(68·5%)
Parent against child under 2 years	123 (8·1%)		
Parent against child 2 years & over	60 (3·9%)	183	(12·0%)
Son or daughter against parent		99	(6·5%)
Siblings (brothers and sisters)		57	(3·7%)
Other relatives in the family (incl. in-laws, aunts, cousins, etc.)		142	(9·3%)
		1527	(100·0%)

semi-skilled workers. Ten per cent of the families were in the higher socio-economic groups living in suburban or middle-class neighbourhoods.

(4) The situations leading to the outbreak of criminal violence in the home were inevitably marked by extreme variety. Some were the culmination of long-standing conflict or discord; others resulted from sexual jealousy or some other serious clash of wills; while others seemed to have been triggered off by some minor incident. There was also a small number of cases in which there was evidence of mental problems: of depression, neurotic symptoms or other forms of mental illness. The causative or significantly associated factor of alcoholic drink is often referred to in the case of violence generally and family violence in particular. Having regard to the social milieu in which a high proportion of the offences occurred, it is perhaps somewhat surprising to find that in 82% there was no indication of drink having been taken at all immediately prior to the offence by either offender or victim. Some drink had been taken in 10% and a lot of drink had been taken in 8% of the cases. *Heavy* drinking by the offender occurred more freqently than *heavy* drinking by the victim, although it should be noted that in 9% of the cases of criminal violence the victim had been drinking immediately prior to the crime (see Table 4.5).

Table 4.5 Drinking and family violence

No information as to drinking by offender or victim	1255	(82%)
Offender having been drinking	138	(9%)
Offender and victim having been drinking	110	(8%)
Victim only having been drinking	24	(1%)
	1527	(100%)

(5) It is only to be expected that the vast majority of crimes of family violence were found to occur during the weekends, and that the most critical times, both during the weekends and during weekdays, were between 6 p.m.

and midnight, the larger proportion involving adult victims occurring between 10 p.m. and 1 a.m. The weekends and evenings are the peak times of leisure activities when members of the family have an opportunity to be together, but the eruption of criminal violence in the family at other times also needs to be separately considered.

(6) In parts of the urban areas chosen for the English survey, where the proportion of coloured inhabitants is mounting, the proportion of their cases of family violence was likewise. However, the incidence is no higher than might be expected having regard to the density of such groups in the locality, their socio-economic status, and the economic deprivation of the districts they inhabit. Seventy-five per cent of the cases of family violence involved the indigenous white families; 17% involved coloured families, and 8% involved familes of mixed ethnic groups (see Table 4.6). In this connection it is particularly important to stress that it is not known to what extent the reporting of criminal violence to the police is influenced by the ethnic origins of the offenders and victims, or those who witness such crimes. (There is some evidence from the recent survey that ethnic minorities are less likely to report crimes of violence to the police than the indigenous white population.)

Table 4.6 Offender and victim of family

White *v* white	1140	(74·6%)
Coloured *v* coloured	261	(17·1%)
Mixed ethnic families:		
White *v* coloured	27	(1·8%)
Coloured *v* white	99	(6·5%)
	1527	(100·0%)

(7) Information on the *modus operandi* of the crime indicates that no weapon was used in 6 out of 10 of the crimes; in such cases injuries were inflicted by punching and kicking. In the 40% of the cases in which a weapon was used, blunt instruments were more frequently recorded than sharp, and more often than not were objects ready to hand and picked up in the heat of conflict, rather than premeditatively selected. The deliberately planned attack was a fairly rare type distinguished in less than 10% of the cases, while the use of fire-arms was noted in less than 1% of all cases of family violence (these were mainly shot-guns and air-guns rather than fire-arms acquired for a criminal attack).

(8) The degree of injury varied enormously from crime to crime: 4% of the cases ended in death; in a further 15% the victim sustained multiple internal injuries, fractured bones or serious stab wounds; in 23% of the cases injuries ranged from extensive bruising to moderate cuts and stabs; in the great majority (60%) the injuries were fairly trivial or merely nominal. In more than half of the cases the injuries were inflicted on the face or head of the victim. (Owing to rounding errors these percentages add up to more than 100.)

(9) The recorded violence between spouses occurred in all age groups although there appeared to be a greater frequency among those of the middle and late 20s, and the late 30s and early 40s; such higher incidence was associable with the earlier period (i.e. the first 3 to 8 years) of married life, and with its middle years, and may indicate periods of potentially high stress between the parties.

(10) In accordance with one's expectations in such a category of crime the previous criminal records of the offenders seemed to have little bearing upon their proneness to domestic violence. It was found that for half of the offenders it was their first court appearance. In a quarter of the cases there was evidence of previous convictions for non-violent offences only (mainly thefts and breakings), while in a further quarter of the cases there was recorded at least one previous conviction for a crime of violence, although most of such offenders also had previous convictions of a non-violent nature which appeared distinctly more habitual than the violent crime; in only 4% were the criminal records of recidivists exclusively related to violent crime.

Among the violent recidivists less than 15% had a previous conviction for family violence; mainly the convictions were for violence in related conflict situations involving neighbours, lodgers, landlords, fellow-employees, friends, or casual acquaintances met in public houses or other places of entertainment, or in the streets. Among one group of the violent recidivists previous convictions for robbery with violence or for attacks on police were recorded.

The prevalence of convictions for property offences in the previous records of the offenders involved in family violence may be partly a reflection of the delinquency in the areas in which the majority lived, but also partly a result of attitudes of the police and prosecution departments in dealing with offenders involved in domestic violence, who had a known previous record of property crime. It could also be argued that the unsuccessful property offender is predictably a person likely to have an unsatisfactory family life; but further research would be required to test whether such a view is correct or not.

(11) The scene of the crimes of violence involving members of the same family, of course, was usually their normal residence, though a small group of cases occurred in the streets, in places of entertainment, or in a nearby shop (see Table 4.7). The cases that occurred in streets were usually the

Table 4.7 Scene of crime of violence

Place of residence	1297	(85·0%)
Streets, etc.	183	(12·0%)
Shops, offices, etc.	20	(1·3%)
In or around places of entertainment, etc.	22	(1·4%)
Family car	5	(0·3%)
	1527	(100·0%)

culmination of a chase from the place of residence; and the victim had fled from the home where the altercation had originated. Some were on the way home from social events, as in the car attacks; but on a few occasions—including some of the attacks by fathers on daughters—a member of the family had gone from the home to seek the relative who was then attacked after an altercation.

ASPECTS OF FAMILY VIOLENCE IN SCOTLAND

A Scottish survey, relating to the Greater Glasgow area, covered crimes known to the police in 1972. Within the Scottish sample there were 190 crimes of violence involving members of the same family. The detailed results of that survey are being published separately, but some of the salient features in comparison with the English sample are perhaps worth mentioning here. First, there was a similar spread of the different kinds of family relationships as found in the English survey: spouses, cohabitees, parents, offspring, siblings, and other relatives. Second, the proportion of female *offenders* in both samples was much the same. Third, the crimes of violence within the family, recorded by the police, in Scotland and England occurred in similar kinds of deprived urban areas. Fourth, the Scottish sample showed a much higher incidence of heavy drinking, both as regards the offenders and their victims. Fifth, since there is a very small coloured population in Scotland, it was not surprising to find that only 4% of the Scottish crimes of violence in the family involved coloured people. The majority of the domestic disputes resulting in criminal violence, in fact, involved persons born in Scotland. The only significant minority involved people born in Ireland. Sixth, the offenders more frequently used weapons in their assaults in the Scottish cases: as in England, these included a large proportion of crimes in which the weapon was some object that was readily available in the home. As a consequence of the use of weapons, the injuries inflicted by offenders convicted of family violence in Scotland tended to be somewhat more severe than in comparable cases in England.

It should be noted that in Scotland a number of cases that were initially recorded as assaults in the family were dealt with in the courts as breaches of the peace. Also, it can perhaps be suggested that the samples of offenders *convicted* of criminal violence in the two countries are not strictly comparable because of the differences in police recording and the prosecution and criminal justice processes. In general, however, the comparisons between the two samples indicate broadly similar problems of a medical, social, economic, and educational nature. There is also an equal awareness in the two countries that many of the issues relating to criminal violence in the family cannot be effectively tackled solely within the criminal justice framework.

CRIMINAL JUSTICE CONTROL OF FAMILY VIOLENCE

The prevention and control of family violence through the criminal justice process involve officials who must make decisions at various stages in any particular inquiry or process, namely, police, prosecuting authority, members of the judiciary, and staff of the penal and social services. As mentioned already such decisions made within the criminal justice system and including the cardinal one, whether to bring a case into that system in the first place, will be influenced by the kinds of facilities available from other control systems: medical, social, educational, pastoral, etc. (McClintock, 1974b). However, preceding any formal measures by officials, the attitudes of those participating in the violent acts (as victims or offenders), of witnesses of the incident, as well as of members of the community with factual knowledge of violent family discord, will all influence whether or not a particular act of this kind is reported to the police in the first place. Their decision made on this point will not only depend upon an assessment of its gravity and its likelihood of occurring again, but also on personal attitudes towards the police, respect for the courts, and the possibility of help from alternative agencies of control.

The secondary, and possibly adverse, consequences of reporting such crime to the police (including the breakdown of the marriage or a possible custodial sentence for the spouse or other relative) will also have to be weighed before the victim takes any action. Discussions with police officers of many years' service, as well as with those currently serving on patrol duties, readily establish the existence of a long tradition in the police of coping with families in difficulties when friction has reached sparking point and needs experienced intervention. Undoubtedly, in the past a great deal of work was done informally by the police to keep family violence within bounds, short of taking steps to prosecute. In varying degrees the police have used their discretion as regards reporting for prosecution and have either issued a warning as to what is likely to happen if such conduct continues or have utilized their liaison with the social, medical or educational services or voluntary organizations to assist in preserving domestic peace. In the last decade or so, one has seen the development in many countries of a more formal and structured approach to those processes, such as the formation of community relations branches of the police, family crises units, and inter-professional committees. These experiments are designed on the principle that intervention, less drastic than that of criminal justice, is likely to be more effective in forestalling or counteracting family violence.

In the urban studies of violence in England and Wales referred to above, it was found that, of those cases of violence in the family reported to the police and recorded by them as crimes, only 2 in 3 resulted in a conviction. The group of cases not resulting in a conviction involved some 500 alleged offenders. The two main reasons why the cases did not proceed to a conviction were: (1) that the police were content to warn or caution the offender (either in situations in which advice and help were available from other services, or where it was judged, in the circumstances, that no further violence would occur),[7] or (2) because the victim or complainant subsequently asked for the charge to be withdrawn and indicated an unwillingness to give evidence if the case proceeded. A few cases, of course, led to acquittals or failed due to legal technicalities. The cases which did not result in a trial tended to be those which were less serious, as regards physical harm to the victim, and those in which the altercation and family broil had been marked by a considerable amount of activity and even initiative on the part of the 'victim'. Clearly, in cases of interpersonal violence the law can only come into operation if there is a labelled 'offender' and a labelled 'victim'; but the social situations in which some incidents of family violence occur make it an extremely difficult task to decide who is really the offender and who the victim; this is so, even when the police have intervened at the scene of the crime or arrived there immediately after its occurrence. The law can in fact be seen as sometimes imposing an arbitrary and unreal distinction between 'offender' and 'victim' in what is a complex social situation of personal relationships and responsibilities. The use by the courts in England and Wales of their power to bind both parties over 'to keep the peace', without proceeding to a conviction, formally recognizes this problem by providing what has been termed 'preventive justice' when dealing with less serious cases of interpersonal violence occurring in various circumstances including that of family conflict. In England the possibility of arrest for breach of the peace is retained (Williams, 1954).

In cases in which the courts have proceeded to a conviction, the degree of culpability and extenuating circumstances of the offender will be reflected to some extent in the kind of sentence imposed. However, the courts also have another particular difficulty when dealing with cases of family violence, namely, that the penalty imposed on the offender such as a heavy fine or custody may, if he is the breadwinner, have immediate adverse effects on the victim as a member of the family. Most sentences are very mindful of these difficulties in attempting to deal with such situations.[8] Custodial sentences are usually only considered in the following circumstances: (1) cases of very serious injury; (2) several offences continuing over a considerable period of time or other aggravating conditions relating to objectionable behaviour; (3) where the aggressor is a younger member of the family, e.g. the son attacking a parent; or (4) where the marriage has broken down and attempts at reconciliation can no longer be considered as appropriate. In all other cases, if at all possible, the courts will deal with the offender by the use of a non-custodial measure.

In the survey of violence carried out in urban areas in England and Wales, 1013 persons were convicted of crimes of violence in the family. Only 164, or 16%, were dealt with by custodial measures, and even then 23 offenders were given orders under the mental-health provisions on account of mental abnormality or illness. The remainder, 849 offenders (84% of those convicted), received sentences of a non-custodial kind. The penalties imposed by the courts upon offenders convicted of family violence were as shown in Table 4.8.

Table 4.8 Penalties imposed by the courts

Custodial:				
(a) Institutions for young offenders	7	(0·7%)		
(b) Imprisonment	134	(13·2%)		
(c) Medical institutions	23	(2·3%)	164	(16·2%)
Non-custodial:				
(a) Fine	353	(34·8%)		
(b) Absolute or conditional discharge	231	(22·8%)		
(c) Suspended sentence	137	(13·5%)		
(d) Probation order	122	(12·0%)		
(e) Otherwise dealt with	6	(0·6%)	849	(83·8%)
Total			1013	(100·0%)

The view of sentencers is that, apart from the cases where supervision is seen as a helpful and appropriate measure to apply, the court has to mark sufficiently strongly its condemnation of the aggressive and violent behaviour brought before it. If immediate imprisonment is not regarded as essential the fine and the suspended sentence are regarded as the two main measures in this sense. Strictly, the decision to suspend a prison sentence should be taken after deciding on imprisonment; most magistrates, however, see the suspended sentence as a separate measure. The conditional discharge order or a binding over after conviction are selected as affording some measure of control where the gravity and aggravating elements are considered to be low. It is of some significance, as regards the control of family violence through the criminal justice process, to note that 1 in 3 of the offenders was fined and 1 in 7 was given a suspended sentence. It should also be noted that in many cases there was a fairly lengthy period between the reporting of the crime of violence and the conviction of the offender; and where the offender had continued to reside in the same home, this is known to have considerable influence on the sentencer's selection of a penalty.

It might be thought that the value of the fines imposed was rather on the low side: in more than 6 in 10 of the cases it was no more than £20. There were undoubtedly many cases in which the sentencer viewed the fine as a mark of public disapproval rather than as a penal sanction imposed for the purpose of individual deterrence. But it also has to be borne in mind that the vast majority of the offenders were from the economically deprived areas, where incomes were low and many of the offenders unemployed, and where the families were usually in considerable economic and social difficulty. In 1 in 10 of the cases the fine was over £50, and over £100 in only four instances (see Table 4.9).

Table 4.9 Amount of fine

Up to £5	40	(11·3%)
Over £5 up to £10	98	(27·8%)
Over £10 up to £20	79	(22·4%)
Over £20 up to £50	96	(27·2%)
Over £50	40	(11·3%)
	353	(100·0%)

As regards length, prison sentences tended to be primarily related both to the gravity of the current offence of violence, and to previous convictions, especially those of an aggressive nature. However, there appeared to be substantial variations according to the judgement of different sentencers as to the appropriate tariff, and there is undoubtedly need for more explicit guidelines for judges and magistrates and trying this kind of offender. The survey revealed that of those sentenced to imprisonment 4 in 10 were given sentences of 6 months or less, while 1 in 10 was given a sentence of over 5 years. Details are set out in Table 4.10.

Table 4.10 Length of prison sentence

Less than 6 months	26	(19·4%)		
6 months	31	(23·1%)	57	(42·5%)
Over 6 months, up to 1 year	18	(13·5%)		
Over 1 year, up to 2 years	19	(14·2%)		
Over 2 years, up to 5 years	26	(19·4%)		
Over 5 years	14	(10·4%)		
	134	(100·0%)		

It is difficult to make an accurate comparison of the criminal justice processes of control of prevention of family violence in Scotland with those of England and Wales. In Scotland a very substantial proportion of offenders, whose offences were initially recorded by the police as assaults, were brought before the courts, by the procurators fiscal, for a breach of the peace, and were not technically convicted of a crime of violence. Only 109 of the 190 offenders recorded by the police as having committed a crime of violence were in fact convicted of an offence in that category. The convicted offenders in the Scottish sample had on the whole committed offences resulting in somewhat more serious injuries; also they tended to have longer previous criminal records and to have a higher total of previous crimes of violence and breaches of the peace. However, even with such differences between the samples, it is noteworthy that in Scotland 56% of the convicted offenders were given custodial sentences, as contrasted with only 16% in the English sample. The percentage of sentences of more than a year were approximately the same for the two samples; but in the lighter sentences there was a very much greater concentration of the very short sentence of 3 months and under in the Scottish sample. The extent of the imposition of fines was approximately the same in the two samples: 1 in 3 of convicted offenders. Fines in Scotland were on the whole much heavier: 7 in 10 of them being over £20 as contrasted with 4 in 10 in the same category in England. This difference remained even after taking into account the change in the value of money between 1970 and 1972. Probation orders were made much less frequently in Scotland than in England. The Scottish courts do not have the power to suspend prison sentences; this may be one of the reasons for the large excess of immediate imprisonments in Scotland over England noted above. The English courts suspended sentence on more than 1 in 7 of their cases of family violence.

CONCLUSIONS

A study of criminal violence in the family reveals a range of complex interrelated issues of both a theoretical and practical nature. It has been stressed that the formal definitions of *criminal* violence have to be seen in the wider context of aggressiveness in the home; what is defined as criminal in respect of aggressive behaviour has to be related to what different social groups view as deviant or morally unacceptable. The amount of criminal violence in the family not reported to the police is not simply an actuarial question but is one that is bound up with the assessment of social attitudes to aggressive behaviour, of the criminal justice system and the ways it operates, and of other systems of social control within society. The extent to which the *recorded* increase in family violence is entirely a *real* one is difficult to ascertain. Undoubtedly there has been a considerable amount of 'hidden' criminal violence in the family both in the recent and in the more distant past. Part of the current increase in recorded family violence may be attributable to an increase in the *reporting* of violent crime to the police because of less tolerance of aggressive behaviour in the family, associated with the greater social and economic independence of women in modern society and what they are prepared to put up with in the home. Furthermore, increases in the reporting of family violence to the police may also, in part, reflect a decline in the informal control and support of the extended family and the neighbourhood or local community when crises occur. It was found that in the majority of crimes reported the injury inflicted was not severe. However, the magnitude of the recorded increases—especially in the major crimes—lead most people to the conclusion that there is a real increase in family violence even though, as with other kinds of violence in society today, it cannot be accurately measured.

Whatever the view as regards the extent of the increase in family violence, that which is reported to the police today constitutes a growing and serious problem. The criminologist is concerned with ascertaining the nature of the problems involved and the ways in which they are dealt with by the criminal justice system and other systems of social control. Recent surveys of recorded criminal violence in the family give some measure of the dimensions of the problems. It is clear that criminal violence in the family involves much more than the battering of wives and children by aggressive males, or the battering of babies by mothers. The mass media have tended to focus attention exclusively on these kinds of family violence. Women commit criminal violence against their husbands and other adult relatives; also children, and especially teenagers, seriously assault their parents or other siblings in the family, while other relatives get involved in serious violence in the home as well.

It was found that there was a wide range of circumstances in which criminal violence occurs in the family, and although it is undoubtedly true that in some cases it is only after a long history of aggressiveness and discord that a complaint of criminal violence is reported to the police, there are also many instances in which the violence has been sudden—almost like an accident—and immediately regretted by all involved. In such cases it is usually the severity of injury that has been the main reason for the incident being reported to the police. The legal notions of 'an offender' and 'a victim' are also not easy to apply to the complex situation in which family conflict develops into interpersonal violence. Furthermore, the use of weapons (including objects readily available), the methods of attack, and the physical injury to the victim, suggest a vast range of motivation and consequences in respect of these crimes; all of which indicate the complexity of the phenomenon and the difficulties in finding adequate explanations for its occurrence or methods for its effective prevention. It is true that a very substantial proportion of the recorded crimes of violence in the family occur in areas of social and economic depression and, as with other forms of interpersonal violence, are significantly associated with conditions of life lacking incentives and basic social amenities. But the recognition of a high association between family violence and economic, social, and personal disadvantages is only a stage on the way and does not in itself constitute a full explanation: further research needs to be undertaken of a more sociological nature.

The methods of prevention and control of family violence within the criminal justice system could well benefit from clearer guide-lines for the police, the prosecutors, and the sentencers, together with a greater liaison between such official bodies. While there are important developments in bringing together administrators in the criminal justice system with those of other social control systems, much more still requires to be undertaken in this respect if such violence is to be prevented or at least adequately and effectively dealt with when it occurs.

Some comparisons between the incidence of family violence in England and Wales and that of Scotland confirm that the two socio-legal systems are dealing with broadly similar problems, although the analysis when carried into detail is found to be fraught with difficulties. However, it would appear that in Scotland imprisonment is more frequently imposed on those convicted of family violence than is the case in England and Wales. Similar problems of criminal violence within the family occur in most European countries although they appear to be less extensive than in Great Britain. But available data are not very detailed and there is need for more rigorous comparative studies of the problem.

NOTES

1 Medical research on injured babies drew attention to the criminal ill treatment (battering) of children; the battered spouse has evoked sympathetic interest from social-welfare services. For recent assessments of various aspects of violence in Britain, see Tutt, 1976.

2 The dearth of socially relevant data applies also to other forms of criminal violence. On the general issue of public opinion and violence, see Lenke, 1974. On the more general issue of knowledge from and the influence of the media, see the US reports of the *National Commission on the Causes and Prevention of Violence* (1969). It must also be pointed out that one of the dangers of formulating views on the basis of abstract data from criminal statistics is that it is likely to lead to a situation in which stereotypes are mistaken for social facts. See McClintock 1974a.

3 For an early study of the problems based on recorded crime in London, see McClintock, 1963. It refers to the category of domestic violence throughout, but see especially 'A note on violence arising from family strife and neighbourhood disputes', pp.248ff. See also McClintock, 1974b. A forthcoming book on urban violence in Great Britain by F. H. McClintock, to be published by Heinemann Educational Books, will contain a more detailed analysis of the trends in known criminal violence over a 20-year period.

4 In England and Wales the police are usually the prosecuting authority except where the Director of Public Prosecutions has to be informed and may take the initiative. In Scotland prosecutions are carried out by public officers, known as procurators fiscal, who are responsible to the Lord Advocate. See R. M. Jackson (1967), *Enforcing the Law*, Macmillan, pp.48ff and A. V. Sheehan (1975), *Criminal Procedure in Scotland and France*, HMSO, chapter 6, pp.125ff.

5 The changes in population during this period are so small in contrast to the crime rates that they can be regarded as constant from a statistical point of view. For a detailed assessment of trends in crime up to 1965, see McClintock and Avison, 1968, and McClintock, 1974a, pp.33ff.

6 Personal communications from a number of senior police officers who analysed their own local statistics on the same basis as that used in McClintock, 1963.

7 This is, of course, a difficult decision for a police officer to make, but experienced officers often say that this can be judged from the attitude of the offender when they first come to the scene of the crime.

8 This is apparent from discussing crimes of violence with magistrates at training sessions, and from the person experience of the present writer who has been a magistrate since 1963 in Cambridge and London.

REFERENCES

Council of Europe (1974) *Violence in Society* (Collected Studies in Criminological Research, vol. XI), Strasbourg: Council of Europe.

Friedmann, Wolfgang (1972) *Law in a Changing Society*, London: Stevens, 2nd ed.

Hadden, T. B., and McClintock, F. H. (1970a) 'Social and legal definitions of criminal violence', *Proceedings of the Fourth National Conference on Research and Teaching in Criminology*, Cambridge: Institute of Criminology (mimeographed).

Hood, R. (ed.) (1974) *Crime, Criminology and Public Policy*, London: Heinemann Educational Books.

Hood, R., and Sparks, R., (1970) *Key Issues in Criminology*, London: Weidenfeld & Nicholson, chapters 1 and 2.

Lenke, L. (1974) 'Criminal policy and public opinion towards crimes of violence'. In Council of Europe (1974), pp.61ff.

McClintock, F. H. (1963) *Crimes of Violence*, London: Macmillan.

McClintock, F. H. (1970) 'The dark figure'. In Council of Europe, Collected Studies in Criminological Research, vol. V, Strasbourg: Council of Europe.

McClintock, F. H. (1974a) 'Facts and myths about the state of crime'. In Hood (1974), pp.3ff.

McClintock, F. H. (1974b) 'Phenomenological and contextual analysis of criminal violence'. In Council of Europe. (1974), pp.125ff.

McClintock, F. H. (forthcoming) *Urban Violence in Great Britain*, to be published by Heinemann Educational Books, London.

McClintock, F. H., and Avison, N. H. (1964) 'Ways of classifying offences for criminological research'. In *Proceedings of the First National Conference in Research and Teaching in Criminology*, Cambridge: Institute of Criminology (mimeograph).

McClintock, F. H., and Avison, N. H. (1968) *Crime in England and Wales*, London: Heinemann Educational Books.

McClintock, F. H., and Gibson, Evelyn (1961) *Robbery in London*, London: Macmillan.

McClintock, F. H., and Hadden, T. B. (1970b) 'Law and social control systems: a functional analysis'. In Jolowicz, J. A. (ed.), *The Division and Classification of the Law*, London: Butterworth.

National Commission on the Causes and Prevention of Violence (1970) *Final Report*, New York: Praeger.

Tutt, Norman (ed.) (1976) *Violence*, London: HMSO (Department of Health and Social Security).

West, D. J., and Wiles, P. (1973) *Bibliography on Crimes of Violence*, Cambridge: Institute of Criminology.

Williams, Glanville (1954) 'Arrest for breach of the peace', *Criminal Law Review*, 578–592.

5

SOCIOLOGICAL PERSPECTIVES ON FAMILY VIOLENCE

Dennis Marsden

Is violence between family members so individual and so far outside normal human nature that it is not amenable to sociological study? Certainly, sociologists have arrived late in the wake of the controversies surrounding family violence, and they have hitherto contributed less than specialists from other fields. In fact it must be admitted that a preoccupation with the workings of the wider society and the normal have hindered sociologists from paying attention to family violence.

However, sociology can help to answer the questions: why is there so much confusion over the nature of violent acts in the family; why is there so much interest in family violence *now*; and how can we make sense of the varied evidence and explanations of violence which derive from different sources and other specialist approaches? Rather than baldly assert our own definition of family violence we will ask throughout, what are the meanings given to violence by others?

'BATTERED BABIES', 'BATTERED WIVES,' AND 'GRANNY BASHING' AS PUBLIC ISSUES

History teaches that there is no simple link between the scale of human misery and the degree of public concern. So if baby battering, wife beating, and more recently granny bashing are now of public interest we must ask why, in C. Wright Mills's phrase, these 'personal troubles' have become 'public issues' (Becker, 1960; Wright Mills, 1970; Timms, 1975).

The discoveries of the phenomena of baby battering, wife beating, and granny bashing have been made in diverse ways. Most notably, there has been a different involvement of officials and academic specialists, a varied basis for the spread of public interest and support, and a contrasting public response.

Battered babies: discovery and official response

The clinicians who first recognized that the X-rays of hospitalized chilren might reveal deliberate violence also coined the label, the 'battered child syndrome' (Kempe *et al.*, 1962). Because of the age of the victims, but also by more sensational alliteration, child abuse became in the press the 'battered-baby syndrome'. A number of scandals of child deaths served to focus attention, perhaps too narrowly, upon attackers who were lower-class men with a fairly unstable record of work and sometimes crime.

Within a comparatively short space of time, Britain has set up a co-ordinated network to watch for and protect children who are at risk in their own homes, even to the extent of taking resources from other needy groups, and currently child abuse is the subject of a parliamentary Select Committee investigation. America lacks the network of surveillance, but goes further in requiring doctors to register suspected cases of child abuse.

Battered wives: discovery and initial campaign

In Britain, violence towards women was rediscovered even more recently, when a centre was opened in Chiswick by Erin Pizzey to give advice, but instead became involved in providing refuge for women who had been badly beaten by men (Pizzey, 1974). Erin Pizzey, herself the wife of a TV reporter, made very effective use of the media (who queued up for information), with TV and radio broadcasts, articles, a best-selling book called *Scream Quietly or the Neighbours Will Hear*, and a nationally shown TV film of the same name. At one point in the campaign I estimated that about 60% of all items in the BBC's press-cuttings file were about Chiswick Women's Aid or Erin Pizzey herself. CWA continued to make news because of endemic overcrowding, which has resulted in widely-publicized conflicts with the public health authorities.

Erin Pizzey has described herself as the child victim of her father's violence towards her mother (she says she keeps CWA open 'for her mother'), a disturbed child, and a potential child beater saved only by an early appeal to a psychiatrist (Kurtz, 1976; *Listener*, 1976). In her book she directly links child and wife battering by asserting 'the child is father to the man'. Men who are violent in adult life were treated violently as children. They became psychologically disturbed but ultimately they came to identify with the battering father, to repeat his behaviour as adults. Some girls with violent childhoods may get almost physically hooked on violence, so that they become attracted to violent men in ways for which they cannot be held responsible. The cycle of violence is reinforced when as mothers, in response to the stress of violence from their husbands, they also beat their children.

CWA in its appeals for help has followed very much the same line of argument (*Nemesis*, 1974a), strongly maintaining that violence occurs at all levels of society, and even that it may be more prevalent among middle-class and professional men (*Nemesis*, 1974b). The failure of police and various officials to use their powers to intervene in what were described as family 'muggings', has been attributed to tacit male approval of, and even secret propensities for, violence.

A heavy emphasis on the ungoverned brutality of the men helped to counter the stereotype that women deserve to be beaten occasionally and may even masochistically approve of violence as the assertion of masculine authority and possessive jealousy. In so far as it caught the public imagination, the issue of battered wives derived some of its impact from the implicit analogy with 'battered babies' and the explicit analogy with the controversy over harsh punishments for street muggings.

CWA was helped initially by a grant from Bovis, the building firm of Sir Keith Joseph, whose now notorious 'cycle of deprivation' speech followed a line similar to CWA's, that pathology was transmitted by the family (Townsend, 1974). CWA also received a grant from the Urban Aid programme, which was actually part of an earlier government response to the threat of violence in inner city areas.

The spread of the Women's Aid movement by feminist groups

The refuge movement has been largely spread by the voluntary activities of feminist groups, for whom the issue of battered wives offered a very practical focus for action. Over 100 refuges have now been set up, and in 1975 the National Women's Aid Federation was established to co-ordinate the movement (although without CWA); it was later funded by the Department of Health and Social Security. Some local refuges also receive Urban Aid grants, and income from the social security benefits of their residents.

Disagreements have arisen with CWA because the feminist refuges seek to provide women with a more political and less individualistic explanation of their plight, as part of a general programme of psychological rehabilitation. Attempts are made to get the women to run the refuges themselves.

Refuges have found themselves in a dilemma because if every applicant was allowed in, the accommodation would become overcrowded, demoralizing the inmates and risking closure. Yet refuges are still unevenly spread and cannot accommodate all the women who call upon them for help. One recent estimate gave the proportion of women turned away as two or three times the number admitted (Harrison, 1975). The dilemma is exacerbated because without the evidence of overflowing refuges, the issue of battered wives may appear to have been successfully handled with no call for further government action.

Tentative government response, and the spread of academic and professional interest

Compared with the swift response to the issue of battered babies, the public and official reaction to battered wives has been more equivocal. From an official viewpoint there has been a problem of inadequate evidence, and the feeling that battered wives were already being catered for by existing services, or that their needs could be met by *ad hoc* arrangements for diverting funds from other purposes. Indeed, were battered wives to be seen as a 'problem' at all (Timms, 1975)?

Early attempts to get Parliament to act followed the line of Women's Aid publicity. Jack Ashley, MP produced statistics to suggest that there might be between 27 000 and 75 000 cases of wife battering in Britain, based on information from Citizens' Advice Bureaux (Ashley, 1973). He secured funds for individual refuges and the NWAF. The DHSS set up a working party, and a parliamentary Select Committee was set up to report first on battered wives, although it was also proposed to look at child abuse (Parliamentary Select Committee on Violence in Marriage, 1975).

These two bodies helped to spread awareness of the issue among officials and academic specialists by sending out requests for evidence. The Scottish Office funded a research project (Dobash, 1975). The British Psychiatric Association produced a review of clinical evidence largely gleaned from criminological studies of child and wife murderers, and from alcoholics (Scott, 1974). A psychiatrist studied residents of CWA (Gayford, 1975). A local psychiatric hospital mounted an incidence study in Colchester (Marsden and Owens, 1975). Groups such as the British Association of Social Workers set up working parties (BASW, 1975); and all over the country various bodies like the police, probation officers, Samaritans, Citizens' Advice Bureaux, social services departments, and voluntary associations, were stimulated to look for evidence among their records and cases.

However, the sudden call for evidence found these bodies, and academic research in general, in some disarray, and produced a range of submissions implying quite different or controversial definitions of the problem. The lack of evidence may be judged from the way the Colchester incidence figure, itself based on only 19 interviews, was used to work out an incidence for wife battering in Wales (Parliamentary Select Committee on Violence in Marriage, 1975).

Although the Select Committee recommended that refuges should be set up in every settlement with more than 50 000 inhabitants, the case was made less convincing by the confession that the varied evidence must be left to speak for itself. There has been no further official action beyond the commissioning of a little more research, mostly psychological.

Granny bashing

Third among these issues, news of granny bashing first appeared in an article in a professional journal, the *Nursing Standard*, and was briefly taken up by the press and TV (*Guardian*, 1976). Old people were said to suffer injuries from their relatives because of various kinds of stress, such as the lack of day care and support facilities for families caring for elderly relatives. The Royal College of Nursing urgently requested information from all its members.

Probably the most interesting thing about granny bashing is that although all kinds of reasons could be suggested why it must take place and should arouse public guilt and outcries, nothing else has happened. After a brief surprised and even jokey treatment by the media, the issue was dropped. This is in marked contrast to the public outcries and scandals which have followed the discovery of violence towards old people in institutions.

Family violence issues in America: a footnote

The issues of family violence in America are different, most notably in being swamped by a wave of concern with violence outside the home such as inner-city crime and murder, campus unrest and shootings, police violence on civil rights marchers, saturation bombing in the Vietnam War, and the effects of television violence on children (Steinmetz and Straus, 1974).

The issue of violence towards women shows the most marked contrast because it has focused on rape, and feminist writers have not pushed any campaign analogous to Women's Aid. Instead, interest in violence in marriage seems to have come most directly from social scientists, particularly Straus (Straus, 1971; Gelles, 1974), and the American Government has now generously funded his research into marital violence (Straus, 1976).

The different development of the issues of family violence in America underlines the importance of the social context, and the involvement of particular movements and academic specialists.

THE CONTRIBUTION OF ACADEMIC SPECIALISTS

We have seen how various non-sociological specialists have been heavily involved in the original discoveries and subsequent developments of controvery over family violence. They have been called in by the media or official bodies to provide explanations which are expected to be somehow more objective and authoritative than public opinion. Yet it is striking that the specialists themselves are deeply divided on the issues of family violence, and it is equally striking how little contribution was made initially by sociologists.

Non-sociological specialists and child abuse

In Britain major specialist controveries surround the possibility that child abuse may be deeply ingrained in the cultural, psychological or genetic make-up of a relatively small number of families, or in failures of early bonding between mother and child (Oliver *et al.*, 1973; Lynch, 1975; Kellmer

Pringle, 1973). The implication is that abused children should be removed early and permanently, to prevent a recurrence of the violence and very expensive calls on agency services in future generations.

An alternative view that battering mothers can be helped has come mainly from a voluntary agency (NSPCC, 1976). One eye-catching study, the *Yo-yo Children*, linked child abuse to parental discord in a situation where mothers, said to be 'immature', shuttled between their violent husbands and domineering and destructive mothers, taking their children with them (Moore, 1974).

Some of the more sophisticated and eclectic studies have built up fairly elaborate biographies of child abusers which describe early defects of relationship, leading to an 'immature' and 'vulnerable' personality, escape into ill-advised and hasty pregnancy, and subsequent repetition of pathological family relationships (Brandon, 1976; Smith, 1974).

Non-sociologists and wife beating

Initial evidence on wife battering came from luridly violent populations which had already been studied by criminologists and psychiatrists, for example child murderers and alcoholics (Scott, 1974). The most prominently publicized research by a psychiatrist has been a study of CWA which suggested that the origins of violence lay in childhood experiences, although interestingly in different patterns, only a minority being violent, the others over-indulgent (Gayford, 1975). In this situation a sizeable minority of children had also suffered violence. The women from the refuge (on the basis of much less evidence) were hypothesized to be psychologically vulnerable to being trapped into unprotected sexual intercourse and pregnancy, the 'Venus fly-trap': in a popular version of this theses the same psychiatrist speculated more wildly about the women's behaviour leading to violence, an indulgence bitterly criticized by Women's Aid (Gayford, 1976; NWAF, 1976).

There are some familiar criticisms of psychiatry which will not be laboured here. At worst the samples from which evidence is drawn are very small and highly selective. The nature of the pathology is assumed to be agreed. Explanations suffer from tautology in identifying, as causes of the violence, 'character defects' the only evidence for which is the violence itself. Tests to establish this tend to be administered with prior knowledge of the violence rather than blind, and without controls to see whether the 'abnormal' characteristics are shared by the general population. Little attention may be paid to environmental stresses (Gelles, 1973).

Some studies do attempt to avoid these defects, and also take note of environment by including occupational status and housing. However, the model adopted tends to see the environment as merely an accumulation of objective 'factors' which may trigger violence.

Traditional sociological discussions of the family

The major reason for the comparative lack of sociological contribution to the controversy about violence seems to be that until recently the family has been regarded by major schools of thought in sociology as a subordinate element in the wider social structure.

Early Marxist perspectives on the family certainly saw relationships between man and wife and children as exploitative and potentially conflictful, but Marx described the first proclamation of the 'rights of the child' as essentially a move against industry, which he saw as responsible for the destruction of the family (Marx, 1946). Officially state-socialist countries today seem coy about revealing any evidences of family violence which could be seen as a failure to plan properly and eradicate old values (Borland, 1976). Also, there are schools of Marxist thought today, French and male, which still insist that all explanation must take place at the level of society and not the individual, so that in so far as they look at the family they tend merely to invent stereotyped behaviour patterns to fit their general analysis (Althusser, 1971).

Industrial sociology might have made more contribution towards an understanding of whether industrial tensions carry over into the family situations, to what extent militants are also personally violent men, whether violent men are frequently sacked or seek out jobs with high autonomy and self-employment, and so on. Yet any discussion of industry–family correspondences seems to have been mainly in terms of the effects of work on the separation of domestic tasks, leisure, and interests, with the wife's acquiescence rather than conflict and violence. One of the most influential recent pieces of research pictures workers as leading lives which are increasingly 'privatized' in the home and spent in close involvement with wife and children (Goldthorpe *et al.*, 1968). By default, then, studies of the family were left mainly to sociologists in the functionalist tradition, who have tried to see society as a smoothly-working system.

The functionalist sociology of the family

The family was seen as a haven of peace, serving a 'tension-management function' for the wider society, the emphasis being on the harmonious, nurturing, and supportive nature of the woman's role in the home, as a counterpart to the husband's stressful task of winning resources from the wider society and setting goals and giving leadership in the family group (Parsons *et al.*, 1956; O'Brien, 1971).

Functionalists have been less inhibited than Marxists in borrowing from psychology and psycho-analysis to explain violence at an individual level. However, when it was suggested that the father's absence at work might cause boys to become compulsively masculine, their aggressive behaviour was seen as channelled into male groups *outside* the family (Parsons, 1947).

Alternatively, there was interest in whether or not violence might be normal in some families, but again such families were seen as away from mainstream society, in a 'subculture' (Wolfgang and Ferracuti, 1967).

This functionalist pattern can be traced through family studies in various areas. Discussions of marital discord took a static view that adjustment in marriage might be better if the backgrounds of husband and wife were similar in age, class, religion, education, and so on (Locke, 1951). Decision making was viewed as the outcome of a more or less even balance of resources (Blood and Wolfe, 1960), or an exchange based on a symmetrical power relationship, where the husband exchanges cash and good behaviour for the wife's domestic skills and services (Cromwell and Olson, 1975). In an 'exchange' view of marriage, skill in interpersonal relationships was also seen as necessary for harmony.

Some predictions about family violence from the functionalist perspective

In fact, although the major interest of functionalists was harmonious relationships, functionalism does lead to some predictions about violence. Discord should arise most often where there is mismatching of backgrounds, where one of the couple lacks resources, or where the 'exchange' breaks down in other ways, through defects of interpersonal relations. And there is some evidence that these predictions work, although with significant modifications: for example, divorcing couples were found to be little more discordant than married couples, since conflict does not necessarily lead to divorce. The wife's superior education can result in violence, but not, interestingly, her inferior education (Gelles, 1974). Violence may increase when women are out of work, but not in all cases (Marsden and Duff, 1975). Attacks are made on women who are depressed, ill, or pregnant (Gelles, 1975; Marsden and Owens, 1975). Similarly, it has been suggested that child abuse may be triggered by a lack of responsiveness in the child.

Functionalist models also predict that there should be a higher incidence of violence where the husband is in a less well-rewarded job. The man's inability to achieve the conventional goals in society and to perform his role of breadwinner may lead to frustration and hence aggression, compulsive masculinity, or criticism from the wife, all of which may result in violence.

A connection has also been suggested between the social position of the parents and the use of corporal punishment in the family, with the middle-class relationship seen as a more balanced, verbally controlled and love-oriented exchange, and the working-class relationship a more arbitrary, non-verbal, physically-controlled exercise of authority (Bernstein, 1973).

These suggestions about the distribution of physically violent acts are superficially borne out by the greater *observed* frequencies of violence between people in lower-paid jobs, and lower-class parents do tend to smack their children harder and more frequently. The women, however, smack more than the men (Newson and Newson, 1970), which is not easily explained by a theory based on *men's* work situation. These researchers did not find the working-class parents lacking in verbal skills so this was not a reason for physical punishment.

Eclectic model building: Straus's behaviourist systems model

An interesting attempt to modify functionalism and to incorporate perspectives from other specialisms has been made by Straus. A view of America as a stably-functioning, non-violent society has become more and more difficult to sustain. For example, it has been pointed out that although the behaviour of violent gangs is officially deplored, it is merely an unofficial or 'subterranean' version of values widely held in American society and pervasive in the mass media (Matza and Sykes, 1961). Straus's response to the various radical criticisms of American society and the family is to suggest what amounts to an inversion of traditional functionalism, and to see society and the family as an interdependent social system of vidlence (Straus, 1973; Steinmetz and Straus, 1974).

The major plank of this systems approach is that violence is learned and reinforced in children through examples in the family and mass media of its effectiveness in achieving desired goals (Henry, 1974). When the child grows up and encounters frustrating contexts in adult life, particularly marriage, he will tend to use the violent behaviour he has learned as a solution, and use it on his own wife and children, whom he has learned are victims (Straus, 1973; Steinmetz and Straus, 1974).

The home is seen as a special institution in society, unusually prone to induce stress and violence (Gelles, 1974; Straus, Steinmetz, and Gelles, 1976). The family demands a high, diffuse, and enduring commitment from which it is difficult to opt out. Family members meet frequently in close interaction, and issues are raised which may not necessarily be resolvable to everyone's satisfaction: the issues are often 'zero-sum games' (where, for example, you can only take your holidays in one place, or decorate a room one colour), so if one party wins, the other loses. Authority in the family is very unequally distributed, as is power, so that some individuals, usually the man, may always tend to win. While negotiation might be beneficial, alone among social institutions the family has no formal mechanisms for such negotiation and problem solving, beyond legal separation and divorce. Nor does society pay much attention to teaching people the necessary knowledge of possible problems they may encounter in the family, and the skills necessary to solve them.

There are powerful norms of privacy, so that there is for the most of the time no outside audience for behaviour in the home, and it is one of the few settings where violence is openly or covertly approved.

If we add all these aspects of the home together we come to the conclusion (remarkably different from the functionalist stereotype) that violence is quite likely to take place between relatives in the home. This analysis can even be taken as far as identifying the times of day and the rooms which are most stressful: the kitchen at teatime where the couple meet, ostensibly for a companionable meal but in fact to discharge the accumulated aggression of the day; the bedroom late in the evening, where the man returns after drinking; but not the bathroom where, despite the adverts, individuals tend to spend time alone (Gelles, 1974).

On this model links between violence in the home and violence in the wider society are said to come through the modification of individual personality to bring approval of violence, so that individuals are prepared to act violently or to support and approve violence by others. Thus, various studies by Straus and his colleagues have suggested statistical associations between corporal punishment and the approval of capital punishment (Gelles and Straus, 1975), between occupational situation, the use or approval of physical punishment, dogmatism, hawkishness (in approval of wartime behaviour and police action), and so on (Steinmetz and Straus, 1974).

Encouraged by evidence of success from these small correlational studies and undaunted by the growing complexity of the arguments and specialist squabbles, Straus has attempted to generalize and recruit support for his model by adding more and more possible elements from sociology and other specialisms. The model now takes the form of elaborate diagrams linking boxes of 'factors' by arrows indicating the processes of 'interaction' (Straus, 1973; Gelles, 1973; Steinmetz and Straus, 1974).

Some preliminary criticisms of Straus's model

Criticism of this enterprise may seem churlish and premature, when it has added considerably to our insights and it is still being pursued with such energy on so many fronts. Nevertheless, it is worth stressing that laying out concepts schematically in boxes does not solve, and may conceal, many value-problems which lie between different specialisms. And in view of its large financial backing, which seems likely to make it influential, some preliminary criticisms must be made of its major emphasis on physical violence learned in the home.

In their eagerness to gain support for their model of violence transmitted through learning, Straus and his colleagues seem not careful enough in their use of data. In fact there is little evidence of transmission of early behaviour patterns (Rutter and Madge, 1976). It is not clear how much violence, of what intensity, needs to be experienced, as victim or witness, in the family or via the media; and how we are to account for violence in men who have not been beaten as children but on the contrary over-indulged. In the evidence cited to show that violence is widespread, the threat of violence is equated with its use; the high proportion of all murders found to be committed by family members is stressed but not the very low number of murders in families; and figures of violence are given for a sample of couples picked because they were known to be violent (Steinmetz and Straus, 1974). There seems to be a tendency to estimate on the high side, and for initial caution to drop away with frequency of citation as time passes.

There are problems at a behaviourist-imitative level, for there seems little similarity between pressing a button to electrocute a man, dropping a bomb from an aeroplane, shooting a student, and being smacked as a child. The simple correlational techniques used to establish connections between approval of such acts and corporal punishment in childhood are theoretically uninformative and probably misleading as to the processes of connection. (Are hawks, for instance, more likely to recall childhood punishment?)

But even if we accept a more complex family learning model, are we any further advanced in the necessary analysis of the vast chain of social and political institutions between the family and the state? Not much attention has so far been paid to the literature on work and inequality (although Straus is not alone in this). It is actually a very difficult and basic sociological and political problem, why many people who work in bad conditions or who are poor do not feel and behave more aggressively at work and in political life (Runciman, 1966; Parkin, 1971).

Correspondingly, although women and children are seen as 'socially-defined' victims, the major focus is merely upon the aspect of physical violence. There is less interest in all the other processes which confine women and children to subordinate status in the family. An essentially functionalist emphasis in Straus's systems theory means that women still tend to be seen as continuing in violent relationships because of their personalities (albeit modified under stress), rather than through the weight of external constraints.

Above all from a feminist perspective, the slightly obsessional preoccupation of Straus's model with physical violence is very restrictive in the meaning it gives to violence. To bring a fuller understanding of this viewpoint we must now turn to the radical, feminist, and Marxist analyses of the family.

RADICAL, FEMINIST, AND MARXIST ANALYSES OF THE SUBORDINATION OF CHILDREN AND WOMEN IN THE FAMILY

The feminist movements which took up the cause of battered wives, and the interest which has helped to make battered babies into an issue, are elements in a much wider intellectual critique of social institutions. This critique pictures violence in the family as the inevitable symptom of relationships which are essentially repressive and restricting. (Increasingly, however, there is less analogous concern with liberating the elderly from the stereotypes of 'ageism'.)

In view of what has been said previously, these broader movements cannot be claimed as the achievement of sociologists for, by default, criticisms of the family at the interpersonal level were left initially to radicals, including psychiatrists. However, much of the analysis is sociological in character; and more recently feminist Marxists have gone further in the attempt to provide a comprehensive analysis at the societal and interpersonal level. For present purposes an attempt to distinguish different schools of criticism would not be particularly useful, nor indeed is it altogether possible, since there is overlap and ongoing argument between the developing perspectives.)

The implication of these critiques of the family would be a fundamental change in the definition of 'violence' and a change in the whole focus of research and the meaning of the evidence.

The subordination of children

Recent critiques of the status of children have focused on the way that the notion of children as 'immature' is used as a justification for denying them opportunities afforded to adults and subjecting them to ideological indoctrination in schools and to physical punishment. Radical psychiatrists have proposed the 'death of the family' (Cooper, 1971). Radical educationists have urged the 'deschooling' of society (Illich, 1973) and 'escape from childhood' (Holt, 1973), and the abolition of corporal punishment in schools (Newell, 1972).

These critiques have tried to shift the emphasis from merely physical to ideological subjection and restriction. It has been underlined that parents still treat their children as 'property' in the sense that they feel they have a right to expect children to respond appropriately in personal relationships and to do them credit in their attainments. Indeed, paradoxically, in a modern situation of child-centredness, stressful demands in the relationships of children with their parents may increase, for example as the need for educational credentials rises (Musgrove, 1966). Thus is might be argued that the concept of abuse should be extended to include mental cruelty as well as physical. Gil has insisted that existing clinical models are far too narrow; they exclude large numbers of cases of violent acts towards children which remain undetected or which are approved as legitimate, while mental abuse is entirely ignored (Gil, 1975). He proposes that we should define child abuse much more broadly as 'inflicted deficits, or gaps, between the rights and actual circumstances of children, irrespective of the source or agents of the deficits'.

This definition would entail that we should cease to look for the causes of child abuse of all kinds, mental and physical, in interpersonal relationships. For while abuse must manifest itself in interpersonal behaviour in institutions like the family and the school, Gil argues that acts of abuse will have their causes in the social structure at quite other levels; namely those which serve to define the nature of the various institutions and the 'victim' status of childhood. He identifies the key problem as inequality; and he argues for redistribution of power and the reduction of oppression in all kinds of institutions, with research aimed at changing the social structure rather than research of a trivial kind at the level of manifestation.

Welcome though such an attempt to gain a 'holistic' view of child abuse might be, the basic approach represents a leap of faith and a statement of ideology, rather than the hard work of sociological analysis which is proposed. The view of the role of inequality in creating stress, and institutions in maintaining domination, is unsophisticated. It is probably still true to say that critiques of childhood have tended to focus more on schools and education (perhaps because of the element of state compulsion in the relationship). They are therefore less well worked out in terms of family relationships than the critiques of the status of women to which we now turn.

The subordination of women

The major contribution of critiques of the status of women to arguments on family violence is two-fold. First, they have focused more attention on the structural and ideological forces in the wider society which tend to lock women into roles within the family. And, second, they have attacked the roles which women are required to play.

Attention has been drawn to the way women's opportunities and rewards in work are restricted because women provide merely a reserve labour force which cushions male workers from the worst impact of low pay and unemployment (Barron and Norris, 1976). And correspondingly, women who are confined to the home serve as a cheap means of caring for husbands and children (Oakley, 1974; Wilson, 1977), and also caring for other dependants: women are the 'community care' which is so much talked about but which attracts so little government cash.

Historically, women's subordination in marriage and work has been embodied in law and in other processes of official machinery. There has been a very marked reluctance to permit women equal grounds for ending marriage, any opportunity to do so, or adequate support to live alone (Chester, 1970; McGregor, 1974). For example, the wife has more difficulty in establishing that she has suffered violence from her husband, and to succeed in law a woman must proceed against her husband herself and must be demonstrably more injured than a non-relative (Inter-Action, 1974). The police are reluctant to intervene in domestic disputes. Social workers adopt the aim, and some like probation officers have the formal duty, of attempting to keep couples together (McGregor *et al.*, 1970; Parkinson, 1969). Social security officials have a statutory duty to ensure that women who apply for support are unsupported by their husband or another man, which sometimes leads them to adopt aggressive or dilatory tactics (Marsden, 1973). Some housing officials have taken the line that women who have left home as a result of marital disputes are not 'homeless' and therefore do not qualify for rehousing; and in addition mortgage and tenancy policies favour male ownership and tenancy (Glastonbury, 1971; SHAC, 1976). It is only in the 1970s that we are beginning to realize just how massive is the discrimination now built into government legislation of all kinds (Land, 1975). Women are more likely to be refused credit and hire purchase. The whole situation may be summed up by saying that women have rights to various systems of resources and derive social status mainly through their relationships with men (Marsden, 1973).

As well as the overt structural constraints which lock women into marriage and child care, there is the underpinning of informal social and ideological controls. These can hardly be appreciated because they are so deeply embedded that they appear natural, and tend to become visible only to those women who attempt to remain unmarried and childless, or to women who become lone mothers (Barker and Allen, 1976; Busfield, 1974; Marsden, 1973). For example, visiting and leisure patterns, neighbourhood life and relationships, are all geared to the higher status of marriage, and of motherhood.

Attention has now been drawn to the role of the mass media and pulp literature in propagating images of happy and trouble-free married life and fulfilled motherhood (Sharpe, 1976). These ideological mechanisms are so powerful that, for example, one group of ordinary teenage girls visualized their status in their 20s as early *widowed* motherhood, so little conception did they have of the realities of marriage and men (Veness, 1962). The conventional stereotype of the detrimental effects of mothers working and academic theories of the child's need for continuous maternal care may be seen as further ideological controls to keep women in the home, since it has been argued that they have no factual basis (Tizard, 1976).

The implications of women's subordination for the study of violence

It will be seen from the kinds of evidence already cited that this critique implies a changed view of family relationships in research. The study of marriage needs to take account of the asymmetrical relationship of males with females, where male gender is a source of authority for the man unless he deliberately relinquishes it or forfeits it by incompetence (Cromwell and Olsen, 1975). The use of interpersonal skills is an aspect of maintaining this domination (Bell and Newby, 1976), and physical violence is merely one among a number of means for the subordination of women (Goode, 1971). Little research has yet emerged from these new perspectives, but in any case the whole focus of research should shift away from violent acts to look at all the institutional forces which define the status of women.

This switch to seeing women as subjected to societal pressures to marry, to have children, and to stay married, suggests a partial reinterpretation of data on women's behaviour which other specialisms have described as pathological. Moreover it leads to a different, woman's view of the generation of stress in marriage.

Thus, we should beware of psychiatric descriptions of 'vulnerable' or 'immature' personalities if these are based merely on an 'unrealistic' view of marriage and motherhood and an eagerness to marry to get away from the parental home (Busfield and Paddon, 1977). We may even question whether women who knowingly marry violent men are very unusual, since in the repertoire of conventional stereotypes there are socially-approved images of masculine protectiveness and possessive jealousy, and the script where the good woman saves the man from the worse side of his nature and marriage settles him down. (Correspondingly, there are some cross-cultural dilemmas about when to describe a man's behaviour as abnormal.)

Stresses arise in the family not simply from the situation of men at work outside the home, nor only from the objective conditions of women's life in the home, but also from the ideological contradictions in marriage. The double standard of man's supposedly larger sexual appetites and woman's purity, sexual deference, and carefully circumscribed sexuality within marriage, may be highly productive of stress and violence. On the other hand, there may be a tension between high and increasing expectations of marriage and the abilities of individuals to develop a relationship felt to be adequate to meet those expectations (men are said to be increasingly frightened by women's sexual demands, and women angry at their men's passiveness; *Guardian*, 1977).

Women who would prefer to work may be locked into a frustrating round of domestic chores and the care of very young children, or dependents, with resulting depression (Fonda and Moss, 1976). Alternatively women may become locked in the routines of compulsive housework and cleaning, which appear neurotic yet represent the epitome of housewifery (Oakley, 1974). Both forms of behaviour seem to increase the likelihood of child abuse or 'granny bashing'.

Whether or not a woman is free to leave a violent and stressful marriage will depend on: her emotional investment in the ideals of marriage and motherhood, contrasting with the alternative identities available to her as a lone mother or worker; her social status in the circle of her friends and how this depends upon her marriage; her financial investment in marriage, that is, the standard of living and financial protection it brings compared with alternative resources or living alone; the possibilities and stigma of gaining alternative income from social security or legal processes; the availability of alternative accommodation; access to the law and willingness and ability to use it; and so on.

This means that the behaviour of some battered women who keep going back to violent men, and who even say they miss them, need not be explained as sado-masochism (Parkinson, 1969) or immaturity (Moore, 1974). In our society such behaviour may be further explicable as the desire not for this particular man and relationship, but for the security and status which a man, *any* man, tends to confer upon a woman in marriage (Marsden, 1973).

In other words, whether or not violence builds up and continues in a relationship is not purely a matter of personality but a complex balance of internalized social ideals and external constraints and opportunities. All these different aspects of control and opportunity will vary with the social class of the woman, and over time, but the trends of variation will not be uniform or in the same direction.

Thus, overall, critiques of women's status in the family would question whether violence can be seen as a set of objectively-defined physical acts whose causes lie exclusively in the personal pathology of the battering husband, the battered wife or battering mother, or the battered child. On this view, we should always consider how far the causes lie also at other more structured levels (and not merely, as Gil suggested, in inequality); and the conception of violence itself should be extended to include any illegitimate exercise of authority, subordination or restriction of growth and autonomy, whether or not the woman acquiesces, and whether or not the marriage is tranquil.

Physical violence remains an important social problem to be dealt with urgently. But even where there is no physical violence or even conflict and resentment of domination, 'structural' or 'sexist' violence may be taking place. Indeed a rise in conflict and possibly in physical violence may be a consequence of any move by women to question and reduce the degree of sexual domination in the family.

THE MEANINGS AND CONTROL OF PHYSICAL VIOLENCE IN INTERPERSONAL RELATIONSHIPS

There remain questions of how physical violence manifests itself in personal relationships, what it means, and how it is controlled. Here we can utilize a further sociological perspective, which itself developed out of the broader intellectual critique of societal institutions which has just been described. 'Interactionism' looks at individuals as actors who make evaluations of actions, negotiate shared meanings with others, and behave according to those meanings. An offshoot, 'labelling theory', looks at the consequences of actions being labelled by observers, and behaviour in response to labels or the possibility of being labelled.

In fact neither of these perspectives has yet been much used in the discussion of marriage (Berger and Kellner, 1964). But some suggestions can be made as to how they may further help us to understand the controversy over the meaning and data of family violence. Of special interest will be an understanding of what influences in the family permit or inhibit the build-up of violence, and how family violence becomes visible to outsiders and what they do about it.

The interpersonal meanings of violent acts: denial and neutralization

There are a number of ways in which a physically violent act may fail to be defined as illegitimate violence. Initially there may be an attempt to deny that the act occurred at all. At one level denial may be seen as a mechanism of personal psychology; but it is also social, an attempt to evade sanctions or an unwillingness to contemplate the loss of self-esteem and the re-evaluation of the self and personal relationships which would have to follow any acknowledgement that a violent act had been committed.

Denial is common in child abuse and occurs also in marital violence. It enables the continuation of the view that a marriage or parent–child relationship is essentially loving and caring, as society says it should be. In middle-class families, where a higher premium is placed on these values, violence may therefore sometimes take the form of a sudden explosion, quickly suppressed, denied or explained away.

Alternatively, the violence may be admitted but it may be neutralized in the eyes of the aggressor by 'blaming the victim'; that is, it may be seen as caused by the victim, or as a just punishment or expression of outrage or a deterrent. Frequently, in fact usually, corporal punishment of children is seen in this way, but there is also a fair degree of covert or unofficial approval of violence towards women in particular sexual and domestic situations (Owens and Straus, 1975).

It might be thought that this view of violence as justifiable would be more common among manual workers, where high levels of violent 'punishment' may be regarded as normal. But it should not be forgotten that in lower middle- or 'respectable' working-class families very high standards of domesticity or children's behaviour may also bring higher culpability in cases of failure, and therefore a higher possibility of pubishments blamed on the victim. The standards of housewifery which cause some women to be intolerant of any childish untidiness or uncleanliness may also provide the standards of behaviour whereby the child can be blamed for causing the violence.

A further alternative is that the act itself may be admitted to have taken place, but the aggressor may claim not to have been fully responsible for it, because of some extraneous uncontrollable factor such as stress at work ('things got on top of me'), alcohol ('I didn't know what I was doing'), or some kind of 'uncharacteristic' mental lapse.

Again, perhaps, such explanations of violence may be more likely to be felt necessary (and more often accepted) in the middle class. But as explanations they raise difficulties. Alcohol may indeed work chemically to lower inhibitions, but drunken behaviour (or for that matter mental illness) does not always necessarily take the form of violence (Gelles, 1974). Moreover a 'loss of control' may still be subject to some deep rules of behaviour which inhibit outright murder, and dictate the greater incidence of the use of weapons by women and the greater likelihood of the use of fists by men.

The negotiation of shared meanings of violence in the family situation: scripts and routines of violence

It might seem probable that the 'aggressor' and the 'victim' would have a different viewpoint on the meaning of violence, the aggressor being more likely to deny, neutralize or justify the action. Yet in the family the aggressor may have the power to impose a particular meaning upon a violent action, while the victim may have a great deal of emotional, social, and even financial, investment in the family ideal and consequently may have a vested interest in accepting a non-pejorative meaning for violent behaviour.

Thus it happens in child abuse cases that both parents may collude in denial, and not simply with the object of evading legal sanctions (the mechanism of families 'scapegoating' or agreeing to persecute one child has been described; Bell and Vogel, 1960). Alternatively both husband and wife may come to accept that a high degree of violence is justified in punishing a child, so that violence becomes 'normalized' in a relationship ('all children need a good smack sometimes'). Similarly husband–wife violence may come to be seen as normal, condonable; or neutralized as an inexplicable interruption in relationships which are otherwise reasonable and loving (as seemed to be happening in the 'Jekyll and Hyde' marriages of women still living with violent men in the Colchester study; Marsden and Owens, 1975).

These shared meanings of violence and partly learned through interaction and trial and error in family situations. Once a spouse or parent learns that violence can be used, it may become ritualized at a high level (Scott, 1974). Violent episodes may become routinized and subject even to set 'scripts' of behaviour and speech. One particularly interesting account of ritualized violence described the home as like a theatre: violence had begun with the wife's challenge to the insecure masculinity of the husband, who had responded with assertively masculine behaviour, violence, which thereafter became more and more frequent and routinized (Feild, 1974). Some men deliberately bring their children in as spectators of violence, to increase their wives' humiliation and anxiety. There may also develop routines for the aftermath of violence, so much so that it has been suggested that some men get hooked on remorse and reconciliation (Berne, 1967).

On the other hand many, perhaps most, couples learn ways of avoiding conflict and violence. Some wives know what to expect of the husband's weekend binges, and they may devise stratagems for avoiding the worst of the violence, by going to bed early or by getting the children out of the way. In a study of unemployed men and their families, conflict and violence arose in some families because the man was at home devalued, interrupting the wife's normal routines and relationships; yet other couples avoided conflict by the wife going out to work, by the husband going out of the house to work in the garden shed or on an allotment, or by the husband engaging in do-it-yourself activities which preserved his masculine status and the sexual division of tasks in the household (Marsden, 1975).

The concealment of violence from outsiders: Jekyll and Hyde marriages

Apart from the stressful nature of home situations, a further explanation of the fact that most violence takes place in the home appears to be that violent incidents are 'managed' so as to conceal them from outside labelling and stigma, and the possibility of sanctions (Dobash, 1975; Gelles, 1974; Marsden and Owens, 1975; New South Wales, 1975). The aggressor attempts to manage the image of family relationships in public, whatever happens 'backstage' in the home (Goffman, 1959). And the victim may actively assist in this process, for fear of herself being labelled a failure.

This has been described as the Jekyll and Hyde phenomenon in the Colchester study, where to the outside world the man was said to appear 'as nice as pie' and 'the life and soul of the party' (Marsden and Owens, 1975). It might be suggested that Jekyll and Hyde marriages will occur in the intermediate strata of society where there are the tightest standards of reserve in personal relationships and the strongest norms of privacy in the home. Some men such as vicars, doctors, lawyers, schoolteachers, social workers, and policemen, who are 'moral exemplars' in society, will stand to lose more from public discovery of any violence, and may therefore more actively attempt to conceal it.

Within the home, too, violence seems less likely to occur when others are present, and not merely because they might intervene. In some families attempts are made to conceal violence from the children, which may mean that children are less likely to be affected by parental violence than is commonly assumed.

Wives may be forbidden to go out in case their bruises are seen, and injured children may be kept away from school or from the sight of health visitors, social workers, and doctors. It has been suggested that much undetected violence towards children occurs between the ages of 1 and 4, that is in the gap between the ages where there is systematic state supervision of children's health. Violence may be directed at particular parts of the body where it will show less: children may be smacked around the head, or a soft weapon may be used, such as a cushion, in granny bashing.

Rarely, still more complicated situations arise, where the aggressor attempts to make the victim appear and feel to be the violent one (the so-called 'gaslight' syndrome).

Outsiders' reactions to violence, and unofficial controls

Apart from the official and legal controls on violence, there are others of a less formal kind, which operate with varying effectiveness to bring support or to inform the authorities and provide escape routes and controls. The most immediate controls will be exercised by relatives and neighbours who may live with or near the violent family. Child abuse is often reported by relatives or neighbours. In an incident of marital violence, when a brother discovered that his sister was being beaten he collected some friends to give her husband a beating.

Neighbours may provide temporary refuge or more permanent shelter, and the offer of accommodation by relatives seems crucial in women's escape from violence (Marsden, 1973). There are stories of how in the past villagers serenaded the aggressor with 'rough music', the rattle of pots and pans, to let him know he should change his ways and that he was being watched. Unfortunately, neighbours' gossip, stigma, and ostracism may be sanctions against the victim as well as the aggressor.

More powerful sanctions are in the hands of employers, who may give the sack (a sanction sometimes brought about by information from relatives). A policeman whose violence was heard by police neighbours lost his job (Marsden and Owens, 1975). The possibility of the loss of income may, however, be a further incentive to the victim as well as the aggressor to conceal violence. Another powerful sanction is that housing authorities may be able to engineer the husband's eviction.

In respect of the causes and control of violence, the army seems especially worthy of attention. Soldiers may be prone to be violent (by virtue of their social origins, authoritarian upbringing, training, contacts with violence, and way of life). Family conditions seem stressful with periods of separation of husband from thewife and children, frequent moves which break the wife's social contacts with relatives and friends, and situations where comparatively young and inexperienced mothers bring up their children without advice from relatives. To make matters worse, the British army is jealous of the intervention of outside agencies and still relies largely on an old style of paternalistic or 'lady bountiful' welfare, carried out by commanding officers and their wives, which has recently come in for criticism on account of its inadequacy and amateurishness (Spencer, 1975).

Factors influencing outside knowledge and intervention

Since many families do not seek outside intervention and may conceal violence, there remains the question of how violence may nevertheless become known to outsiders and officials, and what influences their willingness to intervene. It might be suggested that in general outside intervention will be more likely the closer the family's physical and social links with the surrounding society.

The physical layout of the housing in which the family lives is clearly important. A violent family in an isolated caravan, a farm labourer's cottage, or a detached suburban house, will draw less attention than a violent family living in a high density terrace where the houses have thin walls.

But also influential will be the closeness of the violent family's social contacts with outsiders. In new blocks of flats there may be sound contact but no neighbourliness, especially where the layouts prevent neighbours from meeting, a design calculated to promote hostile reactions to noise intrusion.

Some evidence suggests that violent families are less in touch with the surrounding society (Gelles, 1974). This may mean that violence increases with social isolation, which could be explained as stress or by the lack of outside sanctions. Yet it could also mean that violence itself increases social isolation. In a time of 'tender-mindedness' when violence is publicly disapproved of relatives and neighbours may not want to get involved in distasteful incidents for which there is no familiar idea of what to do. Violent families may themselves remove to escape notice, or there may be a calculated attempt by the aggressor to render the victim more vulnerable by driving away any potential outside audience or source of help (Marsden, 1973).

Even if evidence of violence comes to outsiders' attention, it may not necessarily bring sanctions. Partial concealment, and the differing meanings given to violent actions by the family themselves, can lead to confusion for outside observers, who may in any case disagree among themselves about the meaning of actions and appropriate responses. The failure of social workers and police to intervene in violent families, or the actions of social workers in removing children from home, are highly controversial. It has also been said that the police are sometimes excluded from case conferences on child abuse for fear that they might intervene and prosecute parents (Borland, 1976). Families who look 'respectable' may be less likely to be perceived as violent and to be sanctioned. Where there is a desire for concealment from the authorities, this will be made easier by the greater geographical mobility of the middle class, and their more separated housing.

The different views of violence taken by various agencies, and the different likelihood of sanctions of varying severity, may lead those who seek help to approach agencies very selectively. For example, the middle class may be more likely to approach a psychiatrist or the child guidance services, whereas the working class may approach the police or probation services.

The visibility of violence to outsiders and their willingness to intervene are probably affected by various structural and ideological influences which change over time. For example, in spite of scares about 'granny bashing' there has been a major switch in household patterns in this century, so that old people and younger married couples are now more likely to live in separate households. This means a reduction of stress through crowding, but possibly an increase of stress through isolation, and a loss of visibility to outsiders and access to help for other kinds of violence. However, in spite of more immediate physical separation between households relatives do keep in touch, so it is difficult to assess how far changes in the extended family will have affected knowledge of violence and possible intervention.

Another recent switch in housing patterns is towards semi-detached houses, or blocks of flats where there is propinquity without sociability. This points to a decrease in outsiders' knowledge of violence, a decrease in the possibility of intervention, and a decrease in willingness to intervene.

MAKING SENSE OF THE EVIDENCE ON PHYSICAL VIOLENCE

The discussion of these last two sections can now help further to clarify the confusion which has arisen from the conflicting evidence on family violence derived from various sources and specialisms. It will be apparent that between the occurrence of any physical act in the family and the final categorization of that act as violent, there intervenes a complex chain of social processes. These operate selectively and sequentially to censor or filter out knowledge of the act, so as to reduce the likelihood of its becoming known, and labelled, outside the family, to friends, the general public, officials—and research workers.

It is generally recognized that only a proportion of physical violence comes to public notice. But how great a fraction, and which examples of violence, is controversial. And what is less clearly recognized in arguments is that the violent acts which come to light are not like the separate tips of an iceberg, where the hidden violence comprises merely larger numbers of similar instances, and the visible tips are of the same kind.

Rather the situation might more appropriately be likened to the searchers in the dark with the elephant: each of them grasps a part—the hairy, brush-like tail; the rubbery, snake-like trunk; the columnar, tree-like leg; the scaly, wall-like side—and asserts this to be the true nature of the whole beast. The implications of this situation deserve to be spelled out in more detail, for the violence which comes to light in various samples may yet provide us with a number of sightings whereby we might aim to discover more of the real shape of the 'elephant' of family violence at present concealed in the dark.

A longer historical perspective

Taking a longer historical perspective, it cannot strongly emphasized how much change there has been in all those various cultural and structural factord which influence not only the genesis of violence but also its public visibility and control by outsiders. Major variables are the level of violence in society, which seems to have fallen markedly in public life, and the climate of public awareness and concern about violence as an issue, which seems to be currently high. In a climate where family violence becomes a public issue, people are more likely to perceive acts as violence, and moreover they are more likely to perceive them as calling for intervention, even though the overall level of violence may be much lower.

Falling household size must have drastically affected the pattern of family interaction in all sorts of ways, including marital violence, child abuse, and inter-sibling violence. There has been a vast and very recent change in the composition of households, too, and a switch away from domestic service over a wide social spectrum and not just in the middle class (Lazlett, 1974). The relative isolation of the nuclear family unit within one household is historically a very recent phenomenon. And the state of affairs now, where officials have the right of entry to the home but exercise it very infrequently, is totally different from a situation where the boundaries of the home were much less clearly marked as private territory, and where in consequence any violence must have been visible to a much wider range of outsiders, although possibly the less remarked for the same reason.

It will be apparent that seen in a historical context it becomes even more difficult to assess trends in violence. The questions of definition, and how sheer awareness influences the control and detection of violence, become much more complex.

The overall incidence of family violence today

Various estimations of the physical abuse of children today suggest that something like one-tenth of cases come to light, but perhaps here the difficulties of definition are even greater than with physical violence towards women, since the corporal punishment of children is used in a majority of families at all social levels.

For battered wives all the indication points towards the real incidence of violence, however defined, being much larger than the observed incidence. Any agency may see only a small fraction of violence, with possibly the family doctor being the person most likely to know about violence (Marsden and Owens, 1975). Jack Ashley's startling estimate of 27 000 to 75 000 cases was based on figures from Citizens' Advice Bureaux, yet probably only a small minority of women go to them for advice, since they offer no protection or resources. A crude estimate from the Colchester study was higher, at one in a hundred marriages, but a later check of Colchester's solicitors revealed that they had been consulted by five times as many women suffering the effects of violence as had been estimated in the original study (Colchester Women's Aid, 1976). And even this figure may be low, since people tend to use divorce grounds which are most convenient and least stigmatizing (Chester 1970; Chester and Streather 1972; Goode, 1962; Marsden, 1973). This would indicate an incidence of about 5%. Other evidence seems to place the incidence of violent marriages at between 1% and 5%, of rarely violent marriages at up to 15%, and the remainder of non-violent marriages at around 80% (Chester, 1977).

Studies of court records indicate that the cases investigated by the police are often only one incident in a long history of violence (Dobash, 1975; New South Wales, 1975), while women who apply to the police at all appear to be only a minority.

The distribution of violent acts and marriages by social class

Just as the available evidence does not give any clear indication of overall incidence, so it also fails to describe the social distribution of families in which there was ever a violent act, and the different social distribution of families which continue violent. The distinction is between women who escape and women who do not. It has been stressed earlier how difficult it is to draw up a balance of all the factors which may operate to keep women in a marriage which turns violent. On the whole it might be expected that middle-class women are more prepared and able to escape from violent marriages, because of the greater acceptance of divorce, better access to matrimonial relief through the law, greater earning power, and alternative sources of accommodation. There are reported examples of working-class women who have remained locked for years in violent relationships because of the practical and ideological barriers to escape (Marsden, 1973). Yet this is a generalization only, and will not apply to all cases: the situation of the Jekyll and Hyde marriages has been noted.

Similar class factors may operate in child battering cases to increase the ability of middle-class parents to get help, and to reduce the likelihood of violence continuing and becoming categorized as such.

In addition, it might be suggested that out of all violent marriages, women who go to refuges represent fractions not merely of the more violent but also of the more working-class marriages, and of families who lack informal resources and contacts. (There is other evidence that middle-class women are more likely to seek help sooner, from different sources, whereas working-class women, especially those with more children, may delay seeking help until violence is more severe (Marsden, 1973; New South Wales, 1975).

Selective escape from marriage, to different destinations, could account for differences between refuges and also, for example, for the contrasts between the sample of women from the highly-publicized CWA, and the Colchester Jekyll and Hyde marriages (which were obtained by advertisement and from a variety of other sources). The CWA women had usually become pregnant extra-maritally, the husbands had records of violence in childhood and in adult relationships other than the marriage, violence began early, and it involved children. None of these characteristics featured prominently in the Colchester study, and their incidence in other refuges seems lower that at CWA.

Plainly, if class factors affect the continuation of violence, the likelihood of categorization, and the composition of samples, caution has to be used in building theories upon these samples to try to explain the incidence of violence in different classes.

The suggested connection between child abuse and wife beating

The contrasting CWA and Colchester samples offer a further example of how the same social processes which lead particular families to appear in research may actually shape the theories which may be derived from that research. For *if* one of the reasons why CWA women left their husbands was that the violence turned upon the children and began to repeat itself in their behaviour, then Chiswick may have a considerably higher than average group of families where the children suffered from violence, in contrast to the Colchester study where there was as yet little paternal violence towards the children or evidence of transmission.

Other refuge populations also seem to show less connection between parental and child violence than Chiswick. There is the further, neglected question of how far violent behaviour in children and by refuge mothers towards children may be exacerbated by refuge conditions and other current stresses, rather than resulting entirely from the original violence in the home.

Evidence from police records shows little direct relationship between incidents of marital violence and child abuse. In one study, a quarter of violent cases involved offences committed by husbands and directed at their wives, compared with less than 4% of violence directed at children (Dobash, 1975). In about 50% of cases children were involved as witnesses, but again this relationship may be partly an expression of the requirement that prosecution has to have witnesses, and the incidence of child witnesses of parental violence *might* be lower in the general population.

Similarly, samples gained from an agency specializing in child neglect might be expected to show a higher than average connection between child and parental violence (Moore, 1974; RSSPCC, 1974).

Variations in prognosis for different samples

The different samples investigated by research workers or dealt with by specialists and agencies may also hold out different hopes for amelioration of the violence, depending on their origins. For example, in the case of marital violence it might be suggested that CWA would have a lower incidence of women returning to their husbands successfully (i.e. with no further violence), because the men are so much more publicly and uncontrollably violent. While a better chance of successful return or control of violence might be predicted for women who have Jekyll and Hyde marriages: the violence seems more under the husband's control and may therefore be suppressed if the man realizes his behaviour is visible to the wider society, and if the balance of power in marriage is restored by the woman's freedom to leave the relationship through the provision of refuges.

A further example may be given in relation to child abuse. There seems to be a different prognosis for future family behaviour from violence detected by X-ray diagnosis, by social service visits, by neighbours' reports, and by self-report. Differences in the sources of samples may account for some of the disagreement over whether and in what ways battering parents may be helped.

The problem of the 'vocabulary of motives' in explanation of violence

Finally in this discussion of the meaning of the data, we should recognize more explicitly the problem posed for research by the variations of meaning and explanation given to violence in interpersonal relationships. These meanings constitute variable 'vocabularies of motives' which are used by the actors themselves and by observers to explain violence to themselves and to other audiences. Different motives may be given, depending on the audience.

The existence of vocabularies of motives makes it difficult to assess the evidence on individual factors such as alcohol, or mental illness, or childhood batterings, since in various situations such explanations may be volunteered or omitted as individuals sense their acceptability (Gelles, 1974). Moreover, it seems that people with a particular definition of their own problem will tend to approach those agencies which most nearly fit the definition. For example, if the problem is seen as psychiatric, a psychiatrist may be approached, or if seen as a problem of sheer bullying, the police. There may thus develop a self-confirming, self-selection of particular kinds of cases, offering particular kinds of motivational accounts, through approaching those agencies which are most likely to accept and confirm them.

There are further difficulties in trying to understand violence by questioning the victims, for in some ways the victim may be the very last person to know what it is that triggers off violence in the aggressor. Moreover, some refuges make a deliberate attempt to change the victim's perception. They offer explanations which externalize blame (so as to build up the woman's self-confidence), sometimes by placing it more squarely on early influences in the man's childhood, sometimes by referring it more abstractly to wider social and political processes. While this evidently serves a very valuable function for the women, its awkward implications for research based on motivational accounts gathered from refuge populations will also be clear.

CONCLUSIONS

This chapter has tried to show that we can better understand the issue of family violence if we see it in a broader context of social change and intellectual and political controversy.

It must be stressed that although it proves possible to discuss violence towards women and violence towards children in the same broad conceptual frameworks and from similar sociological perspectives, the indications are that child and wife battering are not as directly connected as some contributors to the public debate have tried to suggest. There may be links in some families, but the connections are complicated and seem unlikely to be found in a majority of cases.

The current wave of interest has little to do with any recent changes in the incidence of violence. Instead it draws its heat from an ever-widening circle of controversy, fuelled by political and intellectual debates about the whole status of women and children, and fanned by the mass media. Growing interest in the problem may itself generate more evidence.

Rather than any recent absolute increase in family violence, we seem to be witnessing a classic 'moral panic'—albeit in a valuable cause—about a phenomenon which appears to question cherished standards (Cohen, 1972). The legitimacy of male and parental authority in the family are under scrutiny. At a time when the use of violence in society is being strongly challenged, the discovery of the continued use of violence in the family conflicts with the ideal that the home should be a source of peace and emotional support and renewal in a complex world.

But while formal sanctions have operated to damp down violence in public life, they have not been extended to family life. There may be a paradox here in the situation of women: the very decline of violence in public life and increase in 'tender-mindedness' may make people more reluctant to credit the continued existence of violence in the home and to intervene. This leaves wives more vulnerable to violence unless and until a deliberate attempt is made to generate wider awareness of their plight, and to provide them with escape routes.

Similarly a growing child-centredness may have led to a disbelief that parents can be violent towards children, thus paradoxically rendering child victims more vulnerable.

There has not been sufficient space to establish fully the validity of critiques of the family. Rather, this chapter has attempted to give sources and spell out the implications of these debates for a shift in the definition of violence away from the merely physical, to put more emphasis on the whole social situation and status of women and children. This status constrains them to receive blows and prevents their escape or, even without physical violence, restricts their growth, aspirations, and autonomy. *An* increase in marital violence may be a consequence of women's challange to their subordination.

The social policy implications of this perspective are very clear. In the short term there should be the provision of networks of surveillance and refuges for the control and immediate relief of physical violence. In the long term there is a much broader need to strengthen all the social policies which will release children and women—and grannies—from their societally-created status as the victims of violence and domination.

A coda: family violence and the 'trained incompetence' of academic specialization

From the point of view of academic research and specialist study the lessons of this analysis of family violence are less clear and not very encouraging. The appearance of a public issue like family violence was a call to academics to emerge for a while from their separate specialisms, to try to negotiate common descriptions of the problem which would be more widely accepted than those current among the coteries of their colleagues in mutually isolated specialisms. A shift away from individual pathology to viewing violence also in a more structural way implies at best some sort of fusion between psychiatry, psychology, and sociology, possibly with a number of other specialisms making a contribution. Unfortunately the issue of family violence also exposes the difficulties of such a joint enterprise.

The separate specialists tend to investigate only selected problems using a limited repertoire of favoured explanations. To make matters worse, they tend to work with the different (in some cases literally) captive samples which are most accessible through the researchers' professional activities, and which are tailored for the specialist perspective. True, specialists borrow from one another, but in a relatively naïve way. 'Sociological' explanations which are sometimes regarded as quite distinct, relying on only 'social' factors, in fact resort to psychiatric or psychological concepts to explain individual behaviour. Psychiatrists and psychologists tend to incorporate 'environment' into their explanations, if at all, only in an impressionistic way as a set of triggering stress factors. Such borrowings in no way represent a fusion of the different perspectives, and tend to ignore value problems and controversies about the use of concepts. The fundamental questions about the impact of social forces on the self tend to get lost down the cracks between the different specialisms.

Thus a major lesson from this analysis of the issue of family violence must be the way the sudden call for evidence demonstrated with unusual clarity the 'selective inattention' with which research approaches social problems (Steinmetz and Straus, 1974), and the 'trained incompetence' of academic specialization (Gil, 1975) which restricts the ability of academics to contribute to public policy debates.

ACKNOWLEDGEMENTS

I would like to acknowledge the help of Joan Busfield, Bob Chester, Stan Cohen, Lee Davidoff, June Freeman, Nicky Hart, Geoff Hawthorn, John Martin, Howard Newby, June Thoburn, Sylvia Walby, and Elizabeth Wilson.

REFERENCES

Althusser, L. (1971) 'Ideology and ideological state apparatuses'. In *Lenin and Philosophy, and Other Essays*, New Left Books.

Ashley, J. (1973) *House of Commons Debates*, Hansard, vol.860, col.218.

Barker, D. L. and Allen, S. (1976) *Dependence and Exploitation in Work and Marriage*, Longmans.

Barron, R., and Norris, G. (1976). In Barker and Allen, 1976.

BASW (1975) Draft discussion paper.

Becker, H. (1960) *Social Problems: a Modern Approach*, Free Press.

Bell, C., and Newby, H. (1976) In Barker and Allen, 1976.

Bell, N., and Vogel, E. (eds) (1960) *A Modern Introduction to the Family*, Free Press.

Berger, P. L., and Kellner, H. (1964) 'Marriage and the construction of reality', *Diogenes*, **46** (1).

Berne, E. (1967) *Games People Play*, Penguin Books.

Bernstein, B. (1973) 'A socio-linguistic approach to socialization: with some reference to educability'. In *Class, Codes and Control*, Longmans, vol.1.

Blood, R. O., and Wolfe, D. M. (1960) *Husbands and Wives: the Dynamics of Married Living*, Free Press.

Borland, M. (ed.) (1976) *Violence in the Family*, Manchester University Press.

Brandon, S. (1976) In Borland, 1976.

Busfield, J. (1974) 'Ideology and reproduction'. In Richards, M. (ed.), *The Integration of the Child into a Social World*, Cambridge University Press.
Busfield, J., and Paddon, M. (1977) *Thinking about Children*, Cambridge University Press.
Chester, R. (1970) 'Sex differences in divorce behaviour', *Journal of Biosocial Science*, Supplement 2.
Chester, R. (1977) Personal communication; figures based on responses to *Woman's Own* questionnaire and Marplan survey for *News of the World*.
Chester, R., and Streather, J. (1972) 'Cruelty in English divorce', *Journal of Marriage and the Family*, November.
Cohen, S. (1972) *Folk Devils and Moral Panics*, McGibbon & Kee.
Colchester Women's Aid (1976) *Colchester's Battered Women Need Refuge*.
Cooper, D. (1971) *The Death of the Family*, Penguin Books.
Cromwell, R. E., and Olson, D. H. (1975) *Power in Families*, Sage.
Dobash, R. E. (1975) Evidence to the Parliamentary Select Committee on Violence in Marriage, 1975.
Field, R (1974) 'Of course only a brute would batter his wife ... but is that the whole story?', *Cosmopolitan*, November.
Fonda, N., and Moss, P. (1976) *Mothers in Employment*, Brunel University.
Gayford, J. J. (1975) 'Wife-battering: a preliminary survey of 100 cases', *British Medical Journal*, 25 January.
Gayford, J. J. (1976) In *Welfare Officer*, January.
Gelles, R. J. (1973) 'Child abuse as psychopathology: a sociological critique and reformulation', *American Journal of Orthopsychiatry*, 43 (4).
Gelles, R. J. (1974) *The Violent Home*, Sage.
Gelles, R. J. (1975) 'Violence and pregnancy', *The Family Coordinator*.
Gelles, R. J., and Straus, M. (1975) 'Family experience and public support of the death penalty', *American Journal of Orthopsychiatry*, 45 (4).
Gil, D. J. (1975) 'A holistic perspective on child abuse and its prevention', *American Journal of Orthopsychiatry*, April.
Glastonbury, B. (1971) *Homeless Near a Thousand Homes*, Allen & Unwin.
Goffman, E. (1959) *The Presentation of Self in Everyday Life*, Anchor.
Goldthorpe, J., Lockwood, D., Bechhofer, F., and Platt, J., (1968) *The Affluent Worker*, Cambridge University Press.
Goode, W. J. (1962) *Women in Divorce*, Free Press.
Goode, W. J. (1971) 'Force and violence in the family', *Journal of Marriage and the Family*, 33.
Guardian (1976) 'Granny bashing' incidents go up', 15 May.
Guardian (1977) 'Passive man', 28 April.
Harrison, P. (1975) 'Refuges for wives', *New Society*, 13 November.
Henry, J. (1974) In Steinmetz and Straus, 1974.
Holt, J. (1973) *Escape from Childhood*, Penguin Books.
Illich, I. (1973) *Deschooling Society*, Penguin Books.
Inter-Action (1974) *Inter-Action Advisory Service Handbook*, London: Interaction Inprint.
Kellmer Pringle, M. (1973) 'Non-accidental injury to children', The Needs of Children, National Children's Bureau, Highlight, no.7.
Kempe, C. H., Silverman, F. N., Steele, B. F., Droegemuller, W., and Silver, H. K. (1962) 'The battered child syndrome', *Journal of the American Medical Association*, **181**, 17–24.
Kurtz, I. (1976) 'How Erin built her battered empire', *Sunday Times*, 28 April.
Land, H. (1975) 'The myth of the male breadwinner', *New Society*, 9 October.
Listener (1976) 'Breaking the chain of family violence', 30 September.
Lazlett, B. (1974) 'Family membership, past and present', American Sociological Association.
Locke, H. (1951) *Predicting Happiness or Divorce in Marriage*, Holt.

Lynch, M. A. (1975) 'Ill-health and child abuse', *Lancet*, 16 August.
McGregor, O. R. (1974) In *Report of the Committee on One Parent Families*, HMSO, Cmnd 5629.
McGregor, O. R., Blom-Cooper, L., and Gibson, C. (1970) *Separated Spouses*, Duckworth.
Marsden, D. (1973) *Mothers Alone*, Penguin Books.
Marsden, D., and Duff, E. (1975) *Workless*, Penguin Books.
Marsden, D., and Owens, D. (1975) 'The Jekyll and Hyde marriages', *New Society*, 8 May.
Marx, K. (1946) *Capital*, Allen & Unwin.
Matza, D., and Sykes, G. M. (1961) 'Delinquency and subterranean values', *American Socciological Review*, 712–9.
Moore, J. G., (1974) *Yo-yo Children*, NSPCC.
Musgrove, F., (1966) *The Family, Education, and Society*, Routledge & Kegan Paul.
Nemesis (1974a) **1** (1); **1** (7).
Nemisis (1974b) **1** (4).
Newell, D. (1972) *A Last Resort*, Penguin Books.
Newson, J., and Newson, E. (1970) *Four Years Old in an Urban Community*, Penguin Books.
New South Wales (1975) *Domestic Assaults*, NSW Bureau of Crime Statistics and Research.
NSPCC (1976) *At Risk*, Routledge & Kegan Paul.
NWAF (1976) *The Existing Research into Battered Women*, NWAF, 51 Chalcot Road, London, NW.
Oakley, A., (1974) *Housewife*, Allen Lane.
O'Brien, J. (1971) 'Violence in divorce-prone families', *Journal of Marriage and the Family*, **33**, November.
Oliver, J. E., and Cox, Jane (1973), 'A family kindred with ill-used children: The burden on the community', *B. J. Psychiatry*, **123**, 81–90.
Owens, D., and Straus, M. (1975) 'The social structure of violence in childhood and the approval of violence as an adult' *Aggressive Behaviour*, **1**.
Parkin, F. (1971) *Class, Inequality and Political Order*, Paladin.
Parkinson, G. (1969) 'Marriage on probation', *New Society*, 22 May.
Parliamentary Select Committee on Violence in Marriage (1975) vols 1 and 2, *Report* and *Evidence*, House of Commons Paper 553–i, HMSO.
Parsons, T. (1947) 'Certain primary sources and patterns of aggression in the social structure of the Western World', *Psychiatry*, **10**.
Parsons, T., Bales, R. F. (1956) *Family Socialization and Interaction Process*, Routledge & Kegan Paul.
Pizzey, E. (1974) *Scream Quietly or the Neighbours Will Hear*, Penguin Books.
RSSPCC (1974) *Report of the Working Party on Marital Violence*.
Runciman, W. G. (1966) *Relative Deprivation and Social Justice*, Routledge & Kegan Paul.
Rutter, M., and Madge, N. (1976) *Cycles of Deprivation*, Heinemann.
Scott, P. D. (1974) 'Battered wives', *British Journal of Psychiatry*, **125**.
SHAC (1976) *Violence in Marriage*, SHAC.
Sharpe, S. (1976) *'Just like a girl'*, Penguin Books.
Smith, S. (1974) 'Social aspects of the battered baby syndrome', *British Journal of Psychiatry*, **125**.
Spencer, John C., *et al.*, (1975) *Army Welfare Report*.
Steinmetz, S. K., and Straus, M. (1974) *Violence in the Family*, Dodd Mead.
Straus, M. (1971) 'Some social antecedents of physical punishment: a linkage theory interpretation', *Journal of Marriage and the Family*, **33**.
Straus, M. (1973) 'A general systems theory approach to a theory of violence between family members', *Social Science Information*, **12**.

Straus, M. (1976), *Family Violence Research Programme*, Department of Sociology, University of New Hampshire.

Straus, M., Steinmetz, S. K., and Gelles, R. J. (1976) 'Violence in the family: an assessment of knowledge and research needs', paper presented to the American Association for the Advancement of Science, February.

Timms, N. (1975) 'Battered wives: a study in social problem definition'. In *Social Policy Yearbook for 1974*, ed. K. Jones.

Tizard, J. (1976) 'Effects of day care on young children' in Fonda N., and Moss, P. (eds), *Mothers in Employment*, Brunel University Management Programme.

Townsend; P. (1974) 'The cycle of deprivation', BASW Conference Paper.

Veness, T. (1962) *School Leavers: their Aspirations and Expectations*, Routledge & Kegan Paul.

Wilson, E. (1977) *Women and the Welfare State*, London: Tavistock.

Wolfgang, M., and Ferracuti, F. (1967) *The Subculture of Violence*, Tavistock.

Wright Mills, C. (1970) *The Sociological Imagination*, Pelican.

6

VIOLENCE IN THE FAMILY: AN HISTORICAL PERSPECTIVE

Margaret May

INTRODUCTION

Just under a century ago the phenomena of the battered wife and child were first widely recognized as serious social problems meriting specific state intervention. Widespread public pressure induced the government in 1875 to establish the first official inquiry into conjugal violence, followed in 1878 by a major attempt to protect wives against physical maltreatment by their husbands, the Matrimonial Causes Act. The 1870s were also marked by growing public awareness of the extent of child abuse, culminating in the foundation of the NSPCC and the first salient legislation, the Prevention of Cruelty to Children Act, in 1889. In the late nineteenth century the problem of domestic violence became a public issue, discussed by press and Parliament and stimulating research into its nature and causes. Widespread public interest, however, soon waned and was only sporadically revived by particularly brutal cases. Indeed the intermittent nature of public concern is the most striking historical feature of the problem, and is reflected in the paucity of historical research into this aspect of family relationships.[1]

THE PROBLEM OF SOURCES

This chapter provides an introduction to the origins of the late Victorian legislation and changing attitudes to, and patterns of, family violence in England and Wales before 1914. Scotland, with its separate legal system is largely excluded from this study. Given the type of evidence available, however, such a survey is inevitably of a tentative and exploratory nature. The difficulties of eliciting patterns of behaviour in such an intimate and private setting as the family today are well known, but are compounded as one moves further back in time. For the nineteenth and early twentieth centuries the quantitative and qualitative source material is both fragmentary and limited, and variations between rural and urban areas and between different social groups preclude firm generalization. Attempts to enumerate the incidence of domestic violence, as today, are particularly problematic. One possible gauge is provided by judicial and police returns, but up to 1853 offences against women and children were not distinguished from other offences against the person in the national returns, and subsequently their familial status was generally not recorded.[2] Moreover nineteenth-century commentators universally agreed that only a fraction of the cases of domestic violence reached the courts. One of the most baffling aspects of the phenomenon to contemporaries was the reluctance of victims to prosecute, and wives 'propensity to perjure themselves in defence of their husbands, one even pathetically claiming to have bitten her own nose'. Non-reporting was particularly serious in cases of child abuse, while limitations on the evidence of spouses and the need for young children to prove they understood the nature of an oath long restricted court proceedings. Moreover some forms of child abuse only became a criminal offence from the 1880s and it was only with the work of the NSPCC that reliable statistics began to emerge.

Literary evidence is also uneven. The available sources include biographical material, the insights provided by journalists and novelists, and the many surveys produced by Victorian and Edwardian social investigators disturbed by new industrial conditions. But few inquiries were specifically concerned with domestic violence and much information arises only incidentally. Moreover the observations of middle-class investigators were inevitably coloured by their own preconceptions of family life and their definitions of 'violence' were highly subjective and variable. Indeed the startling contrast between middle-class assumptions about family relationships and the realities of working-class behaviour formed a recurrent theme in the literature, and provided a major stimulus to reformist activity. The possibility of distortion emerges particularly in the findings of court officials, educationalists and, above all, temperance workers. Ex-wife beaters were prominent among the reformed drunkards regularly paraded at temperance rallies, and temperance workers did much to expose the problem, but their accounts were inevitably influenced by their primary concern with the drink question.

Biographical material often provides more direct insights, though generally restricted to the experience of upper social groups. Childhood recollections in particular frequently refer to parental practices, though spouses tend to be more reticent about their relationships. Perhaps the best known nineteenth-century accounts of family violence were those of the feminists, Mary Wollstonecraft and Caroline Norton. The former was terrorized by her tyrannical father and his assults on her mother, while Caroline Norton's attempts to escape her husband's brutality produced one of the most famous divorce scandals of the Victorian era. But while it is possible to cite many cases of excessive violence, accounts of domestic bliss also abound, so that the incidence of violence is difficult to establish. Similar difficulties arise in interpreting the numerous allusions to family violence in contemporary fiction and lack of space has prevented a detailed discussion of such sources.

The meaning and scale of domestic violence can only be fully assessed in the context of contemporary patterns of power and authority within the family. Historical study of family life, however, is a relatively recent development and, while historical demographers like Peter Laslett (1972) have provided valuable insights into family structure, research into the quality of family life is still in its early stages. Some historians, especially those like E. Shorter who have adopted a cross-cultural and long-term approach, suggest that industrialization has been accompanied by a gradual 'improvement' in the quality of family life, arguing that more democratic affectionate relationships gradually replaced the authoritarian pre-industrial family. Hitherto British historians, however, have concentrated on short-term changes, particularly in the period 1760 to 1840, and on the controversy over the alleged deterioration in family life and intensification of intra-family exploitation accompanying early industrialization.

While this debate, which has been succinctly summarized by H. Perkin, continues, considerable differences of opinion have, as Laslett (1973) observes, also emerged in the few historical studies of childhood. One perspective, building on P. Ariès' seminal work, suggests that from the late eighteenth century particularly it is possible to trace the emergence of a modern concept of childhood and a movement to more affective child-rearing methods. Traditionally, however, the nineteenth century, especially the early decades, has been viewed as a period at least of indifference if not active and cruel exploitation, particularly of child labour, and this remains the dominant impression. But though opinion on the nature of short-term changes in family and child life are divided, it is generally agreed that from the late nineteenth century it is possible to trace a clear 'improvement'.

Within the limitations of the source material, primary and secondary, this chapter, commencing with a survey of family relationships and domestic violence in the first half of the nineteenth century, will concentrate on shifts in public attitudes as indicated by the emergence of new protective measures for women and children and an examination of contemporary explanations of family violence. It will not be able to cover medical sources, which constitute a literature in themselves.

CONJUGAL VIOLENCE IN THE NINETEENTH CENTURY

Early industrial England inherited and in many ways, socially and economically, reinforced an autocratic patriarchal family structure. The expected pattern of family government was both upheld by the law and, from the turn of the century, encouraged by a proliferation of domestic and child-rearing manuals aimed particularly at the newly respectable middle classes. Family counsellors such as the influential Mrs Ellis and Mrs Sandford, and child advisors like Louisa Hoare or the Reverend Lant Carpenter, all enjoined the subordination of wife to husband and children to parents, especially the father. The child's duty was that of 'unquestioning obedience', the wife's to 'submit' and 'defer' to her husband's rule. Such a family structure was seen as a bastion of the social order, and any interference as a threat to social stability. Indeed Mrs Ellis advised the unhappily married wife faced with an ill-tempered husband that her highest duty was 'to suffer and be still' (Ellis, 1845, p.73).

The prescriptions of family counsellors were enshrined in the law. At the beginning of the nineteenth century both wife and child retained the chattel status established centuries earlier. Children, as Jeremy Bentham had approvingly observed, were the property of their parents. Admittedly parents had a moral duty to support, educate, and protect their offspring but, as Blackstone's authoritative *Commentaries on the Laws of England* showed, apart from the Poor Law, there were few means of enforcing these obligations. Similar proprietorial attitudes extended to wives, whose position was frequently compared with that of children. On marriage the law, upholding the Christian doctrine of one flesh, substituted total subjection to the husband for dependence on the father. Children, property, earnings, liberty, even the wife's conscience belonged to the husband. Her legal identity was absorbed into his. In return he was expected to provide the 'necessaries' of life, though separated wives found it difficult to exact maintenance. As the feminist Barbara Leigh Smith bitterly observed, 'a woman's body belongs to her husband' who had the right to forcibly prevent her from leaving him (Smith, 1854, p.6). Early nineteenth-century commentators, however, regarded her special legal status as a privileged one, the mark of a civilized society's concessions to women's frailty and need for masculine protection. To Blackstone women were 'the favourites' of the English law (Blackstone, 1770, I, p.433).

Legal patriarchy was also seen as one guarantee of domestic harmony and in upholding it the law expressly sanctioned a degree of physical force. To ensure the necessary filial obedience the father might 'lawfully correct his child, being under age, in a reasonable manner' and 'delegate' his authority to the child's teacher (Blackstone, 1770, I, pp.452–453). The right of moderate chastisement also extended to the masters of apprentices on the grounds that they were responsible for their trainees' conduct. Similar reasoning underlay the belief still expressed by some legal authorities at the turn of the century that what Mary Wollstonecraft termed the 'divine right of husbands' also included an entitlement to correct wifely misbehaviour. As the much-quoted *Treatise of Feme Coverts* declared, though the law safeguarded the wife against serious injury the husband might still beat her 'for lawful correction' and 'to order and rule her' (Nut and Gosling, 1732, pp.81, 184). This tradition was summarized by Blackstone in the late eighteenth century:

> The husband also (by the old law) might give his wife moderate

> correction. For, as he is to answer for her misbehaviour, the law thought it reasonable to entrust him with this power of restraining her, by domestic chastisement in the same moderation that a man is allowed to correct his servants or children .... But this power of correction was confined within reasonable bounds; and the husband was prohibited from using any violence to his wife .... The civil law gave the husband the same, or larger authority, over his wife, allowing him for some misdemeanours *flagellis et fufibus acriter verbare uxorem*; for others only *modicam castigationem adhibere* ....

Though the ancient right of chastisement had been seriously challenged and modified by the courts since the seventeenth century, legal opinion remained ambivalent and, as Blackstone also observed, 'the lower rank of people, who are always fond of the old common law, still claim and exert their ancient privilege and the courts of law will permit a husband to restrain the wife of her liberty in case of any gross misbehaviour' (Blackstone, 1770, I, pp.444–445). The persistence of this traditional belief, not only among the lower orders, was shown in the publicity accorded the declaration attributed to Judge Buller in 1782 that legally a husband could beat his wife with impunity provided he used a stick no thicker than his thumb. In Wales the permissible form of marital discipline was popularly held to be three blows on any part of the person, apart from the head, with a broomstick! Though unsubstantiated by subsequent legal authorities, Buller's assertion was popularized by several writers and cartoonists, notably Gillray, and reappears throughout the nineteenth century.

Popular belief in a husband's right to chastise his wife was sustained in the early nineteenth century not only by street literature but continuing uncertainty among the legal profession following conflicting court cases. Popular textbooks such as Bacon's *Abridgement* still stated in 1832 that the husband had by law 'power and dominion over his wife' and could 'beat her, but not in a violent or cruel manner' (Parry, 1916, p.44). Judicial reassertion of this power frequently emerged in cohabitation cases since the husband's rights of cutody were embodied in the same ancient dicta. By mid-century, however, J. J. S. Wharton found it necessary to warn that just as the popular impression 'that a husband can get rid of his wife by selling her in the open market place with a halter round her neck' was incorrect, so it was 'a great error to suppose that a husband can chastise his wife'. The links between wife selling and wife beating as indices of the low status of women were to become a pronounced theme in later, especially feminist, writings. But Wharton also revealed a more common social differentiation in attitudes to conjugal violence. Citing earlier writers he suggested that whereas in the lower ranks 'blows sometimes pass between married couples who are, in the main very happy' and amidst those of 'very coarse habits such incidents occur almost as freely as rude or reproachful words', a violent husband in the upper classes was 'unsupportable' (Wharton, 1853, pp.312, 468).

This implicit toleration of some domestic violence among the lower classes compared to the chivalry expected of the upper-class male, analogous to the double standard of morality underlying working-class prostitution, was a recurrent feature of the literature. Despite, or because of, such ambivalent warnings, some legal uncertainty continued. In 1862 Serjeant Woolrych's *Criminal Law* still hesitantly recognized among the 'defences to criminal assault', the 'parent who chastises his child .... or even, as some say, the husband his wife', and many defendants in wife-beating cases claimed this right, some successfully (Parry, 1916, p.46). Uncertainty was only finally removed with the case of *R.* v. *Jackson* in 1891 when in ruling against the husband's right to imprison his wife, the court also revoked the associated dicta on his right to chastise her.[3] From the beginning of the nineteenth century, however, it was agreed that women and children were entitled to protection against excessive violence. Safeguards took several forms, some official, others hitherto neglected by historians.

Firstly, like other injured persons, wives and children were entitled to 'pray the peace' against their aggressors, and magistrates were empowered to bind them over to keep the peace. Early in the century, however, legal protection was often restricted by delays and inadequate enforcement measures. Some improvement came when, as part of his reformist crusade, Peel up-dated the law. Under the Offences Against the Person Act of 1828, magistrates were empowered to punish summarily those convicted of common assaults by fines of up to £5, with a maximum of 2 months' imprisonment for defaulters. Aggravated assaults were to be dealt with by the superior courts. Court records show that some wives, often after long suffering, resorted to the law, as did even a few beaten husbands. Contemporary reports of such cases reveal a picture of bruised and black-eyed women, sometimes pregnant, being attacked by their mainly lower-class husbands, commonly on the slightest pretext on their return from the pub. Assaults involved punching and kicking (sometimes with hobnailed boots) and striking with straps, pokers, tongs, and other household implements. But assault charges by wives formed only a small portion of court business. In London they were often fewer than cases of cruelty to animals protected by a vigilant RSPCA. The fear and shame which intimidated many victims were highlighted by a case in Manchester in 1853. John Eagan, 'a dirty and dissolute shoemaker', was charged with 'brutally beating his wife and three children', one of whom was 'covered in bruises' and whose sight had been impaired. The wife had long lived a 'life of hide and seek', escaping to neighbours or the streets but, fearing further brutality, had not dared to prosecute until her plight was accidentally revealed during a routine sanitary inspection (*The Times*, 26 August 1853).

In theory the abused wife had another recourse since 'intolerable cruelty' constituted one of the grounds for both divorce and separation. Up to the divorce reforms of 1857, however, expensive parliamentary proceedings were beyond the means of almost all women. As Caroline Norton, who 'learned the law respecting women, piecemeal, by suffering from every one of its defects of provision', discovered, separation was also a humiliating and intimidating process (Norton, 1855, p.29). Following her husband's violent attacks, which included throwing an ink-bottle at her head, kicking, and scalding her with a tea-kettle, she sought refuge with relatives, but he continued to harass her and even successfully claimed some of her property which was, legally, still his. Moreover, the fact that she returned to him was thought to condone his cruelty, while, despite the 1839 Infants Custody Act, which she helped secure, the father's rights, even over young children, were still upheld by the courts (Norton, 1854). Yet large families and limited employment opportunities, especially for middle-class women, reinforced wives' dependence on their husbands, while the Poor Law, with its deterrent philosophy upholding the husband's duty to maintain, provided little hope for the deserting wife and mother.

More immediate protection for some came from the traditional practice of community discipline of disorderly households known as 'rough music'. This was a noisy public demonstration, often organized by the village youth, aimed to publicly humiliate those who had violated customary obligations or matrimonial conventions. Its form varied regionally. In some areas the offender's home was surrounded, usually at night, by individuals screaming, blowing cow horns, and beating pots, kettles, and any other noisy instruments. Elsewhere the culprits, often seated backwards on a donkey, were paraded through the streets. Those whose behaviour threatened the traditional patriarchal family structure, like nagging wives or cuckolded husbands were the major targets. Husband beaters, though rare, were favourite victims, and another indication that conjugal violence was not simply a one-way process. Significantly such demonstrations extended to cases of cruelty to children and occasionally to wife beaters, and, from the turn of the century, collective action against the latter became more common. The Reverent W. Cooper reported that for much of the century in southern England 'when a husband had made himself notorious by beating his wife' he was treated to the 'badger's band' (Cooper, 1873, p.390). F. P. Cobbe found a similar expression of popular disapproval, 'riding the stang', common in the North and Scotland (Cobbe, 1878, p.56). The prevalence of such practices throughout the century provides one index both of the extent of wife beating and community hostility to at least the most notorious and excessive cases of domestic violence. E. P. Thompson (1972) has recently suggested that from the early nineteenth century these demonstrations increasingly focused on wife beaters, but how far this indicates a shift in the wife's status or popular attitudes is difficult to discern, and contemporary evidence is often contradictory.

Many middle-class investigators felt that conjugal violence was widespread among the lower orders and that few wives sought legal redress. While some attributed this to legal deficiencies many, like Wharton, maintained the common belief that what Sam Weller termed 'the amiable weakness of wife-beating' was an accepted part of lower-class family life unquestioned by many wives. A discerning few observed that family violence, like drinking, with which it was often associated, had escalated under the strains of industrial society. More commonly, however, it was depicted as one facet of the generalized 'savagery' of the uncivilized masses, reflected in their brutal sports and pastimes, and the frequency of street brawls in which women often participated.

Mayhew's influential study of London street life, first published in the *Morning Chronicle* in 1851, portrayed the undomesticated life-styles of a 'distinct race' which prized physical prowess, particularly as a means of settling disputes. Costermen resembled

> North American Indians in their conduct to their wives. They can understand that it is the duty of a woman to contribute to the happiness of a man but cannot feel that there is a reciprocal duty .... The wife is considered as an inexpensive servant and the disobedience of a wish is punished with blows.

Even severe beatings, not uncommon, were accepted by women as part of their customary role which, Mayhew discovered, extended to courtship where punching 'a gal' was the recognized method whereby youths established 'ownership'. Male costers felt women 'liked a feller for whalloping them', though one coster girl remarked such practices were tolerated from economic necessity (Mayhew, 1861, I, pp.43, 36, 45).

Though Mayhew's street labourers are not a representative group his *Morning Chronicle* colleagues, often with little surprise, noted similar habits among the lower sections of the manufacturing population. Among the Northampton shoemakers one reported a 'large proportion of the homes ... bear witness to the dissipated habits of their occupiers and, in the ruinous condition of the furniture, tell too plainly that the owners were 'quarrelsome in their cups' (*Morning Chronicle*, letter XLVI, 30 January 1851). This common theme emerges in another account of the conditions of the 'manufacturing poor' in the North in the 1840s, which distinguished between the more 'respectable' and the coarser elements typified by a household where the wife had a black eye received 'in a slight skirmish with her husband as they were taking some mild refreshment together' (*Fraser's Magazine*, 1848, p.3). In many districts, particularly 'low neighbourhoods' it was felt that wife beating was taken for granted. Neighbours remained indifferent, as in one street incident where no one offered to interfere, although the woman's face was beginning to 'exhibit both blood and marks; for however that old right of a man to chastise his wife is repudiated in other parts of society ... in these walks the ancient custom still holds good' (Duncombe, 1848, p.73). For many, life in such areas was epitomized by Godwin's account of a Whitechapel chemist's window, advertising 'Ladies and Gentlemen/ are respectfully informed that

/BLACK EYES/ are Effectively Concealed on Moderate Terms ...' (Godwin, 1854, p.3).

Though only incidentally highlighted in early social inquiries, conjugal violence among the lower sections of the working class became proverbial. But apart from occasional sensational cases it roused little concern. This was particularly noticeable in the major discussion of working-class family life in the 1830s and 1840s on the impact of factory employment. One of the most striking features of this debate was the fear that wage-earning wives, and children, had reversed traditional family roles, undermining the father's authority. The rise in wife beating noted by some observers possibly reflected an attempt by some husbands to preserve their traditional mastery. Certainly many commentators were more concerned with the need to reassert patriarchal authority than with its potential or actual abuse.

From mid-century, however, wife beating became a subject of greater concern, manifest in successive attempts to restrict it particularly in the 1850s and 1870s. Reformist efforts were inspired by two main groups: law-enforcement agencies whose concern was part of a more general anxiety over the level of violent crime, and feminists campaigning for the emancipation of women. In the 1850s the chief impetus came from magistrates and police perturbed by inadequate counter-measures, especially for aggravated cases. Police improvements, notably in London, had revealed what one magistrate, urging more effective police powers, described as 'the common practice of ill-using women' by husbands who frequently escaped punishment (PP 1854, LIII, p.145). Disquiet at the limited protection for women and children was inflated by lurid press reports and more general fears for law and order prompted by the abolition of transportation and successive outbreaks of 'garrotting' in 1850s. A man who assaulted his wife might easily attack others or transfer his aggression to the streets.

Judicial concern was expressed in Parliament where Thomas Phinn secured the publication of the first limited return of assaults on women and children by males in the metropolis. The information proved unfortunately varied from court to court, making comparison difficult. But of 6111 cases reported by ten courts between 1850 and 1854, 1059 husbands, 17 fathers, and 110 other relatives were recorded as summarily charged or convicted, though it is unclear how far prosecutors disguised their relationships especially since few courts noted the relationship of unmarried couples (PP 1854, LIII). A high proportion of the other cases involved disputes between neighbours or violence associated with theft. Like many magistrates, however, Phinn was convinced that such statistics, based on court cases, seriously underestimated the scale of wife beating. It was not 'even for blows that wives brought their husbands before the bench ... the woman rarely complained of her husband, or the child of its parent, until the brutality had arrived at such a pitch that life was insecure' (Parl. Debates, 1853, CXXV, 674). Like many others he attributed non-reporting to low penalties, especially for aggravated assaults, and advocated corporal punishment. As *The Times* (12 March 1853) declared, adopting a powerful image, women had less protection than animals! To the frustration of many magistrates wives frequently dropped charges or interceded for their aggressors, Exposed to the husband's 'coaxings and intimidations', those adjourned to the sessions often failed to appear and juries were unimpressed when physical evidence of maltreatment disappeared in the meantime (Parl. Debates, 1853, CXXIV, 1417). The remedy, however, was viewed more in terms of punishing the husband rather than aiding the wife, and few questioned a system which returned her to a convicted husband, or drove her to the workhouse while the breadwinner was in prison.

In March 1853 the Government responded to mounting pressure with a bill to suppress 'the rapidly growing evil' by 'extending the same protection to defenceless women as they already extended to poodle dogs and donkeys' (Parl. Debates, 1853, CXXIV, 1418). Under the Act for the better Prevention and Punishment of aggravated Assaults upon Women and Children, magistrates were empowered to summarily punish those convicted of aggravated assaults on women and on males under 14 with up to 6 months' imprisonment, with or without hard labour, or a fine of up to £20 with similar imprisonment on default, and additionally bind them over to keep the peace for 6 months. More expeditious justice, it was hoped, would encourage 'the victims to complain' and deter brutal husbands (Parl. Debates, 1853, CXXV, 680). This 'Good Wives' Rod', as it was popularly labelled, was little used, however. In the metropolis, for instance, in the 5 years up to 1860 only 1960 were sentenced under the Act, of whom one magistrate estimated less than a third were for assaults on wives. Nevertheless, the measure allayed widespread public anxiety, demonstrating the well-known tendency for people to assume that the passage of legislation had solved the problem.

A few MPs, however, still felt wife beating was increasing and continued to press for severer punishments to reduce non-reporting. Several bills to impose flogging, an antidote canvassed in 1853 but rejected by the Government, were introduced in the late 1850s. Various strands in contemporary attitudes to family violence emerged in the ensuing debates. Most commentators, echoing foreign observers for whom wife beating was one hallmark of the English labourer, saw conjugal violence as a lower-class phenomenon produced largely by drunkenness. Only one noted perceptively that though they formed the majority of victims, if 'the revelations of the Divorce Court' were any guide, 'brutal assaults were by no means confined to women of the lower classes' (Parl. Debates, 1860, CLVIII, 532). This observation pinpointed a major imbalance in the discussions. Since few ventured to study divorce cases and most information was derived from police records, conjugal violence was assumed to be a lower-class trait. Social differentiation also characterized the language adopted: 'wife beating' or 'wife knocking' applied to the lower strata, middle-class women suffered 'cruelty'.

Most discussion centred on the propriety of flogging and the scale of wife beating. Flogging, supported by reference to its efficacy in the forces, was advocated as the only meaningful punishment for such 'brutes', and for the 'moral effect' on 'low neighbourhoods' where most offences occurred. Government spokesmen, however, felt the problem was not increasing, though press publicity had encouraged more prosecutions. As the Home Secretary declared, flogging was unlikely to sweeten subsequent marital relations, and would only deter wives, many of whom already petitioned for their husband's release 'on the grounds that their husband is penitent and the woman is suffering from being deprived of her means of support' (Parl. Debates, 1860, CLVIII, 530). Echoing this mistrust of flogging, a *North British Reviewer*, in one of the first specific studies of conjugal violence, suggested that preventive measures were as necessary as immediate punishment. Though the roots of domestic violence were manifold, and partly a reflection of women's low social status which encouraged abuse, practical remedies could be applied. The immediate cause lay in the ignorance and negligence of the working class wife. Rather than providing the husband with a comforting refuge from the frustrations of work she neglected their home, driving him to the pub, and inflamed him further by a stream of household complaints. The solution to the inevitable quarrel, when nagging wives were often silenced by blows, lay, as Miss Brewster's experiments in Scotland showed, in domestic training for the wife, and, in the longer term, an improvement in working-class housing (*North British Review*, 1856).

The tendency to blame the woman for her failure to conform to the cherished ideal of wifely self-denial and forbearance remained a common theme in discussions of conjugal violence. Even more common, however, was the feeling expressed by the *Saturday Review* that since wife beating could not be cured it was best ignored (*Saturday Review*, 16 May 1857). Faced with such opposition successive bills failed and when, following an 'epidemic' of 'garrotting', the law on offences against the person was revised in 1861, provisions for wives and children remained substantially unchanged. Nevertheless a muted campaign for the flogging of wife beaters, occasionally linked with proposals for divorce, continued in the 1860s.[4]

The 1850s also saw another limited attempt to protect the victims of conjugal violence, the 1857 Divorce Reform Act, passed under strong feminist pressure. Indeed the *Daily News*, predicting an influx of cases, felt the Act gave wifes a new security against wife beating, hitherto 'the premium on concubinage over matrimony in the working classes' (*Daily News*, 28 May 1858). But divorce remained financially impossible for most women, and was further restricted by the need to prove adultery as well as cruelty. More significantly, growing concern with family violence was expressed in the first organizational attempt, hitherto neglected by historians, to aid the victims, The Society for the Protection of Women and Children from Aggravated Assaults. Founded in 1857 it aimed 'to prevent or punish offences and crimes committed on women and children' and functioned mainly as an advisory and prosecuting agency. Though not confined to domestic violence, much of the society's work concerned beaten wives and, less frequently, the battered child. It advertised for information, guaranteeing confidentiality, and provided legal aid and advice. This first attempt to counter family violence, however, had a somewhat chequered history. Significantly it was one of the least known of London's charities and attracted only limited support. Precarious funding limited the society's work but it pressed for legal improvements and endeavoured to publicize the problem, publishing occasional dossiers of its cases, and, in 1864, one of the earliest studies of cruelty to children, *Compassionate Justice*. It was also able to provide considerable fuel when widespread public agitation revived in the 1870s.[5]

This second wave of public concern was spearheaded by feminists affronted by the continuing high incidence of wife beating. The trigger was provided by John Stuart Mill who directly linked the battered wife with the struggle for female emancipation which had developed a coherent ideological and organizational form in the 1860s. Feminist campaigning increasingly focused on women's political and legal disabilities, particularly property and income rights, and the Commission on these incidentally revealed the plight of working-class women bound to dissolute or brutal husbands. The feminist onslaught on the husband's financial control rapidly broadened into an attack on his continued property in the wife, and the gradual assertion of married women's property rights provided both a crucial precedent and a spur for measures to give the wife control of her person, complementing the political drive to abolish her chattel status.

In 1866 Mill presented the first petition for women's suffrage, which one commentator felt promised relief to the thousands enduring the 'miseries of wife-beating' (Westminster Review 7 March, 1866). In 1867 he secured a major parliamentary debate on female suffrage in which he highlighted the battered wife as a central issue of female emancipation, asserting that the existence of wife murder and beating unsuppressed by derisory sentences demonstrated the need for separate representation. The theme of the 'trampled', 'mangled' wife was taken up by several feminist supporters, notably Alfred Dewes. In an influential article in 1868 he declared that while the protection of divorce was denied the working-class wife, sentences were such that it 'still seems to be held by the administrators of the law that the husband has the right of correcting his wife'. The inferior status of women, fostered by the law, was such that 'the lower ranks of people' still 'unmistakeably exercised this ancient right' (Dewes, 1868, pp.122ff.).

Mill himself re-emphasized these themes in *The Subjection of Women*, published in 1869 though written in 1861. Central to his assault on contemporary notions of femininity and catalogue of women's disabilities was the portrayal of marriage as a form of legalized slavery. Though he admitted concentrating on women's legal position, he felt 'domestic slavery' encouraged their devaluation and maltreatment. Among 'the most naturally brutal and morally uneducated part of the lower classes' in particular, it fostered contempt for the wife who appeared 'an appropriate subject for any indignity'. Mill recognized that women were the only objects over whom labouring men, themselves exploited, could exerise any superiority:

> And how many thousands are there among the lowest classes ... who, without being in a legal sense malefactors in any other respect, because in every other quarter their aggressions meet with resistance, indulge the utmost habitual excesses of bodily violence towards the unhappy wife, who alone, at least of grown persons, can neither repel nor escape from their brutality ... with a notion that the law has delived her to them as their thing, to be used at their pleasure .... (Mill, 1970, pp.33, 46, 35)

Brutality, he warned, would continue while women, like children, returned to their tormentors, and declined to prosecute, and he urged that conviction for assault should entitle the wife to divorce or separation.

A hostile press, upholding the cherished belief in masculine chivalry and domestic tranquillity, condemned Mill. Many doubted if legislation could alter the brutal habits of the lower orders, while he was attacked for ignoring 'the reconciling effects of the indissoluble' and even for increasing the pool of under-paid 'superfluous women' with a flood of separated wives (*Blackwood's Magazine*, 1869, pp.317ff.)! But the case of the 'black-eyed women' like Susannah Palmer, who after years of brutality knifed her husband, was vigorously publicized in the feminist press and at suffrage meetings. In 1874 alone 2841 summary cases of aggravated assaults on women and children were reported, with a further 3106 in 1875, of which it was estimated that four-fifths were by husbands on wives (Cobbe, 1878, p.71). To many feminists wife beating, like wife selling, became a symbol of male exploitation and legal oppression, which only women's suffrage could abolish. It provided powerful ammunition for their attack on the so-called 'natural' relationship between the sexes, and emphasized the need for educational and employment opportunities to reduce women's vulnerability. Inadequate protection measures also demonstrated the failings of a male Parliament, and concern with wife beating merged into the fundamental feminist belief, derived from Mill, in the law as a moulder of social behaviour. Changing social attitudes, epitomized in the lower classes by wife beating, depended on destroying a legal structure which taught men 'that their wives are their property' (*English Women's Review*, 1877, VII, p.389). The franchise was a prerequisite for the protection of such women from 'the uncontrolled dominion of the savage passions of men' (Shore, 1872, p.20). Feminist campaigning against this aspect of the 'double standard' provided a new rationale for state action, the assertion of female dignity would facilitate the elevation of men.

Feminist agitation concentrated particularly on establishing the scale of violence and disproving the popular notion that women themselves provoked it. Their efforts were reflected in one of the earliest studies of conjugal violence, Frances Power Cobbe's 'Wife Torture in England', published in the *Contemporary Review* in 1878 and subsequently reprinted as a pamphlet. One of many Victorian spinsters who found a career as a professional social reformer, Cobbe was already an experienced campaigner, partly through her involvement in the crusade against cruelty to animals which was also rousing public interest in the 1870s. She estimated that the number of brutal assaults on women alone averaged 1500 a year, most being by husbands on wives. Though she felt wife beating was more common in the upper strata than 'generally recognized', the 'dangerous wife-beater belongs almost exclusively to the artisan and labouring class'. She also argued, from court cases and statistics, that it varied geographically and occupationally, being concentrated in densely-populated areas with heavy and casual labourers most prominent. Wife torture was attributed to a combination of general and specific factors. It was partly a consequence of lives brutalized by squalid homes and unrelieved 'toil in dark pits and hideous factories'. Second, it was fostered by the 'common idea of the inferiority of women' and matrimonial and legal traditions which led men to regard their wives 'as their things'. Long inured to such customs women themselves took it for granted that 'a husband is a Beating Animal'. Drunkenness, overcrowding, jealousy and 'hetereopathy', an impulse to hurt partly aroused by the victim, were the precipitating factors. Cobbe insisted that in 'wife-beating', as distinct from 'wife-beating by combat', the wife was the undeserving victim. Many were sober and industrious while husbands were drunken dissolutes often with a criminal record. Cobbe's remarkably prescient study also summarized the feminist case against both existing penalties and flogging. Neither released the wife from her tormentor, and flogging only increased her reluctance to prosecute. The solution lay in securing her personal safety and economic independence by applying 'the same redress which women of the richer class obtain through the Divorce Court' (Cobbe, 1878, pp.55ff).

Feminist pressure was reinforced by renewed alarm about violent crime among police authorities in the 1870s following a series of brutal assaults, including attacks on the police. Judicial anxiety, expressed nationally in the press and at meetings of the British Association and the Social Science Association, focused on the need for severer punishments. At the Liverpool Social Science Congress in 1876 Serjeant Pulling, in a dramatic description of the city's 'kicking districts', voiced widespread judicial concern at low penalties and legal procedures which seemed designed to deter rather than aid the wife, whose life consequently was 'simply a duration of suffering and subjection to injury and savage treatment, far worse than that to which the wives of mere savages are used'. He saw the solution in improved procedure, including public prosecutors, and flogging for second convictions. In the ensuing discussions most speakers supported him, though a few felt divorce would provide greater protection for the wife (NAPSS, 1876, pp.345ff). Growing concern fuelled by sensationalist press reports was also reflected in

Parliament where a flogging bill was introduced in 1872, and several members led by Colonel E. Leigh repeatedly pressed for action. In May 1874 the Government commissioned an inquiry into the law on brutal assaults, which revealed a general consensus among police and judicial authorities about the serious level of violent crime, ascribed mainly to drink, and the need for severer punishments.[6] Though much of the report focused on measures for suppressing other forms of violent crime, an overwhelming majority favoured flogging for conjugal assaults, though a few recommended divorce (PP 1875, LXI). To further test opinion the Home Secretary, Cross, introduced a flogging bill in 1875 which produced a debate similar to those of the 1850s; it was withdrawn in the face of heavy opposition led by spokesmen for the Vigilance Society, a 'purity' organization which was campaigning for divorce (Parl. Debates, 1875, CCXXIV, 1853ff).

In 1878, however, while the Home Office reconsidered, F. P. Cobbe, with the aid of Alfred Hill, prepared her own bill. Published with her article on 'Wife Torture', the bill for the protection of wives whose husbands had been convicted of aggravated assaults upon them, provided for judicial separation with custody of the children and maintenance. Cobbe preferred separation to divorce proceedings, fearing the latter might incite assaults by the husband or provocation of one by the wife (Cobbe, 1878, p.87). The bill was introduced with some trepidation into the Commons, but its provisions were incorporated into Lord Penzance's bill concerning the costs of intervention by the Queen's Proctor in matrimonial causes and passed, to Cobbe's relief, with no opposition in 1878.

The Matrimonial Causes Act empowered courts to award wives a judicial separation, custody of children under ten, and maintenance where the husband had been convicted of an aggravated assault, provided they did not commit adultery before or after the award. Despite the innovatory emphasis on safeguarding and maintaining the wife, the numbers claiming separation remained small, and feminist agitation for more thorough protection revived gradually in the 1880s. Greater relief came with the case of *R.* v. *Jackson* in 1891, and, with continuing feminist pressure, the 1895 Summary Jurisdiction (Married Women) Act, which expanded the grounds for separation to include persistent cruelty and wilful neglect. This extension precipitated a flood of applications, and provided a clearer gauge of the scale of matrimonial misery hidden by previous measures. By the 1900s some 8000 matrimonial orders were annually made by the English and Welsh courts and, according to one official, the pressure of claimants was such as to almost overwhelm the magistrates (Holmes, 1900, p.94). Public interest in the specific problem of conjugal violence, always sporadic, was submerged in a wider anxiety at the matrimonial morality of the poor. Mounting judicial concern at the pressure of matrimonial business, combined with growing realization of the difficulties of enforcing maintenance and the problem of illicit unions contracted by separated wives, led in 1909 to the establishment of a Royal Commission on Divorce and Matrimonial Causes. Though concerned with a welter of matrimonial disputes, the Commission, chaired by Sir Gorell Barnes, one of the chief critics of existing measures, provided some insights into the problem of domestic brutality as well as the need for legislative reforms. But the majority of recommendations, including the greater availability of divorce for the poor and improved procedures for enforcing maintenance, were delayed by stiff religious opposition. The problem of the battered wife continued to attract some attention, notably in C. V. Wedgwood's bill of 1910 to provide outdoor relief of up to 10 shillings a week to wives whose husbands were convicted of an aggravated assault on them, and through occasional sensational cases. But further action, as with matrimonial legislation in general, was delayed until the First World War further sharpened interest in family life.

CHILD ABUSE

While public concern with conjugal violence fluctuated, a new and more sustained campaign against child abuse developed in the late nineteenth century. The two were occasionally combined, as in T. D. Selwyn's proposal in 1882 that wife and child beaters should be placed in the public pillory. This suggestion was one reflection both of a radical shift in traditional attitudes to the relationship between parents, child, and state, and more subtle changes in child-rearing practices by the 1880s.

Like women, children were traditionally a subject class. Though protected by similar legal provisions their position was in practice restricted by court procedures and the universal belief in the sanctity of parents' rights, including that of 'moderate' chastisement. Early in the century this was regarded as an indispensable element in child rearing, and physical punishment was part of the normal experience of many children in both private and public settings. How far children suffered intense cruelty, however, is difficult to establish, especially in a society where, with most children forming part of the labour force from an early age, attitudes to their capacities differed from ours. Many people still retained earlier views of children as small but defective adults rather than separate beings with special developmental needs, and in the working classes particularly the worlds of childhood and adulthood were not yet clearly segregated. The low status of children, like women, was conditioned by basic demographic and economic factors. High infant mortality and large families often precluded individual attention and limited parents' emotional investment. High birth rates combined with high mortality also contributed, like the unbalanced sex ratio, to the low evaluation of childhood. In many families children were still seen as a source of income rather than the pivot of family life.

By the 1880s, however, traditional attitudes to childhood were being radically reassessed and child abuse had become a major public issue. This new concern stemmed partly from earlier shifts in upper-class attitudes. It is generally agreed that by the late eighteenth century among the upper strata at least children's needs were becoming more widely recognized. One expression of this was an outpouring of child-rearing literature which provides some insight into expected patterns of parent–child relationships. Though differing in their religious persuasion and educational philosophies, the authors agreed on the twin desiderata of rigorous parental surveillance and filial obedience. They disagreed, however, on the means of instilling appropriate behaviour. Many, especially Evangelical, writers felt with Mrs Sherwood that children were naturally evil.[7] The only effective antidote to this predisposition was regular beating to 'break the child's will'. Though painful to the parent this was vital not only to punish misconduct but redeem the sinner. To spare the rod was not only to spoil the child but to endanger its soul. A substantial minority, however, influenced either by Rousseau's ideas of childish innocence, or Locke's *tabula rasa* theory, counselled moral suasion and condemned corporal punishment as ineffective, damaging to parent–child relationships, and based on a misconceived notion of childhood. Nevertheless obedience remained the cardinal juvenile virtue and appropriate methods for 'training the will' included isolation for varying periods in a corner, cellar or dark closet, dietary punishments, and keeping children in a fixed position. Medical opinion was also divided, and while some counselled mild treatment others still upheld shock treatment including beating or immersion in cold water, especially for the constitutionally weak or lazy.

How far parents followed this conflicting advice is difficult to assess. Much of the evidence is anecdotal, and biographical data reveals a wide range of parental behaviour, from those who rarely chastised their children to households where it was a daily, sometimes savage, occurrence. For many upper-class children early experiences were conditioned less by parents than nursemaids and, for older girls, governesses. That some parents' seclusion from their children led to abuse is clear. In 1800 the *Gentleman's Magazine* reported on a nurse charged with manslaughter when an infant held in the steam above a copper of boiling water as a punishment fell in (*Gentleman's Magazine*, 1800, vol. 70, p.788). In the 1850s Curzon's nanny deployed a wide repertoire of cruelty:

> In her savage moments she was a brutal and vindictive tyrant .... She persecuted and beat us in the most cruel way and established over us a system of terrorism so complete that no one of us mustered up the courage to walk upstairs and tell our father or mother. She spanked us with the sole of her slipper on the bare back, beat us with her brushes, tied us for long hours to chairs in uncomfortable positions with our hands holding a pole or a blackboard behind our backs, shut us up in darkness .... (Rose, 1969, p.20)

Accounts of similar savagery emerge throughout the century, while the recollections of Augustus Hare, Samuel Butler or Dickens' novels, among others, show that parental brutality among the middle class, particularly strict Evangelicals, was not unknown. Boarding-school discipline, for many upper and middle-class children, especially boys, almost a substitute for home life, also produced abuses. Early in the century public schools were notorious for their ferocious punishments and, despite Arnold's reforms, flogging remained an institutional feature well documented by its more sensitive victims, and even cited by ex-sufferers in Parliament as a justification for the punishment of others.[8]

But much biographical material shows that even rigid discipline was often mediated by an affectionate family or school life. How far corporal punishment, sometimes in extreme forms, could be sanctioned, however, emerges in the many debates on its advisability at home and school conducted by correspondents to family magazines in the 1860s and 1870s.[9] The sometimes sadistic discussions ranged from its efficacy, suitable parts of the body, whether clothed or not, the appropriate instrument—with slippers or hands being regarded as less effective than the birch, best used when wet—the number of strokes and the ages at which chastisement should begin and end. Many felt even young babies could be safely beaten or spanked; others recommended corporal punishment well into the teen years for both boys and girls. Some mothers advised strapping the child to an ottoman or the bed to secure the full effect. The most sensational discussion, which included advice on the purchase and manufacture of suitable instruments, in the *Englishwoman's Domestic Magazine*, necessitated separate publication in 1870, partly as the contents were thought too offensive for some readers.[10] Parents and teachers advocated corporal punishment from an early age at home and school, for its educational value in stirring the forgetful and the sluggish, as the most meaningful punishment for children whose capacity for reasoning was naturally limited, and as more effective especially for 'shaming' than alternatives such as bread and water or dark cellars. Significantly, the most ardent advocates were those who claimed to have benefited from beatings in their own childhood. As in earlier debates, however, an equal number expressed horror and disbelief at practices they thought confined to the lower classes, and prescribed affectionate discipline. Though the debate between physical and moral force continued, the value of affective methods was increasingly emphasized by child guidance writers in the late nineteenth century and corporal punishment viewed as a last resort, particularly as the possible consequences for a child's long-term development became recognized.[11]

If middle and upper-class attitudes and practices varied, many commentators felt with the Reverent T. Guthrie that working-class children were 'brought up by curses and blows not love' (Guthrie, 1851, p.10). Early in the century influential middle-class reformers like J. P. Kay and Lord Shaftesbury propagated a picture of callous working-class parents who saw their children as a burden, allowed them to die, even hastening the process for burial club money, maltreated them and exploited their labour. Working mothers were criticized for the high accident rates among children left alone or with unreliable minders or older children, and for their use of narcotics. Parents' apparent willingness to abandon children to charities or prison was seen as another sign of their indifference, and fears of encouraging parental irresponsibility proved a major restraint on reformist activity. Summarizing the findings of many contemporaries a writer in *Fraser's Magazine* concluded that from birth 'the hand of their natural protectors was too often raised against them' and 'the fact is at least certain that among the very poor the ill usage of their children is a crime too common to excite much notice' (*Blackwood's Magazine*, 1850, p.398).

Others, however, were equally disturbed by parental over-indulgence, and there are many reports of parental affection and self-sacrifice. Though neglect and passive cruelty was by today's standards widespread, the scale of active cruelty is difficult to guage. Middle-class reformers, appalled at the harshness of urban life, were prone to exaggerate, neglecting the poverty and ignorance which underlay apparent indifference. The fact that many children of working age stayed with parents until marriage suggests that family ties were strong and M. Anderson's study of early nineteenth-century Lancashire shows that mother–child and often father–child relationships were affectionate, though some fathers were feared as heavy drinkers against whom children sided with the mother. Later the NSPCC certainly found a 'wholesome sentiment' among the poor with over half their cases regularly reported by the general public, particularly the poor. The line between legitimate and unacceptable violence, however, was a highly subjective and uncertain one, and early Victorian attitudes were conditioned by a society still accustomed to high levels of public violence and the public spectacle of physically punishing offenders. Among the lower strata especially, pre-industrial patterns of child rearing which, as Lloyd de Mause has recently shown, were often cruel and insensitive, remained.

That many children suffered considerable brutality is clear. Occasionally, often almost by accident, such cases surfaced in the courts and the press. In 1829, for example, a surgeon who overheard neighbours gossiping exposed one famous case of parental cruelty, while another, that of a 10-year-old Bermondsey girl, was discovered by a passer-by attracted by her cries. At the end of an alley he found 'an emaciated child fastened by her wrists and ankles' to a ring in the wall. On examination her 'body exhibited marks of severe chastisement, scarcely any part of it being without black and blue stripes ... as for her flesh it was around one inch thick in dirt'. At the hearing her father and step-mother, claiming her perversity, had to be protected from an angry mob (*The Times*, 28 April and 1 June 1829).

But the cases of child abuse which reached the courts were rare. In the early nineteenth century, as later, many abused children were too young or defenceless to express their sufferings. The conditions attached to oath-taking by young children often frustrated judicial action, while the traditional emphasis on parental rights led to light sentencing, and policies designed to protect women made no provisions for the peculiar vulnerability of children. While many children suffered in silence those who managed to react against parental violence attracted some attention. Reformatory workers like the chaplain of Preston gaol, the Reverend J. Clay, felt the 'brutality of parents', especially step-parents, was a major cause of delinquency (PP 1852, VII, p.868). Runaways from brutal parents were particularly prominent among the vagrant children who infested urban streets. Mayhew documented many such cases and concluded that the 'brute tyranny of parents' who vented their frustrations 'in the passionate beating' of their children caused much juvenile vagrancy and crime (Mayhew, 1861, I, p.468). Child beggars, some deliberately mutilated by their parents, along with juvenile street traders forced to work by beatings, added to their number. Indeed early in the century the Mendicity Society regularly warned the charitable against such young 'imposters' whose maimed or neglected condition was deliberately induced by profiteering parents. In the 1900s George Sims was still campaigning against such practices, reporting one girl deliberately blinded by her begging mother (Sims, 1908, p. 115).

The link between parental violence and the threat of delinquency or semi-delinquency proved a potent factor in the growth of public concern with child abuse. But the experience of cruelty was not confined to the home. As numerous inquiries showed, children in mines and mills early in the century, especially pauper apprentices, were often savagely beaten, sometimes by their parents, and such practices persisted for much longer in agriculture and other industries. Corporal punishment for even trivial offences also characterized elementary schooling throughout the nineteenth century, despite the efforts of a few progressives. Evidence of abuse led to new regulations in the 1870s and 1880s, but in the 1900s the educationalist Sir John Gorst was still concerned at the excessive reliance on corporal punishment in state schools, a pattern inherited from the public schools (Gorst, 1907, pp.180ff.). Indeed the abolition of corporal punishment was one of the main planks in the abortive school strike of 1911, one of the few mass expressions of children's response to adult treatment.[12]

Until the 1880s, however, the scale of excessive parental violence was often hidden. As a speaker at the 1872 Social Science Congress observed, it was 'too hastily' assumed that 'there was an intuitive and instinctive love of the parent for the offspring sufficient for the protection of the child'. Significantly he felt violence, often excessive, was still the universal mode of child discipline, and drew attention to the possibility that such treatment might scar a child for life (NAPSS, 1872, 1872, pp.304ff.). His address was one sign of the new concern with child abuse which developed from the 1870s, stemming from a new surge of social investigations and the emergence of welfare institutions and professions which revealed the existence and implications of parental cruelty. Fundamental economic and demographic changes underlay the growing concern with child abuse. Economic depression, and growing international competition in the late nineteenth century stimulated a new interest in 'national efficiency' and the conservation of human resources. Anxieties about the quality of the population were reinforced by exposures by recruiting officers during the Boer War of the debilitated condition of the masses, already highlighted by the surveys of Booth and others. Growing concern with the threatened deterioration of the race was heightened by continuing high infant mortality among the poor and the new spectre of a declining birth rate. Combined with the new science of child psychology such concerns contributed to a new evaluation of childhood. Increasingly children were seen not as miniature appendages of their parents but as citizens with their own special developmental needs.

The re-evaluation of childhood in the late nineteenth century was expressed in the twin concepts of 'children's rights' and 'children as national assets'. As the philanthropist Mary Tabor argued in 1888, advocating new protective legislation, children had a natural right to a healthy protected upbringing and the state a vested interest in ensuring parents respected these rights. Brutally used or neglected children, whom she estimated at 5% of the child population, whose development was consequently retarded, represented a loss of manpower and a continuing burden on the rates. Similar concern with child wastage and the citizenship rights of children reappeared in countless 'child life' studies and, from the 1870s, in the reports of schools boards, medical officers, and charities. The establishment of school boards in 1870, and, especially after the introduction of compulsory schooling in 1876, the appointment of school attendance officers, revealed a hitherto unsuspected amount of child cruelty as well as neglect. Many school attendance committees, such as those attended in the 1870s, by Benjamin Waugh, later chief promoter of the NSPCC, or those observed by George Sims in the 1880s, discovered cases of children beaten violently, often by drunken parents, or inadvertently hurt during parental fights (Sims, 1889, p.140).[13] Inquiries into absenteeism also renewed public concern with maltreated street children, a problem which was highlighted by the work of philanthropists like Dr Barnado, and by W. B. Stead's sensational campaign against juvenile prostitution.

The possibility of parental cruelty was also exposed by the prolonged medical battle against infanticide and high infant mortality arising from non-accidental deaths. In the period 1856 to 1860 in London alone, it was estimated that 3901 inquests were held on children under 2 found dead, many of whom were discovered in back alleys, privies, canals, and the river, and a high proportion of whom it was felt were deliberately killed (Ryan, 1862, p.62). Some outraged contemporaries, like Disraeli in *Sybil*, even felt infanticide in Britain was nearly as high as in India. Indeed one London coroner, Dr Lankester, remarked that the police were as accustomed to finding dead babies on the streets as dead dogs or cats (Langer, 1974, p.360: NAPSS, 1866, pp.261ff.). Led by Dr Lankester and Dr W. B. Ryan the medical profession in the 1860s commenced a long campaign to improve the law, particularly by providing for the registration of still births, which they felt were 'induced' by unscrupulous midwives as a means of avoiding prosecution, and to reduce the penalty of capital punishment, which often prevented conviction. It was generally agreed that illegitimate children, especially of domestic servants, formed the majority of victims, and concern for their protection broadened in the early 1870s into a wider movement against the related abuses of baby farming and child-life insurance.

The dangers of fostering were most dramatically exposed by the conviction of Margaret Walters in 1870, following the discovery of 16 infant corpses in south London. This case, which has been well documented elsewhere, led, under pressure from Dr Curgenven's Infant Protection Society, to an Infant Life Protection Act in 1872, though effective legislation was not secured till the twentieth century.[14] The preceding parliamentary inquiry, however, also revealed the problem, noted by earlier writers, of children starved or ill-used by parents in order to profit from burial clubs. Growing public awareness of child abuse was further sharpened by the compulsory appointment of local medical officers of health in 1872. Their reports gradually unveiled the scale of accidental deaths among the infant poor, notably from suffocation or 'overlaying', the incidence of which was highest at weekends and was often attributed to drunken parents or baby-minders. Overlaying, it was estimated, accounted for some 1500 infant deaths between 1890 and 1900 alone (NSPCC, 1903, p.4). It was growing awareness of this and the continuing problem of ill-used street children unprotected by the school boards which prompted the Reverend George Staite's Liverpool appeal in 1881 for a Society for the Prevention of Cruelty to Children. Combined with T. F. A. Agnew's reports on American societies this led to the founding of the Liverpool Society in 1883, followed in 1884, after considerable press publicity, by the London Society. This, as has been described elsewhere, combined with 31 other aid societies to form the NSPCC in 1889 with Waugh as secretary.[15]

The society's work provided the first real index of parental violence, though its energies were increasingly absorbed by 'neglect' cases, and the proportion of cases classified as 'cruelty' declined as the society expanded. But the actual numbers of cases of cruelty rose steadily from 1107 out of 3947 complaints in 1889 to 3991 out of 54 772 involving 159 162 children in 1913. By the 1910s Waugh estimated that an average of at least ten children a day were violently assaulted by their parents (NSPCC, 1910, p.23). Earlier he graphically portrayed the forms this violence took:

> after beating, locking up for the night in a coal cellar with rats; immersing a dying boy in … cold water to 'get his dying done' … breaking a girl's arm while beating her, then setting her to scrub the floor with the broken arm folded to her breast and whipping her for being so long about it; hanging a naked boy by tied hands from a hook in the ceiling, then flogging him … lashing a three year old with a drayman's whip … throttling one boy … thrusting the knob of a poker up the throat of another …. (Waugh, 1894, pp.4–5)

Waugh attributed such behaviour to 'the low estimation of the child' legally sanctioned for centuries, but elsewhere in his annual reports he observed a link between 'lapsed parental instincts' and over-zealous punishment by parents, often beaten themselves, or with over-high expectations of their child's conduct, and in some cases a pathological 'addiction' to cruelty. While over half the cases of child abuse were attributable to drunkenness, one twelfth were the product of such 'morbid moralists', and a further quarter of unnatural 'savages' (NSPCC, 1897, pp.40ff.).

To prevent such cruelty the society, guided by Waugh, developed a number of roles, publicizing the problem and the inadequacies of existing controls, canvassing for new measures and enforcing them. Its legislative campaigns and attempts to expand met considerable resistance, grounded in the entrenched belief in the privacy of the home and the sanctity of parental rights. Even Shaftesbury questioned the possibility of protective legislation. But skilful lobbying and well-primed political advocates blending humanitarianism with economic realism, gradually secured a series of acts which, as Waugh proclaimed, radically altered the political status of the child. The society's first achievement was an amendment in the law in 1885 enabling children's evidence to be received without oath where the truth of what it was saying was otherwise proved. In 1889 with the Prevention of Cruelty to Children Act, it secured entirely new powers to protect the inarticulate child. In addition to further improvements in procedure and arrest, and establishing the responsibility of those who had the custody, control or charge of a child for its proper treatment, the Act made the ill-treatment, neglect, abandonment or exposure of a child punishable by 3 months to 2 years' imprisonment and fines of £25 to £100 with increased penalties where it appeared financial benefit from child-life insurance was involved. The powers of this 'children's charter' were increased by further legislation in 1894 and the society's campaign, aided by its incorporation in 1895, culminated in the wide-ranging Children Act of 1908, sections 1 and 2 of which improved provisions for the protection of infant life and for the prevention of cruelty to children.

The details of this measure, the product of agitation by many child-welfare organizations and the symbol of the new attitude to childhood, are well known, as is the society's second major role, of enforcing them. Under Waugh the society pioneered a new approach to child abuse, based on removing 'the evil from the home, not the child' (NSPCC, 1898, p.57). Prosecution and the removal of the child were regarded as a last resort and the society relied heavily on a system of warnings reinforced by supervision from their inspectors, the 'Cruelty Men'. The society's novel approach, developed especially with 'neglect cases', merged with growing anti-institutionalism in child care, stemming particularly from dissatisfaction with Poor Law 'barrack schools', and alleviated the widespread fear that such care, public or private, also encouraged parental irresponsibility. The society viewed its methods as a means of stimulating this responsibility, directly and indirectly. Waugh placed great emphasis on the society's third role, its educative mission. To 'convert minds' to the new status of childhood and encourage neighbours, the society's key informants, he master-minded a massive publicity campaign, circulating through its ladies' committees leaflets on the society's work, its relationship to the police, the need for legislation and the form it should take, and advice on child rearing.[16] To rouse public support it also organized exhibitions of torture instruments and launched a series of moving appeals, commencing with Waugh and Manning's article, 'The child of the English savage' (1886), later reprinted as a pamphlet, as well as its annual reports and the *Children's Guardian*. Re-education was also the basis of the inspectors' work with parents, in which it was thought with considerable prescience that the rescued child filled a crucial role by rejuvenating atrophied parental instincts.

LATE VICTORIAN AND EDWARDIAN EXPLANATIONS OF FAMILY VIOLENCE

The society's work, together with continuing concern with the protection of wives, prompted several attempts to study the problem of family violence in the late nineteenth and early twentieth centuries. Most accounts were policy oriented, concerned like those of over-burdened NSPCC officials less to explain than to publicize the need for action. Many were impressionistic compilations of case studies rather than attempts to document or measure the scale of family violence, and its incidence often surfaces only indirectly in contemporary social surveys. But, in combination, such studies served to crystallize popular stereotypes of domestic violence and provide a valuable insight into late Victorian and Edwardian attitudes.

As earlier, the most prominent feature of the literature is that family violence was perceived and discussed largely in terms of working-class, and especially lower-class behaviour. Domestic violence in the upper strata was often assumed not to exist, or at least to take less damaging non-physical forms. More frequently it was viewed as an aberration best not discussed. Conjugal violence especially was seen as an attribute of what contemporaries often described as the 'sinking' or more significantly the 'destructive' classes at the base of the social pyramid. Cobbe's belief that wife beating was 'ten-fold as numerous and twenty times as cruel among the lower class' was sustained by many commentators like the lawyer, Arthur Cleveland, in the 1890s and the court missionary, Thomas Holmes, in the 1900s (*Life*, 1894, I, p.218). It was also perpetuated by members of the respectable working class, particularly temperance supporters, who sometimes depicted wife beaters as class enemies. Many, like the journeyman-engineer, Thomas Wright, drew a careful distinction between the steady respectable working man and the 'roughs' defined as having a 'general disposition to noisiness, drinking, fighting and wife-beating' (Wright, 1970, p. 373). The Irish in particular were thought to be prone to conjugal violence. While most observers shared this view a few noted that though rarer and more controlled it was not monopolized by the poor. Cobbe noted that 'the gentleman or tradesman somehow manages to bear in mind the disgrace he will incur if his outbreak is betrayed by his wife's black eye' and limit his cuffs (Cobbe, 1878, p.58). Similarly a London magistrate observed, 'In suburban areas we do not hurt each other with our fists. It can be done more effectively with a look or gesture ...' (Cairns, 1922, p.36).

While wife beating was seen mainly as a lower-class trait, contemporaries were more divided on the social distribution of child battering. Many 'child life' studies, such as Robert Sherrard's *Child Slaves of Britain* or George Sims's *The Black Stain* produced in the 1900s, upheld the view popularized by *The Bitter Cry of Outcast London* that slum children were from infancy 'subject to the most cruel treatment' (Mearns, 1970, p.67; Sherrard, 1905; Sims, 1889). Early NSPCC supporters such as Hesba Stretton also contributed to the impression that cruelty was concentrated among the poor. The NSPCC, however, repeatedly argued that 'cruelty is wholly independent of surroundings and wages', and made valiant efforts to convert the public to this view (Waugh, 1894, p.7). Waugh insisted that a correlation between violence and poverty was 'not justified by the facts'. Any apparent link simply reflected higher visibility and greater willingness to report in slum areas, whereas among the better off in detached suburban housing 'the face discoloured by a dog-whip would be covered with face powder' and suspicious servants, who were rarely believed anyway, dismissed. He found the average weekly wage of parents dealt with by the society was 27s. compared with the working-class average of £1 and that the most refined torture was inflicted by the better off (Waugh, 1910, pp.4ff.). Despite special publicity for middle-class cases—the most famous was that of a doctor and his wife prosecuted in 1887 for thrashing and maltreating their 3-year-old daughter for mis-spelling the word 'fox'—and repeated praise of lower-class parents, the society continued to be attacked as a 'slanderer of the poor'. Some social investigators upheld the society's stand. In London Charles Booth found working-class children were more likely to suffer from spoiling than harshness, and were on the whole subject to 'kindness and affection' (Fried and Elman, 1971, p.249). Nurse Loane's experience in the urban and rural south led her to a similar conclusion. In the North, however, Roberts's study of Edwardian Salford paints a different picture, with savage beatings particularly prominent among those who had experienced military discipline.

The NSPCC was almost alone in emphasizing that violence was a rural as well as an urban problem and in attempting to quantify the level of violence. Its reports do not distinguish the victims of parental violence from other cases, but as early as 1887 Waugh noted 'that the average number in cruelly used families was $3^1/_2$ and the average age of victims ... under 5 years', a feature he re-emphasized in 1894 (Waugh, 1887, p.12; 1894, p.6). From 1899 more detailed statistics were published, showing children under 2 on average formed 14·5% of all cases, with equal proportions of older boys and girls.

Male offenders slightly outnumbered females. Few efforts were made to establish the incidence of conjugal violence, though many commentators remained convinced that court statistics were an unreliable guide. In the 1900s Holmes felt that if all magistrates attended to every wife-beating case 'they would not get through half of them'. Yet wives put up 'with a lot before they complain' and many subsequently lied 'unblushingly' to save their husbands (Holmes, 1900, pp.73–75). Another observer also felt 'wife-beating was still a flagrantly common offence' (Hecker, 1911, p.127). The Gorrell Divorce Commission, too, heard evidence, particularly from women's organizations, of the sufferings wives endured for the children's sake and to avoid publicity.

Explanations of family violence were also often unsystematic. Many could only conceive such behaviour, especially child abuse, in terms of the unaccountable action of 'brutes' or 'madmen'. Apart from vague psychological accounts, a number of alternative social explanations were developed, particularly for conjugal violence which often appeared less abnormal than child abuse. These may be broadly classified as moralistic, environmental, and cultural. Most studies were highly moralistic in character, associating family violence with an irregular family structure, and especially the dissolute habits and ignorance of the poor. Many observers, such as Charles Booth, continued to note that though 'wife beating' was high among unmarried couples, women often saw such relationships as a safeguard, since 'rough labourers behave best ... if not married to the women with whom they live' (Fried and Elman, 1971, p.248). Investigators like W. Clarke-Hall continued to trace a link between child abuse and second marriages, while others such as Sherrard and Cairns re-asserted the myth of the wicked step-mother and the peculiar vulnerability of the unwanted or illegitimate child.

The most common explanation of all forms of domestic violence as earlier, however, was the heavy drinking of the working classes. Observers like Sims in the 1880s and Holmes in the 1900s re-emphasized the violence of drunken husbands, often precipitated by their wives' domestic mismanagement, while the prison chaplain, J. W. Horsley (1898), ascribed half the cases of both wife and child battering to drink. In its evidence to the Gorell Commission the NSPCC similarly attributed a high proportion of conjugal and parental violence to drunkenness as did the Scottish Society. The Liverpool Society reported this was responsible for nine-tenths of child cruelty, a view echoed by Waugh's successor Robert Parr in 1910 (Parr, 1910, p.3). The emphasis on drink partly reflected the influence of temperance workers in exposing the problem, and partly more general public concern from the 1870s with high alcohol consumption and consequent street violence. It was also reflected in the establishment of inebriate reformatories in the 1890s for drunken parents convicted of child abuse, and in the 1902 Licensing Act whereby habitual drunkenness became a ground for separation for battered wives.

Excessive drinking and the innate callousness of the poor were often seen as a sufficient explanation of family violence. Many, however, viewed drunkenness and the associated brutality partly as a symptom of the debilitation produced by slum conditions and, more commonly, as a manifestation of a more general culture of violence among the poor. A few perceptive observers felt drink itself was a reaction to squalid, overcrowded housing and the emotionally impoverished life of the poor. Men struggling for low wages, experiencing little respect or power in their working lives, found a release in the conviviality of pubs and savage mastery at home. Parents in cramped housing with little escape from crying children resorted to rigid, often excessive discipline. Poverty underlay the savage beatings so frequently reported by juvenile mendicants and street sellers, while high mortality rates conditioned many to a low evaluation of human life. As Sims observed in 1889, the 'waste of human life brought about by the conditions in which the poor are allowed to live breeds in them a contempt for the sufferings of others' (Sims, 1889, p.70). Parr, like Waugh, similarly felt that blunted sensibilities and drunkenness sprang from the hopelessness of life in 'sunless streets and mean habitations' (Parr, 1919, p.10).

But environmentalism often merged imperceptibly with cultural explanations, as successive investigators substantiated the impression that conjugal violence especially was such a common feature of slum life as to rouse little attention. Social investigators and slum missionaries, like the Reverend D. Rice Jones, frequently reported that the nights, especially at weekends when the pubs shut, were invariably punctuated by 'women's voices crying "murder!" and the voices of little children screaming with terror while their parents are engaged in a desperate fight ...' (Jones, 1884, p.27). Such experiences were so common that many wives became inured to it and sons simply followed their fathers. Wright in the 1860s felt that among the 'roughs' even 'the beaten woman' saw such behaviour as a 'commonplace' in which no person of a well-regulated mind would interfere (Wright, 1970, p. 134). Like many others in the 1900s Holmes found 'wife-beating so common among a certain class that I have found plenty of wives who take it as a matter of course' (Holmes, 1900, p. 85). Lady Bell's study of Middlesborough steelworkers also showed the pressure on wives, especially in areas of low female employment, to tolerate the breadwinner's behaviour. She found 'wife-beating is not so entirely a thing of the past as some of us would like to think' and many women counted themselves lucky to have non-violent husbands (Bell, 1907, pp. 238–239).

If wives were accustomed and neighbours indifferent, there is evidence that some husbands still saw wife beating as their right. In the 1880s, for instance, Bolton husbands formed a 'wife-Beating Club' to aid members fined for assaulting their wives, and similar groups were reported in Scotland (*The Times*, 18 December 1884; *Scotsman*, 29 October 1874). One Lancashire solicitor even attempted to defend a husband on the grounds that 'in Blackburn and Wigan, it is the usual thing for a husband when he comes home at night to give his wife a kicking and beating' (Corin, 1910, p.128). Some observers felt wife beating was so common as to form part of child socialization. Horrified summer-camp organizers in Birmingham in the 1890s even found that girls playing 'home' included a violent 'father' who gave the 'mother' an unmistakable black eye! (Samuelson, 1911, p.7) Indeed Walter Besant comforted himself that if his typical East London girl's husband drank and beat her 'it would be no new thing' since she had often witnessed her father's or brother's violence (Besant, 1903, p.151).

Similarly parental violence was often seen as learned behaviour and family violence depicted as part of a general culture in which masculinity was equated with aggression and daily life punctuated by street brawls and pub fights. As contemporaries often emphasized, such battles were not confined to men. Female pugilists were regularly reported and the participants described as loud-mouthed viragos lacking domestic skills who often provoked their husbands' drunken assaults with their nagging tongues. Conjugal violence appeared a two-way process, one element in the pent-up savagery of the slums which, as graphically portrayed in Morrison's *Child of the Jago* (1896), extended from neighbourhood battles and juvenile gang fights to matrimonial violence and regular child beating. To many this became the authentic picture of domestic violence, and fears of the barbarity at the heart of the Empire did much to induce state action.

CONCLUSION

Though historical research into changing family relationships is only in its early stages, this preliminary survey has highlighted a number of hitherto neglected aspects. In the first place it shows that domestic violence is not a new phenomenon which has only recently excited public attention as is sometimes suggested in contemporary discussions of wife and baby battering. Indeed though the evidence is fragmentary and impressionistic it appears that the scale of family violence, like public violence, has declined gradually since the early nineteenth century. Moreover recent concern is only the latest of a series of 'rediscoveries' of a problem which has roused sporadic public anxiety since the mid-nineteenth century.

Historically, pressure to mitigate family violence developed largely as an offshoot of broader campaigns to improve the status of women and children, themselves reflections of fundamental socio-economic changes, and fluctuated both with the relative strength of these movements and the level of public concern about public violence. The recognition both of conjugal and parental violence was largely the product of a growing consciousness of other forms of inequality and exploitation, partly stimulated in the case of the former by active campaigning by a few victims such as Caroline Norton. Though the type of provision was moulded by such pressure, legislative intervention was only achieved when, as in the late nineteenth century, the social costs of wasted human resources were recognized, and family violence threatened to spill over into public violence. Child welfare workers like the

Reverend Horsley, echoing the earlier fears of Serjeant Pũlling, felt gutter children and 'hooligans' were simply reproducing on the streets behaviour learnt at home. This close link between family violence and other forms of social disruption discerned by Victorian and Edwardian commentators has had a long-lasting effect on interpretations of the problem.

Perhaps the most crucial aspect to emerge from a historical study is the continuity of popular stereotypes of the violent parent or husband. Despite the efforts of agencies like the NSPCC, many observers propagated an image of family violence as a lower-class phenomenon, the culturally-transmitted product of a cramped environment which limited opportunities for the distillation of aggression, and of a social life centred on pub and street which legitimized physical force. To some social reformers, however, like Cobbe and Waugh, the problem was rooted not only in lower-class customs but in wider social traditions which had long sanctioned the low status of women and children and afforded them few rights. How far and why different interpretations were perpetuated after 1914, however, remains a question for future research.

NOTES

1 The few exceptions include a brief account of protection for wives by McGregor *et al.* (1970), and for children by Housden (1955). Radbill (1975) provides a more sweeping study of child abuse.

2 A further problem is the lack of continuous national returns of summary offences. For the difficulties of using judicial and other returns see V. A. C. Gatrell and T. B. Hadden in Wrigley (1972).

3 *R.* v. *Jackson* (1891), I QB 671.

4 For example, F. W. Newman, 1865, pp.159ff.

5 The society amalgamated with the Associated Institute for Improving and Enforcing the Laws for the Protection of Women to form the Associated Societies for the Protection of Women in 1892. The new body increasingly focused on cases of desertion, seduction, and illegitimacy, the concerns of the Associated Institute. After considerable wrangling with the NSPCC, it agreed to refer cases of child abuse to the latter and concentrate on adult women.

6 The rise in assault charges partly reflected changes in the licensing laws in 1869 and 1872, which one historian describes as producing a 'frightening burst of debauchery' (Checkland, 1964, p.233).

7 Among the methods Mrs Sherwood commended was taking her fictitious family to see a boy hanging on a gibbet, and it was common practice in the early nineteenth century for children to be safeguarded from evil by being whipped on execution days.

8 For example Bamford, 1967; *Fraser's Magazine*, 1854.

9 For example *Family Herald, Queen, English woman's Domestic Magazine.*

10 Supplemental Conversazione (1970). Some writers have seen this as one example of the massive Victorian literature of flagellation; in itself it is suggested a sign of violence in the home. For example Marcus, 1966.

11 For example by 1922 the possible sexual implications of corporal punishment were being noticed in manuals such as Frankenburg, 1946.

12 See Marser, (n.d.).

13 For Waugh's early life see Waugh, 1913.

14 For example McCleary, 1933, 1935; Pinchbeck and Hewitt, 1973.

15 For the early history of the societies see Agnew, n.d.; Housden, 1955; Morton (n.d.), *Early Days.*

16 For example Waugh, 1888, 1890a, 1890b; the society's pamphlets included *Charred, With Many Stripes, The Ways of Child Torturers Illustrated,* and the reminiscences of an Inspector, *The Cruelty Man* (1912). By 1909, 15 000 ladies were involved in circulating literature. On the society's 'educational' role see especially the *Reports* for 1895, 1896, and 1902.

LIST OF STATUTES

An Act for Consolidating and Amending the Statutes in England relative to Offences Against the Person, 9 Geo.IV, c.31, 1828.
The Custody of Infants Act, 2 and 3 Vic., c.54, 1839.
An Act for the better Prevention and Punishment of aggravated Assaults upon Women and Children, 16 and 17 Vic., c.30, 1853.
Matrimonial Causes Act, 20 and 21 Vic., c.85, 1857.
Offences against the Person Act, 24 and 25 Vic., c.100, 1861.
Infant Life Protection Act, 35 and 36 Vic., c.38, 1872.
Matrimonial Causes Act, 41 Vic., c.19, 1878.
The Prevention of Cruelty to and Protection of Children Act, 52 and 53 Vic., c.44., 1889.
The Prevention of Cruelty to Children (Amendment) Act, 57 and 58 Vic. c.27, 1894.
The Prevention of Cruelty to Children Act, 57 and 58 Vic., c.41, 1894.
The Summary Jurisdiction (Marred Women) Act, 58 and 59 Vic., c.39, 1895.
The Children Act, 8 Edw. VII, c.15, 1908.

REFERENCES

Official publications and reports

Note. In this section PP indicates the Sessional Papers of Parliament, with the date of the Session and the volume number. They are listed in date order.

Select Committee on Criminal and Destitute Children, PP 1852 (515) VII.
Return of the Number of Charges Preferred Against Male Persons for

Assaults on Women and Children ... within the Metropolis, PP 1854 (523) LIII.
A Return of the Number of Persons who have been Sentenced to Imprisonment by the City or Metropolitan Magistrates for Aggravated Assaults on their Wives or Other Women, PP 1860 (353) LVII.
Select Committee on the Protection of Infant Life, PP 1871 (372) VII.
Reports to the Secretary of State for the Home Department on the State of the Law Relating to Brutal Assaults, PP 1875 (c.1138) LXI.
Royal Commission on Divorce and Matrimonial Causes 1912–1913 (Cd 6478–82), XVIII–XX.

Books and articles

Agnew, T. F. A. (n.d.) *Work in Early Days for the Prevention of Cruelty to Children.* NSPCC.
Anderson, M. (1971) *Family Structure in Nineteenth Century Lancashire*, Cambridge University Press.
Ariès, P. (1973) *Centuries of Childhood*, Penguin Books.
Bamford, T. W. (1967) *The Rise of the Public Schools*, Nelson.
Bell, Lady (1907) *At the Works*, Arnold.
Besant, W. (1903) *East London* (1903 Edition), Chatto & Windus.
Blackstone, W. (1770) *Commentaries on the Laws of England*, 4 vols, Clarendon Press.
Blackwood's Magazine (1850) 'Public nurseries', **42**, 397–399.
Blackwood's Magazine (1869) 'Mr Mill on the subjection of women' **106**, 309–321.
Brewster, M. M. (1854) *Sunbeams in the Cottage*, Constable.
Butler, Samuel (1903) *The Way of All Flesh*, Grant Richards.
Cairns, J. A. R. (1922) *The Loom of the Law* (1922 edition), Hutchinson.
Carpenter, L. (1820) *Principles of Education, Intellectual, Moral and Physical*, Longman.
Checkland, S. G. (1964) *The Rise of Industrial Society in England 1815–85*, Longman.
Children's Guardian (1887–1914).
Clarke-Hall, W. (1926) *Children's Courts*, Allen & Unwin.
Cleveland, A. R. (1896) *Woman under the English Law from the Landing of the Saxons to the Present Time.* Hurst & Blackett.
Cobbe, F. P. (1878) 'Wife torture in England', *Contemporary Review*, **32**, 55–87.
Cobbe, F. P. (1894) *The Life of F. P. Cobbe, By Herself.* R. Bentley, 3rd ed.
Cooper, W. (1873) *Flagellation and the Flagellants, A History of the Rod in All Ages and Countries*, Hotten.
Corin, J. (1910) *Mating, Marriage and the Status of Women*, Walter Scott.
Dewes, A. (1868) 'The injustice of the English Law as it bears on the relationship of husband and wife', *Contemporary Review*, **9**, 114–125.
Dickens, Charles (1953) *David Copperfield* (1849–1850), Dent.
Disraeli, B. (1954) *Sybil* (1845), Penguin Books.
Duncombe, J. (1848) *Sinks of London Laid Open.*
Ellis, Mrs (1845) *The Daughters of England.*
Ellis, Mrs (1850) *The Women of England, Their Social Duties and Domestic Habits*, Fisher, 9th ed.
English woman's Domestic Magazine (1860–70).
English women's Review (previously *Journal*) (1858–1896).
Frankenburg, C. A. (1946) *Common Sense in the Nursery* (1946 edition) Penguin Books.
Fraser's Magazine (1848) 'The manufacturing poor', **37**,1–16.
Fraser's Magazine (1854) 'Our public schools', **150**, 401–413.
Fried, A. and Elman, R. E. (1971) *Charles Booth's London*, Penguin Books.
Gathorne-Hardy, J. (1972) *The Rise and Fall of the British Nanny*, Cape.

Godwin, G. (1854) *London Shadows, A Glance at the Homes of the Thousands*, Routledge.
Gorst, J. (1907) *The Children of the Nation*, Methuen.
Guthrie, T. (1851) *First Plea for Ragged Schools.*
Hare, A. J. C. (1896–1900) *The Story of my Life*, 6 vols, George Allen.
Hecker, E. A. (1911) *A Short History of Women's Rights*, G. P. Putnam.
Hoare, L. (1819) *Hints for the Improvement of Early Education and Nursery Discipline.*
Holmes, T. (1900) *Pictures and Problems from the London Police Courts*, Arnold.
Horsley, J. W. (1898), *Prisons and Prisoners*, C. A. Pearson.
Horsley, J. W. (1913) *How Criminals are Made*, Unwin.
Housden, L. G. H. (1955) *The Prevention of Cruelty to Children*, Cape.
Jones, D. R. (1884) *In the Slums: Pages from the Notebooks of a London Diocesan Missionary*, J. Nisbet.
Langer, W. M. (1974) 'Infanticide: a historical survey', *History of Childhood Quarterly*, **1**, 353–365.
Laslett, P. (1972) *Family and Household in Past Time*, Cambridge University Press.
Laslett, P. (1973) 'L'Attitude a l'egard de l'enfant dans l'Angleterre du XIX siècle', *Annales de demographie historicale*, 313–318.
Loane, M. E. (1908) *From Their Point of View*, Arnold.
McCleary, C. F. (1933) *The Early History of the Infant Welfare Movement*, H. K. Lewis.
McCleary, C. F. (1935) *The Maternity and Child Welfare Movements*, P. S. King & Sons.
McGregor, O. R., Blom-Cooper, L. and Gibson, C. (1970) *Separated Spouses*, Duckworth.
Macmillan's Magazine (1883) 'Corporal punishment in schools', **48**, 481–484.
Marcus, S. (1966) *Underneath the Victorians*, Weidenfeld & Nicolson.
Marser, D. (n.d.) 'Children's states in 1911', Ruskin History Workshop.
Mause, L. de (1974) *The History of Childhood*, New York Psychology Press.
Mayhew, H. (1861) *London Labour and the London Poor*, 4 vols, Griffin Bohn & Co.
Mearns, A. (1970) *The Bitter Cry of Outcast London* (1883), repr. Leicester University Press.
Mill, J. S. (1970) *The Subjection of Women* (1869), repr. MIT Press (ed. W. R. Carr).
Morning Chronicle, (1851).
Morrison, A. (1946) *A Child of the Jago* (1896), Penguin Books.
Morton, A. (n.d.) *The Directorate of Sir Robert Parr*, NSPCC.
Morton, A. (n.d.) *Early Days*, NSPCC.
NAPSS (National Association for the Promotion of Social Science) (1857–1886) *Transactions.*
Newman, F. W. (1865), Corporal punishments and penal reformation; *Fraser's Magazine*, **71**, 154–166.
North British Review (1856) 'Outrages on women', **25**, 233–256.
Norton, C. (1854) *English Laws for Women in the Nineteenth Century.*
Norton, C. (1855) *A Letter to the Queen on Lord Chancellor Cranworth's Divorce Bill*, Longman, Brown, & Green.
NSPCC (National Society for the Prevention of Cruelty to Children), Annual Reports (various titles), 1889–1890 to 1913–1914.
Nut, E. R. and Gosling, R. (1732) *A Treatise of Feme Coverts.*
Parr, R. (1910) *The Cruelty of the Drunken and How Children Suffer*, NSPCC.
Parry, E. A (1916) *The Law and the Woman*, C. A. Pearson.
Perkin, H. (1969) *The Origins of Modern English Society 1780–1880*, Routledge & Kegan Paul.
Pinchbeck, I. and Hewitt, M. (1973) *Children in English Society*, voll II, Routledge & Kegan Paul.
Radbill, S. (1975) 'A history of child abuse and infanticide'. In R. E. Helfer and C. H. Kempe, *The Battered Child*, 2nd ed., University of Chicago Press.
Roberts, R. (1973) *The Classic Slum*, Penguin Books.
Rose, J. K. (1969) *Superior Person: a portrait of Curzon and His Work in Late Victorian England*, Weidenfeld & Nicolson.

Ryan, W. B. (1862) *Infanticide, Its Law, Practice, Prevention and History*, J. Churchill.

Samuelson, J. (1911) *The Children of Our Slums*, Simpkin Marshall.

Sandford, Mrs (1837) *Woman in Her Social and Domestic Condition*, 5th ed., Longman, Rees, Orme, Brown, Green & Longman.

Sherrard, R. H. (1905) *Child Slaves of Britain*, Hurst & Blackett.

Sherwood, Mrs (1818–1847) *The History of the Fairchild Family*, J. Hatchard.

Shore, L. (1872) *The Political Disabilities of Women*, pamphlet printed by A. Alexander.

Shorter, E. (1976) *The Making of the Modern Family*, Basic Books.

Sims, G. (1889) *How the Poor Live and Horrible London*, Chatto & Windus.

Sims, G. R. (1907) *The Black Stain*, Jarrold & Son.

Sims, G. R. (1908) *The Devil in London*, Stanley Paul.

Smith, B. L. (1854) *A Brief Summary in Plain Language of the Laws Concerning Women*, Chapman.

Society for the Protection of Women and Children (1864) *Comparative Justice*.

Tabor, M. C. (1888) 'The rights of children', *Contemporary Review*, **54**, 408–417.

Thompson, E. P. (1972) ' "Rough music": Le Charivari anglais', *Annales economies sociétés civilisation*, **27**, 285–312.

Waugh, B. (1887) *Tortured Children: A Third Year's Experience in their Defence*, NSPCC.

Waugh, B. (1888) 'Street children', *Contemporary Review*, **53**, 825–835.

Waugh, B. (1890a) 'Baby farming', *Contemporary Review*, **57**, 700–714.

Waugh, B. (1890b) 'Child life insurance', *Contemporary Review*, **58**, 40–63.

Waugh, B. (1894) *Some Conditions of Child Life in England*, K. P. Trench.

Waugh, B. (1910) *Our New Protectorate for Children*, NSPCC.

Waugh, B., and Manning, H. (1886) 'The child of the English savage', *Contemporary Review*, **49**, 687–700.

Waugh, R. (1913) *The Life of Benjamin Waugh*, T. F. Unwin.

Wharton, J. J. S. (1853) *An Exposition of the Laws Relating to the Women of England*, Longman.

Wollstonecraft, M. (1929) *The Rights of Woman* (1792), Dent.

Wright, T. (1969) *Our New Masters* (1873), repr. A. M. Kelly, New York.

Wright, T. (1970) *The Great Unwashed by a Journeyman Engineer* (1868), repr. Cass.

Wrigley, E. A. (1972) *Nineteenth Century Society*, Cambridge University Press.

7

VIOLENCE IN THE AMERICAN FAMILY

Richard J. Gelles

The examination of violence in the American family is an endeavour marked by contrast and paradox. The first major paradox is the fact that the study of intra-family violence was so long in coming. American social scientists have had a tradition of studying violent behaviour and its causes. The major schools of sociology in the United States concentrated on studies of suicide, homicide, and juvenile crime, including gang violence. Social scientists have focused considerable attention on violence on television and its effect on children and adults. Despite this intensive examination of violence in the United States, there was, until 1970, a perceptual blackout on either seeing or studying violence in families. In 1970, a call for papers for the annual meeting of the National Council on Family Relations, which had as a theme 'Violence in the Family', yielded few papers.

The selective inattention to the topic of family violence tended to produce a thesis that violence between family members was either rare, dysfunctional, or a pathology traceable to mental illness or psychopathy. What makes this thesis paradoxical, and what makes the perceptual blackout of violence between family members difficult to understand, is that research carried out in the 1970s (Straus, Gelles and Steinmetz, 1977) indicates that violence between family members is more common in the United States than violence between any other individuals except during war or riots.

This chapter on violence in families in the United States could be subtitled 'A study of paradox and contrasts', because our research on violent families has unveiled a continued series of paradoxes and contrasts between the image of the family and the actual behaviour which goes on behind the closed doors of American households. We have found norms and attitudes in existence which both condemn and approve of using violence on one's intimates. We have discovered that violence between family members, rather than being a minority pattern of behaviour, or a behaviour that is rare and dysfunctional, is a patterned and normal aspect of interaction between family members. Our research has uncovered structural arrangements which enhance and encourage the striking and beating of one family member by another. Lastly, our work on wife abuse and child abuse reveals that the legal system in the United States not only cannot effectively intervene and protect family members, it (the legal system) actually results in situations where the marriage licence becomes a hitting licence!

THE STUDY OF FAMILY VIOLENCE

It was not until the early 1960s that the issue of family violence was brought into focus for the American people. Although pediatric radiologists had developed procedures and protocols for uncovering incidents of child abuse through X-ray diagnosis (Caffey, 1946), it was not until Henry Kempe and his colleagues published their paper on the 'battered child syndrome' in 1962 that the issue of child abuse gained national attention. As a result of Kempe's efforts, a national campaign was mounted, and by the end of 1969 all 50 states had enacted legislation which mandated the official reporting of cases of child abuse. In 1974, the United States Congress enacted legislation which created the National Center on Child Abuse and Neglect whose mission was to study child abuse and create programmes which could test methods of preventing and treating abuse and neglect. Americans were late in identifying wife abuse as a social problem. Erin Pizzey's book, *Scream Quietly or the Neighbours will Hear*, has not been distributed in the United States (up through March of 1977). Interest in wife abuse was aroused in the mid-1970s as a result of the news about Great Britain's concern with battered wives and as a consequence of work by the National Organization of Women (NOW) which made wife abuse a priority issue. However, through the end of 1976 only a handful of scholarly articles had been published on wife abuse and very little precise information on this topic is available.

Why the interest in family violence?

The question arises, if violence between family members has been a part of American family life since the time of the Pilgrims, and if it is an extensive and common phenomenon, why does it emerge as an issue in the second half of the twentieth century? We have identified forces which created the perceptual blackout on family violence and movements which led to attention being given to this topic. The semi-sacred nature of the American family as a social institution tended to create a smokescreen which obscured violence from the attention of the public and social scientists. The American family has traditionally been viewed as the locus of love, peace, and tranquillity. Family life has been idealized in books, movies, and television as the best way to live. The ideology of the tranquil family was enhanced by a paradigm in social science which viewed social systems through a consensus-equilibrium model. Social scientists who employed this paradigm focused on the procreative and regulatory functions of the family. Using this perspective, one sees the family serving to regulate sex and help place members into appropriate status locations. Violence and conflict were conceptualized as dysfunctional for the family and the social system. Given that the family was such an enduring institution, little thought was given to the possibility that violence could be a normal feature of family interaction.

Numerous streams of thought and action converged in the United States in the late 1960s and early 1970s which helped to uncover the hidden side of family life. First, the 1960s in the United States was a decade of violence. Race riots, political assassination, rising rates of interpersonal violence, and a war which produced thousands of casualties drew attention to the topic of violence. The National Commission on the Causes and Prevention of Violence was formed as a response to the assassinations of Martin Luthur King and Robert Kennedy. The commission produced the first comprehensive national study of attitudes and experiences with violent behaviour. The questions which dealt with family violence opened the eyes of many people who had previously thought family violence was uncommon and deviant. The women's movement which aimed at the liberation and equality of women brought women of all ages and backgrounds together for 'consciousness-raising sessions'. A latent consequence of these sessions was the realization that many women had common experiences they previously thought were their own problems—being victims of conjugal violence. Women slowly began to realize that being beaten and battered by their husbands might not be *their own* fault. In addition to the women's rights movement of the 1960s, child advocacy became a growing social movement. The social consciousness of the decade focused on the maltreatment and abuse of children. Attention to the issue of children's rights was usually attracted by presenting pictures of children who had been grievously injured and maimed by their own parents or caretakers. Finally, while the social movements gathered steam, the paradigm of American social science began to change with a 'conflict model' of human behaviour supplementing the 'consensus-equilibrium' school of thought. A conflict model of family relations (Sprey, 1969) was much more suited for the study of family violence than the previous model which focused on mate selection and incest taboos.

THE EXTENT OF VIOLENCE IN AMERICAN FAMILIES

The fact that violent family members are among the 'missing persons' of official statistics on crime and in research on family interaction means that few reliable and valid data are available on which to base estimates of the incidence of family violence. However, by piecing together data from official statistics on child abuse, homicide, and assault; studies of attitudes on violence; and our own pilot studies of family violence, we have been able to construct a statistical portrait of the violent family.

Physical punishment

Perhaps the most common form of family violence is the use of physical force to punish children. Various studies indicate that between 84% and 97% of American parents use physical punishment on their children at some point in raising them (Blumberg, 1965; Bronfenbrenner, 1958; Erlanger, 1974; Stark and McEvoy, 1970).

Child abuse

Incidence data on the extreme forms of parental violence towards children are more difficult to locate. Child abuse is as much a political term, designed to draw attention to a social problem, as it is a measurable scientific term. Efforts to measure the extent of child abuse by totalling the number of reported cases produces information on only the tip of the child-abuse iceberg due to varying definitions of abuse, selective reporting, and varying agency procedures for identifying confirmed cases of child abuse. An example of this variance is David Gil's research findings on the incidence of abuse. Gil identified 6000 cases of confirmed reported child abuse for 1965 (Gil, 1971). For the same period, he asked a nationally representative sample of adults if they knew of a child who had been physically injured by his or her caretakers in the previous year. The extrapolation from answers to this question produced a figure of between 2·5 and 4·07 million American adults who knew of a child who was injured by his or her caretakers (Gil, 1971). Richard Light (1974) modified Gil's extrapolations by considering possible overlap of knowledge, and produced an estimate of 500 000 children abused each year. Other estimates run to as high as 1 million children abused by their parents each year in the United States (*New York Sunday Times*, 30 November 1975).

Homicide

The United States is noted for its high rate of homicide. Statistics indicate that the most common relationship between murderer and victim is a family relationship. In Atlanta, 31% of the 255 homicides in 1972 were the result of domestic quarrels *Boston Globe*, 1973, p.12). The situation in Atlanta is typical of the nation at large where between 20% and 40% of all murders are committed by family members on family members (Curtis, 1974).

Assault

Data on assault are more difficult to interpret because many family members fail to press charges against one another. Yet data on police activities in the United States show that more police calls involve family quarrels than all other criminal offences (rape, homicide, burglary) combined (Parnas, 1967, p.914). In fact, more police officers are killed answering family disturbance calls than die answering any other single type of call (Parnas, 1967). In St Louis, aggravated assault between husbands and wives made up 11% of all aggravated assaults (Pittman and Handy, 1964). In Detroit, family assaults constitute 52% of assault reports (Boudouris, 1971).

Applicants for divorce

Studies of couples in the process of obtaining a divorce also bear witness to the violent American family. Levinger (1966) interviewed couples on their reasons for divorce and found 32% of the middle-class and 40% of the working-class couples discussing 'physical abuse' as a major complaint. O'Brien (1971) reported that 17% of the couples he interviewed spontaneously mentioned violent behaviour in their marriage.

Research on family violence

In 1970 a series of investigations began on the specific issue of violence in the family. These initial pilot studies provided the first specific evidence about the extent of family violence. I conducted in-depth interviews with 80 couples and found that 54% of the subjects mentioned incidents of conjugal violence at one point in their marriages (Gelles, 1974). Murray Straus and Suzanne Steinmetz have studied violence by asking college students to report on their experiences during the last year they lived at home (Straus, 1974a, 1974b; Steinmetz, 1974). The results of these studies show that during one year 62% of the college students used physical force on a brother or a sister. Sixteen per cent of the students' parents had used physical violence on one another. Since these statistics are for only one year, Straus and Steinmetz conclude that they *underestimate* the true level of violence in the students' families.

A recent replication of Straus and Steinmetz's work found that nearly 8% of college freshmen report being physically injured by their parents during the last year they lived at home (Mulligan, 1977).

A national study of family violence

Since the indirect evidence indicated an extensive pattern of violence in American families, we believed that there was a need to document the exact extent of violence in the American household. In 1976 we began a study of family violence based on interviews with a representative sample of 2146 American families. The results will be published in the forthcoming book, *Violence in the American Family*, by Murray A. Straus, Richard J. Gelles, and Suzanne K. Steinmetz; but the preliminary results indicate that violence between family members is a widespread phenomenon in the American household.

NORMS AND ATTITUDES

The data which are available on attitudes towards violence in the home and the information we have accumulated in our interviews with families reveal a striking pattern of opinions concerning family violence. A cross-sectional survey of the population of the United States, conducted in 1968 for the National Commission on the Causes and Prevention of Violence (Stark and McEvoy, 1970), found that one in four men and one in six women would approve of slapping a wife under certain conditions. Reversing the roles, 26% of the men and 19% of the women would approve of a wife slapping her husband. Research on parent-to-child violence indicates that approval for physically punishing a child is widespread (Stark and McEvoy, 1970). Nevertheless, the data on norms approving violence are not necessarily directly related to the actual behaviour in question. Many individuals might say they approve of an act and never engage in it, while many others might disapprove of a behaviour but engage in it all the time.

Our investigation of attitudes towards family violence has produced numerous contrasts and paradoxes. When we first began to study family violence we searched through the content of various mass media to see whether family violence was portrayed in television, movies, novels, or even comic strips. Our conclusion was that violence was *never* portrayed in *normal, average families* by the mass media. When a family member struck another on television, in a book, or even in the comics, the offender was either a criminal, deviant, or someone who was not an American (the most family violence in a comic strip in the United States occurs in 'Andy Capp' which is a story of an unemployed Englishman and his wife). This was startling to us since the American mass media are so often accused of being too violent. We assumed that violent media would at least reflect norms and behaviours in the society, but in the case of family violence, we were wrong (Steinmetz and Straus, 1974).

A second contrast is revealed in a story often cited by Murray Straus (1973, 1974a). Straus tells of a couple in a counselling session where the husband admits to hitting his wife on several occasions. The husband goes on to say that he thinks what he did was wrong and that he regrets hitting his wife. When asked why he hit his wife, the man stated that he could not control himself. At this point the counsellor asked, 'Why don't you stab her?' That the husband did not stab his wife or even consider it, illustrates that he was in fact under control but that he was operating under a set of implicit norms which allowed him to hit his wife and not stab her. Thus, the conflicting norms which allow family violence but which limit certain excesses as deviant can be found in operation in the same man at the same time.

There are other examples of how social norms and attitudes produce a 'licence' to hit family members. Field and Field (1973) found that police in Washington, DC, use a 'stitch rule' to decide when they should arrest an abusing husband. If the wife requires a specific number of sutures to close a wound, that is grounds for taking her complaint seriously. Calvert (1974) points to the fact that the California Penal Code establishes different grounds for assault complaints—wives must be more seriously injured by their husbands to file a charge of assault than individuals struck by non-family members. Truninger (1971) argues that the court system in the United States is mired in a mythology about conjugal violence and is often ineffective in dealing with acts of violence towards women. This ineffectiveness often becomes grounds for men to hit their wives in that they perceive the court's lack of concern with spousal violence as being tacit approval.

Our interviews with families on the subject of family violence uncovered another dimension of the norms and attitudes towards family violence. We found that victims and offenders in acts of intra-family violence were able to justify even serious and often dangerous physical attacks. Husbands and wives would frequently agree that the victim of a spousal attack 'got what s/he deserved' or 'needed' to be struck (Gelles, 1974). Even wives who had ribs broken and jaws fractured would sometimes claim that they deserved to be hit by their husbands. When we spoke with parents about hitting their children, most parents stated that they were doing something that was in the best interests of the child. Children who were hit by their parents 'needed it' or 'deserved it' because their parents believed that they would be better off if discipline was swift and strict.

The contrasts and paradoxes surrounding family violence lead to the conclusion that norms exist in American society which *simultaneously* encourage and approve of the use of physical violence and also condemn the violence in the home. American parents are told that 'sparing the rod will spoil the child' while at the same time child abuse laws are passed which limit the use of the rod. Official response (or lack of response) to complaints of wife abuse or spouse abuse lends support to the claim made by Straus (1973) that the marriage licence in the United States is a hitting licence. Our interviews illustrate how individuals will accept and approve of an act in their home which they would condemn if it happened to them in the streets or a tavern (Gelles, 1974). It is clear that these contradictory norms make it difficult at times to fully grasp exactly what the subjective meanings of violence are when it occurs in the family.

THE ROOTS OF FAMILY VIOLENCE

Despite the documented evidence that family violence is an extensive pattern of interaction in the United States and despite the evidence that it is often approved and considered normative in families, the issue of violence between family members has only recently surfaced in the research of American social scientists. Consequently, much is left to be done in terms of identifying which kinds of families are prone to violence and what factors are causally related to intra-familial violence.

The early work on child abuse, wife abuse, and other forms of family violence has largely served to identify factors which *are not* causal factors. Beyond that, we have been only able to propose micro-level and macro-level variables which seem to increase the potential of violence occurring in our society and in particular families.

What does not cause violence

The early perceptual blackout which prevented scientists and much of the public from realizing that violence occurred in large numbers of American families was partially due to the fact that social scientists and the public alike tended to see violence, child abuse, and wife abuse as being caused by psychological disorders or 'sickness'. Much of the early scientific work on child abuse and wife abuse proposed that abusers were 'sick' or suffering from deep-seated personality disorders (see for example the work of Kempe *et al.*, 1962; Steele and Pollock, 1974; Galdston, 1965; Snell, Rosenwald, and Robey, 1964). Much of this early research was based on case studies with limited sample sizes and the theories which were developed were based on *post hoc* analyses of the cases (Gelles, 1973; Spinetta and Rigler, 1972). When closely scrutinized, the data used to build the psychopathological model of violence tended not to be supportive of the propositions advanced by the researchers. Although one could not totally rule out psychological factors as causes, it did appear that they were not necessary or sufficient factors in bringing about violent acts.

A second set of proposals offered a sociological explanation of violence. This perspective argued that family violence was related to social class—the lower the class, the more likely there would be violence in the family. Although the official statistics bore out this hypothesis, the statistics themselves are subject to error. Lower-class individuals may be more likely to show up in official records of wife or child abuse because they are more likely to do these acts, get caught doing these acts, or both (Gelles, 1975). What ever the reason for the differential distribution of abuse cases, it appears that social class in and of itself is not a sufficient explanation for violence (Straus, 1977).

Another theoretical approach to family violence is to lay the blame on structural stress. However, preliminary evidence from our research (Mulligan, 1977) shows that stress as a single factor is not sufficient to explain the extent and severity of family violence.

Having ruled out *single factor causal* models from the psychological, sociological, and social psychological perspectives, researchers now face what they should have expected all along, that the causes of family violence are multi-dimensional and multi-variate (Gil, 1970). Thus, the search for the roots of family violence in the United States led to identifying factors which are associated with family violence, then towards building a theory of family violence. The theory-building part of the endeavour is still going on (see Gelles and Straus, 1977 for more detail on building an integrated theory of violence); thus this chapter will focus on the factors which have been found or which are considered to be associated with intra-family violence in the United States.

Norms which tolerate and mandate violence

One of the first factors we found associated with family violence is that violence is frequently tolerated, often valued, and sometimes mandated in marriage. Although we argued previously that there are conflicting norms which simultaneously condemn and condone violence in marriage, the resolution of this paradox is that in most instances marriage licences are viewed as hitting licences (Straus, 1973). Violence in child rearing is not only accepted, it is encouraged and mandated. The most controversial aspect of our public presentations in the United States has been our equating physical punishment of children with violence—we claim spankings are violent. Each time we have made this statement in a public forum in the United States or Canada, we have been criticized by members of the audience who steadfastly believe that it is a parent's duty to be strict and to punish his or her child for the child's own good. When we conducted our interviews on family violence (Gelles, 1974) many of the respondents said they were glad their parents had used physical punishment on them and some said they wished they had been hit more often (for their own good).

The norms which allow violence in the family are indicative of the general norms in the United States towards violence. It would appear that violence is an accepted part of our society and is quite often considered to be an appropriate solution to problems or frustrations. More than 50% of American households contain guns—most of them handguns. Seventy per cent of the population agrees that a boy should have a few fistfights when growing up. Almost half the population believes that teachers in schools should have the right to hit a pupil, and more than 60% of Americans are in favour of the use of capital punishment (Stark and McEvoy, 1970; Gelles and Straus, 1975).

While it is true that the actual level of violence in the United States is exaggerated by Americans and Europeans alike, the fact remains that Americans do have a great propensity to approve of using violence instrumentally to solve problems or expressively to show one's feelings.

Structural sources of violence

The research on family violence indicates that it does occur in families of all class levels. Incidents of infanticide, filicide, child abuse, and wife abuse are found in homes of blue-collar workers as well as professionals. While the official statistics tend to over-represent lower-class families because of their social marginality, there is reason to believe that violence is more common in blue-collar and lower-class families. Data gathered using interviews and self-reports indicate that these lower-class families tend to report more violence in them (Gelles, 1974).

The explanation for the association between class or social position and violence is thought to be that structural stress is disproportionately distributed in American society, with more stress and frustration occurring in lower social class families (Coser, 1967; Merton, 1938). Unemployment, economic problems, unwanted children, illness, and other stress-producing events are more likely to occur in low income or low socio-economic status families. Violence is often an adaptation to structural stress and family members tend to victimize one another in attempting to adapt to the stressful situations they find themselves in (Gelles, 1974).

Sexual inequality

Another structural attribute of American society which tends to produce family violence is the socially structured inequality between men and women. American men are constrained through social norms and social convention to be dominant in the family. Men are socialized to believe that they ought to be the leader and instrumental head of the household. Women, on the other hand, are constrained by the burden of child care. They are the ones who typically give up their jobs when they have a child and they tend to have career paths which adapt to those of their husbands' in terms of location and hours.

The socially structured inequality between men and women is also found in a society which labels occupations as 'men's work' and 'women's work'. Our research on family violence illustrates that violence between husband and wife is common when men cannot hold down the dominant position that they see society mandating for them. Thus, husbands who make less income than their wives and who hold less prestigious jobs than their wives, and who believe that they should be the dominant member of the family, will tend to use violence as a resource to secure the dominant role. Women, on the other hand, are more likely than men to use physical violence on their children. In instances where mothers abuse or kill their child, the root cause seems to be the child being perceived as interfering with the mother's desires or goals for herself (Gelles, 1973).

Social–psychological factors

The family is an interaction setting where roles are assigned on the basis of age and sex rather than interest or ability. There are specific social–psychological variables which tend to be associated with the use of violence in the home. In many instances conjugal violence which is initiated by the husband is thought to be an expression of 'compulsive masculinity' where a man uses violence as a form of expression and as a way of establishing a masculine identity after being raised by women (Parsons, 1947). Other researchers view violence as a means of establishing a positive self concept after experiencing socially devaluing experiences (Kaplan, 1972). A third line of reasoning traces violence to somato-sensory deprivation where violence is a consequence of a lack of intimacy, love, or physical affection (Prescott and Douglas, 1976).

Our research indicates that there are two main social–psychological forces which are associated with family violence. The first is the fact that the family serves as a training ground for violence. Research on murderers (Guttmacher, 1960; Palmer, 1962; Gillen, 1946), child abusers (Steele and Pollock, 1974; Bakan, 1971; Kempe *et al.,* 1962; Gil, 1971), and wife abusers (Gelles, 1976) all confirm the hypothesis that the more violence he experiences in growing up, the more likely an individual is to use violence as an adult. In fact, the more violence a woman experiences as a child in her family of orientation, the more likely she is to be a *victim* of violence in her family of procreation (Gelles, 1976). The explanation for this relationship might be a genetic one (violent genes are passed on), a psychological one (being a victim produces psychic trauma), or a social–psychological one (seeing violence produces a 'role model' for violence in the family). We tend to believe that the social–psychological explanation is the most viable. Children who see and experience violence when growing up tend to use these experiences as guides for dealing with problems in their adult families.

A second factor which increases the extent of violence in the family is privacy. The increasing nuclearization of the American family (Glick, 1975), which is a consequence of fewer children being born, smaller households, and fewer families living with relatives, has lessened the amount of social control which can be exerted on conjugal dyads. Thus, with high privacy and low social control there is no one available to act as a referee or a 'second' when conjugal conflict festers. In many families the lack of a third party to intervene may accelerate the conflict into a violent episode.

Summary

Although our research is far from producing a tight theory of the causes of family violence, we can propose that there are numerous structural and social–psychological variables which interact to increase the likelihood of violence taking place in American families. In addition, the structural arrangement of American society which produces social inequity between classes of individuals and between the sexes, together with norms favourable to using violence to solve problems, interact to produce the rather high level of family violence found in the United States. Although these factors are probably not unique to the United States, they do help explain why Americans are so prone to be violent towards those they claim they love.

SOCIETAL RESPONSE TO THE PROBLEM OF VIOLENT FAMILIES

Although the issue of violence in the home has attracted considerable attention from the American mass media, politicians, and social service personnel, Americans are far from addressing the actual causes and possible solutions to the problem. The American judicial system has traditionally been reluctant to become involved in intra-familial matters. Courts often are mired in a pool of mythology concerning child abuse and wife abuse. Many judges do not want to intervene in what they believe to be private matters. Thus, few cases of wife abuse ever end in the courts, and only the most severe instances of child abuse are handled by criminal or family court systems. Forty-eight of the 50 states refuse to recognize that a woman could be raped by her husband, and thus women are not allowed to prosecute their spouses for acts of sexual violence.

The social service system, which is a billion dollar a year enterprise in the United States, has historically ignored or passed over serious facets of family violence. In 1976 there were only six functioning shelters for battered wives in the entire United States, while there were 85 refuges in Great Britain. Complicated federal and state regulations mean that social services are available for low-income families, while well-to-do families with problems of abuse and violence are often cut off from the organized efforts to intervene and strengthen families.

Ultimately, the failure of legal or social systems to actually deal with or attempt to prevent acts of family violence might be a consequence of the norms which state that a 'man's home is his castle' and that violence between intimates is a private matter better left to families to resolve.

The future situation, however, is not as bleak as the past or current situation in the United States. Organized political efforts such as the Women's Liberation Movement and the Child's Rights Movement in the United States have resulted in revisions of state and federal laws pertaining to individual rights in families. Civil and criminal suits brought by victims of family violence are forcing social and legal systems to address the problem of victims of domestic violence. The Federal Government established an office to co-ordinate child abuse and neglect research, prevention, and treatment efforts in 1973 and more extensive national efforts are now under way to deal with all aspects of family violence. We see the possible outcome of these activities as a real questioning of the norms which condone violence and a growing realization that family members are not for hitting.

ACKNOWLEDGEMENT

This paper is part of a research programme on intra-family violence supported by grants from the National Institute of Mental Health (MH 27557) and the National Center on Child Abuse and Neglect and Office of Child Development (90–C–425).

REFERENCES

Bakan, David (1971) *Slaughter of the Innocents: a Study of the Battered Child Phenomenon*, Boston, Mass.: Beacon Press.

Blumberg, Myrna (1965) 'When parents hit out', *Twentieth Century*, 173(winter), 39–44.

The Boston Globe (1973) 'Home strife number one cause of murders in Atlanta', *Boston Globe*, 6 February, 12.

Boudouris, James (1971) 'Homicide and the family', *Journal of Marriage and the Family*, 33 (November), 667–682.

Bronfenbrenner, Urie (1958) 'Socialization and social class through time and space'. In E. E. Maccoby, T. M. Newcomb, and E. L. Hartley (eds), *Readings in Social Psychology*, New York: Holt, 400–425.

Caffey, John (1946) 'Multiple fractures in the long bones of infants suffering from chronic subdural hematoma', *American Journal of Roentgenology, Radium Therapy, Nuclear Medicine*, 56, 163–173.

Calvert, Robert (1974) 'Criminal and civil liability in husband–wife assaults'. In Steinmetz and Straus, 1974, 88–90.

Coser, Lewis A. (1967) *Continuities in the Study of Social Conflict*, New York: Free Press.

Curtis, Lynn (1974) *Criminal Violence: National Patterns and Behavior*, Lexington, Mass.: Lexington Books.

Erlanger, Howard B. (1974) 'Social class and corporal punishment in childrearing: a reassessment', *American Sociological Review*, 39 (February), 68–85.

Field, Martha H., and Field, Henry F. (1973) 'Marital violence and the criminal process: neither justice nor peace', *Social Service Review*, 47 (2), 221–240.

Galdston, Richard (1965) 'Observations of children who have been physically abused by their parents', *American Journal of Psychiatry*, 122 (4), 440–443.

Gelles, Richard J. (1973) 'Child abuse as psychopathology: a sociological critique and reformulation', *American Journal of Orthopsychiatry*, 43 (July), 611–621.

Gelles, Richard J. (1974) *The Violent Home: a Study of Physical Aggression Between Husbands and Wives*, Beverly Hills: Sage Publications Inc.

Gelles, Richard J. (1975). 'The social construction of child abuse', *American Journal of Orthopsychiatry*, 45 (April), 363–371.

Gelles, Richard J. (1976) 'Abused wives: why do they stay?', *Journal of Marriage and the Family*, 38 (November), 659–668.

Gelles, Richard J., and Straus, Murray A. (1975) 'Family experience and public support of the death penalty', *American Journal of Orthopsychiatry*, 45 (July), 596–613.

Gelles, Richard J., and Straus, Murray A. (1977) 'Determinants of violence in the family: toward a theoretical integration'. In 'Contemporary Theories About the Family, ed. W. Burr, R. Hill, F. I. Nye, and I. Reiss, New York: Free Press.

Gil, David G. (1971) 'Violence against children', *Journal of Marriage and the Family*, 33 (November), 637–748.

Gillen, John Lewis (1946) *The Wisconsin Prisoner: Studies in Crimogenesis*, Madison: University of Wisconsin Press.

Glick, Paul C. (1975) 'A demographer looks at American families', *Journal of Marriage and the Family*, 37 (February), 15–27.

Guttmacher, Manfred (1960) *The Mind of the Murderer*, New York: Farrar, Straus, & Cudahy.

Kaplan, Howard B. (1972) 'Towards a general theory of psychosocial deviance: the case of aggressive behaviour', *Social Science and Medicine*, 6 (5), 593–617.

Kempe, C. Henry, Silverman, F. N., Steele, B. F., Droegemuller, W., and Silver, H. K. (1962) 'The battered child syndrome', *Journal of the American Medical Association*, 181 7 July, 17–24.

Levinger, George (1966) 'Sources of marital dissatisfaction among applicants for divorce', *American Journal of Orthopsychiatry*, 26 (October), 803–807. Reprinted in Paul

H. Glasser and Louis N. Glasser (eds), *Families in Crisis*, New York: Harper & Row, 126–132.

Light, Richard J. (1974) 'Abused and neglected children in America: a study of alternative policies', *Harvard Educational Review*, 43 (November), 556–598.

Merton, Robert K. (1938) 'Social structure and anomie', *American Sociological Review*, 3 (October), 672–682.

Mulligan, Martha A. (1977) 'An investigation of factors associated with violent modes of conflict resolution in the family', unpublished MA thesis, University of Rhode Island.

O'Brien, John E. (1971) 'Violence in divorce prone families', *Journal of Marriage and the Family*, 33 (November), 692–698.

Palmer, Stuart (1962) *The Psychology of Murder*, New York: Thomas Y. Crowell Company.

Parnas, Raymond I. (1967) 'The police response to domestic disturbance', *Wisconsin Law Review*, 914 (fall), 914–960.

Parsons, Talcott (1947) 'Certain primary sources and patterns of aggression in the social structure', *Psychiatry*, 10 (May), 167–181.

Pittman, David J., and Handy, William (1964) 'Patterns in criminal aggravated assault', *Journal of Criminal Law, Criminology and Police Science*, 55 (4), 462–470.

Pizzey, Erin (1974) *Scream Quietly or the Neighbours Will Hear*, Harmondsworth: Penguin Books.

Prescott, James W., and Wallace, Douglas (1976) 'Developmental sociobiology and the origins of aggressive behavior', Paper presented at the 21st International Conference of Psychology, Paris.

Snell, John E., Rosenwald, Richard J., and Robey, Ames (1964) 'The wifebeater's wife: a study of family interaction', *Archives of General Psychiatry*, 11 (August), 107–113.

Spinetta, John J., and Rigler, David (1972) 'The child-abusing parent: a psychological review', *Psychological Bulletin*, 77 (April), 296–304.

Sprey, Jetse (1969) 'The family as a system in conflict', *Journal of Marriage and the Family*, 31 (November), 699–706.

Stark, Rodney, and McEvoy, James, III (1970) 'Middle class violence', *Psychology Today*, 4 (November), 52–65.

Steele, Brandt F., and Pollock, Carl B. (1974) 'A psychiatric study of parents who abuse infants and small children'. In Ray E. Helfer, and C. Henry Kempe (eds), *The Battered Child*, Chicago: University of Chicago Press, 89–134.

Steinmetz, Suzanne K. (1974) 'Occupational environment in relation to physical punishment and dogmatism'. In Steinmetz and Straus, 1974, 166–172.

Steinmetz, Suzanne K., and Straus, Murray A. (1974) *Violence in the Family*, New York: Harper & Row (originally published by Dodd, Mead & Co.)

Straus, Murray A. (1973) 'A general systems theory approach to the development of a theory of violence between family members', *Social Science Information*, 12 (June), 105–125.

Straus, Murray A. (1974a) 'Leveling, civility, and violence in the family', *Journal of Marriage and the Family*, 36 (February), 13–30.

Straus, Murray A. (1974b) 'Cultural and social organizational influences on violence between family members'. In Raymond Prince and Dorothy Barrier (eds), *Configurations: Biological and Cultural Factors in Sexuality and Family Life*, Lexington, Mass.: Lexington Books–D. C. Heath.

Straus, Murray A. (1977) 'Normative and behavioral aspects of violence between spouses: preliminary data on a nationally representative USA sample', paper read at the Symposium on Violence in Canadian Society, 12 March 1977.

Straus, Murray A., Gelles, Richard J., and Steinmetz, Suzanne K. (1977) *Violence in the American Family*, in press.

Truninger, Elizabeth (1971) 'Marital violence: the legal solutions', *The Hastings Law Journal*, 23 (November), 259–276.

8

VIOLENCE AND THE FAMILY: SOME MEDITERRANEAN EXAMPLES

Peter Loizos

INTRODUCTION

This chapter describes a situation found in rural communities of the Mediterranean, in which violence between family members may, in local thinking, be necessary and proper to preserve the future integrity of the family itself. The situation provides a contrast to the liberal, egalitarian, and reforming assumptions which, one suspects, are held by most of the people who will read this book.

The argument is that the belief in family honour as a moral code may lead to violence, particularly by men against related women. People from communities to be described here have emigrated to industrial societies, where even after a generation or more of residence, they often maintain the honour code, and so come into direct conflict with the law, or with the public morality of the wider society.

Anthropologists usually try to examine a practice in terms of the institutions which accompany it. The theme of 'violence in the family' invites such a treatment in two ways. One, which cannot be followed up here, would be to examine all contexts of violence in a particular society, since it is to be expected that particular societies have attitudes to violence in general which would help make greater sense of *family* violence. Unfortunately there have been few studies of Mediterranean communities which provide full enough information for such an approach. Another possibility is to examine some of the rights and duties of family members in a number of societies, to see how far the use of violence can be seen as a legitimate right which accompanies certain roles. The chapter will take this second course, using the idea of honour to provide a perspective on particular family relationships.

The chapter first discusses the elements of the honour code, and reviews some recent attempts to explain it. The nature of parental authority is then considered, first in the disposal of children's labour in South Italy, and then in terms of parental obligations to make economic provision for children at marriage. Instances of violence in support of family honour are then discussed, with examples from Portugal, Sicily, Greece, and Cyprus in turn. In conclusion some questions are raised and possible areas of comparison suggested.

THE HONOUR CODE

Pitt-Rivers (1977, p.1) has stressed that the nature of honour codes has varied from one period to another, from place to place, and from class to class. It usually includes most of the following features: first, the total social reputation of a family, its 'honour', depends in the last resort on men both protecting their womenfolk and controlling their sexuality. Fathers, brothers, and husbands must see to it that mothers, sisters, daughters, and wives are not seduced, and do not indulge in dalliance. The men of a family may feel the need to kill an actual or potential seducer; in extreme cases a father should kill his daughter, or a brother his sister, if she has dishonoured the family by condoning her own seduction.

There are some other features which tend to go with the code. Typically, men see women as their moral and spiritual inferiors, and women pay lip service, at least, to this view. Men think that their authority should be accepted without question by women in most matters, and if women contest a decision, which inevitably they do from time to time, then they are likely to be beaten. Parents are usually under a customary obligation to give property to their children, either at marriage, or later. Marriage is not the result of two people freely choosing each other, but is arranged by the family acting in concert, or by the exercise of parental veto. Although this code is being challenged by forces of change in rural communities, it has proved tenacious to a surprising degree.

A number of terms have been used to describe it. Goode (1964, p.112) writes of *machismo*, i.e. male-vanity cultures. The phrase 'honour-and-shame' (Peristiany, 1965) suggests that men have their honour at risk, to women who should show a proper sense of 'shame', that is modest conduct, in dealing with unrelated men, a theme which dominates English nineteenth-century fiction from Jane Austen to Arnold Bennett. The expression 'double standard' points to the contrast between men who are free to have sex with any woman they can seduce, and women who only have sex with one man—their husband. For those concerned with the emancipation of women, such situations (with whatever labels) present type cases of male chauvinism and of women 'unconscious' of oppression.

Attempts to explain the code

A number of studies have given excellent accounts of how honour codes work in particular societies. A classic study of northern Greek shepherds is that by J. K. Campbell (1964), and a younger scholar has attempted a slightly more materialist approach in describing a South Italian town (Davis, 1973). There have been only a few comparative studies, or authors who sought to explain why honour codes exist in the particular forms they do.

Pitt-Rivers (1965, 1977) seeks to explain why the word honour tends to have two apparently contradictory meanings—virtue and precedence. The Legion of Honour, a Nobel Prize, and a knighthood are all honours accorded 'for virtue'; yet all too often there are grumbles that such honours have been wrongly bestowed, in recognition not of virtue but of power or favouritism. Recent criticisms of honours granted on the resignation of Sir Harold Wilson are perhaps an extreme case of a well-established type of complaint. Pitt-Rivers argues that such a conflict over two opposed definitions of honour is the very stuff of social life. Within a social structure, persons or groups struggle to make their private definitions of events accepted as 'reality'.

Pitt-Rivers discusses the failure of European states to put down aristocratic duelling. Aristocrats regarded themselves as above the law and public morality. He notes that 'street-corner society', the world of criminal fraternities, also defines its honour as a law unto itself. The origins of the word 'outlaw' are perhaps suggestive in this respect. But whether outlaws or not, criminal groups often simply consider legal codes as irrelevant to their private honour.

There is, then, a fundamental conflict between honour and legality, as Pitt-Rivers makes clear; and he points to peculiar similarities between the two systems:

> Authority as political power claims always to be moral authority, and the word therefore enjoys the same duality as honour from the moment that the legitimacy of the use of force is disputed. It cannot admit that its actions are devoid of legitimacy. (1977, p.15)

To consider Islamic societies in detail is outside the scope of this paper, but one study should be mentioned because it implicates religion in supporting the honour code, and apart from a few suggestions by Peristiany (1965, p.183) this relationship is virtually unexplored for the Christian Mediterranean. Antoun (1968) argues that the Quran and Islamic law emphasize honour with what he terms the modesty code. He further suggests a logic which works in local belief systems, and is reminiscent of 'labelling' in deviance theory: Arab village men attribute moral weakness and strong sexuality to women; they must then maintain strong institutional checks on female behaviour, to protect their own honour. These include child betrothal, infibulation, virginity tests, early arranged marriage, and the rapid remarriage of widowed or divorced women. In criticism of Antoun it should be noted that such practices as infibulation, virginity tests, and cliterodectomy are performed by women on women, but he might argue in reply that they are done to conform with dominant *male* ideas about honour. Whichever view one takes, these acts are surely clear instances of violence within the family? Antoun maintains that women are only rarely killed for sexual transgressions in the Arab world, but he is clear that if they are tempted to rebel against the honour code, fear of violent reprisals by their male relatives is a powerful deterrent.

Religion comes a very poor second to ecology, in Jane Schneider's (1971) wide-ranging comparative analysis of the honour code. She pays much attention to the problems of organization which pastoralists and agriculturalists alike face: they must keep together stable workforces, when there are strong pressures towards splitting up. Islam and Christianity are important to her only in so far as they have furthered agriculture over pastoralism. She argues that when the state was weak, and scarcely exercised any control of law and order in rural communities, then there was fierce, endemic competition between groups for vital scarce resources—pasture, arable land, and water.

> Thus honour can be thought of as the ideology of a property holding group which struggles to define, enlarge and protect its patrimony in a competitive society (1971, p.2)

In such a situation women are seen and treated as a form of property; but property with a difference:

> In other words although women are contested resources, much like sheep, and given a competitive society, subject to usurpation, they can be socialized to bear part of the defensive burden themselves. (1971, p.20)

The honour code is a unifying ideology for a group of related men. They form a unit of common defence since they 'own' the honour of their women relatives, they stand or fall by it; it makes or breaks them.

Davis (1977, pp.89–100) has praised this explanation, while pointing out some of its weaknesses: it ignores urban and aristocratic sources of honour; and it does not explain the persistence of the honour code when underlying ecological situations have changed. Davis places honour alongside class systems and state bureaucratic institutions as one of the three forms of stratification which co-exist in Mediterranean societies. He also argues that although the code is invoked about matters sexual, in South Italy at least people talk frequently of their readiness to kill for honour, but only rarely do so. They find ways of accommodating to attacks on their moral integrity. The commoner form of assassination is that of a neighbour's character, over some trivial item of household duties, rather than a sexual escapade. One might add that gossip and slander fall short of physical violence, but they may give rise to it. They are certainly violent behaviour. Within the family, verbal attempts to control the behaviour of others is often psychologically violent in a similar way.[1]

A Gloss on Jane Schneider

In this section one of Jane Schneider's key arguments will be made slightly more explicit. There is no need to follow her final resort to ecological determinants of the honour code. When government is weak the prime problem for small groups is self-defence. Until recently, government in rural communities of the Mediterranean was little more than the collection of taxes, and so relations between groups with opposed interests were regulated only locally, if at all. Violence as a means of settling disputes was rather common. While legal codes, courts, and government authorities existed in regional capitals, rural people probably avoided recourse to them if they could because their judgements were too often uncertain, corruptible, incomprehensible or, in terms of local values, simply irrelevant.

In such a situation the final safety of an individual depended on his social identity, as a member of a group, usually a group of kin, who stood together in defence. This safety included both the safety of his person, and of his property. As Jane Schneider emphasized, the honour of the group was a property (in both senses) of its women, and the women, in a sense, were property of the men.

It then becomes possible to understand the subordination of women within a particular group, and the possibility that they might suffer violence from their own kinsmen, as a cost, or by-product of the group's defence policies, and the specially 'protected' nature of women. By giving the smallest encouragement to an outsider, a woman could put her male kin into a situation where they should endanger their lives to see that she remained chaste. There was some ambiguity here: women symbolized the closed solidarity of the defence group, yet were also its weak points. For in the logic of local cultural codes, uncontrolled female sexuality signalled a lack of power and authority in the related men, an inability to dominate, to assert male strength. Such weakness within meant weakness in external relations, too. To complete the vicious circle, a group tried to communicate its full strength to the outside world by the fullest subordination and most blameless 'purity' of its women.

The situation was never static since groups were always in competition for power and prestige, and continually watched each other for evidence of weaknesses. The strong could afford to punish the lightest chance word from the weak, who in turn were careful not to give offence. Between groups of equal power there was antagonism, tension, and a dialectic of challenge and response, as Pitt-Rivers has made clear. One of the most recent analyses of the feud (Black-Michaud, 1975), an institution intimately connected with honour codes, suggests that it is a way of imposing temporary dominance while avoiding the higher costs of all-out violence between competitors. Honour becomes a language of power relations, with some resemblance to modern diplomatic communiqués.

FAMILY AUTHORITY AND CHILDREN'S LABOUR

The honour code is linked to the authority of men over women, and male household heads over women and children. In many societies rights of the household head over the labour and over the person of junior members were extensive, and similar to property rights. In a serious crisis, for example when a household was faced with starvation, a junior was sometimes sold into slavery, or into debt-bondage, or sent into domestic service to insure the survival of the others. Such extreme situations did not prevent relations of affection within the family in more normal times, but these were also accompanied by strong authority relations. Fathers usually expected to command their sons to labour on family land, if they wished to be fed. With such rights of command over labour were also, very frequently, duties, particularly the duty to contribute to the costs of a child's marriage. Such 'costs' often involved the transfer of substantial productive resources, in land, livestock or cash. Such marital provision is common in the Latin Mediterranean, and land has been scarce for hundreds of years. The *Observer* newspaper (Mather, 1976) recently gave some details of such patriarchal authority as it still survives in a region of South Italy.

In a region near Bari, called La Murgia, 'boys aged between 11 and 14 are taken away from home and school and sold to landowners who put them to work on these bleak, lonely hillsides'. Since 1967 this kind of child labour had been illegal in Italian law, but local courts in 1976 were hearing their first cases, following the suicide of a 14-year-old boy. In 1972, when the boy was 11, his father had signed an (illegal) contract with a farmer in which he received the boy's wages of £27 a month, plus 8 kg. of cheese. The boy had been working 15 to 18 hours a day, having 6 days off a year.

The article called this a system of slavery but this is journalistic licence. The boy's person had not been sold, although his labour had been; the farmer did not own the boy, but solely the right to his labour. By contemporary British standards it is certainly a brutal and lonely life for a child. But in northern Greece young boys might well be working similar hours for their own families, without any pay at all. The big difference, from the point of view of their personal satisfaction, is that at night or at frequent intervals they would return to their own families. The article on La Murgia says that only 13 000 out of the local population of 45 000 have jobs, though it is not clear if the 45 000 is the total population or the 'adult' workforce. In either case unemployment is high, and this is surely a key fact. In nearby Pisticci, Davis (1973, p.15) reports that in 1965 bus drivers worked an average of 110 hours a week with 2 weeks' unpaid holiday a year. Because by local standards their jobs were secure and well paid, they were actually *envied.*

At marriage in this part of South Italy men are given a share of family property. The parents, in other words, recognize an economic obligation to provide for their children when they marry, by what is in effect a capital transfer. In a sense, and depending on his particular family, the shepherd boy may have been working for his own marital portion, a brutal form of enforced saving, but not, in insecure rural societies, a very unusual situation. In rural Cyprus, before 1945, similar agreements seem to have been quite common; sometimes a young man worked for a peasant farmer for many years, living in his house and eating at the same table. In some cases I recorded, such men ended up by marrying the farmer's daughter and obtaining property with their brides. In other cases, their wages were saved and used to buy land; commonly the employer paid the boy's father, who then used the money as he saw fit. Such domestic authority also commonly extended to the arrangement of marriages. In rural Cyprus, until recently, parents arranged the marriages of their children. There was no courtship between boy and girl, who were lucky if they were consulted at all. Recalcitrant girls were beaten for refusing a spouse chosen by their parents; today if such beatings occur the parents would be considered 'old-fashioned' or 'backward' by many families. But in fact young women still tend to behave in conformity to parental expectations, although change is rapid (Loizos, 1975).

Cutileiro reports on the south-east Portuguese villages he studied that a man reaches full manhood only when he marries, mature bachelors being regarded as 'odd'. After marriage a man becomes head of a family, and owner or guardian of family property, and his wife may not dispose of her property without his consent.

> He becomes for the first time the full trustee of a woman's honour, and her behaviour is intimately tied up with his reputation and the fate of their family. The risk of his wife's adultery (and even the most carefully chosen wife may err in this respect) is the risk of perpetual dishonour.... Marriage is therefore a dangerous proposition, but the courage and ability to face it are the marks of a true man.... If a man praises his wife in conversation, he will first make some qualification, making it clear that because she is a woman she cannot be expected to attain moral perfection.... (Cutileiro, 1971, pp.100–108)

If a woman becomes the object of public disapproval or gossip, for such actions as spending too much time outside the home on errands, or 'protecting' their daughter's fiancé, the husband

> gives her a thorough beating to remind her who is master in the house. In many cases these beatings have little effect, but when they are made public by the neighbours who heard the wife's screams, there is general approval. (*ibid.*, p.103)

This picture of subordination is modified by the fact that wives usually control family budgets, the husband handing over wages on a Saturday night if he is a poor wage labourer or salaried worker. Poor women, because they are also wage earners, cannot be secluded at home in the way that richer women are, and are the objects of seduction attempts by wealthier men, a fact also reported in Southern Italy by Davis, and observed by myself in Cyprus. Most observers of these rural families note that the formal public dominance of the husband, reflected in a number of small things (such as men eating before women eat, women not speaking in front of guests until they are spoken to, women not smoking, etc.) is offset, contradicted, or modified, by important rights, usually economic, which wives have over husbands. Davis (1969, 1973) sums this up neatly by saying that in the South Italian town he studied the man's rights are sexual and his duties economic, while his wife's rights are economic and her duties sexual. This means that men must provide for their families, not squander family resources; their sexual adventures with other women may be passed over by their wives and local opinion providing they do not cost too much. The wives must submit to their husband's sexual demands, but must not themselves have extra-marital liaisons. The ideal rural Mediterranean wife is a virgin at marriage and thereafter knows sexually her husband only. Sexual intimacies between engaged couples occur but if the engagement is broken off the girl may find it hard to get any partner who is not himself socially blemished by poverty, a previous marriage, or some other personal disability.

A similar picture emerged from a book about a Sicilian community, studied by C. Gower Chapman in 1928 but only recently published. Marriage was arranged by parents, with dowry given on behalf of a daughter; love matches were frowned on, although youngsters sometimes performed 'runaway' marriages. Sometimes parents threatened a child with violence is he or she rejected a match. The need to endow daughters made them a burden to parents, and it was not considered desirable for unmarried girls to work for wages, so unlike their brothers they could not make much financial contribution to a household except through their unpaid domestic and agricultural labour. The earnings of unmarried children went into a common fund administered by the parents.

> Ordinarily economic independence is only attained at marriage, and the capital necessary for the founding of a new home comes as a donation from the parents of the contracting parties. Relations between husband and wife are cooperative even though the woman is 'always subservient' to her husband. (Gower Chapman, 1973, p.35)

The ethnographer, a young American woman, continued:

> The report current in Sicily that in America women are in authority

> over men is a constant source of marvel and disapproval. It is a thing of the other world, entirely unreasonable, and Sicilian women are the first to condemn it. Man commands because it is his right by greater intelligence and by wider strength. He occasionally expresses his authority by virtue of his greater strength. Wife beating is not only recommended in proverbs and found frequently in folk tales; it is a not infrequent occurrence in daily life.... At the same time it would be improper to represent the Sicilian woman as a much abused creature. She may be the occasional victim of her husband's displeasure, even when she herself is not the cause of his ill-humour; yet on the whole the relations between married persons are friendly and harmonious. (*ibid.*, p.36)

Large household expenditures were customarily approved by both husband and wife; but her property and her dowry remained hers all her life. Women of the upper classes never travelled away from the house without a chaperone, and for longer journeys, without a male protector. The double standard prevalied here too:

> The chastity demanded of women and so jealously guarded by their male relatives is in no way expected of their brothers. A woman is weak, a ready victim to the blandishments of men, who are ever in pursuit. (*ibid.*, p.41)

Men were considered socially superior to women because they 'provide food and are natural protectors and masters of women'.

One further example of how men dominate women will be given. In the Greek mountain village described by Juliet du Boulay (1974), in one of the most sensitive and penetrating recent analyses of rural male/female role relations, men were seen as superior in a number of ways. If challenged 'the man can always rely on the use of force as his final and invincible argument' and even a man living and working on his wife's property

> can and does put an end to prolonged arguments or grumbling with a blow or two; and although there is only one house in Ambeli in which the wife is beaten frequently by her husband, there is hardly a woman who cannot relate tales of how she has been struck by her husband for argument, opposition, or some indiscretion. (du Boulay, 1974, p.104)

On the same page the author sets out the oppositions implicit in the villagers' conception of male and female nature (see Table 8.1). Men saw women as holding the house together, essential partners who could make or break the family unit. A really good woman transcended any 'inherent' flaws in her nature and could relate to her husband on more equal terms, as a spiritual partner, if still an inferior.

Table 8.1 Greek villagers' conception of male and female nature

Men	Women
Adam	Eve
Superior	Inferior
Right	Left
Closer to God	Closer to the Devil
Intelligent	Unintelligent, 'stupid'
Strong-minded	Credulous
Cool-headed, brave	Fearful
Reliable	Unreliable
Strong	Weak (seen also in the aspect of sensuality)
Responsible	Irresponsible

THE ECONOMICS OF HONOUR

An excellent study of 'honour' crimes in contemporary Greece examined 197 cases reported between 1960 and 1963. The author noted that in traditional rural society a woman who had been dishonoured by unchastity or unfaithfulness was not permitted to commit an act of violence except against herself—that is, she was supposed to commit suicide.

> Male members of the family, on the contrary, must defend their honour and the family honour in an aggressive, violent manner by assaulting or killing the dishonoured woman and/or those responsible for the dishonour ... killing in defence of family honour was not considered to be a crime; it was, on the contrary, a socially expected and approved behaviour. (Safilios-Rothschild, 1969, p.206)

She notes that as Greece became more urban, and more rural families moved to cities, so women tended to be employed and paid as individuals, to have more freedom from family control. The former 'passivity' of women in matters of seduction and jilting gives way to an active role. They are less likely to be killed by family members or kill themselves, and are more likely to punish the man who has wronged them by a murder or by a violent attack on him, typically by throwing acid into his face.

She stresses that in rural areas neither partner could initiate divorce as a legitimate way of dealing with an unsatisfactory marriage, unlike Muslim countries, where typically men can easily divorce their wives but often women would have greater difficulty in divorcing their husbands.

> The wife is supposed to love, cherish and support her husband for ever, regardless of what he is or what he does. The husband, on the

> other hand, in the case of dissatisfaction may rely on beating or on the interference of her parents in order to make her obey him and perform her household tasks, the two main expectations he has from his wife. (*ibid.*, p.212)

It is also worth noting an economic aspect of female 'purity', male 'protection', and the arrangement of marriage by the whole family. Safilios-Rothschild reports that a father killed his daughter and her fiancé because the fiancé was asking that the dowry be doubled after learning that his future wife was pregnant from a previous affair. Crudely speaking, in Greek culture dowries have to go up as a woman's purity goes down. So a girl who has behaved in an uncontrolled manner costs her family more in economic endowments to the future union, as compensation for her fiancé's taking 'second-hand goods'. The article notes that rich girls do not need to be completely chaste in order to marry, but poor girls must be beyond reproach. In a central Italian village, the poorer people say: 'Gentlemen's horns are made of straw' (i.e. the disgrace from being cuckolded is short-lived like straw, not durable like horns) and in Sicily men used to say: 'The dowry hides the defects of the bride.' In Greece the way the law dealt with honour crimes was also characteristic of Mediterranean double-standard sexual morality. Husbands who had killed wives for infidelity were frequently acquitted; and brothers who killed a 'dishonoured' sister got lighter sentences than those who had killed the sister's lover, or both parties. (Safilios-Rothschild, 1969, p.215) In this society, women are worth less, and can cost the family its fortune and its honour; or so it seems to men.

VIOLENT MEN SEEN AS INADEQUATE

This brief survey has highlighted an aspect of violence in the family. A fuller treatment would need to consider all the contexts of violence in each society, as well as the range of non-physical means for controlling behaviour, including verbal abuse, gossip, slander, child-rearing methods, and so forth. There will also be important local variations within societies, and the pace of contemporary change, the rise in secondary education, and changes in the economic and legal position of women do not leave such patterns untouched. Some of the accounts cited here were recorded 40 years ago in a poor, isolated, and backward rural community. Sometimes, a careful ethnographer has given us an essential qualification to the rather dark-toned picture sketched so far. J. K. Campbell, writing of a northern Greek shepherd community he studied in 1955, tells us that the wife's adultery is perceived by her hsuband as the ultimate act of disobedience, and if a husband surprised the guilty parties in the act, he ought to kill his wife first, and only then her seducer. It is not surprising that the flat refusal of a wife to do her husband's bidding is rare, since the sanction is likely to be a beating with a stick.

> The Sarakatsani of both sexes accept the right of a husband to strike a disobedient or erring wife. It is true, however, that men who are continually beating their wives (and certain men in the community have this reputation) are held in considerable contempt. (Campbell, 1964, pp.152–153)

Laurie Arnold, who studied a grape-growing village near Limassol, Cyprus, in 1974, found men had the right as household heads to discipline both wives and children, but that for them to do so by violence was not usual, and to do so in public was reprehensible. The men who beat their wives regularly also beat their children. She adds significantly that the threat of violence was an everyday part of life, not only over political issues in the coffee-shops, but in quarrels between neighbours or over economic issues, such as rights of way, and land boundaries (personal communication).

There are several points to bear in mind, then, when trying to assess the material presented here. The 'brute fact' of men beating women is part of several other issues. One of these is local attitudes to the *general* subordination of women to related men, particularly wives and daughters to husbands and fathers. Linked to this is the moral obligation upon men as family heads to provide economically for their dependents, and to protect them against seduction and insult at the risk of their own lives. The third key factor is the fairly commonplace use of violence, or the threat of violence, in many areas of social relations, the banality of violence, to paraphrase Hannah Arendt. Finally, there is some reason to suppose that while occasional beating is widely regarded as legitimate, regular or frequent beating is a sign of the inadequacy of the man.

Readers impelled to censure such situations would do well to ponder related aspects of recent British social history. For example, the rights of ships' captains to order corporal punishment upon crew members in the British Navy, which continued into the early nineteenth century; the use of corporal punishment in British schools; the brutality accompanying children's labour in factories during the early industrial revolution; and the extent to which that revolution received an important impetus from the 'peculiar' institution of slavery (Williams, 1964). These are very recent situations in British history; if we now pride ourselves on our progress and liberalism in certain respects, we should also appreciate that the rapidly changing rural societies of the Mediterranean need to be understood in the context of their particular histories—and of our own.

It is worth raising a number of questions which deserve further thought. How much brutality towards family members appears within urban subcultures in which violence is commonplace, casual, normal? Do such subcultures make important distinctions between violence within the family and violence outside it? When and how is violence seen as legitimate? Do women accept men's authority as legitimate? What are the limits to such authority? What does the term 'jealousy' mean in British society, and in different class cultures? How much of the anger felt by 'jealous' men and women is related to some internal, and highly personal feeling of inadequacy, and how much of it is related to some 'external' shame they feel at *public* humiliation, betrayal, loss of face? Are men who live in stable communities, with encompassing communities of social control, more likely to beat wives, or less likely? How often does violence against women follow criticisms by the women of the men's alleged failure as providers or protectors? How frequently do women strike the first blow? These questions are not raised to suggest fundamental similarities between industrial urban contexts and the rural situations surveyed here, but they would certainly be worth consideration, in any attempt at contextual understanding of violence in the family.

ACKNOWLEDGEMENTS

I would like to thank Laurie Arnold, of the Manchester University Department of Anthropology, for helpful comments and for permission to cite some unpublished field notes; also Gill Shepherd and John Martin for helpful comments.

NOTE

1 Sydel Silverman (1968) has made a valuable analysis of the absence of the honour code in Central Italy, in contrast to South Italy, and since it employs arguments similar to those used by Jane Schneider, its omission by Schneider is unfortunate. John Davis (1977) has uncharacteristically overlooked the important paper by Antoun (1968).

REFERENCES

Antoun, R. T. (1968) 'On the modesty of women in Arab Muslim villages', *American Anthropologist*, **70**, 671–696.

Black-Michaud, J. (1975) *Cohesive Force*, Blackwell.

Boulay, Juliet du (1974) *Portrait of a Greek Mountain Village*, Clarendon Press.

Campbell, J. K. (1964) *Honour, Family and Patronage: a Study of Instititions and Moral Values in a Greek Mountain Community*, Clarendon Press.

Cutileiro, J. (1971) *A Portuguese Rural Society*, Clarendon Press.

Davis, J. (1969) 'Honour and politics in Pisticci', *Proc. Roy. Anth. Instit.* (annual), 69–81.

Davis, J. (1973) *Land and Family in Pisticci*, Athlone Press.

Davis, J. (1977) *People of the Mediterranean: an Essay in Comparative Social Anthropology*, Routledge & Kegan Paul.

Goode, W. J. (1964) *The Family*, Prentice-Hall.

Goody, J., and Tambiah, S. J. (1973) *Bridewealth and Dowry*, Cambridge University Press.

Gower Chapman, Charlotte (1973) *Milocca. A Sicilian Village*, Allen & Unwin.

Loizos, Peter (1975) 'Changes in property transfer among Greek Cypriot villagers', *Man*, **10** (4), 503–523.

Mather, I. (1976) 'The misery of the shepherd boy slaves', *Observer*, 19 December.

Peristiany, J. G. (ed.) (1965) *Honour and Shame: the Values of Mediterranean Society*, London: Weidenfeld & Nicolson.

Peters, E. (1975) Introductory essay on the feud in Black-Michaud, 1975.
Pitt-Rivers, J. (1965) in Peristiany (1965).
Pitt-Rivers, J. (1977) *The Fate of Schechem, or the Politics of Sex. Essays in the Anthropology of the Mediterranean*, Cambridge University Press.
Safilios-Rothschild, Constantina (1969), ' "Honour" crimes in contemporary Greece', *British Journal of Sociology*, **XX**, 205–218.
Schneider, Jane (1971) 'Of vigilance and virgins', *Ethnology*, **9**, 1–24.
Silverman, Sydel F. (1968) 'Agricultural organisation, social structure, and values in Italy. Amoral familism reconsidered', *American Anthropologist*, **70**, 1–20.
Williams, E. (1964) *Capitalism and Slavery*, Deutsch.

PART III

Social Policy and Social Action

9

FAMILY VIOLENCE AND SOCIAL POLICY

J. P. Martin

INTRODUCTION

In one sense the subject of this chapter does not exist. There is no comprehensive set of provisions, based on a clear underlying philosophy, designed to solve the problems created by violence in a family setting. What does exist is a range of measures, not designed for the purpose but nevertheless having some bearing on the matter and capable, in a characteristically English way, of almost interminable adaptation to meet the most immediate difficulties. Any description and interpretation of these provisions necessarily has an omnibus character; it will err on the side of inclusion, and it may create an illusion of greater administrative coherence than is really justified. However the attempt must be made in order to provide some context for the detailed discussions of social work and other methods in later chapters.

'Social policy' is used here to refer to measures taken by publicly funded organizations, which may be said to imply a degree of governmental concern. This can be shown at various levels.

The lowest level may simply involve noting the existence of a problem and somehow assuming that the services to meet it are adequate. Thus, for example, medical services might patch up the injuries of a battered wife, or a court might grant her an injunction, but neither action would face the underlying problems and motives of those involved. Of such stuff too are the more bland parts of the Government's *Observations on the Report from the Select Committee on Violence in Marriage* (DHSS *et al.*, 1976), for example its response to the committee's urging of the need for medical education to take the problem into account:

> the Department of Health and Social Security has drawn the attention of the Education Sub-Committee of the General Medical Council to the relevant passages of the Committee's report and has

> written to the Council for Postgraduate Medical Education. The Council for Postgraduate Medical Education in turn referred the matter to a meeting of the Advisory Committee of Deans. The Deans agreed with the view of the Select Committee as to the important role of those concerned with medical training in ensuring that doctors are aware of the need for vigilance in cases of marital disharmony and of the possible need, with the consent of the patient, to take further action and alert others to the situation. (para. 24)

Bureaucratically correct, no doubt, but hardly stirring stuff.

The second level is that where special procedures are devised to facilitate dealing with a problem. Thus, in the face of child abuse, area review committees have been set up locally to consider procedures and policy, while the actual children thought to be at risk have become the subject of case conferences. Such developments, while not involving an explicit assignment of resources, do nevertheless imply a shift of bureaucratic attention so that at least more time may be spent on a particular activity, albeit at the expense of something else less in the public eye. For example some Manchester social workers started a women's aid organization called Shield, and had a meeting with their director to keep him informed about what they were up to. He not only helped in various ways but tactfully 'recognised that we were using a lot of our working time dealing with Shield business and said that if we used our discretion in this he had no objections' (National Women's Aid Federation, 1975, p.38).

The third level is where resources are explicitly assigned for a given purpose, and policy entails financial decisions—grants are given, buildings provided, expenses paid and so on. In hard times such decisions may indeed be proof of sincerity, but in prosperity they may signify little more than the bonhomie of the man who contributes to a collection to establish his liberal generosity and, in the process, protects himself from the inconvenience of further importunity.

For convenience we may call these three levels of provision 'nominal', 'procedural', and 'material'—and we shall use these short titles in the rest of this chapter.

Margaret May's historical survey (chapter 6 in this book) has shown how public concern about family violence waxed and waned during the nineteenth century and up to the First World War. There is no reason to doubt that similar fluctuations have continued since. During the early 1970s, however, both major forms of family violence were drawn to public attention. There was a series of deaths of children in some form of public care, of which the most notorious was that of Maria Colwell who was killed by her step-father early in 1973, while the battering of wives was brilliantly publicized in Erin Pizzey's book, *Scream Quietly or the Neighbours Will Hear* (Pizzey, 1974). Following this the House of Commons appointed its Select Committee,

originally relating to Violence in Marriage, which produced an interim report in 1975 (SC, 1975). Since then it has been reconstituted with a wider brief and significantly a new title 'Violence in the Family', and has sat during the parliamentary sessions of 1975–1976 and 1976–1977.

The trauma of these events have left their mark on English social policy. 'Non-accidental injury' and 'wife battering' have become familiar phrases on the social-work scene and a wide variety of attempts have been made to develop existing services or support new ventures in local areas. The task of this chapter is to provide a broad description of what has been attempted and to discuss the difficulties encountered and the lessons to be learned.

As this is an undeveloped and fragmented area of social policy we should begin by considering what requirements an adequate policy should satisfy, and this should give us some criteria against which to judge existing provisions. The following are suggested as a starting point:

(1) Children or women at risk should be located or identified sufficiently quickly to prevent further harm being done to them.

(2) The process should be sensitive enough to identify those at risk without unnecessary over-identification. It should not be forgotten that identifying a person as being at risk simultaneously attaches a conspicuous label to the person(s) suspected of violence. Experience in criminological prediction has shown that prediction devices which appear to predict potential delinquents with some accuracy often do it at the price of considerable over-prediction, i.e. many whom they tag as likely to be delinquent do not become so in fact (Wootton, 1959; Simon, 1971). The ease with which similar over-prediction can occur in child-abuse cases has been demonstrated by Light (1973) who calculated that, on various assumptions, there might be a risk of between 68% and 85% of the parents suspected of abusing their children being incorrectly labelled. As he says, 'this seems unacceptable' (p.571).

(3) The labelling process should allow for de-labelling. No one should be stigmatized as potentially violent for longer than necessary to protect those at risk.

(4) When danger becomes apparent effective protection should be swiftly available.

(5) Protection of those in danger should not take an unnecessarily provocative form. Many of those concerned, whether adults or children, may find themselves in the same household again, and whatever protective action is taken should not leave scars which might arouse further tension and violence.

(6) Long-term solutions should be sought.

(7) Because of the potentially drastic effects of any family violence, particularly towards children and pregnant women, policies should aim at prevention as far as possible.

(8) While potential victims must be protected, and this may involve urgent and drastic action, long-term decisions should avoid haste. The

repercussions of family break-up are sufficiently far-reaching to demand careful concern for natural justice.

In spite of the overlap between the two main forms of abuse, the exposition will probably be clearer if, in the main, services relating to abused children and to battered women are treated separately.

SERVICES RELATING TO ABUSED CHILDREN

Sources of information

Although the research literature on child abuse is extensive, as shown by Letitia Allan's contribution to this book (chapter 3), not much of it is concerned with the organization and operation of services intended to deal with the problem. For this we have to turn to a more scattered literature, of which the main sources are, perhaps, the reports of the various inquiries concerned with notorious cases, and the evidence submitted to the Select Committee on Violence in the Family up to the end of 1976. Although the published reports relate to cases which particularly attracted public attention they constitute, as it were, a series of test cases from which certain lessons about organization can, and have been drawn. Many of the most obvious have formed the basis of the circulars subsequently issued by the Department of Health and Social Security (DHSS). Such circulars, however, being intended to provide administrative guidance may understate their rationale, while their desire to play down contentious issues may inhibit the statement of what needs to be said. There is, therefore, a case both for re-stating conclusions already drawn and examining some of the arguments more closely. Furthermore, the passage of time has given some opportunity of seeing how new procedures appear to be working so that the conclusions can be slightly up-dated.

Looking at 'failures', however, has its dangers. It can give misleading impressions, for example of the roles of men and/or step-parents in child abuse. Its value is in examining *procedures*, which should be able to cope with all cases.

The most significant of the published inquiries are briefly outlined below in order to bring out the salient points for those without access to the reports. (Bibliographical details are given at the end of this chapter.) In chronological order of the dates on which the children died, they were as follows:

Graham Bagnall died 28 May 1972 at the age of 2, having been born on 20 May 1970. His condition had been a matter of concern since he had been about 10 months old, and at thirteen months he had been in hospital 'with injuries consistent with "battering" '. Three months later his elder brother (then 3 years of age) was also admitted to the same hospital with suspicious injuries. Meanwhile Graham had been boarded out in an approved foster home: the possibility of adoption by the foster parents was discussed but rejected by Graham's parents (actually mother and step-father) when they understood the implications of adoption (presumably its permanence). While Graham was in foster care his mother gave birth to her third child, a daughter. Graham was returned to the parents because there seemed to be no grounds for opposing their request. Six weeks later he was found dead in his cot. Subsequently both were convicted of manslaughter. His step-father was educationally subnormal, he had been to an approved school and was known to have been aggressive/violent on three occasions. Report published Salop County Council, January 1973, with supplementary report by Shrewsbury Group Hospital Management Committee, March 1973.

Maria Colwell died on 7 January 1973 at the age of 7, being one of the nine children that her mother had borne by that time. She spent some years in the foster care of her aunt, but was returned to the care of her mother and step-father (Mr Kepple) at the age of 6 years and 8 months, being placed under a supervision order from that date. The family was visited by a variety of social workers, and concern about Maria was expressed by her class teacher at school and by neighbours. Nevertheless in spite of all this evident concern she was battered to death by her step-father, and was also found to weigh only about three-quarters of what would have been expected from her age and height. Mr Kepple was convicted of manslaughter and sentenced to 8 years' imprisonment. He had had a poor physical health record and had been convicted of relatively minor offences of violence on two occasions. An inquiry was held by a committee appointed by the Secretary of State for Social Services and its report was published in 1974 (DHSS 1974a).

David Lee Naseby died on 19 May 1973 at the age of 4 months. He was an illegitimate child and was killed by his step-father, who had a previous history of mental illness and at least one conviction for assaulting the mother, and for being drunk. He was subsequently convicted of murder. During the baby's short life the father was very aggressive towards the hospital staff and the baby was apparently assaulted on several occasions, at least once during a visit while he was an in-patient. The report was published by the Staffordshire Area Health Authority in 1974.

Max Piazzani died on 4 August 1973 at the age of 4 having starved as a result of wilful neglect which had occurred over a period of $3^1/_2$ years. His parents were subsequently convicted, sentenced to 2 years' imprisonment, which on appeal was reduced to 18 months on the ground that 'the emaciated condition of this little boy was not due to deliberate starvation, but was due to inability of this ailing baby to absorb and digest and to be nourished by food that he was given'. There was a history of conflict between the family and the medical profession and, owing to illness, regular visits by the health visitor had ceased 9 months before Max's death. The committee of inquiry was set up, and its report published jointly, by the Essex Area Health Authority and the Essex County Council in 1974.

Lisa Godfrey died on 23 October 1973 at the age of 3 years and 7 months, having been injured by her mother 5 days previously. The mother had been under the immediate supervision of a probation officer but had also attracted the attention of the health service and of social services. All three authorities combined to produce the report. Mrs Godfrey was actually on probation for defrauding the Department of Health and Social Security, but the family had a history of varied troubles including debts, marital difficulties, and quarrels with neighbours. The father had a criminal record. In the home he was a rather shadowy figure who took little, if any, responsibility for the children. Mrs Godfrey, therefore, bore the brunt of the family's numerous problems. The report was published in 1974 by the three authorities jointly (London Borough of Lambeth *et al.*, 1974).

Susan Auckland was killed by her father on 11 July 1974. She was the second of his children whom he had killed; he had previously been imprisoned for the manslaughter of his 9-week-old daughter in 1968. He was then sentenced to 18 months' imprisonment on grounds of diminished responsibility. He subsequently continued to show instability and violence both by battering his wife and by assaulting his parents and sister. After his release from prison in 1969 the Aucklands had three more children and, for most of the period till Susan's death, he was out of work. His wife's capabilities as a housewife were distinctly limited and he was accustomed to batter her, probably out of frustration. Just over 3 months before the killing Mrs Auckland decided she had had enough battering and left home. Within a few days the major administrative changes in the social services and the National Health Service took place on 1 April 1974 and this disrupted the help the family had been receiving. Susan spent a short period in care, and was then returned to her father who was looking after all three children. Finally, early in the morning of 11 July, John Auckland killed his youngest child; there was also evidence that at about the same period his other daughter was also ill-treated. He was subsequently sentenced to 5 years' imprisonment for manslaughter. The report was published by the Department of Health and Social Security in 1975 (DHSS, 1975b).

Three other cases have attracted sufficient attention to be the subject of published inquiries, but will not be outlined here in order to avoid an excessive amount of case material. Virtually all the points which they raise also appeared in other reports. They will, however, be referred to where appropriate and the names should be mentioned for the sake of completeness. Steven Meurs died at King's Lynn in April 1975 (Norfolk, 1976), Neil Howlett was killed in Birmingham also in 1975 (Birmingham, 1976), and Wayne Brewer was killed in Somerset in 1976 (Somerset, 1977).

The identification of children at risk

The principal policy conclusion that seems to have been drawn from the cases mentioned above has been that the prime need was better identification of children particularly at risk of serious abuse. The reaction to each case has been one of surprise that the danger had not been sufficiently appreciated, with the result that appropriate action (whatever that might have been) had not been taken. This verdict was natural enough for in none of these cases did the death occur as a bolt from the blue. The time-span over which abuse probably took place usually amounted to several months, and there was often a record of social service contact of some kind with the abusing family over a period of years before the crucial incident. It is this fact that gives all the social agencies such a heavy responsibility. No precautions can be taken against the isolated, unpremeditated, and unexpected assault, but to overlook warning signs is another matter.

Even the few cases mentioned above indicate that no service can claim an irreproachable record. Each has, at some point, failed to appreciate the implications of what was later seen to be evidence that things were going wrong. The significance of injuries has not been appreciated by hospital staffs and/or general practitioners (e.g. Naseby and Godfrey cases); health visitors have not realized the implications of being refused access to a child (Meurs); the police visited Maria Colwell's house on several occasions without fully realizing what was happening; NSPCC supervision failed (Bagnall and Colwell); and Lisa Godfrey's mother was under the supervision of a probation officer at the time of Lisa's death. In almost all cases local authority social workers, often inexperienced, had some responsibility.

There was no shortage of warning signs. They have included complaints from neighbours, observations reported by teachers, a variety of injuries, fear on the part of the child, drunkenness or patent irresponsibility by parents, hostile and threatening behaviour towards social workers or nurses, and even what were, in effect, cries for help from the batterer. The report on Lisa Godfrey had a particularly clear account of warning signs, including several admissions by her mother that she was losing her temper and hitting Lisa.

Likewise the report on Neil Howlett listed four occasions when it would have been appropriate to hold a case conference at which all the relevant facts might have been brought together and their implications assessed.

Case conferences

The committees of inquiry realized that they were being wise after the event in pointing out that in most of the cases the dangers to the children would have been much more apparent, if not obvious, had the information already in the hands of public agencies been collated and considered as a whole. It is not surprising, therefore, that from an early stage in the series of cases the solution of holding a multi-disciplinary case conference has been advocated. Indeed on the basis of its own research the NSPCC was urging the setting up of a central register of children at risk as long ago as 1972 (*The Times*, 8 September 1972). Although the DHSS had issued several circulars in the early 1970s, together with the report of the Tunbridge Wells Study Group (White Franklin, 1973), the present system was effectively inaugurated with the issue of the DHSS Circular LASSL(74)13 on 22 April 1974.

In its circular the DHSS gave a rather brief indication of diagnostic figures and suggested procedures for dealing with children thought to be at risk. It then went on to recommend the setting up of area review committees for each major local authority area to decide on matters of general policy, and the calling of case conferences to consider each case of suspected non-accidental injury to a child. Suggestions were made as to the membership of each type of body. In particular it was stated that

> A central record of information in each area is essential to good communications between the many disciplines involved in the management of these cases. Area review committees should give urgent consideration to setting up within existing resources an adequate system in their area for this purpose. Authorities might wish to consult the NSPCC who have carried out a study of suspected child abuse in which they considered the question of registers. (DHSS, 1974b, para. 17)

By January 1977 area review committees had been set up by 100 counties and boroughs. Most of these were under the chairmanship of the director or senior members of the Social Services Department; outside London, however, chairmen were quite often drawn from the medical profession, usually area community physicians or specialists in child health. The recent circulars, particularly one issued in February 1976 (LASSL(76)2), gave quite a lot if information about the state of organization at that time, and also included specimens of procedures worked out in two areas which could be used as models. All areas were instructed to set up central registers which were to be kept on a highly confidential basis but, nevertheless, ready of access to 'all the caring professions relevantly concerned'. On paper, therefore, the organization should be reasonably comprehensive.

The role of the police

In practice various difficulties have arisen, most of which have been mentioned in evidence to the Select Committee. The issue that seems to have aroused the most intense feelings is the involvement of the police in case conferences. The 1974 DHSS circular made police attendance appear a matter of marginal importance—'Others who may be invited when appropriate include police surgeons, police officers ... ' (para. 16(c)). Understandably the police tended to feel that this undercut their law-enforcement task, and undervalued their potential contribution. As a speaker at the Police Superintendents' Association of England and Wales told their annual conference,

> 'Battered children' cases were kept from police attention' 'because the social services are at pains to avoid us knowing. They do not consider that these cases can appropriately be dealt with [by] the criminal law. This ... is, of course, directly opposed to our duty and is contrary to the spirit of the existing legislation and to the natural spirit of justice.' Social service actions had created a separate category of offences of assault, which did not find its way into the courts at all except in so far as the child was given proper care. 'There is no action against the parent or the adult responsible.' (*The Times*, 2 October 1974)

There was no mistaking the bitter tone of the discussion, and it was echoed with only a little more restraint in much of the evidence given to the Select Committee. This evidence, however, was somewhat inconsistent; it seemed that co-operation between the police and other services was at its lowest in London but elsewhere was sometimes good. There were, moreover, signs of change; as Dr Hodgson (an area specialist in community medicine) put it:

> the problem is not that [paediatricians] feel the police will prosecute; it is the fact that once you notify the police, the police have an obligation to investigate. The mere process of investigation, [paediatricians] feel, often destroys what fragile contact they have with the parents ....
>
> We have got about eight paediatricians, and there was possibly only one of them who had anything like the attitude to police involvement that is common in social service departments. Now the position is changing. There has been an increasing number of case conferences ... where the police were never before involved and where the police have been asked to case conferences. The medical

> profession are surprised at their expertise and their knowledge in these cases and the fact that they are not as obtuse in their management as they had anticipated, and this prarticular problem of communication is being bridged. (SC 1977, Evid.Q.27)

Perhaps even more significant is the fact that the Department of Health and Social Security and the Home Office have finally come off the fence about the role of the police in case conferences. The latest circular, of November 1976 (LASSL(76)26), asserts that the police should be involved 'as closely as possible in the case conference structure'.... 'Area Review Committees should work towards police attendance at all case conferences ... but this can only be achieved through agreement and the establishment of mutual confidence.' The circular goes on to urge chief officers of police to make available to case conferences 'the details of any relevant previous convictions concerning a person involved in the care of (or a member of the same household as) a child who is the subject of a case conference'. This would not constitute a breach of the Rehabilitation of Offenders Act 1974 (paras 8 and 9).

Anyone who has read the official inquiries can be in little doubt that had case conferences been held, and had information about criminal records and styles of behaviour been available from the police, rather different decisions might well have been taken. This would probably have affected all the cases where children were killed by men. Ironically these were also cases where even suspicious and concerned doctors, including paediatricians, were unable to mobilize their concerns in an effective manner. The departmental encouragement of police involvement may therefore have derived, in part at least, from a recognition of the limitations of clinicians and social workers faced with the need to investigate suspicious circumstances in the face of non-co-operation or hostility.

The case was well argued in the Metropolitan Police evidence:

> You may ask, 'Why Police? Could not the Social Worker or N.S.P.C.C. Officer make the necessary investigation? If this were done we should avoid the possibility of prosecution which, in the event may disrupt the family life and so not be in the child's long term best interest.'
>
> My answer is that only Police have the training and experience to deal with this type of case, which may be as difficult as a murder enquiry—since in neither case can the victim help. This is a case for a thoroughly competent and experienced C.I.D. Officer. An investigation irrespective of prosecution is no more likely to disrupt family life than is the position where the true facts are not acknowledged openly, but are nevertheless known within the family. To bring the facts into the open, face them squarely and accept the consequences may well be the first step in rehabilitation. (SC 1977, Evid.p.37)

It would be difficult for members of what are sometimes called the caring professions to deny a conclusion so consistent with their basic philosophies. There are signs that social workers, at least, are adopting a more realistic attitude; as one director of social services put it to the Select Committee:

> We are concerned to protect the child. We sometimes feel that we are unable to do so because the medical profession cannot trust us to become involved without involving the Police, and *indeed in many cases it would be totally impossible for us to protect the child without involving the police* [my italics]. Yet we are often conscious of the holding back of information about children who need protection because of the fear of possibly heavy-handed police intervention.(SC 1977, Evid.Q.1)

In any case the risk of 'heavy-handed police intervention' should be seen in perspective. While the police are indeed under an obligation to investigate suspected crimes the form and extent of such an investigation is not laid down. There may be no prosecution either because a caution might be sufficient or because it may be impossible to prove the case to the standard of 'beyond reasonable doubt' required by the criminal law. The figures do not suggest that recent practice involves an unduly hasty recourse to law, if only because it is often very difficult to judge what was or was not accidental. Dr Hodgson emphasized the difficulty of diagnosis and told the Select Committee

> It is often an assessment of the total family situation, of what is going on in the family and the possibilities for the future, that determine the diagnosis, rather than saying that there has been an incident of battering which is just a little bit beyond what is acceptable ... [this can be particularly difficult] because of the cultural mix in many of our boroughs.... [Teachers] were confused about what was acceptable as a physical attack on children, particularly in some cultures, and what was not. (SC 1977, Evid.Q.19)

One suspects that it is these difficulties, perhaps more common than the rather clear-cut cases the police were talking about, which have led some case conferences to decide that in about 50% of cases the injury was accidental (Q.29). This was borne out by the figures quoted in the annex to the DHSS circular of February 1976 which related to the last 9 months of 1974, and which derived from areas including 90% of the child population of England. From a total of some 5700 known or suspected cases only about 19% were referred to a juvenile court. Where this was done nearly 75% resulted in care orders and about 14% in supervision orders, so that in total about 90% of such cases were placed under some form of supervision. Only about $3^1/_2$% of cases led to prosecution of the parents; when this happened the most frequent outcome appeared to be the making of a probation order (33%); immediate custodial sentences were imposed on 20%, and suspended on

13%. Information about the remaining disposals was not given, but on this evidence it can hardly be argued that policies were excessively punitive. Assuming that about 10 000 adults might have been involved the proportion ending in custody appears to have been about one third of 1% (DHSS, 1976, para.33).

Perhaps the wisest comment on police involvement came from Mr P. J. Owtram of the NSPCC who said,

> I think we would like to suggest that at all times the Police should be encouraged to review the consequences of their actions, so to speak ... it is very difficult to say, in a particular case, that the Police should definitely not take action—say in regard to prosecuting the parents—... but ... over a course of time the sort of action the Police are taking should be subjected to the same sort of evaluation as other agencies have to use 'was it really protective towards the child to do this?' (Q.245)

The role of the medical profession

Whereas the police have rightly been able to complain of being brought into child-abuse cases too late, the same cannot be said for the medical profession and the health visitors. They were involved to some degree in every case. It should not, however, be inferred from this that they were invariably ineffective. For the most part the reports have not been seriously critical of clinical attention as such, and consultants in particular seem to have picked up signs of abuse in the children referred to them. It was not surprising that family doctors tended to be less acute, partly because such cases are rather rare in general practice, and partly because until recently GPs were not so aware of the problem. Even in a practice sensitized to child abuse because of its connection with a hospital specializing in abuse cases the incidence was no more than one abused child for every 150 children under the age of 10 (Beswick *et al.*, 1976).

General practitioners seemed to find it difficult to suspect their own patients, partly because of the very infrequency of child abuse and partly, no doubt, because of the role conflict involved—the parents are his patients too. The difficulty of gauging the situation was the greater when no health visitor was attached to the practice and the doctor therefore had no observer who could visit the home fairly often on his behalf.

What does seem to be clear is that the traditional practice of clinical medicine, centred on clinic or consulting room with doctor and patient in a one-to-one relationship, has grave disadvantages when confronted with child abuse. Clearly the expert clinician can and will identify and treat the injuries; he will probably also have suspicions as to their cause. At this stage, however, the limitations of his role begin to appear. For one thing, he probably only has access to his patient (the child) via the parents (who may be the batterers); sometimes, in a subtle way, parents manage to divert the doctor's attention so that he regards them, too, as his patients, and hence concern for his relationship with them may constrain him from passing on information about the child who is the person at risk. Similarly, neither he nor the health visitor has the right of access to the home, so that apart from his own observation he tends to depend on the parents for information. Furthermore, once the child's injuries have been adequately treated he has no strong grounds for keeping contact, and more urgent cases to see. Hence, whatever his concern the doctor in his traditional role is almost helpless. His concern must be conveyed to others if preventive action is to follow. How to do so is the problem.

There was some disagreement among the medical witnesses before the Select Committee about the most effective procedure. No one was in favour of statutory notification and the British Paediatric Association maintained that

> the safety of the child and the well being of the family can best be ensured by the procedure of a multi-disciplinary case conference, leading to registration of the family locally as being at risk, with court proceedings if appropriate, rather than by statutory notification by a single individual. (SC 1977, Evid.p.141)

The association emphasized the difficulties presented by child-abuse cases and thought that 'if anything it (Non Accidental Injury) is still being under diagnosed'. This was thought to be due to 'a lack of understanding and of expertise in the management of psycho-social problems by some family doctors and clinic medical officers', and also to 'a failure of recognition of possible non accidental injury in some Accident and Emergency Departments'. Both failures stemmed from the limitations of medical education; it was even

> difficult to persuade [family doctors] to attend case conferences concerning a whole family which, one would feel, is the example par excellence of a situation which should concern the family doctor deeply. That this comment has to be made reflects the fact that the subject of child health is a relatively new one; many doctors in the past have not had a broad training in the social aspects of child health which we hope and believe that medical students and doctors on G.P. vocational training schemes are now getting. (SC 1977, Evid.p.143)

The specialists in community medicine emphasized the difficulties of the accident and emergency departments: there was a rapid turn-over of junior staff, access to longer-term records might be difficult at short notice, while a responsible consultant was needed to oversee the management of all cases concerning children in the hospital.

Some doctors criticized the whole idea of case conferences and wanted either a single decision maker or a small 'diagnostic conference'. Advocates of the single decision maker, however, did not wish him or her to be a member of the medical profession. It would be particularly difficult to cast the GP in this role because of the problems he might face if the child was removed from the family on his decision and yet he was still the family doctor. Some even harked back to the 'old child care officer who did such a superb job, but we have lost her, or him'! In the last resort, however, it had to be recognized that the only services with legal backing were the police and the social services, so they had to be involved. There was considerable agreement that the trouble was not so much the idea of case conferences as the way they were conducted that was at fault. As the paediatricians put it

> the average case-conference consists of 12–15 people and lasts for an hour and a half or more. It is thus a costly procedure which occupies many man hours of highly paid workers' time, which might be better spent in research or in direct contact with patients or clients. (SC 1977, Evid.p.143)

If the conferences are too long, it was said, everyone tends to send a deputy, and then no decisions get taken at all. The doctors also criticized the normal practice of holding conferences in the middle of the day which 'is not appropriate for doctors and nurses but ... easier for social services people and teachers'. The most important need, however, was for the conduct of the conferences to be disciplined in order to avoid waste of time.

On the whole it seems that the medical contribution to the handling of child-abuse cases is necessarily somewhat limited for the reasons stated above. At the level of diagnosis and the direct treatment of injuries medical care is indispensable, and clearly diagnostic information must be supplied to the case conference. How far this should be done by the doctor in person seems debatable, though clearly if the system was well run this would be preferable. It seems, however, that the functions of the case conference need closer examination.

Registers of children 'at risk'

The concept of the case conference is simple enough. Almost all the reported cases, and particularly that of Maria Colwell, might have had different outcomes had all the available information been brought together and looked at dispassionately. As counsel to the Colwell inquiry said, 'There was a failure to devise a system whereby [the social worker] was kept informed of what others knew concerning a child in her care' (*The Times*, 8 November 1973). Even before the report was published the East Sussex County Council set up an area review committee and started to compile a register (*The Times*, 29 August 1974); 2 years later it listed nearly 900 children. It was claimed that, as a result, 'cases are being brought to light before there is a serious injury and a local paediatrician is treating fewer children with less serious injuries', and the director of social services was able to maintain that 'We are now pretty confident that there is a very much lower risk that a child will die in the same circumstances as Maria' (*The Times*, 7 July 1976).

Despite the obvious advantages of some sort of register they have been heavily criticized. The first categorical advice to set up registers was given in a DHSS circular of 22 April 1974 (LASSL(74)13) but the recommendation was not very specific. It simply advocated 'A central record of information in each area' and suggested 'Authorities might want to contact the NSPCC who have carried out a study of suspected child abuse in which they considered the question of registers' (para.17). Faced with such guidance it was not surprising that responses and their effectiveness varied. As one told the Select Committee, 'I think we had a register simply to comply with the first DHSS Circular' (SC, 1977, Evid.Q.16). Two years later the system was tightened up by a further circular which both required all area review committees to set up registers and specified in some detail what information was to be collected (DHSS, 1976). Strangely enough the circular was not very specific about the purpose of the register, but its wording implied a concern for 'forming a reliable estimate of the incidence of non-accidental injury' while at the same time acknowledging 'particular local needs'. In evidence to the Select Committee an area review committee chairman commented that the DHSS 'do not seem to specify what the purpose of the register should be'. She suggested that there were two quite different needs: establishing incidence and being useful to social workers or casualty officers who needed to check quickly on the background of individual children with whom they might be dealing in circumstances which aroused suspicion.

There was evidence to suggest that the latter function was not being discharged satisfactorily. Paradoxically this was because of another DHSS concern, also legitimate, that the confidentiality of the register should be preserved with great care. As a result registers have to be kept under lock and key by senior officials and difficulties are said to have arisen of getting access to them in emergencies, often late at night. This may happen in a large county where the child is being treated in one town while the register may be kept many miles away; equally, in large metropolitan areas abusing parents are apt to take their children to the casualty departments of a series of hospitals, often crossing administrative boundaries in the process. Clearly a simpler and more flexible system than some of those now existing needs to be established if effectiveness is to be achieved. Cumbersome thoroughness is not the answer.

The DHSS was right to stress confidentiality because of the possible stigmatizing effects of it becoming known that a child had been placed on the register. Known batterers may meet severe ostracism; Maria Colwell's mother was 'turned away by shopkeepers, and ... lost her job. [She] received many unpleasant anonymous letters' (*The Times*, 7 December 1973). Informally one is told that child abuse has had so much publicity that some parents of genuinely accidentally injured children are anxious about taking them to hospital for fear of being suspected. This was graphically illustrated in the case of *In re Cullimore (a minor)* (*Times Law Report*, 23 March 1976). The parents had a child with brittle bones and were suspected of battering—there was conflicting medical evidence, an unsuccessful prosecution of the parents at the Central Criminal Court, and a long battle between the parents and the, no doubt anxious, social workers. Far from the social workers being lax, the president of the Family Division was reported as saying

> Social workers and others were apt to see the matter in black and white, and some could make no allowance in their own minds for the possibility that the parents were not at fault.
>
> The dilemma was that if the injuries were wrongly held to be non-accidental, the parents who were both 25, could suffer unjustly and be held in hatred, odium and contempt and pilloried in public while the child would be deprived of the loving care of parents and spend its formative years in an institution. If a diagnosis of 'brittle bones' was made and that was wrong, the child was gravely at risk if allowed to continue living with brutal parents.
>
> His Lordship had no criticism to make of the local authority, the social workers, doctors, specialists and nurses, who could not be blamed for being cautious! 'He set aside the place of safety order and granted her care and control to her parents.'

The fine balance and need for careful judgement was also illustrated by a case in which a mother was incorrectly reported to the NSPCC 'the mother was upset by the visit [of the NSPCC inspector] and the false accusation against her, as a result of which her health was affected'. She then sued the NSPCC claiming, among other things, that it was negligent in not checking that the allegation 'was made bona fide and not maliciously'. The case went ultimately to the House of Lords which ruled that the NSPCC held a special position under the Children and Young Persons Act 1969 and, in Lord Hailsham's judgement, 'the public interest was that the parties with *locus standi* to bring care proceedings should receive information under a cloak of confidentiality' (*Times Law Report*, 2 February 1977).

While priority must, as this judgement shows, be given to protecting the interests of the child, registers must be seen for what they are, administrative devices which at their best are no better than the information fed into them. Their effectiveness may be seriously diminished either by being incomplete, due to ignorance or lack of faith by those supposedly supplying information, or by being inaccessible when most needed. Furthermore there is a distinct danger that the existence of a register may take on the function of a bureaucratic shield against criticism of the authorities concerned. A register which is not backed by adequate resources of staff and facilities to undertake the necessary child-care work has all the solidity of a piece of theatrical scenery, and the director of social services who points proudly to it may best be likened to Sheridan's celebreated Mr Puff in *The Critic*.

Having put names on to a register there is the further problem of how long they should stay there. While in the interests of child saftey it is important to have warning lists, such stigmatizing labels should not be attached longer than is necessary. As the National Association of Probation Officers (NAPO) put it,

> the stigma which attaches to inclusion in the register and the fact that many families will be included on the basis of uncertain indications ... [makes] it very necessary ... that there should be recognised procedures for the removal of names, so that families do not remain on the register unnecessarily. (NAPO, 1976)

Practice evidently varies. The DHSS (1976) reports

> Some authorities never remove children from the register because a significant number of 'genuine' accidents can build up a picture of a child at risk. Others destroy records if an injury proved to be accidental. A number of registers incorporate a procedure for regular reviews through the case conference system or a reviewing committee. These ensure that the case is followed up by the appropriate staff, and provide checks that the child has been placed in the right risk category and that where appropriate the record card is either removed from the register or categorised as inactive. (para.21)

On this question the DHSS is studiously neutral, only recommending regular review in order to take account of other children in, or entering, the household who might come to be at risk. Otherwise it places its faith on the confidentiality of the register. It is difficult to see why it did not favour reviews of the kind described in the paragraph quoted above, except perhaps that the English administrator confronted with claims for natural justice is apt to seek refuge under the cloak of confidentiality.

Social services departments

The series of child deaths described earlier in this chapter could scarcely have occurred at a worse period in the history of social work in England. In April 1971 the social-work functions of local authorities were extensively reorganized, while in 1974 the main structures of both local government and the National Health Service were radically changed. The 1970s have, therefore, been a period of administrative upheaval, and services concerned with child welfare have been particularly affected. In 1971 the previously separate children's department of local authorities were combined with other welfare services to form social services departments whose remit covered all the personal social services. This followed the recommendations of a committee chaired by Lord Seebohm (1968) and frequently referred to in evidence given to the Select Committee. In 1974 many previously autonomous local authorities with their own social services departments were combined into larger units known variously as counties, metropolitan districts, and London boroughs. The net effect was to create a system of large social services departments, described by one director as 'vast', and the Select Committee was told that most employed between 1500 and 5000 staff, with a few even larger.

These changes had several relevant major consequences. First, they gave local authority social work a more hierarchical and, some would say, unnecessarily cumbersome structure. Second, the creation of many senior posts meant that these tended to be filled by the most experienced field workers so that the actual social-work tasks increasingly devolved upon young and inexperienced workers. Third, departments were urged or required to increase their commitment to provide for the mentally and physically handicapped, so that resources were stretched and establishing priorities became a major problem. As the directors of social services put it, the 'expectation[s] of social service since the Seebohm reorganisation in 1971 have increased out of all proportion to the growth in resources ...'. Concern about non-accidental injury had its price:

> we, as managers, have had to withdraw resources from other client groups, particularly those that, in our view and in the view of many of our councils, required to be positively discriminated in favour of, such as the mentally handicapped and physically handicapped .... (SC 1977, Evid.Q.373)

When the report on the death of Neil Howlett was published the director of social services for Birmingham commented,

> We are becoming a big children's department, and other groups are suffering because of the concentration on child care. Don't think it is a panacea for all social ills. If the social workers had been visiting weekly, a blow could still have killed Neil in between visits. (*Guardian*, 26 November 1976)

The problem, moreover, is not merely one of deciding between services for children as against other groups, but of how to care for which groups of children. With some unanimity the directors thought that a policy of concentrating on the extreme cases was mistaken; first because of the sheer difficulty of assessing risk with any precision, and, second, because a much larger number of children 'may be lying in the margin of child neglect, and indeed possibly suffering more than some victims of violence, but from an emotional point of view' (p.253). It is not possible to prove this, but several inquiries made the point that the children who died were not regarded as being especially at risk: Maria Colwell's social worker thought that six out of 70 children on her case-load were at risk, but Maria was not one of them (and it was perhaps to the social worker's credit that the other six survived). Similarly the Birmingham social services department did not regard Neil Howlett as being in danger, although this view was later disputed by the committee of inquiry which concluded that 'it ought to have been plain that the children were at risk of non-accidental injury' (Birmingham, 1976, p.12).

In arguing for general preventive measures in a situation where identification of those at risk is difficult and time-consuming the directors have a strong case. When, however, they bemoan that

> we find it impossible to determine priorities between them (i.e. different groups of people in need) other than on the basis of value judgements, except perhaps where we are using a crude criterion of life and death ... (SC 1977, Evid.p.252)

they appear to betray some moral naïvety, born perhaps of the emphasis in social-work training on being non-judgemental. It is difficult to see how priorities can ever be determined except by making choices on the basis of an underlying morality, and it would not seem odd to a layman to regard the life or death of children as the proper subject of value judgements.

It seems, therefore, entirely proper to set up administrative systems as far as possible to identify children at risk so that they can be protected. The question then is, how best to do it?

On this, the clearest message is that there is no certainty, and the clarity of the moral position is obscured by the practical difficulties. The basic problem was graphically put by one witness to the Select Committee.

> Of 332 on our register [Lambeth] 77 are in an establishment of some kind, or are fostered, or are in a hospital.... In other words, we have only physically protected 77. The other 240–250 are all at home with their parents and are on our register as subject to the risk of battering. (SC 1977, Evid.Q.7)

There was an acute awareness of the fundamental dilemma:

> We often walk along knife edges, I think, but the alternatives are not as happy as you might think. If you think of the high turnover in children's homes and the shortage of long term foster parents, to take a child away from home is not suddenly producing a panacea;

> it may be turning out an equally unhappy and disturbed child at 18 as if it had stayed with its parents. (SC 1977, Evid.Q.22)

In short, one kind of safety may be achieved at the price of a different kind of risk. With a death rate of children on registers of even less than 1%, to attempt support in the home is not entirely unreasonable. Its validity may, however, depend on developing better social-work methods.

This chapter is not concerned with social-work methods as such, but it is clear from the inquiries and the evidence to the Select Committee that there are things even the most conscientious visiting cannot do. As the director of social services for Somerset said of Wayne Brewer:

> This child was at risk from an impulsive kind of violence. Unless you are there 24 hours a day it is difficult to protect a child in those circumstances, and difficult to know exactly what goes on in the privacy of the home. (*The Times*, 13 October 1976)

In this case the magistrates issued a supervision order with a recommendation that social workers should visit 'three or four times a week'; a requirement making impossible demands on the social services department as its director made clear in a letter to the clerk of the court. It was also liable to be counter-productive. The family doctor 'commented on the amount of visiting with the family and wondered if this did not, in fact, add to the pressures already facing them' (Somerset Area Review Committee, 1977, §7.11). What, after all, must it be like to be visited almost daily by suspicious social workers? Jordan has indeed argued that

> anxious visiting by social workers of families actually increases battering. In the tragic cases we have all heard too much about, the clients were not new referrals who had not been investigated quickly enough, but cases known for a considerable period.... [Clients] often act out their rebellious anger with us on their children. (*The Times*, 3 October 1975)

Fortunately a variety of experiments have been attempted, some discussed in Jacquie Roberts's chapter of this book and others described to the Select Committee, and there must now be an onus upon social services departments to learn from them and apply their lessons systematically on a larger scale.

Such developments demand two things—staff with appropriate expertise, and the resources to implement them. Both pose serious problems for the departments. It is difficult to estimate what is needed in terms of financial resources as so much depends on the policy being followed. For example, the immediate follow-up of the Maria Colwell case by the East Sussex County Council involved 71 recommendations. These were accepted although they were expected to cost an extra £250 000 a year on the social services budget.

The money was likely to be spent on employing 'more social workers and clerical staff to support them' (*The Times*, 30 April 1975).

One limitation, in the view of the directors of social services appearing before the Select Committee was an excessive commitment to residential institutions.

> In my authority only twenty-five percent of the social services expenditure goes into domiciliary services of all kinds and seventy-five percent goes into looking after a few thousand elderly handicapped people and children in residential care. (SC 1977, Evid.Q.382)

> If every authority just had ten fewer children in residential care in the long run they could save £30 000 at current prices, which would be enough to employ seven or eight social workers to assist in maintaining children in their own families. (SC 1977, Evid.Q.399)

This argument, though appealing in principle, depends on the ability of those social workers to protect children effectively, both by their own efforts and by mobilizing community resources, whether by persuading more parents to foster children at risk, or by encouraging child-minding, play groups, and so on. Without question the directors' top priority was a general programme of care for under-5s.

This leads on to the question of expertise. The major theme of the Seebohm report was the desirability of developing general purpose social services departments, and this was related to an emphasis on the 'generic' training and practice of social work. As we have already shown, this trend has not been welcomed by other services, who hark back, perhaps too nostalgically, to the days of the child-care officer and her special expertise. The directors have certainly denied that the change has had all the ill effects attributed to it, but it seems that a degree of specialization is creeping back. Not only are there specialist appointments, such as the child-abuse specialist from Hammersmith who gave evidence to the Select Committee, but significant parts of departments seem to be moving towards specialization as in Birmingham ('We are becoming a big children's department'). Perhaps this is not surprising as whatever the department's policy a large part of its work will inevitably involve families with children.

It certainly seems that some retreat from the undervaluing of expertise implicit in at least the more simplistic notions of generic social work is under way. Child abusers are unquestionably difficult to work with, and there is a particular need to keep up with developments in methods as reported in the literature. Commenting on the appointment of a specialist worker one said:

> I think it has been a great reassurance that somebody has had a little

> more time to read the mass of literature that is available and avail themselves of the expertise, and that other people can draw on that. (Q.2)

This specialist also had a small case-load of 'hard-core' cases and so can also help by example.

Staff support has become a major problem. Both the various professional associations and the directors of social services have stressed the drastic effects which the public inquiries have had on the morale of social workers. One was 'booed and shouted at' when giving evidence at an inquiry; the term most frequently used to describe the experience was that they had been 'pilloried'. Undoubtedly it must sometimes have felt like that at the receiving end, and it should be remembered that organizations were criticized as much as people, while other professions did not escape censure (even if expressed somewhat drily as in the Auckland report). Moreover in view of the lessons learned from the inquiries it would be a serious loss if such reports were not published, and it is important that the public responsibility of the services should not be denied in the interests of protecting the professionals concerned.

'Pillorying', however, need not happen; the Wayne Brewer inquiry examined its evidence thoroughly while preserving the anonymity of those involved. There is, however, a danger in the trend towards such inquiries being both private and unpublished. Although the Wayne Brewer report seems to have been admirably comprehensive, the principle that inquiries should be conducted by the body responsible for running the service should be resisted. In any case the 'in-house' report automatically runs the risk of being labelled a white-washing exercise (as in the Bagnall case where the hospital authority even published its own report to correct what it regarded as a misleading social services one). Admittedly an area review committee is in a somewhat different position, having no direct responsibility for the operational services, but even so there is a risk of role conflict. In the Wayne Brewer inquiry this possibility led to the Chief Constable vetoing the inclusion of one of his superintendents in the investigating panel. It is, therefore, an important point of principle that inquiries should be held by bodies with a significant representation of independent people whether as members or, at the very least, assessors. The unpublished inquiry likewise suffers from an inherent implausibility, quite apart from breaching the principle that the funding of public services entails a substantial degree of *public* accountability.

A better protection for morale would be a more realistic public and, above all, media view of what can reasonably be expected of social workers. The medical analogy is not perfect as cures are even harder to come by in human relations, but as one witness put it to the Select Committee,

> What I would crave is understanding. If a doctor loses a patient, all the staff say 'Well, he made a jolly good try to keep that person

> alive.' The boot seems to be on the other foot with social workers. (SC 1977, Evid.Q.22)

The history of volatile public concern about family violence does not, however, inspire confidence that this understanding will be achieved.

Professional workers must, therefore, in large measure look to themselves for support. This is a matter of both departmental and professional organization. At a departmental level this is clearly understood; it was one of the themes running through the evidence given to the Select Committee by senior social workers. One director of social services put it categorically:

> I think there had to be public enquiries and the criticism made of main grade social workers. I think it is regrettable that more responsibility in every case was not accepted by the top management and the councils ... clearly we are responsible, and if somebody has got to be held responsible it should be the directors of social services and the committees who decide what resources they should have to do their work. (SC 1977, Evid.Q.379)

For its part the British Association of Social Workers (BASW, 1975) has issued a Code of Practice for Social Workers dealing with children at risk. It claims to set 'a minimum level of professional capability' to which all social workers and social services departments should aspire. It appears to expect such standards of professional and bureaucratic thoroughness that it makes one wonder whether its authors had really thought out the difference between minima and maxima, and whether such standards are achievable by human social workers in the everyday world. Counsels of perfection should not be eschewed, but neither should they masquerade as minimum standards. There is, in any case, a trace of ambivalence about hierarchy. On the one hand, in a code of 13 sections the social worker is enjoined to consult the supervisor at some 14 points, while at the same time it asserts that 'it is essential that the supervisor ensures that prime responsibility for the quality of the social worker's professional practice is vested in the individual social worker'. The conception of what it is possible to do is just as stretched for the supervisor, who 'has a duty to ensure that the work-load carried by social workers does not exceed a level which would prevent the social worker from visiting children on her caseload in accordance with the plan and timetable deemed appropriate'. How this is to be reconciled with the shortage of staff proclaimed by the directors is not apparent.

It is difficult to know how much significance should be attached to such a code. On the one hand it undoubtedly points to important matters, but one has an uneasy feeling that if anything should go wrong it will only increase the possibilities of shifting responsibility. The safest course for all concerned will be to ensure records are immaculately kept and that everything is reported up and down the line whenever possible.

Probably such codes, even if slightly portentous, do some good, but their importance can only be marginal against the fact that effective social work depends on having sufficient adequately trained workers and relevant facilities.

The role of voluntary services

Social work with children is the responsibility of social services departments, and they deploy by far the largest number of workers. They, together with the Health Service, have also been responsible for pioneering various innovations in methods of care such as those described to the Select Committee. Credit, however, should be given to the National Society for the Prevention of Cruelty to Children. Building on its long tradition of concern, it initiated important developments, not only in the form of some of the research which drew fresh attention to child abuse, but also in the setting up of a number of special units which attempted to provide new solutions to the problem. Whatever the degree of success achieved, and unfortunately the results so far do not give much ground for optimism, the evidence produced should be given considerable weight in deciding future policy (NSPCC, 1976, chapter 10). Furthermore, the existence of the system of NSPCC inspectors, and the society's privileged position in being able to initiate care proceedings, have value as a specialized alternative agency for identifying children at risk which some people might be more ready to approach than the more cumbersome and official social services departments.

Exactly how the lessons learned by the NSPCC are to be applied remains to be seen, but thus far at any rate the society has certainly fulfilled the innovatory function traditionally ascribed to voluntary agencies.

The role of the juvenile courts

It seems to be generally accepted that the law relating to child abuse is reasonably adequate (see, for example, Raisbeck, 1976; Metropolitan Police, 1976) and that such problems as occur are related either to procedure or to the sheer difficulty of obtaining evidence. At this point attention should be focused on the juvenile courts because all involuntary care proceedings have to take place in them.

The cases which specifically raised queries about the courts' role were those of Maria Colwell and Wayne Brewer. In Maria Colwell's case the crucial decision was that of the Hove juvenile court which revoked the care order and, in effect, decisively confirmed her hitherto provisional return to her mother's care. The proceedings were described as follows:

> Mrs Kepple was legally represented and gave the only evidence that was called. The Court had a full report from (the social worker) on behalf of the local authority, and we accept that of its kind it was

> probably of the standard expected in general terms. (DHSS, 1974a,§67)

The committee of inquiry was divided on the merits of the report, but did not disagree that the evidence about Mr Kepple's relationship with Maria was misleading—Mrs Kepple had simply asserted that her husband 'treats Maria as one of his own children'. The majority report maintained that the social worker should have challenged this assertion but this seems unreasonable as, unless directly questioned on it, she would probably have felt such an intervention would only have made for difficult relations with the family afterwards. Then went on to comment that

> in a difficult case such as this one, even if the application is not contested, legal representation on both sides is helpful. It is not for us to consider the much wider and more radical proposition of independent representation for the child. (DHSS, 1974a, §68)

The committee's reluctance was not shared by others and, thanks to the advocacy of Dr David Owen, Lady Masham, and others, the Children Act 1975 came to include a series of sections (64–66) enabling the child to be separately represented before the court or, in Scotland, at the children's hearing or before the sheriff. This provision was due to be put into effect from 26 November 1976, but only in some court proceedings. The Minister of State for Health commented that

> We are not overlooking parents' rights, but where there is a conflict of interest, as there was in the Maria Colwell case, we are saying that the child's interest must be given first consideration. (*The Times*, 6 September 1971)

Admirable though this may sound it is surely no different from the principle adopted by the Hove juvenile court in deciding to confirm Maria's return to her mother.

There are problems of practice as well as principle. First, on what information is the court to decide the child needs separate representation? The parents would be unlikely to suggest such a thing, while the social services department would in any case regard itself as acting throughout in the best interests of the child. It would, therefore, not be very ready to advocate the appointment of a guardian *ad litem* unless, of course, it saw this as a way of getting the best of both worlds, enabling the parents to be opposed, as it were by proxy, while adopting a more neutral position itself. Perhaps the only adequate solution, on these lines, is that of the committee set up by Justice (1975) which recommended that

> In all proceedings relating to the welfare of a child, the law should

> provide that the child be made a party to the proceedings and be entitled to separate legal representation. (p.15)

The second difficulty, which follows from acceptance of the principle of separate representation, is, 'How is the child's representative to be instructed?' The vast majority of abused children are under 5 years of age, and even if they are older, as was Maria Colwell (just over $6^1/_2$ at the Court hearing), they may not understand what is going on, or may fear for the unknown consequences of opposing their parents. It puts the lawyer in a difficult position; as Michael King (1975) has commented, 'Few lawyers have the necessary knowledge of child welfare to make an expert assessment of what course of action would be in the child's best interest.'

The fundamental weakness of all the proposals for the representation of the child is that they are attempts to improve the adversary system of court proceedings. This procedure, long established and derived from the criminal courts, rests on the assumption that it is the task of the court to adjudicate between opposed views of the disputed issue. As such it implies a relatively passive court, much dependent on the advocates appearing before it. As Glanville Williams has observed: 'This relative inactivity of the judge is a feature of English procedure going back to the Middle Ages' (quoted in Elston *et al.*, 1975).

It is very doubtful whether such a role is really appropriate in matters involving such delicate judgement as the care of children. The difficulty is that the court is likely to be considering an application by one party, often a parent or local authority, and the legal process of focusing on this issue may lead to a discussion of only those parts of the situation thought by the advocates in the case as likely to support their 'side' in the dispute. To those whose concern starts with the welfare of the child this approach is profoundly unsatisfactory. Much of the medical evidence to the Select Committee was strong on this point. To give only one example:

> the appearance of a child in a juvenile court for care proceedings is often mistakenly viewed as a battle for the care of the child, instead of a procedure necessary for the well being of the family as a whole and for the safety of the child. The care proceedings are 'for' the family and not 'against' the parents. (SC 1977, Evid.p.142)

The essential point is that the issues tend to become narrowed to an artificial 'dispute', and neither the court nor the advocates may have the knowledge and skill required to make the independent assessment of the situation which the court hearing exists to achieve. In the related area of divorce proceedings the recent paper by Elston *et al.* (1975) has, similarly, made clear the limitations of the adversary procedure when it comes to considering the welfare of children affected by undefended divorce cases.

It would seem that there is a strong case for considering a major modification of the existing procedure. The Finer Committee (Finer, 1974), and some evidence to the Select Committee, advocated a specialized family court, while an alternative model is offered by the children's hearings set up by the Social Work (Scotland) Act 1968. Their effectiveness is not beyond controversy, but there is a fairly strong body of evidence in their favour (Spencer and Bruce, 1976; Martin and Murray, 1976). It was noteworthy that the panel reviewing the Wayne Brewer case—where the child was returned to the parents against the advice of the social services department—discussed the 'Adversarial System' in several paragraphs of their report. They mentioned all the points raised above, being particularly aware of the difficulties of the social worker in a polarized situation with the danger of 'being seen, at least in the eyes of the parents as both prosecutor and adviser to the Court' (Somerset, 1977, §4.29). On the other hand they recognized the need for vigorous testing of the evidence and the value of established procedures in doing this. However they clearly had grave doubts about its flexibility and objectivity, and concluded that a

> careful comparison could usefully be undertaken of the way in which care proceedings are conducted under [the Scottish and English systems] and whether there are any differences in the outcome of such proceedings. (Somerset, 1977, §4.32)

At this stage it is not possible to reach a definitive conclusion, but it certainly seems that the proper role of whatever body considers care proceedings should be to investigate the total situation, being able to call for new evidence if important questions are unanswered, rather than attending only to what is put before it by the advocates in the case.

SERVICES RELATING TO BATTERED WOMEN

Cause for concern

Our previous discussion could take it for granted that child abuse was a bad thing, universally condemned, which all right-minded people would try to prevent. One cannot be so confident about views on the treatment of women. The reasons for this are explored in other contributions to this book; here it is sufficient to note that a major influence on the provision of relevant services is a degree of moral uncertainty as to how seriously the phenomenon of battered women should be taken. This is not surprising. To consider almost any provision for women in a family situation is to raise a carpet under which much dust has been swept. All manner of issues may arise, such as the equality of women in the family, the extent to which a husband is entitled to expect services from a wife, responsibility for the care of children, the tenancy of the home, and the extent to which the law should intervene in marital relationships. To treat these matters as open questions may be deeply threatening to many people, and in Britain it has perhaps been easier at times to evade the principles and deal in piecemeal and pragmatic arrangements. Policies, and above all their interpretation, have tended to be determined by traditional, local, and even personal considerations. As a result attitudes may range from sympathetic support to what one witness to the Select Committee described as 'disdain and some derision' (SC 1975, Evid.p.296).

In the absence of real consensus it is worth restating the reasons for treating wife battering seriously.

First, there cannot be any doubt that some of the wife battering reported to the Select Committee would have satisfied the legal criteria for being classified as assaults occasioning actual, or even grievous, bodily harm. Some were the subject of prosecution; others, though apparently involving as much injury, were not. They were, therefore, at least *prima facie* breaches of the criminal law. Such behaviour, moreover, can be a significant burden on the police. The Select Committee was told that 'a recent survey carried out in a city centre division of one of our larger cities showed that 22 per cent of all weekend emergency calls for police concerned domestic disturbances' (SC 1975, Evid.p.362). In extreme cases violence against women may result in death, and in fact murders of wives and girlfriends form a significant proportion of all homicides (Gibson, 1975).

Second, the effects of marital violence are almost always bad for the children. This conclusion was emphasized by every witness before the Select Committee who had had any direct experience of the families concerned. For example, one child-guidance expert said:

> when we come across cases in which there has been violence between the parents in the family or constant friction or arguments it has the most disastrous effect upon child development. I do not think there is any more traumatic experience for any growing child ... and it produced a very damaged personality. (SC 1975, Evid.Q.903)

Similarly Dr Gayford commented

> The pattern of the children is extremely disturbed indeed. Many of the males are very violent. It is even dangerous for another male or other children to spar with them because they do not fight in the usual way that a child will do. They attack; they go for the eyes, mouth, etc. Some of them have become too violent to be kept in school. (SC 1975, Evid.Q.28)

No doubt children of women who passed through the Chiswick refuge might have been extreme cases because of their mobility, but the general point was reiterated many times before the Select Committee and never seriou disputed by any witness.

Third, one may question the moral basis of marriages in which disputes between the partners are regularly solved by the use of superior force. It makes a mockery of the notion that one loves and cares for the other, and human relations are liable to become increasingly crude and unconstructive.

Altogether, marital violence should be taken seriously for the suffering it entails, for its potential as serious crime, and for its damaging effects on the children who are so often its unhappy spectators.

Sources of information

Services of relevance to battered women in Britain are not the subject of an extensive literature. There are a few specialized papers and reports by organizations working in the field, but pride of place has to be given to the House of Commons Select Committee on Violence in Marriage which published its *report* in 1975. In due course the appropriate government departments produced their *Observations on the Report from the Select Committee on Violence in Marriage* (DHSS *et al.*, 1976) which brings the history of developments more or less up to the end of 1976 and provides a convenient summary of the main facts. The most important source, however, is afforded by the *Minutes of Evidence* submitted to the Select Committee. They include numerous memoranda and transcripts of the 15 meetings at which oral evidence was received, amounting in total to 482 pages. Finally, on the legal side there is the important Domestic Violence and Matrimonial Proceedings Act 1976, and the detailed Law Commission *Report on Matrimonial Proceedings in Magistrates' Courts* (1976). The existence of this published material will allow discussion to be brief as the detailed arguments are fairly accessible and do not need repetition.

Problems to be solved

The problems facing battered women are many and complex. Some can be solved with sympathetic help from social services, but others may be so intractable that solutions seem impossible, and return even to an unsatisfactory husband may appear the lesser evil.

The first need is comparatively simple, to get away from being battered or otherwise harassed. Essentially this involves either restraining the husband by threat of legal sanctions or ensuring the physical separation of husband and wife. The latter may entail excluding the husband from the home, or the departure of the wife to a safer place. This stage has some of the characteristics of an armistice, with one member possibly exhibiting extreme reluctance.

Once a degree of peace has been achieved all concerned need to take stock of the situation. This process should not be hurried, and the relevant services should concentrate on providing such support and advice as is necessary while at the same time postponing the more irrevocable decisions on such matters as the tenancy of accommodation.

The long-term problems of a woman whose husband cannot or will not change his ways are likely to be serious. She will in effect have to become head of a single-parent family or enter some form of communal living; she will have either to work to support herself or live on supplementary benefit; she may need to find another home (possibly in a different part of the country); if she moves to another area she and her children may have difficulty in adapting to new customs and making friends; if she is not utterly fed up with men she will come to want male company if only because our social institutions tend to assume that men and women are linked in couples, and very few women have had much experience of living on their own.

Finally the difficult decisions have to be taken—whether to separate permanently or return, and on what basis. This may involve legal and administrative decisions with, no doubt, some bureaucratic delay.

The identification of battered women

Before considering specific services two important general points should be made. First, whereas several official agencies include dealing with abused children as a prime responsibility this can hardly be said in respect of battered women. Recent discussion, therefore, has been much concerned with the application, and sometimes adaptation, of existing services to cover what may appear to be rather exceptional needs. Second, babies and small children are obviously dependent and need adults to protect them from abuse; battered women, on the other hand, are likely to be above the age of majority (18 in Britain) and, however intimidated in practice, will have the legal status of adults. Inevitably these facts, with, perhaps, a lack of consensus on the social importance of wife battering, have led to a non-interventionist attitude on the part of almost all official agencies. The onus is on the woman to ask for help and, in the process, identify herself as being abused by the man with whom she lives.

At first sight any woman ought to know whether she is being battered and the problems of knowing how injuries occurred that so tax those investigating child abuse are non-existent. Obviously a woman knows if she is being assaulted physically or mentally but there is abundant evidence that she may find it difficult to determine the abnormality or unreasonableness of what is being done. Many are ashamed to admit their suffering, or feel unable to act for fear of the consequences to themselves, their children, and possibly their relatives. The crucial fact is that for a woman to identify herself as battered involves her in taking decisive action which cannot later be concealed; hence the vital need to secure her safety when she takes her decision.

The role of the police

Paradoxically the role of the police in relation to battered women could almost be described as the mirror-image of that relating to abused children. With children their complaint is that they tend to be excluded but, with some exceptions, battered women complain of police unwillingness to intervene.

Considering all the available evidence it seems that police practice is likely to be the resultant of some four or five main influences, the balance of which will differ from area to area.

The first practical difficulty which policemen are likely to quote is the ambivalence of those involved in the domestic dispute. This may take the form of the quarrelling couple uniting to turn on the policeman or, more likely, of the wife withdrawing, on the day after, any complaint she made at the time of the incident. Although the complaint may be withdrawn because of the woman's feeling of vulnerability the resulting situation is bound to be an embarrassment to the police officer, particularly if he has charged the man, as later withdrawal has to be justified, probably to the Director of Public Prosecutions. A few experiences of this kind will be enough to make patrol officers wary of intervening any more than they can help, and this caution is no doubt reinforced by police folklore relating to such incidents. It is, perhaps, illustrated by a senior policewoman's comment to the Select Committee

> I think quite often … the husband gets round the wife, deliberately does a reconciliation, if only a temporary one. A lot of these men are very crafty, and these poor gullible women fall for it! (SC 1975, Evid.Q.1560)

Underlying this, however, is a more general belief in the value of the family and, maybe, a realistic view of the alternatives:

> We are, after all, dealing with persons 'bound in marriage', and it is important, for a host of reasons to maintain the unity of the spouses. Precipitated action by the Police could aggravate the position to such an extent as to create a worse situation than the one they were summoned to deal with. The 'lesser of two evils' principle is often a good guideline in these situations. (SC 1975, Evid.p.366)

Although the 'unity of spouses' may leave much to be desired, and although 'bound in marriage' has a custodial ring to it, the values implied are clear enough. Given the widespread acceptance of marriage as a social institution it would be unreasonable to expect the police to take a different view unless given a clear lead in a situation where some improved alternative for the wife might exist.

Several events of recent years point the way to such changes. Even before the Select Committee reported some provincial police forces had quite firm policies. For example, in Manchester, over a 12-month period in 1975–1975.

> 192 husbands have been charged with wife assault. Of these 160 were committed within the matrimonial home. So the evidence was there and the police took action. I feel the way in my force is the best way, arrest, in custody, and before the court next morning. (SC 1975, Evid.Q.1562)

In its report the Select Committee recommended that 'Chief Constables should review their policies about the police approach to domestic violence' and there is now some evidence of the results that can follow from doing this. The Chief Constable of Bedfordshire, a county with a population of 494 000, monitored the results of adopting the recommendation that

> where there is evidence of any injury the police should be ready to arrest the man there and then, subsequently to charge him and either keep him in custody until his appearance in court or, should this not be feasible, escort the woman and children to a Women's Aid refuge or other safe place. (SC 1975, p.xvii)

During a 6-month period, 288 acts of violence in the home came to the notice of the police. In 36% of these cases 'complaints were substantiated, arrests made and proceedings commenced'. It is significant that under this procedure, once charges had been preferred only one in six complainants withdrew their complaints before the date set for the court hearing, a fact which may serve as a comment on the supposed unreliability of women in these circumstances. Indeed the chief constable was led to end his report on the experiment with the question,

> Does the substantiated 36·1% of the total reports of violence indicate that the former low-profile policy of the police and their reluctance to arrest was misplaced? (Bedfordshire Police, 1976)

The other factor which might change police attitudes, and appears to have done so at Chiswick, is an increasing recognition of the seriousness of the criminality of the assaults by some men. There seems to be practically no limit to the degrading behaviour that some will indulge in, while the really obsessional may pursue their wives relentlessly. There was even a case of a man using his car to ram a hostel for battered wives—he 'clambered from his wrecked car shouting, "I'll smash the place down". Police were called ... ' (*Guardian*, 22 April 1976).

Until May 1977 a further difficulty was the fact that, unless the police felt that an assault was so serious as to require prosecution, it was easy for them to minimize their involvement by saying that it was a civil matter and that the wife should seek the protection of an injunction. This would have to be enforced by officials of the court rather than by the police. This blurring of responsibility led, at its worst, to some very unsatisfactory situations such as those described by the Lambeth Community Law Centre in its *Annual Report* for 1976.

> In the case of assaults by husbands on their wives, where actual bodily harm or even grievous bodily harm has resulted the police almost invariably have refused to take any action saying 'It is a domestic matter and we cannot interfere.' In some cases they will take the woman concerned to the nearest hospital or to relatives or friends.
>
> The police seem to be remarkably ill-informed about the rights and remedies available to battered women in this situation, and in some cases gave advice which frankly we consider wrong.

Much of the ambiguity of the police position should, however, be removed by recent, and also promised, legislation. The Domestic Violence and Matrimonial Proceedings Act 1976 not only enables a county court judge to issue injunctions but also to attach a power of arrest so that in certain cases a constable may arrest without a warrant if he has 'reasonable cause for suspecting' a person to be in breach of the conditions of an injunction.

It would be unrealistic to expect established police attitudes to change very rapidly, but it seems likely that the balance could shift towards a more interventionist policy as a result of the lead given by the Select Committee and by the passing of the 1976 Act. It will be necessary to devise efficient procedures for informing the police of the existence of injunctions and, in due course, orders issued by magistrates, but the president of the Family Division of the High Court did not think there need be any difficulty about this (SC 1975, Evid.Q.1814). Police training will, therefore, have to be revised to take these changes into account; if at the same time other chief constables follow Bedfordshire in implementing the Select Committee's recommendations the formal position should alter significantly. Changes in attitudes will take longer, and may depend on factors outside the police, such as the success of the refuge movement and the effectiveness of the follow-up action.

The role of the medical profession

Very little of the evidence to the Select Committee was from a medical point of view, and the problem of wife battering has simply not been seen as a medical issue. Clearly, specific injuries have been treated, and many of Dr Gayford's sample of women had sought help from their general practitioners, but the orthodox practice of medicine seems to have had little more to offer barring some relief of the patient's anxiety. This is not surprising, for how can a problem be tackled by treating only the victim? The question of influencing the behaviour of wife batterers has largely gone by default, principally because neither researchers nor clinicians seem to have been able to study the men concerned. In the long run this must be important because if these men are to live with women at all they need to learn how to do so more peacefully, but this may be an educational rather than a medical problem. In the short run perhaps the most valuable medical contribution would be greater alertness to the possibility of injuries being caused by battering, and a consequential readiness to inquire into what has happened and refer the woman to the appropriate source of help.

The role of the legal system

The legal system has two distinct functions to perform in relation to battered women. It must ensure their safety, and ultimately it must decide, or at least confirm, whatever long-term arrangements are made concerning marriage, parental responsibilities, and property. Its effectiveness in doing so turns, above all, on ready access to good legal advice. This is not to say that all the problems can be solved by the effective use of the legal measures that are available, but the law provides a framework within which solutions to the human problems can be attempted; without some recourse to the law the victim is likely to go on suffering, with it her position should be improvable to some degree.

This section will concern itself primarily with procedure, rather than with the content of family law, partly because this is a period of changes (the results of which are still uncertain) and partly because the burden of evidence to the Select Committee was that the crucial problems concerned access to law and the effectiveness of its implementation. There is no dispute that in England and Wales the criminal law relating to assault is adequate and can be applied to domestic disputes given the will to do so (in Scots law the position is different because of the requirements of corroboration). Likewise the Domestic Violence and Matrimonial Proceedings Act 1976 and the proposals of the Law Commission on Matrimonial Proceedings in Magistrates' Courts which the Government has accepted (Hansard, Written Answers to Questions, 16 November 1976) should meet many of the criticisms prevalent when the Select Committee was set up, and it would be premature to comment in detail.

The first major problem for a battered women is to realize that the law may provide a way out of her difficulties and to summon up the will to embark on such a course of action. The Lord Chancellor's Office is certainly aware of the problem; one of his staff told the Select Committee,

> the problem is much more serious ... many battered wives would not know they ought to go to a solicitor. That is the real problem as the Lord Chancellor sees it. (SC 1975, Evid.Q.1646)

> The Lord Chancellor is anxious to help through citizens' advice bureaux which exist all over the country. We are in the process of setting up an arrangement whereby citizens' advice bureaux liaise with the courts so they have access to a solicitor either on a rota system or because they have their own honorary legal adviser who can start things off. The citizens' advice bureau has the number of the court and can start in that way; anything to start these people in the system; the system works once they can get into it. (SC 1975, Evid.Q.1647)

Getting into the system, for women who may be unsophisticated and are likely to be demoralized, is not easy. Psychologically it is an irrevocable step; a private problem has been brought formally into the open, an act that cannot later be undone. It involves the woman in defining herself (not only individually, but probably as a mother) as having been sufficiently maltreated to take the public action of labelling herself as a victim. She may well seek legal help in a rather timid manner, possibly never having dealt with a lawyer before.

Clearly a good and sympathetic solicitor can provide the necessary legal services, but the situation is one which demands a blend of swift action and wise counselling over a longer period. No doubt informal arrangements can be made locally between lawyers and other organizations giving support, but in larger urban areas law centres may have an advantage. As the Lambeth Community Law Centre put it

> The Law Centre because of its wider experience of the problems faced by battered women and its ability to act outside the financial constraints of private practice, can provide not only a legal service but also personal support .... In addition, with the exception of a few private firms who have the experience and the ability to deal with battered women many solicitors in private practice not only do not have the time to explain the unwieldy and confusing court procedure but [are] often [unable] to recognise a real emergency. Many women are deterred by formality and lack of understanding and often are left unaware of alternatives open to them if they do not wish to return home. (Lambeth Community Law Centre, 1976)

The second problem for a battered woman is to secure her own protection from further violence until a longer-term course of action has been decided. The formal procedure for achieving this is to obtain a court order forbidding her husband to assault her, and possibly also excluding him from the matrimonial home. Concise accounts of the procedure and its problems prior to the coming into effect of the Domestic Violence and Matrimonial Proceedings Act 1976 are given in Raisbeck (1976) and Gill and Coote (1975). Following the 1976 Act the process should be significantly easier, and, if the

Law Commission's proposals are enacted as promised magistrates' courts will be able to make 'personal protection orders' and/or 'exclusion orders' (Law Commission, 1976). Both the actual and the proposed changes will have the effect of localizing the making of injunctions or orders, thus increasing the accessibility of such legal remedies.

There is no guarantee that a court order will be obeyed. The Select Committee was given graphic accounts of breaches of injunctions and, in the last resort, all a court order is doing is to put a price on the repetition of violence. For the breach of an injunction this price is usually a period of imprisonment for contempt of court until the court is satisfied the contempt has been purged. The period in prison may have a calming effect, but it might lead to increased enmity on the husband's part and so be counter-productive. It is, moreover, the wife who has to make the application for her husband to be committed to prison, and this she may be reluctant to do either out of fear or compassion. If he goes she will have to face him saying that she sent him there; if he loses his job because of it she will not only be blamed but may lose financially as well. It is not easy for a threatened woman to take such a stand. However, under the 1976 Act, the decision may be taken out of her hands for a constable may arrest for breach if the injunction has had a power of arrest attached to it. Such a power can only be attached, however, if the judge is satisfied that the victim has already suffered actual bodily harm, so that the woman (or her child) has to take at least one assault before being given what should be extra protection. In the last resort, as Raisbeck (1976, p.105) says,

> the law ... cannot prevent violence, especially in such an emotional atmosphere as that which obtains in the nuclear family. It can merely provide a legal framework within which interested parties are given power to act.

There does not appear to be any reliable information on the effectiveness of the various measures available to the courts. Up to 1976 injunctions have been difficult to enforce (Lambeth Community Law Centre, 1976) and even the Bedfordshire survey of men prosecuted for domestic violence did not give any follow-up information for the period after sentence. It did, however, indicate the sentences or orders imposed by the magistrates and these are of interest. A total of 79 cases were dealt with in ways shown in Table 9.1. It is clear that in these magistrates' courts domestic-violence cases tended to be handled on a conditional basis, presumably on the assumption that the couples concerned would be more likely to sort out their own affairs under the mild constraint provided by the court. This might well be so and, if it worked, would be a satisfactory outcome. However, these are not constructive measures and it is surprising that the help of the probation service was so little used.

Only about a quarter were given punitive sentences. Most of these were

Table 9.1 Sentences or orders imposed on Bedfordshire men prosecuted for domestic violence

Punitive sentences: immediate imprisonment	4%
fines	22%
Probation	6%
Conditional disposals with/without other penalties (Suspended imprisonment, conditional discharges, binding over to keep the peace, etc.)	52%
Other	16%
	100%

fines, which might bear as heavily on the wife as on the husband. Altogether the rationale of the punitive sentences is obscure, although it should be said that the Glasgow courts seem to have been far more punitive (SC 1975, Evid.p.294).

The crucial test of all these policies would be whether they worked, but on this we have no information. Obviously it is needed, and it should also be remembered that mere lack of violence tells little about the quality of family life. Clearly there is a need for research follow-up in order to establish what measures are most effective.

It is also worth referring to two other points which were mentioned before the Select Committee. One is the desirability of establishing a system of family courts which would handle all matrimonial matters and questions of the custody of children as advocated by the Finer Committee (Finer, 1974). If this were done it would presumably be possible to achieve greater continuity in the handling of cases, and also more expertise on the part of judges; by expertise is meant, not merely knowledge of the law, but also of the circumstances in which family problems come before the courts. Particularly if adequately backed by social workers such a court would almost certainly develop into a more positive and constructive agency than the present disparate set-up with its fluctuating membership.

Finally it is worth noting that the eligibility of battered wives to receive compensation from the Criminal Injuries Compensation Board is being reconsidered. So far they have been regarded as ineligible, but a consultative document has been circulated by the Home Office: the outcome of these consultations was not referred to in the Government's observations on the report of the Select Committee (DHSS *et al.*, 1976).

Local authority services

Local authority services are likely to vary greatly in what they provide for relatively small groups who combine the disadvantages of presenting difficult problems and of rousing ambivalent feelings in many people. Battered women clearly fall into this category, and the Select Committee commented on the discrepancies between local authorities in their relationships with

Women's Aid groups, some of which 'left much to be desired' (SC 1975, §27). It is an area of activity where a little local initiative can easily tip the scales and much will depend on the attitudes of senior officials and the chairmen of the relevant committees.

Potentially, local authorities might help battered women by providing social work, by supporting refuges, by being co-operative over housing, and by providing day care for children so that their mothers can go out to work.

It was notable that no witnesses had much that was positive to say about social work as such in this context. At best social workers might introduce women to refuges or other advisory services, but it did not seem that they could do much more than this. The question is explored more fully in a later chapter; here it is sufficient to say that to social workers the likely combination of having to face an unco-operative and intractable man, to protect the children, and to explore the whole situation carefully must present severe difficulties. Set against these are the needs of other clients probably easier to help. In such a setting to pass a woman and her children on to a refuge with its supporting women's aid organization may well be the most effective form of social work available.

The largest single source of funding for voluntary organizations to establish and operate refuges appears to have been the Urban Programme administered by the Home Office. However, under this scheme organizations are still dependent on the local authorities, first, to apply for funds on their behalf, and, second, to provide 25% of the total cost if the application is successful. Their support is crucial. By late 1976 this had been given by 35 of the local authorities in England and Wales (DHSS *et al.*, 1976, p.30). It is, however, also possible to support refuges under housing and/or public health legislation, or by private funds; in fact about 60% of refuges were supported by these means rather than by the Urban Programme, but details have not been publicly stated.

The most difficult problem both for battered women and for the local authorities concerns housing in both its short- and long-term aspects. The Select Committee received evidence of widely varying practices, and this has since been confirmed by a survey, *Violence in Marriage*, undertaken by Shelter Housing Aid Centre (SHAC, 1976). This was based on the histories of 57 women in London who went to the centre for help during 1974–1975. The most important findings were: first, that women found it difficult to get comprehensive advice and tended to be passed from one agency to another; second, that 'not one single wife whose matrimonial home had been a council tenancy remained there', and no fewer than 31 out of 37 were refused help by the local housing authority; third, that wives in owner-occupied property seemed far more likely to be able to remain in the matrimonial home.

In fairness to the local authorities it should be said that SHAC may have dealt with extreme cases; others may have been successfully housed. The Select Committee received quite a lot of evidence that when all other issues had been resolved council-house tenancies would probably be assigned to whichever parent had care of the children after a divorce, but in the meantime there were enormous variations in practice. Some witnesses advocated a general policy that council-house tenancies should be held jointly by husband and wife, but it was by no means certain that this would solve the interim problem while other disputed issues were being settled. It might be that an injunction to exclude the husband from the home would be a successful temporary way of securing the wife's position, always provided she could afford the rent, or get it from social security. A number of authorities, however, made offers to allow wives to take over tenancies on condition they paid off rent arrears run up by their husbands. It does not seem that the ostensible helpfulness of such transfers was adequately matched by an understanding of the precariousness of the wife's position.

Perhaps most difficult of all is the position of women who feel they have to leave privately-owned or rented accommodation. Despite central government policy their claims for housing are likely to seem very weak to a local authority when compared with those on waiting lists already. Particularly bad will be the plight of women married to the obsessional husbands described by Dr Gayford in his chapter of this book; their only hope is to leave their home area and settle elsewhere. A series of moves may well be arranged through refuges, but to get somewhere more permanent after this may be very difficult.

The government's position has been made clear in the departmental *Observations on the Report from the Select Committee on Violence in Marriage* (DHSS *et al.*, 1976). In the long term the Government will

> place the statutory responsibility for accommodation for the homeless in England and Wales on housing authorities .... (§48)

This allocation of responsibility was urged on local authorities in a joint circular on 'Homelessness' by the DHSS and the Department of the Environment in February 1974 (DOE 18/74), and it included a paragraph on problems arising from the break-up of family relationships (Minutes of Evidence, p.178). Unfortunately the paragraph merely lamented the difficulties of such situations and ended on a note of bureaucratic helplessness—'Such cases call for the closest co-operation between housing and social services authorities or departments.' Faced with such guidance it is not surprising that local authorities continued in the diversity of their existing ways and that no note of urgency was heard until the Select Committee began its work and the departments had to begin to justify their activities. All too often women who, in desperation, left their husbands and homes were simply regarded as not being homeless because they left voluntarily rather than being evicted. It is only too easy to see how the battered wife might meet, and feel forced to accept, the assertion from the clerk across the counter to the effect that, 'Well, you've *really* got a house, we can't help you when others have been waiting for years and haven't got anywhere at all .... '

Although it is now said that

> it is the Government's view that when a woman and her children leave the marital home the family should not be pressed to return but should, unless they can find alternative accommodation, be treated as a homeless family and given priority for housing (DHSS *et al.*, 1976,§49)

it is not clear how this view has been put across, and at most it only amounts to advice. It is advice, too, which may go against the grain of what housing authorities believe to be right, as one DHSS official put it to the Select Committee,

> Where the whole tenor of housing policy has been to distribute council tenancies as fairly as possible to people who have been on the waiting list or displaced by redevelopment, the idea of a new category in prime need of accommodation is one that needs a great deal of discussion ... it is a long job to plan a successful change-over, and it has not taken place in all areas. (SC 1975, Evid.Q.599)

Generally speaking the council-house system, as at present administered, presents several obstacles to the battered wife. If she wants to stay in the family home she may have difficulty in being granted the tenancy, while if she leaves she may have serious problems in finding short-term accommodation—councils may have nothing to offer and private rented accommodation is particularly inaccessible to a woman with young children and little money. Once in the queue for permanent council housing she may find that the usual type of 'points' system for housing allocation puts her at a disadvantage. This will be all the more acute if she is so terrified of her husband that she feels she has to settle in a different area where she will have no credit for length of time on the waiting list. Even late in 1976 the Lambeth Community Law Centre was commenting that.

> It is the experience of the Law Centre and the Women's Aid Centres, ... that even if the husband has been excluded from the matrimonial home by the court ... the women are justifiably afraid to return since the husband knows the address. In that situation the Housing Department seem to take an unnecessarily long time sometimes as much as ten months, or even years, to arrange for a transfer. (Lambeth Community Law Centre, 1976)

None of these difficulties is insuperable, but their solution demands some administrative imagination, flexibility and, above all, a willingness to regard the problem as serious enough to merit sympathetic attention. This requirement may be the hardest to satisfy, and it may have led a somewhat frustrated Minister of Housing and Construction to lament to the Select Committee that

> What I regret ... is not so much ... disputation on policy but the fact that some local authorities have not paid sufficient attention to the need to consider this situation at all. In the administrative delays which you can get in making these kinds of decision the family can suffer unnecessarily if psychologically and administratively a local authority is not geared to handling this kind of problem. (SC 1975, Evid.Q.833)

It is not possible to say much on the extent to which battered women are able to secure day-care facilities for their children. If a woman on her own is trying to support herself and her children by working then it is very likely that this will only be possible if day care can be arranged for any children of pre-school age. The adequacy of provision varies greatly from area to area and there is no means of knowing how many battered women who would like to use them are unable to do so for lack of facilities. Nevertheless the point of principle must be made that if battered women are to become economically independent, for many of them this will only be possible if the problems of the day care of small children can be solved.

Central government services

In England and Wales the only central government department which might provide direct services for individual battered women is the Supplementary Benefits Commission (SBC) which pays cash benefits on a means-tested basis to anyone whose income is low enough to qualify. Its benefits tend to be known colloquially as 'social security' or 'the dole'. The SBC came under relatively slight criticism in the evidence to the Select Committee, mainly centring on the handling of individuals at 'counter-level'. As one social worker delicately put it

> When a woman is seeking finance or housing assistance she has first to get through the system and it is not always the case that official policy is satisfactorily implemented at 'counter level'. I think this is a problem we must look at very carefully—to ensure that policies are implemented at very simple levels. (SC 1975, Evid.Q.1456)

Since the Select Committee reported, the SBC's instructions to its staff have been revised to stress the need to 'treat a battered woman no less considerately and helpfully than other claimants whatever the circumstances of their claim' (DHSS *et al.*, 1976, §57). It is not known what effects this instruction has had. The procedure itself is set out in Appendix 6 to the *Observations* (DHSS *et al.*, 1976) and the main potential source of difficulty would seem to be the possibility that the SBC might seek to enforce the husband's maintenance obligations. 'Reasonable' offers from husbands are said to be acceptable, but otherwise the commission might itself take proceedings or try to persuade the wife to do so. There are obvious possibilities that women might be put under some pressure by individual SBC staff, but the official policy is that

> There is no question of benefit being withheld as a constraint to force a woman to return to her husband or it being paid conditional on her willingness to institute proceedings for maintenance against him. (DHSS *et al.*, 1976,p.32)

Apart from help given to individuals by the SBC most central government action is indirect, being intended either to influence local policy (as in housing) or to help groups (such as Women's Aid groups seeking to establish refuges) via local authorities. Hence the only direct assistance given by the DHSS has been to the National Women's Aid Federation to support its central office (£25 000 a year, plus a small capital grant), and a temporary series of grants to Chiswick Women's Aid currently scheduled to end in July 1977. Similar, but even more modest assistance has been given in Scotland by the Scottish Education Department (DHSS *et al.*, 1976, §59–60).

Under its Urban Programme the Home Office has given significant support to the creation of refuges and other services. The complete list of projects is given in Appendix 5 to the *Observations*, but in 1976 expenditure was 'expected to amount to over £420 000 with central government contributing 75% and local authorities 25% of the cost'. Other help was being given, to a total of nearly £200 000 a year, through the Job Creation Programme of the Manpower Services Commission. The Urban Programme figures include both capital and non-capital costs. It is difficult to know whether further capital grants will be made, but up to and including 1976 they totalled £296 000 spread over 21 projects in England and Wales, an average of about £14 000 each, though the range was wide. Non-capital grants are usually made on a 5-yearly basis, so that the total of £185 000 per year would probably add up to more than £900 000 over 5 years. The amounts ranged from a few hundred pounds to nearly £14 000 per year: six projects were receiving £10 000 or more, and the mean was £5600.

While these are not, by the standard of government expenditure, large amounts they may make all the difference to the organizations concerned and are likely to be highly cost-effective. In a period of increasing stringency the central departments (and the co-operating local authorities) deserve considerable credit for their contribution, even if it was partially in response to the pressure created by the existence and work of the Select Committee. As a response it was positive and fairly quick. Apart from itemizing the grants mentioned above it is impossible to be precise about the adequacy of what has been done. It is clear that in this respect local government has been truly independent, with the result that attitudes have ranged from highly co-operative to unhelpful. The Urban Programme could only help where local authority support already existed; if it did not, then central funds could not normally be made available.

Judging from the evidence to the Select Committee the DHSS developed a fairly positive attitude, the Home Office was helpful through the Urban Programme but less so in other respects, the SBC maintained it was helpful all along and the Lord Chancellor's Office and the judiciary made some positive suggestions. Difficulties seem to have been greatest in some local areas which proved unsympathetic and unresponsive to the persuasion of the central departments. Unfortunately this in turn has affected the more helpful areas which have had to bear more than their fair share of the costs involved.

The role of voluntary organizations

Voluntary organizations have played a vital part in the development of services to assist battered women. Indeed, had they not done so the Select Committee might not have been set up, and the developments it has stimulated might not have taken place. Battered women appear to constitute quite a small section of the population and this, coupled with the complexity of their problems, made it unlikely that local authorities would be keen to initiate services for them. Women's experience, therefore, tended to be that

> their treatment by statutory bodies is very, very limited ... largely because the statutory authorities have not had the resources to offer ... in the form of practical alternatives to going back home. (SC 1975, Evid.Q.1096)

In such a situation any major initiative would have to be taken by a private body.

There was no shortage of organizations able to offer advice. There is a national network of Citizens' Advice Bueeaux, the Samaritans also cover most of the country as does the National Marriage Guidance Council. Other organizations may be strong in particular localities. The statutory Probation and After Care Service also has a long tradition of matrimonial conciliation work and its officers are attached to every magistrates' and Crown court in the country with some liaison work in the divorce court but, judging from the Home Office evidence to the Select Committee (pp.410–411), this is becoming a less significant feature of the service's work.

To operate effectively advice-giving bodies depend on there being at least a degree of consensus between the people being advised. Marital violence, however, is likely to happen in a situation which has more of the characteristics of a battle for power, and the stronger person may be seeking surrender rather than agreement. If so it will probably be the weaker party who seeks advice, and the stronger in one way or another will simply not see it as in their interest to co-operate. This is particularly likely when people feel their rights have been denied, and their pride and sense of adequacy are threatened. It is not surprising that in predominantly one-sided situations advice-giving has its limitations and that, in consequence, while such bodies may be consulted by many women they lack the resources to intervene effectively once the violence has exceeded a rather trivial level.

When, therefore, in the early 1970s Mrs Pizzey (1974) began to publicize the problems of 'battered women' and to indicate that a refuge was available she was making the first genuine innovation that might radically change their prospects. In the face of previously unmet need Chiswick Women's Aid was almost overwhelmed and its saga of overcrowding, moves, and conflict with public authorities began. The phenomenal development of the refuge movement is described elsewhere in this book by Dennis Marsden and Joy Melville; here we shall only consider the broader issues of policy which seem likely to confront the movement.

The first is the question of adequacy of the present network of refuges. So far, refuges have tended to suffer from overcrowding and, in view of their uncomfortable conditions, this would suggest there is still some unmet need in the form of women who would go to them if more places were available. How far this has been a matter of a 'backlog' of pent-up need, and how far the number of women will be added to by each generation remains to be seen. In the mid-1970s there were clearly sufficient battered women to justify the existence of a hundred refuges. This is in a country with an estimated population of 9 million married women between the ages of 20 and 54, an average of roughly one per 90 000 in these age groups (OPCS, 1972). This was still a very much lower level of provision than that recommended by the Select Committee—one family place per 10 000 of the population—but that recommendation depended on very tentative assumptions both about the incidence of battering and the extent to which the victims would resort to refuges. At present, however, the discrepancy between the recommendation and the actual provision—by a factor of at least three, assuming refuges accommodate an average of ten families—is so great that further growth would still seem possible in present conditions. What is uncertain is what changes may occur in the fairly near future.

There are quite strong grounds for thinking the future will be different. Paradoxically they stem from the very success of the Women's Aid movement. It would be surprising if the recent and projected changes in the law, coupled perhaps with changes in police attitudes, did not have some deterrent effects, while the broader influences of the women's movement and the publicity given to battered wives may lead to more general changes in social attitudes to marriage and family life. Such developments would tend to reduce the need for refuges as such, though the supportive and counselling role of women's groups might become more important. On the other hand if these same changes lead more women to question the state of their own marriage their tolerance of violence may be reduced, thus leading to more reporting of abuse. At this stage it is impossible to gauge what the net effect will be.

The second major point is that the establishment of enough refuges is not an end in itself. It is an important means for securing the safety of women threatened with injury in their relationships with men, but what it provides is essentially first aid. The women who use refuges still have as their major problems how to live, in the long run, either with or without their husbands. At the moment there is virtually no systematic knowledge of what happens to women after they leave refuges, and yet this must be crucial in deciding what policies to adopt. We need to know how women who return to their husbands fare; whether there is an uneasy and sullen truce, whether violence starts again after a while, or whether the shock has made the husband appreciate his wife rather more than he did? Could any counselling be attempted and, if so, did it help? Conversely, if there is a final separation what price do the wife and her children have to pay in the form of difficulties and reduced standard of living; who gives help and what is most effective; how does she cope with her shattered morale and problems of identity as a woman? Such questions badly need to be answered if all the care and energy put into the provision of refuges is to lead to something which, in the end, is more constructive.

To indicate a need for further research is almost a ritual activity among academics, but in this case the justification is unusually strong. It is not a matter of further, but of basic research; research, too, which may well have a direct effect on the lives of several thousand unhappy women and children, and maybe unhapp y men as well. Whether or not such research could be done by the women's movement, it could certainly only be done with their support.

The third point is the need to do something about the most difficult problem of all, the men. Very little is known about the careers of battering men and they are a daunting subject for research because they may be aggressive, evasive or both.

Nevertheless the need to tackle their problems effectively, and not just deter them, should not be overlooked in the heart of concern about injunctions and law enforcement. There is great scope for experiment, and Women's Aid has been responsible for the opening of one centre for violent men (reported on briefly in chapter 12); it is to be hoped that more will be attempted. Anything of this kind is likely to present problems because of the difficulty of getting men to co-operate. They may be less put off by voluntary agencies but, on the other hand, an obvious possibility would be to use the experience and skills of the probation service—present use is minimal. In such situations, after all, only the courts have any powers, and it is not clear why they should be reluctant to use them if they regard battering as a serious matter.

To get battering taken seriously is a task already undertaken with some success by Women's Aid, but clearly more remains to be done, particularly in regions of the country, such as the North East and in Scotland, where traditional male attitudes appear to be strong (Select Committee, Minutes of Evidence for 5 and 7 May 1975). Much has been due to Mrs Pizzey's flair for publicity, but there is always the danger that repetition will lessen the impact of shock tactics of this kind. It would seem increasingly important to broaden the debate so as to discuss and assert the standards by which violence in marriage should be judged.

Of course battered women are important, but essentially they represent, as it were, a series of test cases of the more important issue of fairness in relations between the sexes. Their problems should lead on to reappraisals of what is appropriate conduct in marriage. This is not necessarily to question the institution of matrimony as such—marriage is probably too widespread for that to be a profitable approach—but there is scope for querying some of the 'rights' to which some marriage partners think they are entitled by virtue of the fact of being married. The emotions of men who batter appear often to be based on the notion that they own their wives and children and have rights over them like any other piece of property. In particular, they seem to feel entitled to particular types of responses from them, irrespective of their own behaviour. A sense of the reciprocal obligations in marriage is absent or warped, and clearly many battered women have little conception of how unreasonably they are being treated.

Several implications follow from this. First, a number of myths should be dispelled. Perhaps the most common is that battered women are really masochists who enjoy it. Undeniably some women may be provocative, but no one who has read of the bizarre and gross violence recounted by Mrs Pizzey, Dr Gayford, and many others can deny that such behaviour is just cruel, and goes far beyond anything that might be enjoyed by a masochist (who would be unlikely to complain in any case). Another myth is that battering is a product of the inability of some working-class couples to communicate any other way. This too does not survive the evidence of non-violent working-class marriages and of violent middle-class ones (English newspaper readers were recently treated to extensive accounts of the sufferings of a rich man's wife who finally killed him with his own shot-gun when in fear of yet another beating; she was acquitted of his murder).

The most important myth is the romanticized view of marriage. The notion that a girl achieves ultimate success in life by marrying is reiterated in fiction and many women's magazines almost every day. Its result may be illustrated by an amusing case of a married 16-year-old girl whose father was fined for failing to send her to school. The case even achieved fame in being the subject of a leading article in *The Times* newspaper—entitled 'Home in time for tea'. Mrs Groves had married a professional footballer and they appeared to share an attitude to woman's social role 'redolent of the Middle Ages', as *The Times* put it. Her husband said

> I don't care whether she knows who won the Battle of Hastings so long as she knows how to cook my tea.

His wife, a sixth-form pupil (i.e. in a high grade) endorsed this view, saying,

> There is no point in my going to school any more. My life is looking after Alan and our home. (*The Times*, 31 December 1976)

Affectionate care as such is not to be despised, but when one considers the evident talents that have been suppressed one may wonder whether, in the long run, either Mr or Mrs Groves have gained as much as they might have done.

The underlying problem is that the view of life given by so much romantic literature, and inadequately countered by education, is a poor guide to the real problems of living. Dr Sidney Brandon, Professor of Psychiatry at Leicester University, and an authority on family violence (Brandon, 1976), aptly summarized it:

> Children are taught about sex, but not about love, about rights but not about responsibilities and about the joys or marriage and parenthood, but not about the strains of living together and the insistent demands of small children. (*Social Services*, 2 May 1977)

Finally it seems important for women to be encouraged to achieve a degree of economic independence so that, if necessary, they are able to support themselves and their children. The wife who contributes to the family income probably stands a better chance of being regarded as a partner and, at the same time, both she and her husband know that she is not totally dependent on him. None of this will be protection against the extreme pathological batterer, but at best it will minimize unreasonable behaviour and at worst it will make escape somewhat easier.

Influencing opinion and attitude in these ways can be done by individuals as much as by voluntary bodies, but the latter may have better access to the media and a better-documented case. In the last resort the point to be got across is, as the Chairman of the Equal Opportunities Commission put it recently—'marriage is not a terminal occupation' (*The Times*, 23 November 1976).

GENERAL CONCLUSIONS

This section will consider some general questions common to services for abused children and for battered women. It will not summarize the more detailed discussions of the previous sections.

The first point concerns the attitudes of neighbours which, at the stage of identifying family violence, can be crucial. The evidence seems to be that when violence occurs in families, particularly of the more serious kinds, the batterer makes efforts to isolate the victim(s) to prevent the knowledge of what is going on from spreading. This applies, of course, to women and older child victims; very young children cannot speak for themselves, so if covering up is attempted it is usually a matter of concocting stories for the benefit of general practitioners or the staff of hospital emergency departments. If a degree of isolation is achieved the battering, particularly of women, may take place over considerable periods, often of many years. Such cultivated isolation itself appears to be an important indicator that something suspicious may be going on—for example, the mother of the lady who killed her violent husband (referred to above) said after the trial,

> we were banned from seeing (her) and even the children ... it will be wonderful getting to know the children when we never could when they were little.

In spite of such attempts at concealment, if there are neighbours it is unlikely they will remain in total ignorance for very long.

Knowing that violence is occurring in a family poses tricky social problems for the neighbours. In England, at least, there is a fairly strong principle that what people do in their own homes is their affair, so that intervention can only be justified in exceptional situations. What is regarded as exceptional is a matter for social definition, and the more uncertain, or even scared, the neighbours may be the more likely they are not to risk intervention. A difficult balance has to be struck between turning a blind eye to a woman or child's danger, and perhaps encouraging, and acting on, gossip. At the moment it seems that, in England, there is a rather greater danger from non-intervention than intervention. A vivid example of the strange interactions that may occur was given recently in the *Guardian*, 17 May 1977:

> there's always someone desperate for help, ostracized in her street because she has a bruised face, she's 'different' and nobody wants to know.
>
> In the case of Jane, a 28 year old former primary schoolteacher with three little daughters, openly vicious behaviour from her town-house estate neighbours was the cause of months of extra unnecessary suffering. Dog shit was lined up along the dividing wire mesh back-garden fence so that her girls might dabble their exploring fingers in it; abusive language was shouted over the front fence with the threat to 'black the other eye for you'; and a newspaper cutting was sellotaped to Jane's dustbin, with the headlines 'Husbands of Battered Wives should go to Prison'.

What a complex of emotions was there. Maybe Jane and her husband were ostracized for committing the grave English offence of embarrassing the neighbours.

The use to be made of neighbours', and even family members', opinions is also particularly perplexing for social workers. They can so easily be accused of acting on rumour, but it is also true that the neighbours are around most of the time and are likely to know what has been going on. Certainly some of the notorious child-abuse cases, particularly that of Maria Colwell, might not have reached the point they did if the apprehensions of neighbours and relatives had been given more attention.

It must be admitted, however, that intervention by one private citizen in the affairs of another is by no means easy. Probably the only things which will make much difference will be rather broad changes in public attitudes to marital violence and, indeed, to notions of privacy. The notion that each nuclear family should have a home of its own is admirable in many respects, but if in the process neighbourliness declines then the isolation and defencelessness of those within it may be increased. In the short run perhaps the only change that might make a difference would be a greater awareness on the part of social workers that if neighbours do voice suspicions then they should be taken rather seriously.

The second main point is simple but important. It is that, to a remarkable degree, the victims of family violence present problems that cross the traditional boundaries between professions providing services. The police, lawyers, the courts, medical practitioners—both general and specialist—even social workers, all reach the limits of their own competence and, to be effective, must call on the help of others. Co-ordination and co-operation is much more than a matter of case conferences, it is a question of seeing the task as a whole, and of understanding how it must be shared. Any one profession, by itself, is probably incompetent, in the sense of being unable to solve the total problem. Professional pride, rather than being harboured for defensive purposes, should be displayed in ability to co-operate fruitfully with others. It is the co-operative relationships that should be seen as natural.

How is effective co-operation to be achieved? The answer to this question depends both on achieving a better understanding of what is effective, and on getting this across systematically during professional training. Earlier parts of this chapter have referred to the astonishing ignorance of the results of attempting to help in cases of family violence. This is true not only in the long term, which might be understandable, but even in the short run. There is limited evidence about the fate of battered children, but virtually none about battered women. Is it, therefore, surprising that each profession tends to be concerned only with its little bit of the action? What is lacking is a standard by which the contribution of each service can be judged. Such a standard can only be supplied by a clear statement of long- and short-term aims, and by carefully compiled evidence of what has actually been achieved. There would seem to be no reason whatsoever for the techniques of evaluation developed in other areas—ranging from the evaluation of penal measures to medical audits—not to be applied to the handling of family violence.

Research evaluation is bound to take time; meanwhile something can still be done about the training, including post-experience training of the relevant professions. The message to be got across is very simple. It is that these problems are too complex to be solved by any one profession acting alone, and that solutions in terms of a single discipline are not sufficient. The acid test is the long-term welfare of the victim, and the contribution of each service should be assessed in this light. The question Mr Owtram applied to the police in respect of children (see above, p. 210) should surely be generalized and extended:

> at all times all professionals should be encouraged to review the consequences of their actions ... was it really protective and constructive towards the woman/child to do this?

There is probably no cause to question the ethics of any of the professions involved so far as they relate to direct contacts with clients, but greater weight should probably be given to the need to regard co-operation with other professions as a part of professional duty. The social workers' code of practice (BASW, 1975) recognizes the need for co-operation, and is thus a step in the right direction, but even this does not seem to embody quite the right spirit of humility, for example

> The social worker has a duty to apprise herself of the limits of professional competence *of other workers* and the legal and administrative frameworks in which they operate in order to work effectively with other professionals on behalf of children at risk. (my italics).

In itself this is sensible enough, but the spirit that needs to be encouraged, in *all* professions, is one that recognizes the inevitable limits of their own competence.

Such an attitude is not easy to learn, and it is understandable that professional training concerned with developing expertise underplays its limitations, but it is vital nevertheless. The inquiries which have followed the tragedies that have taken place have had the merit of showing that no service is perfect, and that human error can always occur. It is important that these lessons should be learned and professional practice improved accordingly. It is natural for the professional associations to want to protect their members in these circumstances, and natural justice demands that they should be properly heard, but the argument that public inquiries should not be held, or that the reports of private ones should not be published, is one that should be resisted. If deaths or serious injuries occur public confidence is likely to be shaken in any case, and a private inquiry is likely only to increase unease. We should forget neither the cardinal principle that people should not be judges in their own causes nor the probability that hushed-up disasters will rebound on those who would keep them quiet.

It is, however, disquieting to read the comment of Olive Stevenson, head of the Department of Social Policy and Social Work at the University of Keele, on the difficulties of applying these lessons to be learned from the tragedies. As the author of the minority section of the Colwell report in which she argued in support of the social workers concerned, Miss Stevenson cannot be accused of lack of sympathy. In a recent paper, however, she asked,

> 'Why, for example, does accurate recording still not take place? Why are ineffective visits not reported as a matter of concern? Why are case conferences not called? Why are G.P.s "bad attenders at meetings"? Why does simple routine information not get passed on? It is increasingly rare for a child at risk not to be identified; it is what happens (or does not happen) after that that is critical.' There was still the fantasy 'it could not happen to me' bringing together a 'curious mixture of anxiety and curiousness,' revealed in all the reports on non-accidental injury. (*Social Services*, 2 May 1977)

Clearly self-criticism and the capacity to learn from mistakes must be developed in the course of all professional training. Subsequently it must be the task of management not to suppress it, but to add support and develop sufficient *esprit de corps* to cope with the failures that are inevitable in human enterprises.

At a policy-making level the problems of family violence have been handled in ways which might almost have been taken from a textbook on government. In each area a voluntary organization has played a major role in initiating a service and/or conducting experiments. Central government has tried to give guidance (not always clear to the recipients and sometimes contested by them), with some financial support filtered through local authorities. Local authorities, dealing with what to some is very much a marginal concern, have displayed the whole range of responses from careful and constructive planning to the dragging of feet. Given the range of attitudes that must prevail it is also clear that though central government may exhort, its requests unless backed by money tend to lack effective force. Its powers in such matters are of persuasion rather than command.

Finally we can return to the distinction we drew at the beginning of this chapter between provision of services at nominal, procedural, and material levels and, in the light of our discussion, make a rough classification of the help that has been given.

It does not seem as if, so far, work in the legal sphere has been greatly affected. Neither the police nor the courts have had to undertake significant amounts of extra work in respect of children or women, so their contribution should be classed as nominal. However, actual and prospective changes in the law may well change this substantially: the police are likely to have to intervene more often in marital disputes, while they seem to be invited to case conferences about children more often than in the past. It is also clear that the legal profession itself could greatly increase its work in relation to marital violence if access to the law became easier (possibly through law centres and/or a family court if these were to be introduced). No doubt there is a great deal of legal work waiting to be done. Its strong social element, however, may not make it attractive to the profession as a whole.

With notable exceptions much the same can be said of the medical profession. On the whole the medical services have not altered their traditional patterns of work, and to that extent their contribution must be classed as nominal. The few special units, such as the Park Hospital, devoting considerable and specialized resources to the care of abused children and their families clearly represent material provision. Attendance at case conferences would rank as procedural.

The social services departments, being general-purpose organizations, make a contribution that, on published information, cannot easily be classified. The case-conference system seems to make quite large procedural demands and, if the Sussex experience is anything to go by, some extra material provision has been made to cope with the problems of child abuse.

Both central and local government have made some material provision for battered women, though varying greatly from area to area. This has taken the form of supplementary benefit and support for some women's aid organizations through the Urban Programme. There is no real means of judging the adequacy of this aid, except that at present the supply of help does not seem to have equalled demand.

On the whole the deployment of material resources has been small in relation to the scale of the organizations concerned. Apart from social services and their concern for child abuse, which has led to both procedural and material provision, other major services seem to have remained in the nominal category. Major changes will depend on changes in attitudes and legislation, both of which are likely only to follow from increased knowledge and changes in public attitudes to the legitimacy of violence in the family.

ACKNOWLEDGEMENTS

I have attempted to pick the brains of many friends and colleagues in the course of writing this chapter. In the end it is difficult to identify specific suggestions, but all those with whom I have discussed these matters have helped by giving information and allowing me to test ideas. They are too numerous to name, but their interest has been much appreciated. The draft has been read, in whole or part, by Joan Higgins, Sheila Martin, Joy Melville, Jessica Pickard, Rosemary Polack, and Jacquie Roberts. Their comments have been invaluable, but they are not responsible for any errors that remain, or for the opinions which are my own.

BIBLIOGRAPHICAL NOTE

This chapter uses many references to parliamentary papers, press reports, and other contemporary sources. They have been accommodated in the standard system of references in the following way.

(1) Press reports—references are given in the text only, specifying the newspaper and its date.

(2) Articles in newspapers are treated like articles in journals and are listed in the bibliography under the author's name.

(3) Reports and/or minutes of evidence of official or other committees are listed in the bibliography under the name of the chairman, or the title of the committee, or the responsible department, whichever seems most appropriate in each case. A brief citation is given in the text.

(4) Parliamentary papers in due course are assigned volume numbers within the complete set of papers published within a parliamentary session, but this is not done until sometime later. If this information is known the session will be indicated in the reference. However, they also have either House of Commons Paper Numbers (HC ...) or Command Paper Numbers (Cmnd ...) and these are stated in the references below. The position is further complicated by the fact that the chapter draws heavily on the work of, and minutes of evidence received by, two House of Commons Select Committees. Evidence to such committees is often published in daily parts with one HC number. However if the evidence is reprinted with the report later it may be given another HC number which will cover the report *plus* evidence. The references below are to the daily part numbers.

The first Select Committee, which sat during the session 1974–1975 and reported in July 1975 was known as the Select Committee on Violence in Marriage. For the purposes of citation in the text of this chapter references to the report will be abbreviated to SC 1975. References to the minutes of evidence will be abbreviated to SC 1975 Evid. followed by either the page number (for written evidence), e.g. SC 1975, Evid. p.296, or the question number (for oral evidence), e.g. SC 1975, Evid. Q.28.

The second Select Committee, known as the Select Committee on Violence in the Family, was set up on the recommendation of the first and sat during the sessions 1975–1976 and 1976–1977. It reported in May 1977. For purposes of citation it will be abbreviated to SC 1977, with its minutes of evidence treated similarly to the 1975 committee.

REFERENCES

BASW (British Association of Social Workers) (1975) 'Code of practice for social workers dealing with children at risk', *BASW News* (London), 4 September; also reprinted in Select Committee 1977, Evid. pp.233–240.

Bedfordshire Police (1976) *Report on Acts of Domestic Violence Committed in the County Between 1st February and 31st July 1976*, Bedford: Bedfordshire Police.

Beswick, Keith, Lynch, Margaret, and Roberts, Jacqueline (1976) 'Child abuse and general practice', *Brit. Med. J.*, **2**, 800–802.

Birmingham Area Health Authority and City of Birmingham District Council (1976) 'Joint Enquiry arising from the death of Neil Howlett', Birmingham: Birmingham District Council, Social Services Department.

Borland, Marie (ed.) (1976) *Violence in the Family*, Manchester: Manchester University Press; Atlantic Highlands, New Jersey: Humanities Press.

Brandon, Sidney (1976) 'Physical violence in the family: an overview'. In Borland, 1976.

DHSS (Department of Health and Social Security) (1974a) *Report of the Committee of Inquiry into the Care and Supervision Provided in Relation to Maria Colwell*, London: HMSO.

DHSS (Department of Health and Social Security) (1974b) 'Non-accidental injury to children', Circular LASSL(74)13; CMO(74)8, 22 April.

DHSS (Department of Health and Social Security) (1974c) 'Non-accidental injury to children', Circular LASSL(74)27, 6 November.

DHSS (Department of Health and Social Security) (1975a) 'Non-accidental injury to children: model instructions for accident and emergency departments', circular from Chief Medical Officer and Chief Nursing Officer; CMO 6/75, 13 February.

DHSS (Department of Health and Social Security) (1975b) *Report of the Committee of Inquiry into the Provision and Co-ordination of Services to the Family of John George Auckland*, London: HMSO.

DHSS (Department of Health and Social Security) (1976) 'Non-accidental injury to children: area review committees', circulars LASSL(76)2, CMO(76)2; CNO(76)3, February.

DHSS (Department of Health and Social Security), Department of the Environment, Home Office, Scottish Office, and Welsh Office (1976) *Observations on the Report from the Select Committee on Violence in Marriage*, Cmnd6690, London: HMSO.

DHSS (Department of Health and Social Security) and Home Office (1976) 'Non-accidental injury of children: the police and case conferences', joint circular LASSL(76)26, HC(76)50, Home Office circular 179/76; 18 November.

Elston, Elizabeth, Fuller, Jane, and Murch, Mervyn (1975) 'Judicial hearings of undefended divorces', *Modern Law Review*, **38** (6), 609–640.

Essex Area Health Authority and Essex County Council (1974) *Report of the Joint Committee Set Up to Consider Co-Ordination of Services Concerned with Non-Accidental Injury to Children*, Chelmsford: Essex Area Health Authority and Essex County Council.

Finer, The Hon. Sir Morris (Chairman) (1974) *Report of the Committee on One Parent Families*, Cmnd 5629, London: HMSO.

Gibson, Evelyn (1975) *Homicide in England and Wales 1967–71*, Home Office Research Studies, no. 31, London: HMSO.

Gill, Tess, and Coote, Anna (1975) *Battered Woman: How to Use the Law*, London: Cobden Trust. (This has been updated to take more recent changes in the law into account. The new version is: Coote, Anna and Gill, Tess, with Richardson, Jo (1977) *Battered Women and the New Law*, London: National Council for Civil Liberties.)

Hansard (House of Commons) (1976) HC Debates, vol. 919, 16 November 1976, Written Answers to Questions, col. 448–449.

Justice (1975) *Parental Rights and Duties and Custody Suits: Report of a Committee* (chairman: Gerald Godfrey, QC), London: Stevens & Sons.

King, Michael (1975) 'Will a child really benefit from having his own lawyer?', *The Times*, London, 18 July.

Lambeth Community Law Centre (1976) *Annual Report 1976*, London: Lambeth Community Law Centre.

Law Commission (1976) *Report on Matrimonial Proceedings in Magistrates' Courts*, session 1975–1976, HC 637, Law Comm. no.77, London: HMSO.

Light, Richard J. (1973) 'Abused and neglected children in America', *Harvard Educ. Rev.*, 43 (4), 556–598.

London Borough of Lambeth; Inner London Probation and After-care Committee; Lambeth, Southwark and Lewisham Area Health Authority (Teaching) (1974) 'Report of the Joint Committee of Inquiry into Non-Accidental Injury to Children, with particular reference to the case of Lisa Godfrey'.

Martin, F. M., and Murray, Kathleen (1976) *Children's Hearings*, Edinburgh: Scottish Academic Press.

Metropolitan Police (1976) 'Memorandum submitted to the Select Committee on Violence in the Family', SC 1977, Evid. pp.35–43.

NAPO (National Association of Probation Officers) (1976) 'Evidence for submission to the House of Commons Select Committee on Violence in the Family', (mimeographed), 21 June.

National Women's Aid Federation (1975) *Battered Women Need Refuges*, London: National Women's Aid Federation.

Norfolk County Council and Norfolk Area Health Authority (1976) 'Report of the Review Body appointed to enquire into the case of Steven Meurs', Norwich: Norfolk County Council and Norfolk Area Health Authority.

NSPCC (National Society for the Prevention of Cruelty to Children) (1976) *At Risk*, London and Boston: Routledge & Kegan Paul.

OPCS (Office of Population Censuses and Surveys) (1972) *Population Projections No. 2, 1971–2011*, London: HMSO.

Pizzey, Erin (1974) *Scream Quietly or the Neighbours Will Hear*, Harmondsworth: Penguin Books.

Raisbeck, Bert L. (1976) 'The Legal Framework', in Borland, 1976.

Salop County Council (1973) 'Report of Working Party of Social Services Committee. Inquiry into the circumstances surrounding the death of Graham Bagnall and the role of the County Council's Social Services', Shrewsbury: Salop County Council.

Seebohm, F. (Chairman) (1968) Report of the Committee on Local Authority and Allied Personal Social Services, Cmnd 3703, London: HMSO.

Select Committee on Violence in Marriage (1975) *Minutes of Evidence*, session 1974–1975, HC 248 i–xv, London: HMSO.

Select Committee on Violence in Marriage (1975) *Report*, HC 553–i, London: HMSO.

Select Committee on Violence in the Family (1977) *Minutes of Evidence*, session 1975–1976, HC 350; session 1976–1977, HC 67; London: HMSO.

Select Committee on Violence in the Family (1977) *Report*, session 1976–77, HC 329–i, London: HMSO.

SHAC (Shelter Housing Aid Centre) (1976) *Violence in Marriage*, London: SHAC.

Shrewsbury Group Hospital Management Committee (1973) 'Report of a Committee of Enquiry of the Hospital Management Committee into the circumstances leading up to the death of Graham Bagnall insofar as the Hospital Authority were concerned'.

Simon, Frances H. (1971) *Prediction Methods in Criminology*, Home Office Research Studies, no. 7, London: HMSO.

Somerset Area Review Committee for Non-accidental Injury to Children (1977) 'Wayne Brewer: Report of the Review Panel', Taunton: Somerset County Council.

Spencer, John, and Bruce, Nigel (1976) *Face to Face with Families*, Edinburgh: MacDonald Printers Co.

Staffordshire Area Health Authority (1974) 'Report of the Committee of Enquiry set up to enquire into the circumstances surrounding the admission treatment and discharge of Baby David Lee Naseby, deceased, at Burton-on-Trent General Hospital from February to May, 1973', Stafford: Staffordshire Area Health Authority.

White, Franklin, A. (ed.) (1973) 'The Tunbridge Wells study group on non-accidental injury to children: report and resolutions', Spastics Society Medical Education and Information Unit (available from DHSS).

Wootton, Barbara (1959) *Social Science and Social Pathology*, London: George Allen & Unwin.

10

SOCIAL WORK AND CHILD ABUSE: THE REASONS FOR FAILURE AND THE WAY TO SUCCESS

Jacquie Roberts

INTRODUCTION

The social workers' statutory responsibility for children is frightening. They are expected to protect any child whose 'proper development is being avoidably prevented or neglected', whose health is being avoidably impaired or neglected, or who 'is being ill treated' (Section 1 (2), Children and Young Persons Act 1969). For the social worker, therefore, child abuse must include inflicted injuries, physical neglect, and emotional abuse and deprivation. A wide range of tasks is involved, including the immediate protection of the child, crucial decisions about the child's future, and rehabilitation of the abused child, siblings, and parents.

This chapter looks at child abuse from the viewpoint of the majority of social workers in Britain who are employed by local government social services departments. It is they who ultimately hold the statutory responsibility for the protection of abused children.

As each case is different it is not my intention to set out rigid rules and guide-lines. Instead, I intend to discuss those factors associated with child abuse which produce major difficulties for the social workers responsible for the child's protection. I will draw from some of the growing literature concerning child abuse, from the experience of special units such as those of the NSPCC, and especially from the one known best to me, the Park Hospital for Children. This is a children's psychiatric hospital in Oxford where residential assessment and treatment for abused children and their families has been developed since 1964. Over 200 abused children have been known to the hospital.

In recent years there have been a few dramatic failures in child protection in Britain, leading to much publicity. The best-known example was a 7-year-old girl called Maria Colwell who was murdered by her step-father. Another child, Stephen Meurs, died at the age of 1 year 3 months from severe malnutrition. In both cases a social worker and an NSPCC officer had visited the family at home and this led to official inquiries into the provision and co-ordination of services to the families. Social workers and their agencies were severely criticized.

Against this background it is necessary to consider the difficulties faced by social workers concerned with child protection. This will show that it is surprising that the failures have been so few. By learning the pitfalls we may be able to gain a wider understanding of child abuse and develop new ways of working with abused children and their families.

In the first part of the chapter, the reasons for failure will be considered in five main sections. (1) The personal difficulties that child abuse generates in social workers and their colleagues. (2) The complexity of the problem which creates uncertainty for those who are expected to 'treat the families'. (3) The characteristics frequently observed in abusing families which make the social workers' task especially difficult. (4) The problem of co-ordination of several professions. (5) The statutory responsibilities and agency demands which, paradoxically, obstruct rather than facilitate effective social work. The second part of the chapter will show how the difficulties not only explain why social workers could easily fail, but also point to alternative attitudes and approaches in the treatment of child abuse. The wide range of factors associated with child abuse points to the necessity of a shared team approach and a need for greater flexibility in social-work methods and in the use of resources. Finally, a discussion of the complex process that leads to child abuse can be shown to provide clues for prediction and prevention. In the future, child protection services in social work should no longer be 'the ambulance at the bottom of the cliff' (Gelles, 1973).

REASONS FOR FAILURE

(1) Personal attitudes

It is necessary to consider personal attitudes and difficulties first, as they are so fundamental to the rest of the problems discussed in this chapter.

Feelings about inflicted injury to children may be so powerful as to inhibit anyone's approach to the problem. Violence from an adult towards a helpless child rouses aversion and anger. And yet, social workers have to combine their natural reaction with tolerance and understanding of the aggressor. Imagine the hospital social worker's conflict when confronted with the following case.

> An 8-month-old baby girl with head injuries is admitted moribund to the paediatric ward. She is having continuous convulsions; her

life is at stake. It is discovered that the parents delayed at least 24 hours before seeking medical advice. The doctor concludes that the injuries can only have been caused by hard and persistent blows to the head. The parents, meanwhile, express their fear by making loud and angry criticism of the hospital staff; they threaten to take the child away from the ward. The nurses too are angry and cannot bear to talk to the parents. In spite of all this, the social worker is expected to get the parents to talk, assess accurately the social history, and home circumstances and obtain a legal order to keep the child in hospital. He wants to gain and maintain the parents' trust but at the same time he is under pressure to gather evidence to support the diagnosis of child abuse.

A major problem for the social worker is that violence produces fear. It produces fear in witnesses, victims, and perpetrators alike. The social worker is frightened for the child; it could happen again. He is also frightened of the parents' reaction to his suspicions. The child is petrified and very confused that the sometimes loving caretaker turns into an uncontrollable, savage aggressor. The parents, too, are frightened. They fear punishment and blame. Many fear for the child's safety as they love their child and do not want him to die any more than anyone else. One mother has said to me, when describing the incident in which she broke the leg of her 4-month-old baby:

> Don't get me wrong—I loved him—I've always loved him—even when I was being so cruel to him.

When parents are frightened they become defensive, hostile, and unapproachable. If the social worker is also frightened, the parents can sense his fear and not feel safe enough to entrust him with their problems. More than any other social-work problem, child abuse demands considerable personal strength before even approaching the family.

In the reports published by committees of inquiry concerning the deaths of several children, individual social workers have been identified and blamed for not protecting the child. I quote from the report of the Review Body inquiring into the death of Stephen Meurs:

> Mrs F. [social worker] in her commendable efforts to get on terms of understanding with Mrs M. [Stephen's mother] failed to attach sufficient weight to information reaching her from other sources and was too easily persuaded that these were malicious rumours. (Norfolk County Council, 1975)

The massive press coverage given to such cases produces yet another fear for a social worker—'next time it could be me'.

It is therefore not only the actual abuse that rouses painful feelings. The social worker has an awesome responsibility for the child's welfare, observers are ready to critize mistakes, and yet, no one knows exactly how to deal with the problem. The result is often anger and frustration when faced with an abused child for whom there is no simple and obvious solution.

There are different ways of reacting to the feelings generated by child abuse. Some people deny the existence of child abuse. Others find it easier to contemplate the terrible suffering of a battered child if those responsible can be neatly categorized as insane, deprived, or delinquent. Yet, Kempe (1971), the first person to describe the 'battered baby syndrome', noticed that

> a great number of parents do not fit the stereotype of drunk fathers or inadequate mothers.

If anyone strongly believes that only the poor and criminal harm their children, then he is failing to recognize a large section of battering parents (Lynch and Ounsted, 1976). Before one can be open and honest towards abusing parents one must face up to the fact that anyone has the potential to harm their child.

Overcoming personal difficulties is still only the first step for the social worker, as cases have to be shared with others, all of whom may have different attitudes towards the problem (Carter, 1974; Oppé, 1975). Social workers may have to discuss cases with someone who denies the existence of child abuse or may be expected to collaborate with someone who believes that permanent separation of the child from his parents is the only solution. Other workers, the press, neighbours, and family members can all increase the social worker's anxiety by off-loading on to him their own fears and concern for the child.

Child abuse, therefore, is a painful problem, and probably the most difficult the social worker can expect to meet. It is now even written into the Code of Practice set out by the British Association of Social Workers (BASW) that the social worker

> has a duty to recognise the high level of anxiety which working with children at risk [of abuse] creates in herself and in other people. (BASW 1976)

There is no written evidence to show what effect this personally-demanding work has on social workers, but it is worth pointing out that special units in the child-protection field have definite policies for limiting the amount of work with child abuse. At the National Center on Child Abuse and Neglect at Denver, social workers are employed on a rotation scheme, first working directly with the families, and then in an administrative post. At the Park Hospital, Oxford, it is considered essential that all members of staff also work on cases that have no connection with child abuse. The NSPCC special unit staff believe that social workers can only cope with ten to twelve cases at one time.

(2) The complexity of the problem

The varying explanations, definitions, types of parents, and associated factors may all confuse rather than aid the social worker in his understanding of child abuse in one case. As Letitia Allan has clearly shown in chapter 3, there are conflicting explanations of child abuse, and there is a continuing debate concerning the aetiology of human violence in general. It is difficult for the social worker to know how much credence to give research results when even carefully-conducted research is shown to have shortcomings (Smith *et al.*, 1974). An inevitable result of conflicting information is confusion and uncertainty for those who are expected to set up adequate methods of treating the problem.

The problem of varying definitions of child abuse also has a bearing on social workers' responsibility. The legislation quoted at the beginning of this chapter indicates a very wide definition of child abuse. On the other hand, the British Association of Social Workers (BASW, 1976) has recommended that registers of children at risk should be strictly limited to those 'who have been injured, or who are at risk of *physical* abuse, including neglect'. As a definition of child abuse this would be too restrictive, as there is some evidence to suggest that it is often not the actual physical injury that has the most damaging effect on the child's development (Jones, 1976; Martin, 1976). When a child is protected from physical injury he may still be suffering emotional abuse. This was noted by Jones (1976) in a reappraisal of the NSPCC's battered-child research project:

> Only slight positive changes were noted in most aspects of parent/child relationships. The majority of children had homes where empathy and sensitivity to their needs were lacking, where inconsistent, often harsh discipline remained the mode.

Official concern over cases of 'non-accidental injury' has limited social workers' definitions of child abuse and blunted their awareness to the wider implications of the problem. Serious forms of child abuse may produce no visible trauma. When an injury does occur it is merely another symptom of the underlying disturbed family relationships.

Not only can child abuse take many forms but also very different types of people abuse their children. A description of six sets of abusing parents known to a family doctor in England clearly shows the diversity of cases (Beswick *et al.*, 1976).

(a) An unemployed father and a mother who had two former husbands.

They lived in a crowded caravan with four children. This family is a well-known problem family where neglect and probably abuse has continued intermittently for years.

(b) An apparently stable middle-class family who had rejected an adopted child. Adoption breakdown may be a precursor to child abuse.

(c) Two parents who were young postgraduate students. Intellectual strain in the parents made the baby's intrusion dangerous. Their intelligence did not protect them from abusing their child.

(d) A wealthy upper-class family where the child was attached to his nanny and crises occurred in her absence. Material wealth did not prevent his abuse.

(e) A psychotic mother and a criminal psychopathic father who met in a local psychiatric hospital. This has been called 'assortive mating' by Ounsted and Lynch (1976).

(f) A lonely young woman who was totally isolated because of a recent move into an army camp, and because of her husband's frequent postings abroad. When difficulties with her child increased, she had no one to turn to.

Similarly, a review of all 50 abusing families admitted to the Park Hospital family unit between January 1973 and June 1975 shows that all socio-economic groups were represented. The parents' ages ranged from 16 to 50 years, and those of the children from 14 days to 12 years. The number of children in each family ranged from one to four. In some families all the children were at risk, in others, only one child was singled out for abuse. No one psychiatric diagnosis could be applied to the parents (Lynch and Ounsted, 1976). This means that treatment has to be varied and adapted to each individual family. While the development of an agreed typology of abusing parents is an attractive idea for the social worker, it could result in too rigid an application of services.

The overt factors that precede abuse are different in every case. In some instances, illness in the mother and neonatal illness in the child seem to be the most important associated factors (Lynch, 1975). In other cases many problems have built up over the years and culminated in a final outburst towards the child (Baldwin and Oliver, 1972). It is necessary to look beyond isolated events to understand child abuse and researchers are forming the opinion that there is a constellation of associated factors (see, for example, Gelles, 1973). Factors build up over a long time to form a very complex process, as illustrated in the following example (and see Figure 10.1).

Paul and Susan were, to many people, the least likely parents to abuse their children. They were hard-working and respectable members of society. Their twins, Mark and Michelle, aged 3½ months, were admitted to hospital with multiple fractures of varying ages. After a delay, when hospital staff refused to believe that the children had been battered, Susan admitted to the abuse.

The process leading to the final breakdown began in the childhood of both parents. The mother came from a sibship of two and was reared in a strict, materialistic family, with the highest standards of cleanliness and decency. She left school and became a successful secretary. Aged 19, after a courtship of 6 months, she married. Her husband came from a sibship of two. He had had an unsettled early childhood, but was subsequently reared quite happily by an aunt and uncle. He did not see his own parents. He worked as a clerk in a supermarket, but his wife persuaded him to change his occupation and work as a driver-salesman, a risky but rewarding employment. The couple decided to buy their own house on a mortgage. The house was to be perfectly furnished; Susan was very house-proud. Their first child, Justin, was a planned baby and was born 2 years and 5 months after they had married. The pregnancy was complicated by hypertension and ended with a caesarian section for foetal distress. Subsequently mother and child made excellent progress and went home together. The baby thrived and conformed to everyone's picture of the ideal baby. On the surface everything seemed to be going well for the family, but the father was working intensely hard, was dominated by his wife, and driven to maintaining high standards of living. Then, despite some apprehension on the mother's part, a second pregnancy was planned, and the perfect two-child family sought. Twins were conceived!

The pregnancy was complicated with illness. Because of this the elder child was moved from relative to relative, while his mother was in hospital for 6 weeks. The father meanwhile was working hard for more money. The babies' deliveries were normal but the mother became ill shortly after the births. When the twins came home, the baby boy was difficult to bath and the baby girl difficult to feed. The elder brother returned home, and was demanding and aggressive. He rejected his mother who was, by this time, feeling physically very ill. Susan was offered a home help, but such was her need to keep everything perfect, she spent much time following her round and tidying up after her.

Susan's response to the stress was to set higher and higher standards. She became increasingly tense. She asked various visitors for help, but was reassured that she was doing well. The boy twin was crying incessantly and the girl twin was failing to gain weight. The elder brother was having temper tantrums. Her husband tried to help, but was, by this time, overwhelmed by his responsibilities at work. Their marriage was breaking down; their sex life was non-existent. Successive vigorous assaults on the children occurred, and the twins finally came to the hospital's notice.

Figure 10.1 Critical path of family

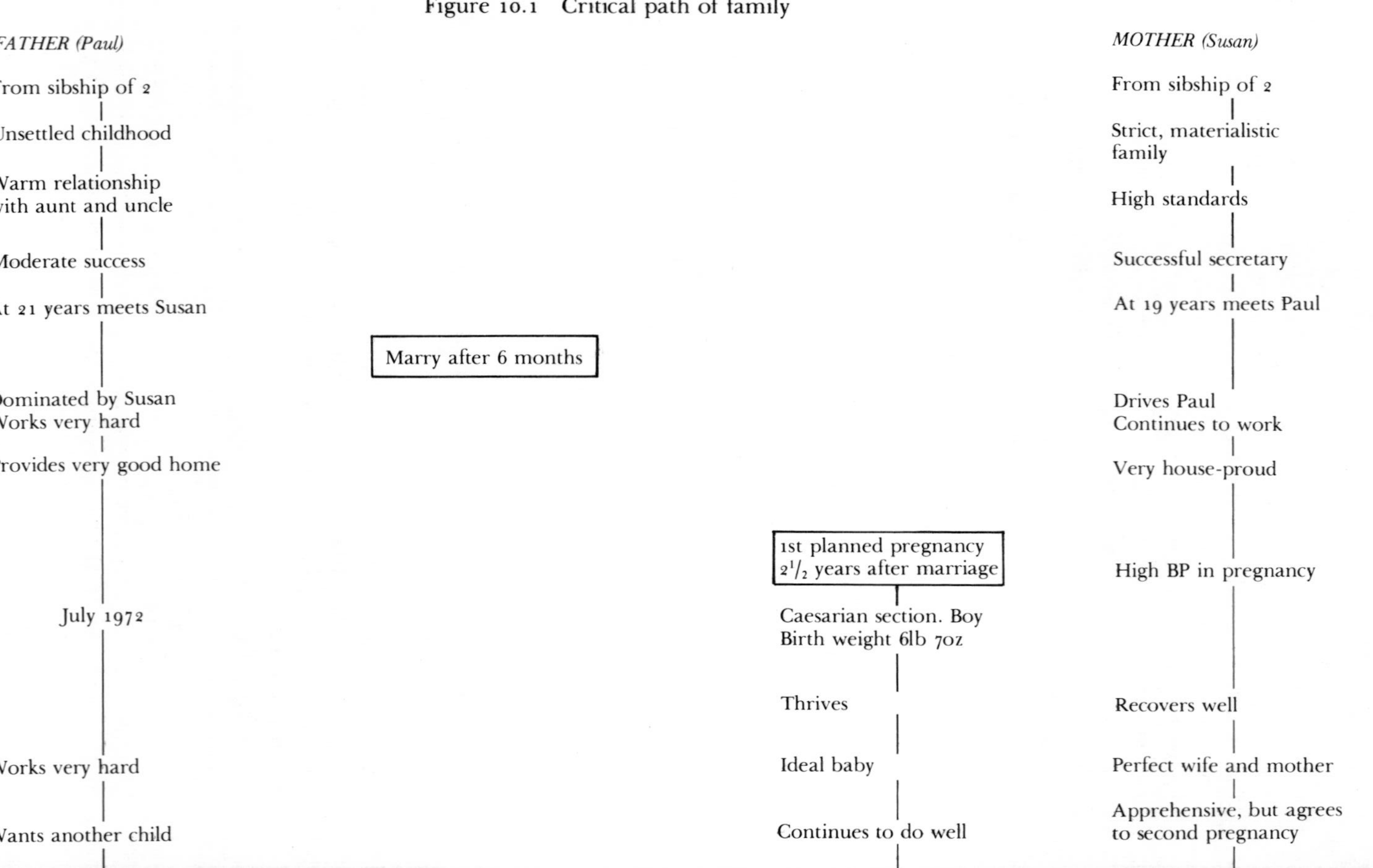
FATHER (Paul)
From sibship of 2
Unsettled childhood
Warm relationship with aunt and uncle
Moderate success
At 21 years meets Susan
Dominated by Susan
Works very hard
Provides very good home
July 1972
Works very hard
Wants another child
Marry after 6 months
1st planned pregnancy
$2^1/_2$ years after marriage
Caesarian section. Boy
Birth weight 6lb 7oz
Thrives
Ideal baby
Continues to do well
MOTHER (Susan)
From sibship of 2
Strict, materialistic family
High standards
Successful secretary
At 19 years meets Paul
Drives Paul
Continues to work
Very house-proud
High BP in pregnancy
Recovers well
Perfect wife and mother
Apprehensive, but agrees to second pregnancy

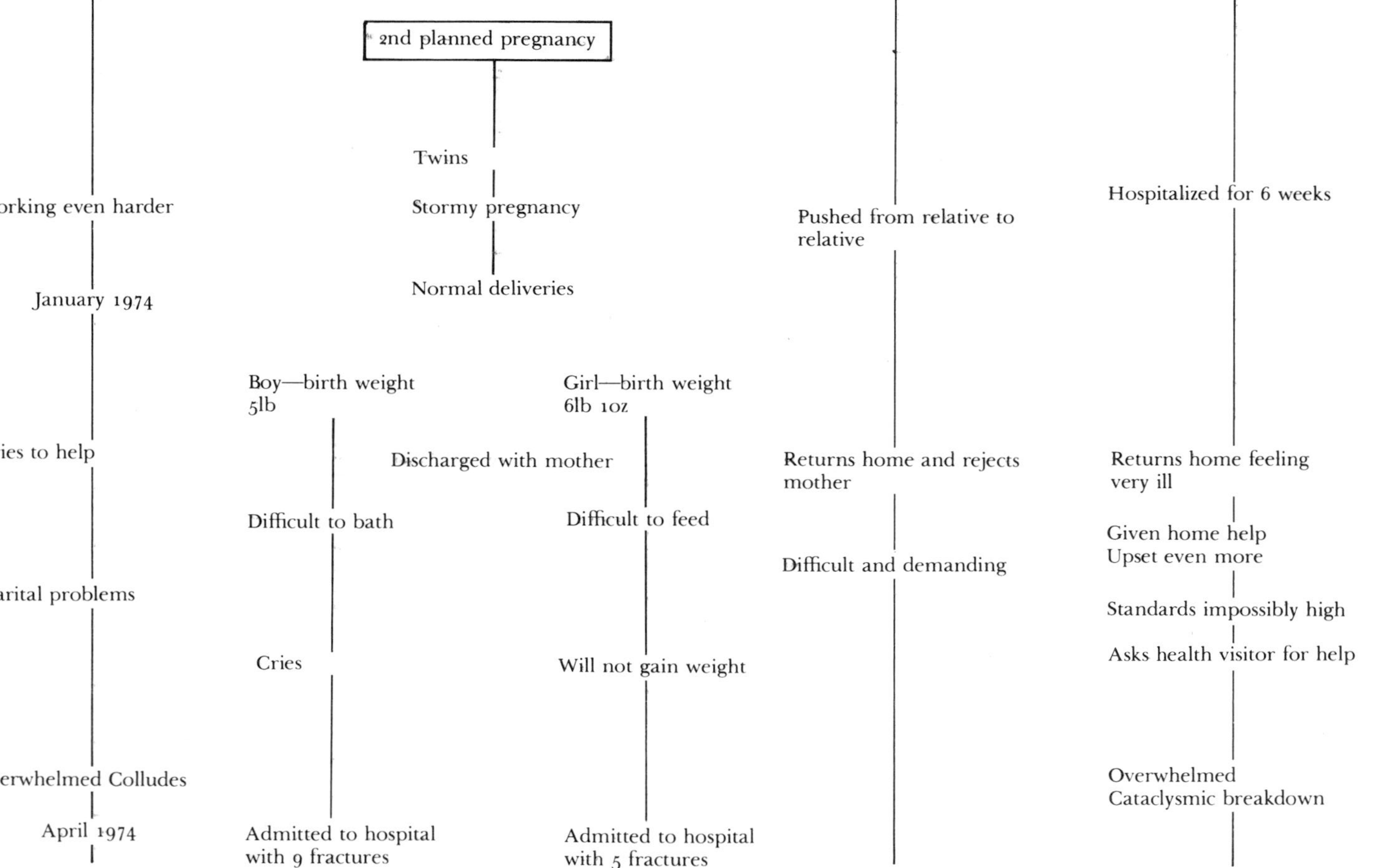
2nd planned pregnancy
Twins
Stormy pregnancy
Normal deliveries
Working even harder
January 1974
Tries to help
Marital problems
Overwhelmed Colludes
April 1974
Boy—birth weight
5lb
Difficult to bath
Cries
Admitted to hospital
with 9 fractures
Discharged with mother
Girl—birth weight
6lb 1oz
Difficult to feed
Will not gain weight
Admitted to hospital
with 5 fractures
Pushed from relative to
relative
Returns home and rejects
mother
Difficult and demanding
Hospitalized for 6 weeks
Returns home feeling
very ill
Given home help
Upset even more
Standards impossibly high
Asks health visitor for help
Overwhelmed
Cataclysmic breakdown

An understanding of why this mother assaulted her children can only be gained by observing the whole process from the beginning. The history began with the parents' childhood. Paul was deprived of his own parents early on and Susan had a very rigid upbringing. Susan's need to conform led her to agree to a pregnancy for which she was not ready. Illness added tension and stress to all the members of the family. The unexpected—twins—rocked the boat. Then, to top it all, the twins were difficult children. They did not conform to high expectations. Tensions built up affecting work, marriage, and home life. During the difficult time of bathing and feeding the twins, the final breakdown occurred.

(3) Family characteristics

In spite of the conflicting evidence from research, it is certain that there are characteristics shared by many abusing families. These are the characteristics which explain why social work in child protection is so difficult and why abusing families are the social worker's most difficult clients.

Mistrust

It is now well documented that parents who inflict injuries on their children have often had a deprived, violent or unhappy childhood (see, for example, Steele and Pollock, 1968; Baldwin and Oliver, 1972). This leads to an inability to establish deep and trusting relationships. As they embark on adult life, they have not yet passed the emotional developmental hurdles of childhood which have been conceptualized by Erikson (1950). Consequently, their links with their own parents may be very close and dependent but at the same time full of bitter resentment. Poor relationships with parents may drive them into liaisons with partners from similar backgrounds, often at an early age.

> A young woman, Sally, was physically and emotionally neglected by her own mother. She hated her mother and ran away from home at 16 years to join the army. She became pregnant soon afterwards and married at 17 years. Regularly she would return, quite excited, to her parents' home for a 'holiday'. All these 'holidays' ended prematurely with a family row and much ill feeling. Sally would depart bitterly disappointed, desperately upset at her mother's attitudes towards her, and vowing never to return. When asked why she repeatedly returned, she replied that she always had high hopes—that next time everything would be all right. She was still desperately seeking her mother's good will and approval. Sally is now having immense difficulties in coping with her own child—she can give the child nothing emotionally, only basic food and clothing.

Their upbringing can breed an overwhelming sense of worthlessness. As E. Davoren (1968), the first social worker to write about the problem, comments:

> They look to others to criticise them, to outrank them, to show their superiority to them and to leave them feeling more helpless than ever.

It is of paramount importance to the social worker that the lack of trust and antagonistic attitudes make the clients most difficult to understand and tolerate. Such parents refuse all offers of help, in spite of their real desire to be cared for. They often seem to do their utmost to undo the benefit of any services offered. These are the parents who say, 'If only we had a nursery place for Jonathan, everything would be all right.' The social worker then spends a lot of time and effort obtaining a nursery place. After one or two attendances, the parents then fail to take their child along—saying that it was no help after all—or they cannot be bothered. It is extremely difficult to persist in the face of such despondent and negative attitudes, but if the social worker does give up, this will only confirm the parents' fear that nobody does care for them. When demands on a social worker's time are great, and some other clients show their gratitude, it is very tempting to close a difficult case and describe the parents as 'resistant'. The social worker cannot look to such parents to give him encouragement in his work.

Mistrust helps to create the social isolation frequently observed in these families (see, for example, Schneider, 1972; Smith *et al.* 1974; Baher *et al.*, 1976). They are unable to make friends; they choose to live in isolated places; they have no one to turn to when in trouble. Social workers have the extremely difficult task of helping them establish links with the community and family they have rejected.

Abusing parents resent people in authority. Because of their childhood experiences they find it difficult to understand that someone can care for them and also exert authority.

> A young man, Freddie, broke the leg of his son, Simon, and severely scalded him. He had spent most of his childhood in a children's home. He trusted no one and was resentful of anyone with official authority. He never did well at school. He often lost jobs through having rows with the man in charge. The very sight of a policeman turned him to violence. And yet Freddie was desperately looking for the controlling father he had never had. He despised his social worker who exerted no control. He needed control and warmth, discipline from someone he could trust. Eventually, he developed an excellent relationship with an older consultant who exerted authority and managed to combine it with a caring attitude.

It is all too easy for a social worker to create either a resentful overdependence or outright hostility in such cases.

Marital problems

Abusing parents almost invariably have marital problems. For example, Baher *et al.* (1976) report that in 72% of their cases 'the marital relationship was a major source of tension in the family'. These findings are supported by other evidence discussed in Letitia Allan's chapter.

It is self-evident that the parents' difficulty in forming relationships extends to their marriage. If an emotionally deprived person marries someone from a similar background, neither partner may find what they need in the other.

> Sarah and Bill each had had a deprived childhood. Sarah's parents divorced when she was 3 years old. She was raped twice by her step-father and had a very poor relationship with her mother. When Bill was 4 years old, his father died. Six months later, his mother battered him. He was taken into care and spent the next 4 years in numerous foster homes and children's homes, until he was finally adopted.
>
> Sarah and Bill married after a month's courtship when they were both in their teens. They planned a baby as soon as possible. When the baby arrived, they were both ill. The baby also became ill with pneumonia.
>
> Neither Sarah nor Bill had enough to give each other emotionally and on top of that they had a new, demanding, sickly baby. Frequent rows developed, often resulting in blows. When the baby was admitted to hospital for pneumonia she was found to have 6 fractured ribs and many bruises. The parents did not deny that the injuries were inflicted.

The inability to form stable marriages is reflected in the disproportionate rates of unsupported mothers (18%) and divorced or separated parents (24%) in the Park Hospital series (Lynch and Ounsted, 1976; cf. also Smith *et al.*, 1974; Skinner and Castle, 1969). In some cases the marital conflict results in violence. Approximately a third of mothers from abusing families claim that they have been injured by their husbands, but it must not be forgotten that wives, too, are sometimes the aggressors.

Family-planning difficulties are closely connected with the marital problems as ambivalence towards marriage and associated unhappy sex lives affect attitudes towards contraception. It is yet another symptom of both personal identity and marital problems that the parents fail in constructive family planning, the result of which is an unwanted pregnancy. Just as in Sarah and Bill's case, while the parents are still emotionally unstable and immature, they have children whom they expect to meet their own needs. Our research has shown that at least 50% of parents who abuse their children begin reproduction under 20 years, as compared with 16% of our local population (Lynch and Roberts, 1977).

The prevalence and obvious importance of marital problems add to the range of skills required of a social worker. It is still too often the practice that social work is carried out during the working day, mainly with the mother of the family. Baher *et al.* (1976) report that 'the focus on the mother was often established at the beginning as she was more easily accessible' and this led to successful marital therapy being set up in only two out of 14 cases where it was attempted. For too long now, fathers have only been brought into treatment incidentally after initial contact with mother and child. As the father's predicament is usually equal to that of his wife, it is essential to approach both parents at the same time with equal opportunities for treatment. If such needs are ignored the problems could be exacerbated (Pickett and Paton, 1976). The father may be very jealous of the attention given to his wife and therefore undo any of the good done. One father had reported that his resentment of the attention given to his wife after she abused their child resulted in uncharacteristic bouts of heavy drinking. One-sided attention towards the wife can also reinforce the husband's impression that he has no part in the problem. One woman was desperately unhappy in her marriage and took out her misery on her 2-year-old child. Her husband told me that there was nothing wrong with him or his children—'It's just the wife, who's mental.'

Disturbed children

Protection of the child from further injuries is a necessary part of social work with abusing families, but it is not the whole solution. By the time the social worker is called in to help in cases of child abuse, it is probable that the injured child is quite disturbed and needs treatment for his emotional as well as his medical problems. Eighteen out of 104 cases of actual physical abuse known to the Park Hospital initially came to notice because of 'behaviour problems'. Experience in group treatment in the community has also revealed that children 'at risk' and abused children frequently have behaviour problems requiring special help (Ounsted *et al.*, 1974; Roberts *et al.*, 1977).

> Rebecca began attending a therapeutic playgroup when she was 18 months old. She was grossly underweight and whined constantly. The mother reported that she woke several times a night, crying. When her mother left her in the play group, she cried continuously for an hour. Her language development was retarded and she was totally unable to play. In spite of great excitement and activity among the other toddlers, she spent several sessions curled up in the

> foetal position refusing to do anything. Only after weeks of special play therapy did Rebecca begin to put on weight and develop into a chattering extrovert toddler.

The social worker's task must extend beyond the modification of parental attitudes towards a normal child. These parents, who would have difficulty in coping with any child, need extra help with children who have very real behavioural and developmental problems. Baher *et al.* (1976) report that 'whether the child is removed from home or remains with his family, it is likely that specific and intensive therapeutic intervention will be required if there is to be any chance of undoing the long-term distortion in the child's relationship with the mother'. Unfortunately, the short-term crisis intervention often demanded in these cases has inevitably put the emphasis on child protection.

The emotional problems of the abused child play a crucial part in the future success of the management of these cases. It has been observed at the Park Hospital and elsewhere that the long-term effects of child abuse can make the child difficult for anyone to love and care for. The rate of foster breakdowns for this type of child is high. Parker (1966) in his study of long-term foster placements found that children with behaviour problems and those with mental handicap were more likely to suffer a fostering failure; abused children so often fall into this category.

One of the most disturbing factors for the abused child can be indecision about his placement. Insecurity in the parental home can all too easily be followed by further unsettling changes in arrangements for his care.

> A little girl, Brenda, was battered twice by her mother. As a result, by the time she was 9½ months old, she had already spent 4½ months of her life in hospital. She then spent 17 months with foster-parents, but she was returned to her natural parents, with whom she had only ever previously spent 5 months. Her parents separated and Brenda went to live with her father and relatives. When she was 3 years old, her mother visited and attempted to strangle her. She was moved again, this time to relatives in another town. Little is known about the next 4 years, but when Brenda was 8 years old she was taken into care for the second time. She has had several changes of placement since and is now in a children's home, aged 10, displaying severe behavioural problems.

Parent/child relationships

Inflicted injuries on a child do not appear out of the blue. Usually, the parents have had child-rearing problems for some time. It is very important to understand the parents' view of the child as they often have unrealistic and rigid expectations of his behaviour and development. Kempe (1971), who originally observed this phenomenon, reports that there is a 'premature demand for satisfying behavioural response from the infant', and 'parental disregard of the infant's own needs, wishes and age-appropriate abilities'. What can appear to be normal boisterous behaviour to a visiting social worker is only too likely to provoke severe discipline from abusing parents. Like all parents, they invest a lot in their children, but unlike most parents they are unable to adapt to the inevitable disappointments and failures. Abusing parents' high expectations of the child are closely connected with their own low self-esteem. The child must achieve where they have failed. If the child fails to live up to their unrealistic expectations, they cannot tolerate a repetition of their own failure. Take the following tragic example:

> Gillian as a child was classified as educationally subnormal. She was deprived and rejected by her parents. She and her educationally subnormal brother were taken to live in a children's home when she was 3 years old, while her brighter, more intelligent sister continued to live with her parents. Gillian spent all her childhood in the children's home. The only communications she had from her parents were sinister, threatening letters from her father demanding money. Gillian's one desire in life was to form the happy family that she had never had. She had a brief affair with a passing fairground man and became pregnant aged 20 years. The son she bore was severely mentally handicapped; she battered him. He was taken into care, where he later died. She soon became pregnant again and this time married a few months after conception. Another handicapped child was born. He was slow to feed; he had few responses; he gave her little in return for her devotion. When he was a year old she broke his arm when wrestling to put on his coat. This child was also taken into care. Eighteen months later a third child was conceived. This time everything had to go well. However, even with a normal newborn baby, Gillian was totally unable to give the expected maternal care. The baby was there to give *her* the family and love she so desperately wanted. She was very impatient with him, and he was difficult to feed. Consequently, in a feeding battle, she bruised his face, and he too was taken into care.

Careful observation of abusing parents' verbal and non-verbal interaction with their children is needed to understand the relationship between parent and child in a case of child abuse. Research in this field is still very new but some etiological studies are now being conducted in order to understand more about parent/child interaction (e.g. Appleton, 1976; Burgess and Conger, 1976). Their preliminary findings support the impressions of many people who have worked with abused children and their parents. Speech delay is common (Blager and Martin, 1976). The abused child is often isolated from his peers and his mother fails either to talk to him or play with him. Because of this he becomes inhibited and unable to play. He does not touch his mother often; he watches her from a distance. When severe abuse has occurred, a child will display 'frozen watchfulness', first described by Ounsted (1972). The parents, in their turn, are inhibited. They find it difficult to cuddle their child or to get down on to the floor and play with him. Very little positive verbal encouragement is given, while reprimands are frequent.

Parents and their abused children require treatment both separately and together in their interaction. Such work demands tremendous sensitivity on the part of the therapists in order to balance out the parents' and the child's desperate needs for attention (see Reavley and Gilbert, 1976).

If the child is receiving special treatment, the parents also need help in adjusting to the changes in the child. This treatment must keep pace with the child's speed of development. To meet this urgency it would seem that more than one therapist is needed. This must be beyond the capabilities of a single social worker, who has neither the time nor the training.

Ill-health

Apart from the immediate severity of injuries, there is plenty of evidence to show that abuse causes long-term ill-health. Rates vary according to the index samples studied, but an abused child is at risk of brain damage, eye damage, other physical defects, and retarded development, in addition to the obvious emotional problems (see especially Martin *et al.*, 1974; Martin and Beezley, 1976).

Research has shown that there is a greater prevalence of ill-health in the families of abused children even before the abuse occurs. In a study which compared 25 abused children with their 35 unharmed brothers and sisters it was found that, for the abused group, there was an increased incidence of illness for both the mother and child during the pregnancy and neonatal period (Lynch, 1975). When abused children are compared with other children there is still a markedly increased incidence of severe neonatal illness requiring admission to a special care nursery; 42% compared with 10% (Lynch and Roberts, 1977).

The effects of ill-health, especially if it has gone unnoticed and undiagnosed, can add to stress. Illness in either parent may cause separation which in turn increases parent/child difficulties. The authors of *At Risk* (Baher *et al.*, 1976) report medical problems for 28 out of 43 parents. Frequently mothers admitted to the Park Hospital have had minor illness, most commonly gynaecological complaints, severe headaches, and iron deficiency anaemia. More serious diagnoses have included chronic renal disease, multiple sclerosis, leprosy, tuberculosis, distrophia myotonica, and a cerebral tumour (Lynch and Ounsted, 1976). Problems such as blindness or congenital abnormality have also been found to put the child 'at risk' by making the child a more difficult one to love and understand. It is easy to comprehend a mother's difficulty in loving and accepting a child who cannot even see her.

Emotional and psychiatric ill-health can play an important part in the process that leads to abuse. The rate found will depend on the definition used and the sample studied. Almost all abusing parents have symptoms of anxiety and/or depression (Steele and Pollock, 1968), while approximately 10% of abusing parents are thought to be psychotic (Kempe, 1971). When parents suffer from a psychiatric illness they require considerable attention and treatment in their own right. If they also have a dependent child, there arises a major problem for the social worker who has to balance out the needs of the parents versus the child. In spite of feeling a great deal of compassion and concern for the parents, the social worker often has to do what will cause them the most distress—take their child away from them. Those with a psychosis must be identified; it is often impossible for them to relate to their baby normally. The very act of battering may be part of their delusional system and removal of their child is a necessity.

Anxiety and depression are often symptoms which can be presented to the GP in isolation from the underlying problem (Pickett and Paton, 1976; Beswick *et al.*, 1976). It is all too easy for doctors to treat such complaints with tranquillizers, although it has been shown that these drugs can have the paradoxical effect of increasing aggression (Grey, 1976). They remove inhibitions in much the same way as alcohol.

The high incidence of ill-health requires a social worker's willingness to take part in the family's medical assessment and care. Social-work help cannot be given in isolation when families have these very real medical problems that need treatment. Health and social-work agencies are often geographically and ideologically separated, and it requires extra motivation and effort to combine the two services.

Resulting chaos

Abusing parents not only have difficult personalities, but also their whole life-style is typically chaotic. Baldwin and Oliver (1972) report a considerable catalogue of interrelated problems, and research has shown the prevalence of extremely 'diffuse' social problems (Lynch *et al.*, 1976). For example:

> Mr and Mrs B both came from violent and unhappy homes; they met in the child psychiatrist's waiting room. Mrs B had spent her childhood being blamed by her mother for the traumatic caesarian section which had brought her into the world. This created a terrible fear in Mrs B of illness and hospitals.
>
> Soon after the marriage, Mr and Mrs B went to live in a very

> isolated cottage, miles away from any town or village. They cut themselves off from other people because Mr B was pathologically jealous of his wife's attention to anyone but himself. Mr B was a farm labourer; he did not earn a high wage. Consequently, financial problems dogged their marriage. They lived in rented accommodation and it was of poor standard. When Mrs B became pregnant, she was not pleased as she much preferred animals to children. She then became ill during the pregnancy and was admitted to hospital terrified. Her one fear that had obsessed her all her life came true: she had a caesarian section. The new baby was very ill and under special medical care for weeks. Mrs B left the hospital and forgot her baby. She and her husband could not afford the transport back to the hospital to visit. The baby's arrival home was greeted with cold displeasure by both parents. Mrs B could not stand his nappies or his vomiting. Mr B became intensely jealous of the baby. After a couple of months the baby came to the notice of the hospital as bruised and grossly underfed.

As the parents' lives become more confused the further they move away from finding a solution. It has been noted that such families tend to escape into a world of unreality (Ounsted and Lynch, 1976). A common reaction is to try to run away and start afresh. Some families develop rituals to cover up the underlying chaos. The superficially good image is often set up to create the right impression. I have noticed a number of families where a high standard of housekeeping and mothercraft has masked a basic lack of mothering. Busy social workers are in danger of trusting such presentations because discovering the unpleasant truth could create more problems for them.

When only one social worker is trying to help a family with such diffuse problems, he too can feel so overwhelmed as to be drawn into the chaos, as observed by Pickett and Paton (1976). The parents easily divert attention from the children by making their own very urgent demands for help. Such constant demands can make the social worker angry or make him avoid the family, and the busier he is, the less likely he is to tolerate their intensity. On the other hand, if the social worker over-identifies with one of the parents he may lose touch with the reality of the total family circumstances, and lose his sense of perspective.

Yet somehow these families need help and guidance to sort out their diffuse chaos. If the social worker is working alone on such a problem he is unlikely to be able to grapple with all the problems at once.

In such circumstances, the developmental and behavioural problems of the child are easily overlooked. Special attention to the parents, with incidental treatment for the child such as nursery admission, is simply not enough to change the overall poor parent/child relationship (Baher *et al.*, 1976). Major injuries may be averted, but the child can still be miserable, ill, and a behaviour problem.

(4) Multi-disciplinary co-ordination

This ugly phrase describes a very difficult task often allocated to the social worker with primary responsibility for the child's protection. The number of professionally-qualified workers from various disciplines involved in a case of child abuse can reach two figures (London Borough of Hillingdon, 1976), the number of decision makers being increased by representatives from each rung in the hierarchy. The end result is often a considerable problem for the person working directly with the family. He may have to consult a number of interested parties, all with differing attitudes, in addition to undertaking the complex work with the family. Professions are prejudiced against each other and have different responsibilities (Armstrong, 1974). One case conference may be attended by the paediatrician, who is primarily concerned with the child's health and development, the psychiatrist who is concerned with the understanding and treatment of the parent's emotional disorder, the social worker who has to help every member of the family, as well as provide adequate legal evidence for obtaining protection of the child, the social worker's senior who is concerned with his agency's accountability, and the policeman, whose duty it is to investigate a crime. And yet, co-ordination of all these disciplines is essential. The social worker finds this time-consuming communication and co-ordination conflicting with direct work with the clients.

The committee of inquiry into the care and supervision provided for Maria Colwell (DHSS, 1974) reported 'lack of, or ineffectiveness of communication and liaison'. Since then, the 'case conference' has been set up as the panacea for all inter-professional difficulties. However, setting up a forum for communication does not necessarily determine that meaningful communication will occur. Varying professional backgrounds may produce major obstacles to the function of the case conference. Klein (1956), in her analysis of 'decision making as instrumental behaviour', shows that 'the more similar the members' frames of reference are, the less time it would take for a group to come to a decision'. Communication difficulties that occur in ordinary daily contact are not necessarily diminished by setting up a meeting.

A case conference can often appear to be set up merely to allay the anxieties of the workers. I quote an author of a *Lancet* editorial (1975), a paediatrician, who had to cancel a spina bifida clinic to attend his second case conference in one week.

> The Friday conference, like the others, was attended by 8 highly trained, highly paid professionals, who sat solemnly round a table discussing a robust healthy child with a bruise on his bottom.

(5) Agency demands and the traditional practice of social work

Social workers have a statutory responsibility to protect the abused child and have to act as representatives of their agency. This means that social workers have the difficult task of combining authority and control with a caring attitude towards the abusing parents, who find it difficult to accept care and control from one person, as they have seldom experienced this from their own parents. This can result in either unmanageable hostility or a passive acceptance of the social worker. In the latter case, it is extremely difficult to know whether any real progress is made, or whether the family simply knows what the social worker needs to hear in order to record 'progress'.

Both the central government and local government social services departments have reacted to the dramatic press reports mentioned earlier because reports criticized agencies as well as individuals. This has led to a number of new bureaucratic procedures. So far these have seldom been accompanied by extra resources, but rather appear to be arrangements for protecting the agency's image—arrangements which do not necessarily help the individual social worker or the client. For example, most social service agencies now have registers of abused children and children 'at risk of abuse', the purpose of which has yet to be clarified. Presumably a register should be available for all practitioners from different disciplines to consult if there is concern that a child's injuries may have been inflicted. If the child's name is on the register then the practitioner is given added information. In some areas, however, the register is not even available on a 24-hour basis and cannot be consulted by hospital doctors. There are also disadvantages in 'at risk' registers. Some social workers will be tempted, because of other pressures of work, to consider placing a name on an 'at risk' register as an adequate form of protection in itself. On the other hand, if, when a child's name is put on the register, a whole departmental procedure is set in motion, some people will be reluctant to put forward names. There is also the danger that a comprehensive family assessment could be replaced by a brief check down the list of names. If a social worker is faced with an injured child and does not find the child's name on the register, he may be lulled into a false sense of security. Thus, agency demands in bureaucratic organizations can often seem to over-ride professional judgement in individual cases, which increases anxiety and frustration for the social worker who may feel he is not getting the right sort of support.

A social worker's commitment to his agency may condition his assessment of problems so that they are 'defined in terms of agency function' (Evans, 1976). For example, cases are often assessed as to whether there is enough legal evidence to justify the agency going to court for a care order. For the child's benefit, the family's problems may require a lengthy and wide-ranging assessment, whereas the agency's function demands quick investigation of the injuries and proof of abuse. There may sometimes be a conflict between the agency social worker's responsibility and what are considered to be the child's best interests. For example, workers from the NSPCC special unit in Manchester have noted that 'by far the most effective form of supervision in the home' is when 'the child is on a care order but living at home on trial' (Pickett and Paton, 1976). And yet in order to obtain a care order, it is necessary to prove in a court of law that the child has been ill-treated by his parents. If legal proof has been established, people are entitled to ask how it is possible for the child to be returned to his parents' care and be safe. On the one hand, this proves to be a successful form of rehabilitation, and on the other hand, it is contrary to the agency's interests, should subsequent injuries occur.

The organization of the agency also affects the type of social-work method used. In the majority of social-work departments today, social workers are all allocated 'case-loads'—lists of individuals or families for whom they assume a primary responsibility. This system tends to commit the social worker to the traditional model of treatment, irrespective of his own philosophy. Traditional social work is based on the individual or the one family. A typical description is given in the Younghusband (1959) report, p.7.

> The purpose of social work is to help individuals or families with various problems, and overcome or lessen these so that they may achieve a better personal, family or social adjustment. The function of social workers is to assess the extent of these problems, to give appropriate help and to offer a supporting relationship when this is required which gives people confidence to overcome difficulties.

This traditional method of social work is often called 'casework'. As Noel Timms (1970) has explained, the word casework was used originally in a non-technical sense to refer simply to the method of working 'case by case' as opposed to solving people's problems by a general solution. It is extremely difficult to describe what a social worker does when he does 'casework'. Some definitions are tautologous. For example,

> Casework is a personal service provided by qualified workers for individuals who require skilled assistance in resolving some material, emotional or character problem. (Younghusband, 1959, § 638).

In general, it would probably be fair to say that social workers mainly use their abilities to form good relationships with clients in order to help them understand their problems and be rid of them, or at least minimize any detrimental effects. Social workers use a wide range of resources, but the good, trusting relationship is considered central. The reference point is the individual or the one family. Otherwise the work has another label, such as 'group work' or 'community work'.

Obviously, in work with abusing parents, the establishment of a trusting relationship is essential. Without it, every other form of intervention would lose its value. However, a therapeutic relationship is a necessary but not sufficient condition for successful work with such families. There are a number of reasons why this traditional conceptual model has its drawbacks in child-protection work. I will mention just a few. First, the number of conflicting interests in one family indicate that a unitary family approach is inappropriate. Maybe more than one social worker has to be used. Second, attention to one individual family member is not adequate for treating the complex family relationships. For example, marital difficulties require direct intervention. Third, there are the important interaction problems between parents and children which need direct treatment. Basically, the casework model is probably very useful in helping individuals and families with 'defined' social problems, but it needs supplementing when dealing with the very complex and 'diffuse' social problems of abusing families and their children (Lynch, Roberts, and Gordon, 1976).

The concept of the social work 'case-load' almost precludes the idea of really sharing the family's care with other agencies. It can highlight a kind of isolated possessiveness and increase the likelihood of treatment being on a one-to-one basis. Many abusing families tend to be isolated socially and the traditional social-work approach holds the risk of reinforcing that very isolation, and, in a strange way, paralleling the isolation on the social worker's side. One only has to think of the visits that the social worker makes in his car to mother and children in the middle of the afternoon. He spends an hour in the house and then drives off. He seldom sees the family in the context of the social group, therefore missing out a major part of the assessment of the problems.

There is some evidence that the success of individual work with parents is limited. In a follow-up study of 50 abused children, Martin and Beezley (1976) found that the 'current behaviour of parents towards a previously abused child' was 'disheartening'. Parents of 21 children had received psychotherapy. Ninety per cent of these 21 children were at home with their natural parents, a mean of 4·5 years later. The authors found that 'even though the children were no longer being battered in the technical or legal sense, 68% were still experiencing hostile rejection and/or excessive physical punishment'. To put these findings into perspective, it must be added that of those children whose parents had not had any formal treatment, only 40% were still with their parents, and of that number, 83% were 'the objects of rejection and excessive physical punishment'. From the results of this study and that of the NSPCC (Baher *et al.*, 1976) one must surely question the justification in continuing a form of treatment that has such limited success.

THE WAY TO SUCCESS

In the first part of this chapter we have seen that there are many reasons why social workers might not succeed in protecting the child. Even when this is done the current definition of success (i.e. reduction of physical injury) is too limited, and will not alter the cycle of child-rearing techniques which produces the next generation's battering parents. A wider range of treatment methods is needed for both abused children and their families.

In this second part, I would like to explore some ways of improving existing services which could go a long way to change the emphasis from protecting children from physical injury to ensuring them a better quality of life.

(1) Sharing

The wide range of a violent family's problems shows that social workers must work closely with other professions. The families need the expertise of a number of agencies, especially health and social services. At present, contact between the professions is invariably on a consultation basis, some workers only meeting at occasional case reviews. Because the problems are so intertwined it would be logical to have an integrated and unified treatment plan, where the family can see people from different disciplines actually working together and sharing common philosophies. This has been one of the main conclusions reached at specialist centres, whether working in residential or community settings.

For example, in the Park Hospital the residential treatment for abusing families was developed by a co-ordinated team of different disciplines already in existence for other purposes (Lynch *et al.*, 1975). The team is a mixture of well-qualified professional staff and experienced, down-to-earth auxiliary personnel. There is a shared responsibility for all aspects of work and information collecting is not left to one person. The different dimensions of the family's problems can all be assessed simultaneously by people with different skills. Varying treatment approaches can be used in parallel. For example, psychotherapy can be offered alongside practical teaching about feeding and changing a baby's nappy. Many families do need both forms of help. For them, any insight gained from psychotherapy loses its value when it comes to mixing a baby's feed. While the parents are receiving help, the abused child and any siblings must be given direct attention for any medical and behavioural problems. Only in this way is it possible to avoid the drawbacks of the traditional approach which expects the therapeutic relationship with the parents to filter through to resolve all the family's problems.

When working closely with colleagues it is possible to share with them the distressing and anxiety-provoking nature of the work. It is impossible to deal with these families in a confident, constructive, and non-punitive manner if one is the only therapist conducting most of the work alone and isolated from adequate support (Pickett and Paton, 1976). The hierarchy in social services departments is supposedly set up to support the field worker but I suspect it rarely fulfils this function. Smith and Ames (1976) have recently argued that the organization of social services departments into Area Teams does not necessarily encourage those conditions which increase professional support.

These conditions are, according to them, effective communications between colleagues, mutual responsibility for professional tasks, and a 'supportive' style of management. Perhaps better support would be obtained if social workers actually shared cases with each other. Smith and Ames (1976) report one such American experience where:

> every client's social service needs are divided up to ensure that each team member works at meeting only one or a few of them. Thus, a single client often does not relate exclusively to one worker, but to several.

In my experience there is no better understanding and support than that obtained from peers who have equal responsibility for and commitment to the families. This is even more effective when members of different professions are included. A group of workers is more able to avoid the attitude—'image protection'. How many decisions are being made which are actually contrary to a child's interest with the principles of 'save us from a Maria Colwell scandal' behind the decision making?

Sharing the responsibility and work with others can give social workers a much more balanced perspective of the clients' problems and can give them other workers' views on their own judgements which may be clouded by over-involvement. If a number of equally committed people are available and regularly seeing family members, then the possessiveness that can develop in having a case-load is diminished and the danger of the solitary worker being drawn into the family's closed system is averted. When working together with a group of people it is easier to be open and honest in one's reactions and about statutory responsibilities. One cannot expect trust from anyone unless one is honest. This applies to colleagues as much as clients.

One of the main problems for local authority social workers is that they have little chance of limiting the overwhelming demands caused by abusing families. Action is often needed at a moment's notice. If one social worker has no way of limiting these demands, he will be continually diverted from long-term planning and therapy by constant 'crisis' requests. As already noted, several specialist units have imposed limits on any one individual's commitment to such families, which is easier to do when the work is shared. This also helps the parents to know realistically that there are limits to workers' tolerance and commitment.

It is plain that what is needed in cases of child abuse is total family care. Above all, the families need someone to reach out to them. Compared with others, these families both need and want more attention, although they fail to show the expected 'motivation'. The concept of a concerted effort by a team of people to provide family care could be criticized as unrealistic because of lack of money and resources, but experience is showing that much can be achieved by changing attitudes and adapting existing facilities.

(2) Flexibility

As the problems of abusing families are so diverse, greater flexibility is needed in social work. As long as the child is protected, the social worker is under no obligation to do only 'casework' because statutory responsibilities do not dictate the method of working. Continuation of traditional methods is so often an outcome of huge lists of clients and so the only way to initiate experiments in different ways of working with these families is to release some social workers from their individual 'case-loads'. They could be involved in a more flexible organization of resources rather than doing casework. Maybe one case of child abuse needs a social worker/co-ordinator with access to a range of therapeutic methods and other workers.

The following section explores some ideas of ways in which already existing facilities could be adapted to provide a wider range of treatment.

Residential care

Residential facilities for the whole family such as that at the Park Hospital can provide a more comprehensive and accurate assessment. The combination of medical treatment, practical help, and various forms of therapy makes it possible for children to be rehabilitated with their parents without prolonged separation (Lynch *et al.*, 1975). Family residential treatment is expensive but it is often an alternative to long-term care of the child and maybe a prison sentence for the parent, both of which cost a great deal.

Long-term residential care for the child who is separated from his parents is often considered the last resort. This is because research has shown (Dinnage and Pringle, 1967a) that children who have been in long-term residential care have far worse life chances than their peers. Indeed, institutional care is often associated with later adult problems such as delinquency, mental illness, and illegitimate pregnancies. Thus, the emphasis in child care is on preventing the need for residential care in the first place. This leads to tremendous problems for residential workers.

> The knowledge that one's work involves painful experiences for children and that the care offered is inevitably second-best ... must lead to disillusionment and denial for some workers. (Dinnage and Pringle, 1967, p.25)

Nevertheless, some children will continue to need residential care and there is a great need to make this a positive rather than a negative experience.

Hazel (1976), while she too argues that residential establishments will always be inadequate as long-term substitutes for homes and families, feels that using residential care in more specific, defined tasks could help the whole of British child-placement policy. It also makes sense in the treatment of abused children and their families.

The special needs and behaviour problems of rejected or ill-treated children indicate that simply providing substitute care is not enough to prevent further problems. Residential establishments can develop special therapeutic treatment for abused children as seen in the next case study.

> Jane and Ruth were separated from their parents on a care order. Ruth had been battered by her mother. She was 18 months old and a whining, difficult, and unlikeable child. Jane, aged 3, in order to avoid danger, had developed the adaptive behaviour 'frozen watchfulness'. These two children were tolerated by foster-parents for only a few weeks. After the foster-placement broke down, they were taken to a residential nursery where they were given special therapeutic attention from nurses and trained residential staff, who can take time off from difficult children. After 2 years of specialized help the children are radically changed. Jane talks spontaneously to visitors; she can face new places and new people. Ruth is happy and relaxed. Both children are developing normally. They can now be fostered with far less risk of breakdown.

Residential establishments could be given the specific purpose of assessment and treatment of such difficult children with a view to eventual placement in families. This is done already in several European countries (Hazel, 1976). In Sweden, apparently, it is the task of all residential homes to ensure that the child leaves it (Hazel, 1976). Likewise, in Germany, disturbed children may be admitted to a 'therapeutic institution' which acts as a centre for 'the training and support of qualified foster-families to whose care the children are gradually transferred'. Maybe we should be concentrating on making residential homes a good alternative care rather than a second-class substitute care, imitating 'normal' family life.

Foster care

The behaviour problems of even very young abused children indicate that specially selected and trained foster-parents are needed to provide more than a substitute family. Just as experiments are beginning in using professional foster-parents in the rehabilitation of the older or disturbed child, so a special type of foster-parent could be used specifically for abused children.

In foster care the focus is on the child, but often in cases of child abuse someone is needed to foster the parents as well.

> Gillian D has two children in foster care. One is with a wealthy childless couple who are the same age as Gillian and her husband, David. During visits, Gillian feels very uncomfortable and senses an atmosphere of rivalry; she does not visit often. Her younger son is with her middle-aged sister-in-law. She is a motherly person, with

> the same standard of living and financial worries as Gillian. She has successfully brought up her own two children. She welcomes Gillian and David to her house at all times and includes Gillian in caring for the child, teaching her what to do. Gillian looks on her sister-in-law as a mother and does not resent being taught. This foster-mother has had no formal training but is exceptional in her ability to empathize with the natural mother while still providing a mother's care for the foster child. This arrangement is helping Gillian and David through a difficult marriage. Gillian does not feel that she has lost her baby and therefore has not replaced him with another.

Foster-parents could be recruited specifically for meeting the dependency needs of such vulnerable parents, if those foster breakdowns which are caused by the parents' overwhelming demands and disruptive visits are to be prevented. There is in fact conflicting evidence about how much natural parents' visits are associated with foster breakdown (Dinnage and Pringle, 1967b), but it is still rare for foster-parents to see working with the natural parents as part of their brief. Foster parents working with abused children would obviously need supervision, training and higher pay. These could be some of the 'professional' foster-parents who are beginning to make a contribution to child care in England as described by Melville (1976).

Family aides or lay therapists

These are usually untrained, sometimes unpaid helpers who work in the families' houses as a kind of 'good neighbour'. The purpose of using such voluntary help is to replace the sort of person of whom the parents are deprived. They are considered an essential part of dealing with the problem of child abuse (Kempe, 1971). The middle-aged woman who has successfully brought up her own family can mother the parents and be a grandparent for the children; she does not have the official authority the parents distrust. Her brief is *not* to supervise the child or do the housework but to help the parents, so that they feel she is as interested in them as the children. Then they are able to model their own behaviour on hers and gradually adopt more successful methods of handling children.

Abusing parents are difficult, which is why they do not have neighbourly help in the first place. Voluntary helpers therefore need both supervision and support in their work. There is probably some reluctance about handing over responsibility to such untrained personnel. Indeed, the NSPCC research team admitted that they were probably 'too wary' about using voluntary aides and perhaps too 'protective' of both clients and staff. In this case it is salutary to remember that the majority of families *are* 'helped' by untrained friends, neighbours, and relatives and that is why they do not need the help of social workers.

Practical help

Jean Packman has recalled that the original child-care officers in Family Service Units were issued with boiler suits (Packman, 1975). An ability to adapt quickly to solving practical problems can often be a way of gaining the trust of parents who are unlikely to respond immediately to verbal psychotherapy. Help with practical problems is often taken as a demonstration of care. Mayer and Timms (1970) vividly describe the reactions of clients who had requested material assistance from social workers and had been refused.

> They were consumed with worry over debts, the possibility of an eviction, the cutting-off of their electricity, and it is absurd to expect that the urgency of their needs could be met by a non-material approach, whether ... offering insight, providing friendship, or the opportunity to unburden themselves to a sympathetic listener. It was 'offering a suit of clothes to a drowning man'. (p.140)

Practical help for abusing parents should never be underestimated. For example, I have taken a mother and baby in a car to a distant hospital clinic and found it an infinitely better use of time than a discussion over a cup of tea about how difficult it is to get to the hospital. First, it demonstrated in real, concrete terms that I could help. By doing this I gained the woman's trust and confidence. Second, it was possible to participate in what the woman was doing. I understood more about the woman's fears of her children misbehaving in public and experienced the same frustration in being kept waiting for a long time. She gained more help from me and I gained more understanding of her and her children than I would ever have done in a normal visit.

Something of a tradition has grown up in social work that time spent on practicalities is 'beneath' a qualified social worker. This has been one of the undesirable consequences of the concern for developing the professional status of social workers, and it was given powerful support by the Younghusband (1959) report which recommended the creation of 'welfare assistants' to 'relieve trained and experienced staff of a proportion of the simpler work and straightforward visiting', helping 'people who require material help, some simple service or a periodic visit' (§ 562). Clients, however, do not perceive their problems in this neatly-stratified way so that reluctance to include the more 'simple' tasks in social work with abusing families, does, I believe, reduce a social worker's ability to gain their trust and hence their motivation in more complicated psychotherapeutic work. Equally, practical help such as rehousing and the provision of home helps cannot alone solve these families' problems.

Day care

Day nurseries and playgroups are obviously important in providing alternative day care for abused children. Such facilities provide an opportunity for them to form relationships with adults and children outside the immediate family. Abused children are so often deprived of this experience because of their parents' isolation. This service could be extended even further by including parents more and by developing special methods of helping parents and children together.

Day care for the whole family is now being developed in NSPCC special units and in some social services departments. This can provide the total family care that is needed and it is considerably cheaper than residential treatment. Day care could be used more flexibly (see Urwin, 1974). Children could be cared for at particularly stressful times—for example, the younger child at teatime when his father and siblings return home for the evening; or the school-child during holiday time.

Group therapy

It is likely that group therapy is an appropriate form of treatment for abusing parents because they all require help with interpersonal skills and social isolation. As D. S. Whitaker (1975), an experienced group therapist, says:

> All of the following can occur more readily in a group than a one-to-one situation: social comparison, testing out new interactive behaviours, learning interpersonal skills, learning to co-operate to a shared goal, reassessing personal goals and values through comparing oneself with others ... learning through feed back, expanding one's own repertoire of behaviour through observing others, alleviating isolation and loneliness.

However, group therapy, which is specifically for abusing parents, remains a relatively undeveloped area (but see Paulson and Chaleff, 1973). The best-known example in the States is the self-help group called Mothers Anonymous, begun in 1970 and described by Kempe and Helfer (1972).

It is therefore worth describing in detail the following project in which I took part as it is an example of how group therapy can be provided for both mothers and children 'at risk'.

Two therapeutic groups, one for mothers and one for children, were set up by a family doctor and staff from Park Hospital. The aim was to provide treatment for parents with the sort of child-rearing problems often found to be the precursors of child abuse. We did not set out to treat very disturbed parents who had seriously injured their child. Close links between the two groups were to be maintained in order to give specific help with mother/child relationship problems. The groups were part of a wider management plan in the general practice (Beswick *et al.*, 1976) and based on the model of former groups run by Park Hospital staff both in the hospital and the community (Ounsted *et al.*, 1974).

There was a prolonged planning stage where uncertainty was expressed about changing the traditional doctor and social-worker approach. People found it difficult to visualize the GP combining the role of personal doctor with that of group therapist. This delay initially caused frustration, but we have found that the frequent discussions have had a long-term beneficial effect on the management of child abuse.

Previous experience had indicated that two therapists for the mothers' group would be required, preferably male and female. A doctor and a social worker, myself, acted as co-therapists. An occupational therapist, skilled in play therapy, ran the children's group. She was assisted by two volunteers and two senior pupils from the local comprehensive school.

Only women with pre-school-age children were considered and the types of cases included were based on former group-work experiences:

(a) Mothers with serious difficulties in coping with their child.
(b) Cases of child neglect or failure to thrive.
(c) Children identified as being at risk of abuse. In some cases the mothers may have admitted fears of harming their child.
(d) Some cases of actual abuse and emotional deprivation.

Careful selection of actual participants was made in order to form a compatible group. This was carried out at a meeting of group therapists, social workers, health visitors, family doctor, and Park Hospital staff. Two examples will suffice:

(a) A young woman who resented motherhood and was driven to the abuse of her difficult second child because of overcrowded living conditions and the child's recurrent infections. This child, a 20-month-old boy, did not speak. His mother was very worried that he was retarded. Both he and his elder sister (aged 4) had a sleeping problem.

(b) An emotionally-disturbed couple who were seeking a medical diagnosis for their child's unexplained failure to thrive. The child was admitted to hospital with chronic constipation. He could not walk at the age of 2 years. The clinical investigations proved negative and further inquiries revealed gross marital and family disturbance. This child also had a sleeping problem.

In retrospect we realized that having very clear aims and making very careful selection contributed to the success of the whole project.

After cases were selected, both parents were visited by a social worker in order to assess in detail the family's problems. Although it was to be a mothers' group, fathers were included in the assessment and planning; it was necessary to obtain their support. The formal assessment showed both parents that there were serious plans for treatment—the mothers were not told to drop in for coffee and chat. Several parents remarked on how important this was to them at the beginning. The social worker also visited after the end of the project to assess any change or progress.

The groups ran every week for 6 months and took place in the local health centre. The mothers were encouraged to spend time in the children's group at the beginning and end of their own group so that the therapists could help directly with mother/child relationships.

The aim in the mothers' group was to encourage maximum interaction in order to increase the mothers' self-respect and confidence. By doing this, we expected the mothers to learn from each other, help each other, and extend their contacts outside the group. The family doctor was careful to avoid being the 'doctor' talking to his patients. He managed to keep surgery consultations separate from group discussions and avoided breaching confidentiality. The mothers were encouraged to proceed at their own pace and discouraged from talking to the therapists as experts. At first there were attendance problems and it was necessary to invest a lot of effort in persuading some mothers to attend. Their apprehension and fear of gossip soon diminished when they realized that the doctor would not reveal their secrets.

The main problems presented by the mothers were those typical of child abusers. These were lack of self-respect, social isolation, poor relationships with parents and husband, and unrealistic expectations of their child. It was in the latter stages of the group that the therapists noted major changes in all these areas. The women had much more self-respect; they had learnt that they were not alone with their problems. They discovered their own areas of competence, and their sense of uselessness diminished as they discovered that they could help others. Their social isolation was greatly alleviated as they often went home with each other and met outside the group. All the mothers became more trusting people and several friendships were formed. In general, they changed most noticeably in their ability to 'get on with other people'. They became much more independent. They gained from each other and from the children's group a far greater knowledge of child rearing and realistic standards of child development. They had received help in adapting to changes in the child's behaviour, especially the increased independence. The independent assessor also noted these changes and commented on a reduction of tension in the women's homes.

The children all revealed some disturbance. The main problems were the child's inability to separate from his mother, inhibited behaviour (i.e. suspicious watchfulness and lack of motivation to move, speak or play), aggressive and attention-seeking behaviour, and delayed development. It was essential to have clear, consistent policies for dealing with all these problems. The aim was to help the children to play, both individually and in a group.

Toys could be used to assess the children's development and allow them to express their emotional problems indirectly.

Careful handling of both mothers and children was needed for dealing with the separation problems. A predictable routine was set up. The children were not cuddled if distressed, but distracted and encouraged to play. In a few weeks, clinging over-attachment was replaced by a happy independence. Participation in the group helped all the children to learn to play. They gained social skills from their contact with other adults and children. Their inhibitions disappeared as they relaxed and established regular trusting relationships. Silly and aggressive behaviour was diverted into constructive play. As the children became happier and more independent they made noticeable advances in development. For example, the child with a failure-to-thrive problem was walking after the first 6 weeks and gained 2 kg. in weight in 2 months.

For disturbed children like these, the importance of special therapeutic care cannot be emphasized enough. The group scheme would not have been nearly so successful if the children's group had merely served as a simple, care-taking function during the mothers' treatment. In conclusion, I feel that group work is important for social work in child abuse, as it can provide a counterbalance to individual casework, and the overdependence that can be created by intensive therapeutic relationships.

Life-lines

In abusing families, it is typically during a crisis that the child ends up abused, and the long-term family problems mean that crises inevitably recur. The families admitted to the Park Hospital for residential treatment are followed up after discharge. Experience of this indicates that, for some, crises do recur. But what is most striking is that, after treatment, they are more able to ask for help before it is too late.

> Freddy, some time after discharge, lost his car licence and then lost his job. The ensuing money problems and marital tension put all the children at risk. He asked the hospital for help. The whole family were admitted for a few days. They were taken away from their problems for a short period, given a safe place, and helped to plan a way out of their financial mess.

Whatever form of therapy the abusing family is receiving, there must be some sort of life-line available, so that they can obtain immediate help at any time of the day or night. Thus, most special units have a 24-hour telephone life-line as an essential part of their service. If the family does not have easy access to a phone, it may be necessary to install one for the child's sake. A telephone life-line could be provided by a local health-services team who could keep a list of the most vulnerable families, knowing when to respond with action.

Those who provide a life-line must be able to offer an immediate place of refuge for the child. Such a facility provides relief for the families and workers alike. There are a variety of places which could provide the 'crisis' bed, paediatric wards, residential children's homes, and foster-parents (see Baher *et al.*, 1976 for use of 'drop-in' foster-mothers). If residential homes provided this sort of service, it would give them an active part in the prevention of family breakdown which could boost the morale of the staff.

(3) Early recognition and prevention

The resources I have considered need not be used only in the treatment of actually abused children and their families, but all of them can be adapted to help parents with the sort of problems that predispose to child abuse. This will only be possible, of course, if we can identify those problems that do lead to abuse.

For this reason it is helpful to regard the family characteristics and stressful events as parts of a long and complex process. Early recognition could be facilitated by a technique designed to elucidate the process rather than concentrating on an isolated cause. Such a technique has recently been developed at the Park Hospital, where the events in each family member's biography are set out in sequence to form a 'critical path', as seen in Figure 10.1. Thus, it is possible to observe clearly the temporal coincidence of stress for each family member and the individual's problems may be viewed against the background of the total family circumstances. In Figure 10.1 it is possible to see the build-up of tension surrounding the twins' birth, each family member having problems which affected the others. When there was no way out, the whole thing exploded. Timely relief from the twins could have prevented the abuse ever happening.

To support the idea of prevention there is an increasing amount of evidence that early recognition of abusers is possible. Indeed, we have found that abusing parents can be identified actually in the maternity hospital. We compared the pregnancies and early histories of abused children with a control group of unabused children born in the same maternity hospital (Lynch and Roberts, 1977). Far more abusing mothers were under 20 years old when having their first child (50% compared with 16%). The abusing parents were far more likely to have been referred to the maternity-hospital social worker (58% compared with 6%). The mothers of the abused children had emotional or psychiatric disturbance recorded more often in the antenatal notes (46% compared with 14%). The abused children were far more likely to have been ill neonatally and admitted to the special-care nursery (42% compared with 10%). What is most striking is that the maternity hospital staff actually recorded concern in the notes about the abusing parents' ability to care for their baby in 44% of cases, compared with only 6% of the controls.

This study shows that maternity staff are identifying the parents who are likely to abuse their child, yet without providing the right sort of help. This is because of their reluctance to label anyone a potential baby batterer; but any family with such problems deserves a comprehensive assessment. Subsequent intervention need not stigmatize, it could be very simple—anything from health visitor's visits during the pregnancy to a mothers' group at the well-baby clinic. Only a very few families will need the intensive help available at a specialist unit.

All those concerned with the care of children and their families have a professional duty to understand more about the process which leads to abuse. Isolated incidents should always be viewed in the light of the total family history. Otherwise a number of predisposing factors could be regarded merely as irrelevant and unconnected events. For example, parents may take a child to the doctor in the morning complaining about a sleeping problem, and then to the social worker in the afternoon complaining about their damp caravan. If both these requests are dealt with in isolation, the parents' underlying predicament with their child has not been understood. This could lead to despair and increase the risk of abuse (Beswick *et al.*, 1976).

If early identification is to lead to prevention, social workers must be prepared to invest their effort and resources in preventive services. Any increased expenditure on prevention would be more than justified by fewer cases needing expensive medical and social-work care after battering. Unless we move the focus of attention from the 'ambulance at the bottom of the cliff' to fixing the road at the top (Gelles, 1973), many children will suffer unnecessarily, and some will even spend the rest of their lives in institutions for the mentally subnormal.

ACKNOWLEDGEMENTS

This chapter was written while I was employed by Action Research for the Crippled Child and seconded to the Park Hospital, Oxford, by Oxfordshire Social Services Department. I am particularly indebted to Dr Margaret Lynch for her comments, and I would also like to thank Dr Christopher Ounsted, Mr Michael Mogg, and Miss Teresa O'Hanrahan for their advice.

REFERENCES

Allan, L. J. (1978) Chapter 3 in this volume.

Appleton, P. (1976) 'Ethological methods of studying the behaviour and development of young children from abusing families'. Martin, 1976.

Armstrong, D. (1974) 'Hospitals: problems of boundary'. In *The Maltreated Child*, ed. J. Carter, London: Priory Press Ltd.

Baher, E., Hyman, C., Jones, C., Jones, R., Kerr, A., and Mitchell, R. (1976) *At Risk: An Account of the Work of the Battered Child Research Department NSPCC*, London: Routledge & Kegan Paul Ltd.

Baldwin, J. A., and Oliver, J. E. (1972) 'Epidemiology and family characteristics of severely abused children', *Brit. J. Prev. and Soc. Medicine*, **29** (4).

Beswick, K., Lynch, M. A., and Roberts J. (1976) 'Child abuse and general practice', *British Medical Journal* (2), 800–802.

Blager, F., and Martin, H. P. (1976) 'Speech and language of abused children'. In ed. H. P. Martin, 1976.

BASW (British Association of Social Workers) (1976) *Code of Practice.*

Burgess R. L. and Conger R., (1976) 'Family interaction. Patterns related to child abuse and neglect', paper presented at International Congress on Child Abuse and Neglect, Geneva, September.

Carter, J. (1974) 'Problems of professional belief'. In *The Maltreated Child*, ed. J. Carter, London: Priory Press Ltd.

Children and Young Persons Act 1969. S.1 (2) and S.2 (1).

Davoren, E. (1968) 'The role of the social worker'. In *The Battered Child*, ed. R. E. Helfer and C. H. Kempe, Chicago: University of Chicago Press.

DHSS (1974) *Report of the Committee of Inquiry into the Care and Supervision Provided in Relation to Maria Colwell*, London: HMSO.

Dinnage, R., and Pringle, M. L. K. (1967a) *Residential Child Care: Facts and Fallacies*, London: Longmans.

Dinnage, R., and Pringle, M. L. K. (1967b) *Foster Home Care: Facts and Fallacies*, London: Longmans.

Erikson, E. H. (1950) 'Eight ages of man'. In *Childhood and Society*, Harmondsworth: Pelican.

Evans, R. (1976) 'Some implications of an intergrated model of social work for theory and practice', *Brit. J. of Soc. Work*, **6** (2), 177–200.

Gelles, R. J. (1973) 'Child abuse as a psychopathology: a sociological critique and reformulation', *Amer. J. Orthopsychiat.*, **43** (4), 611–621.

Grey, J. (1977) 'Drug effects on fear and frustration'. In *Handbook of Psychoparmacology*, ed. L. Iverson, S. Iverson, and S. Snyder, New York: Plenum Press, *in press.*

Hazel, N. (1976) 'Child placement policy: some European comparisons, *Brit. J. of Soc. Work*, **6** (3), 315–326.

Helfer, R. E., and Kempe, C. H. (1972) 'The child's need for early recognition, immediate care and protection'. In *Helping the Battered Child and His Family*, ed. C. H. Kempe and R. E. Helfer, Philadelphia and Toronto: Lippincott.

Jones, C. (1976) 'The fate of abused children', paper presented at symposium on Child Abuse, Royal Society of Medicine, 2–4 June. To be published, ed. A. White Franklin, Academic Press.

Kempe, C. H. (1971) 'Paediatric implications of the battered baby syndrome', *Arch. Dis. Child.*, **46**, 28.

Kempe, C. H., and Helfer, R. E. (1972) 'Innovative therapeutic approaches'. In *Helping the Battered Child and his Family*, ed. C. H. Kempe and R. E. Helfer, Philadelphia and Toronto: Lippincott.

Klein, J. (1956) *The Study of Groups*, London: Routledge & Kegan Paul Ltd, p.131.

Lancet (1975) 'The Battered', editorial, 31 May.

London Borough of Hillingdon Social Services Research (1976. 'Staff costs of child abuse in Hillingdon', London Borough of Hillingdon, March.

Lynch, M. A. (1975) 'Ill-health and child abuse', *Lancet* **2**, 317.

Lynch, M. A., and Ounsted, C. (1976) 'A place of safety'. In *Child Abuse and Neglect. The Family and the Community*, ed. R. E. Helfer and C. H. Kempe, Cambridge, Mass.: Ballinger, chapter 11.

Lynch, M. A., Ounsted, C., and Steinberg, D. (1975) 'Family unit in a children's psychiatric hospital', *British Medical Journal*, **2**, 127.

Lynch, M. A., Roberts, J., and Gordon, M. (1976) 'Early warning of child abuse', *Dev. Medicine and Child Neurology*, December.

Lynch, M. A., and Roberts, J. (1977) 'Predicting child abuse: signs of bonding failure in the maternity hospital', *British Medical Journal*, **1**, 624–626.

Martin, H. P. (1976) *The Abused Child*, Cambridge, Mass.: Ballinger.

Martin, H. P., and Beezley, P. (1976) 'Therapy for abusive parents: its effect on the child'. In Martin, 1976, chapter 20.

Martin, H. P., Beezley, P., Conway, E., and Kempe, C. H. (1974) 'The development of abused children', *Advances in Pediatrics*, **21**, 25–73.

Mayer, J. E., and Timms, N. (1970) *The Client Speaks*, London: Routledge & Kegan Paul Ltd.

Melville, J. (1976) 'Paid to foster', *New Society*, 21 October.

Norfolk County Council (1975) 'Report of the Review Body appointed to enquire into the case of Stephen Meurs', Norwich, December.

Oppé, T. E. (1975) 'Problems of communication and co-ordination'. In *Concerning Child Abuse*, ed. A., White Franklin, Edinburgh, London, and New York: Churchill Livingstone.

Ounsted, C. (1972) 'Biographical science. An essay on developmental medicine'. In *Psychiatric Aspects of Medical Practice*, ed. B. Mandelbrote and M. Gelder, London: Staples Press Ltd.

Ounsted, C., and Lynch, M. A. (1976) 'Family pathology as seen in England'. In *Child Abuse and Neglect. The Family and the Community*, ed. R. E. Helfer, and C. H. Kempe, Cambridge, Mass.: Ballinger.

Ounsted, C., Oppenheimer, R., and Lindsay, J. (1974) 'Aspects of bonding failure: the psychopathology and psychotherapeutic treatment of families of battered children', *Dev. Med. Child Neurol.*, **16** (4).

Packman, J. (1975) *The Child's Generation*, Oxford and London: Blackwell & Robertson, p.56.

Parker, R. A. (1966) *Decision in Child Care. A Study of Prediction in Fostering*, London: Allen & Unwin.

Paulson, M. J., and Chaleff, A. (1973) 'Parent surrogate roles: a dynamic concept in understanding and treating abusive parents', *Journal of Clinical Child Psychology*, **11** (3), 38–41.

Pickett, J., and Paton, A. (1976) 'Protective casework and child abuse: practice and problems', paper presented at symposium on Child Abuse, Royal Society of Medicine, 2–4 June. To be published, ed. A. White Franklin, Academic Press.

Reavley, W., and Gilbert, M. (1976) 'The behavioural treatment approach to potential child abuse—Two illustrative case reports', *Social Work Today*, **7** (6).

Roberts, J., Beswick, K., Leverton, B. and Lynch, M. A. (1977) 'Prevention of child abuse. Group therapy for mothers and children in the community', *Practitioner*, **219**, 111–115.

Schneider, C., Pollock, C., and Helfer, R. E. (1972) 'Interviewing the parents'. In *Helping the Battered Child and his Family*, ed. C. H. Kempe, and R. E. Helfer, Philadelphia and Toronto: Lippincott.

Skinner, A. E., and Castle, R. L. (1969) *Seventy eight Battered Children: A Retrospective Study*, London: NSPCC.

Smith, G., and Ames, J. (1976) 'Area teams in social work practice: a programme for research', *Brit. J. of Soc. Work*, **6** (1), 43–69.

Smith, S. M., and Hanson, R. (1975) 'Interpersonal relationships and child-rearing practices in 214 parents of battered children', *Brit. J. Psychiat.*, **127**, 513–25.

Smith, S. M., Hanson, R., and Noble, S., (1974) 'Social aspects of the battered baby syndrome', *Brit. J. Psychiat.*, **125**, 568–582.

Steele, B. F., and Pollock, C. B. (1968) 'A psychiatric study of parents who abuse infants and small children'. In *The Battered Child*, ed. R. E. Helfer and C. H. Kempe, Chicago: University of Chicago Press.

Timms, N. (1970) *Social Work*, Routledge & Kegan Paul Ltd, London: P.90.

Urwin, K. (1974) 'Social services: problems of resources'. In *The Maltreated Child*, ed. J. Carter, London: Priory Press Ltd.
Whitaker, D. S. (1975) 'Some conditions for effective work with groups', *Brit. J. of Soc. Work*, 5 (4), 423–439.
Younghusband, E. L. (1959) *Report of the Working Party on Social Workers*, London: HMSO.

11

WOMEN IN REFUGES

Joy Melville

'I've wanted to leave for years, but what can you do when you've got three kids? Where can you go?' Remarks like this, from women who have undergone physical or mental abuse from their husbands, have always been unanswerable. Up to about 150 years ago, a man had the 'right' under English law to chastise his wife; and until refuges were set up in the early 1970s most women had no alternative to putting up with violence. By the end of 1976, over 100 refuges had been established in Britain. Many of these were seriously overcrowded, and there was a need for far more, but a start had been made. This chapter attempts to sketch the main features of this experience, and consider what lessons can be learned from it.

THE WOMEN'S PLIGHT

Attitudes to battered wives are still ambivalent and sometimes hostile. The founder of a Midlands refuge said that when she stood in the street with a placard to get support for opening the refuge, women themselves came up to her and said: 'Just let a man hit me, I'd soon show him. Those women must like it.' It's also claimed that some women 'enjoy' being beaten, finding it 'erotic'. But what erotic pleasure is there in being kicked in the stomach when pregnant, or having your jaw broken? 'We have had terrible cases,' said one refuge. 'One of our women was lashed with a hosepipe. Some say the women exaggerate: we need to make people understand what these women put up with.'

The accounts of 'Some Violent Families' at the beginning of this book have given an impression of the sorts of lives some women have endured for considerable periods before enough was enough. Many people would ask: 'Why stay with a husband under these conditions? Why not leave immediately violence takes place?' But few who have not faced physical assault can understand that, immediately afterwards, a woman's power of making decisions can completely disappear, and she will resort to routine tasks like tidying the drawers or cleaning the stove.

Just to walk out of the house, with nowhere to go, is almost impossible. A woman can rarely get any money from social security before she leaves home because, technically, she has a home and financial support from a husband. (Sometimes, if legal proceedings have been started, financial aid is given.) Normally the woman has to leave, find a place to live, and then wait until she is seen by a social security officer. If she just walks out with the children there is a real risk they may be taken into care even though the mother naturally does not want to be parted from them and, in any case, this is only a short-term solution. If they should be taken into care this would put the woman in the 'single, homeless' category, and would stop her being considered for council accommodation. She may have no place at all to go to. The Select Committee on Violence in Marriage confirmed that they had

> received evidence that some battered wives who leave home are told by local authority officials that they cannot be regarded as homeless so long as they have a marital home. We believe this advice is wrong and that all local authorities should be made fully aware of their duty to provide temporary accommodation for battered women. (SC 1975, § 26)

If the woman merely takes out an injunction against her husband, charges him, or starts divorce proceedings, she might have to go on living with him in the same house. To a woman who may have been badly beaten in the past this might be a terrifying and unacceptable prospect. She may indeed not be protected at all. One woman, giving evidence to the Select Committee, said:

> I have been to the police. I nicked my husband. He gave me ten stitches, and they held him in the nick over the weekend and he came out on Monday. He was bound over to keep the peace, that was all. On the Tuesday he gave me the hiding of my life. (SC 1975, § 10)

Even a social worker calling, or a follow-up visit by the police, can provoke the husband into renewed violence. Some women fear despairingly that even if they get away, their husband would inevitably find them and take his revenge. However if the wife stays in a violent environment her mental or physical health will suffer, and she will turn to her doctor for help. But doctors invariably prescribe tranquillizers, which solve nothing.

FOUNDING REFUGES

For solving the battered woman's dilemma the founding of the 'refuge' system was of the utmost importance. In fact it came about almost by accident. Erin Pizzey started Chiswick Women's Aid in 1971 from a small house in Chiswick, merely as a community centre, where women and their children could meet to escape from the isolation and loneliness of which so many of them complained. The plan was for them to talk about the things in their lives which they found unacceptable and try to change them.

In describing the venture in her book, *Scream Quietly or the Neighbours Will Hear* (1974), Erin Pizzey says that the subject of wife bashing was being discussed, and one mother of nine children suddenly admitted that her husband had beaten her all her married life. She had gone to the social services, but they had just told her to go home. The group checked out the position with the social services departments of surrounding boroughs, all of whom confirmed that once a woman leaves home she has voluntarily made herself homeless, so is not entitled to assistance. One social worker even said: 'It is not the policy of the social services to interfere with the sanctity of marriage.' Other women who came to the house in Chiswick admitted to having been battered, and started to use the house as a refuge to get away from the violence in their own homes. Radio, television, and newspaper reports brought even more women (some 5000 in the first $2^1/_2$ years); and letters from battered wives came from all over Britain. Chiswick Women's Aid turned into a crisis refuge for such wives and, due to the publicity that Erin Pizzey successfully fostered, the problem at last got much-needed national attention.

Erin Pizzey told me that, for her, it was a personal thing:

> Although I did not see my mother beaten, she cried an awful lot behind doors. I went for help. And so years later, when a woman stood there and took off her sweater and showed me her bruises and said, 'No one would help me,' I saw it had not changed from my time. Something had to be done.

In April 1974, the first Women's Aid National Conference was held. Chiswick Women's Aid agreed to appoint a national co-ordinator, and the Department of Health and Social Security gave a grant for this purpose. A second conference was held in January 1975, when there was a resolution calling for a national organization. The intention was that local groups would operate individually, but would be linked at a national level for information, publicity, and negotiations. Delegates decided to set up a National Federation—but at that point the Chiswick group withdrew, preferring to operate entirely on its own. By mid-1976, the National Women's Federation had 71 groups, with 16 more applying to join. There were also seven groups in Scotland.

The federation is particularly anxious to encourage the women in refuges to regain their self-respect and confidence. The refuge is not just meant to provide a roof over their heads, but to help them become more independent and self-reliant by running the refuge themselves, taking the day-to-day decisions, and sharing problems with the women there. The moral support they give each other, and the friendships they make, are particularly important to women who have previously suffered severe isolation because of their situation. They go with one another to court, for example, or take each other's children out. Most important, they can see that there are others like themselves, who have been treated equally badly, so that they need no longer feel the problem is theirs alone.

Any Women's Aid group wanting to set up a refuge can get all the information and advice it needs from the federation—including research pamphlets and a kit for new groups. The administration needed to set up a refuge can be extensive. York Women's Aid, for instance, which started in November 1974, produced a report on battered women from such sources as doctors, social services, Samaritans, and the police, and sent it to heads of social services, community, and women's organizations, and so on, with an invitation to a public meeting. It also distributed some 1500 leaflets and, before the meeting, put posters up in the centre of town and the council-housing estates. The meeting, to publicize the aims of the group, was packed out. But such efforts can be unrewarding: the Hastings group, for example, wrote to 400 people in the town to invite them to a similar meeting, and only received about 15 replies. They then wrote to 75 doctors and got three replies.

Members of the Women's Aid groups vary in age (though most are in their 20s or 30s), professions, and politics. The women involved in York Women's Aid originally came from the Women's Action Group connected with the university, but the group now includes working women from the town and social workers. At Norwich, it was the Women's Liberation group which first discussed the idea of a refuge. One thing all members of the Women's Aid groups have in common is a feeling of outrage at the violent way so many women are treated.

The decision to start a refuge can come about quite spontaneously. The Leicester group, for example, got together in April 1974 because one or two women, and some social workers, thought a refuge was needed. There were a few paragraphs in the press about the group, with a contact phone number, and battered women started to ring up. They would ring weekly or monthly to see if a house was yet available for a refuge. Some had their bags packed secretly. The refuge opened in the December of the same year, catering for about nine families. The group then managed to get a second house, so that there were on average some five to six families in each house at any one time.

Getting a house is the main problem would-be refuges face. This, as shown below, can take many forms. For example, one would-be refuge in the Home Counties was told 'There is no need for a refuge in this town, it is a terribly nice place.' Only after the Women's Aid group had sent the council reports from the police, hospital workers, and social workers supporting the need was a house rather reluctantly granted. Another group was offered a dilapidated old mansion, mainly inhabited by vagrant alcoholics, on the condition it raised some £4000 to pay for mending the roof, floors, and windows and put in baths, heating, and so on. While arguing with the council over who should pay, the place burnt down. Three months later the group was offered another place, needing £1000 to make it habitable. The council again would not pay, and the refuge was only opened after a large groceries chain made a house available. It seems a particularly short-sighted attitude: many battered wives are on the housing list as homeless families, and it would obviously help the situation if some of these could be housed together.

A major frustration is the time taken to achieve anything; sometimes the reasons may be genuine, other delays may be caused by the dragging of feet. For example, the National Women's Aid Federation, in a letter to the clerk of the Select Committee on Violence in the Family (9 March 1976), reported that one of their groups had been campaigning in Bath for 18 months for a house, but were still without anything at all. In Cockermouth and Swindon, where the groups did have accommodation, the local authorities were unwilling to pay for the cost of fireproofing the premises, which meant that the groups themselves would somehow have to raise the money for this. In Scotland, the Glasgow group was still in a tenement block as the council, despite promises, had not provided alternative premises. In Dundee, after waiting 2 years, the group had finally been offered a flat, instead of the house which was really needed.

The long struggle of Dorset Women's Aid to get a house for them to use as a refuge culminated in the publication of a report which included the entire correspondence with the local council, along with cuttings of local press coverage (Dorset Women's Aid, n.d.). The frustrations of dealing with the stonewalling tactics of local councils are clearly shown by a succession of letters from the County Council, such as the following:

> There is little I can add to our previous correspondence. However sympathetic one may be to your committee's objectives, the 'provision' of a house as a Refuge for battered wives would—since the Social Services Committee own no vacant houses—involve its purchase, and there would necessarily be a continuing commitment to give financial support to its running costs. The present financial climate is such that a significant extension of service such as this is just not possible in the light of increasing numbers of people needing help ....

By the end of 1976, 37 projects had been approved for grant aid under the Home Office's Urban Programme, and expenditure was expected to run at about £420 000. Under this programme 75% of the cost of an approved project for 5 years is paid to an organization which is supported by a local authority. The local authority must pay the other 25%. This procedure has probably led to an unrealistically low provision of refuges because, as the Select Committee pointed out:

> Several local authorities have so far refused to support applications for urban aid, since they are unwilling to pay their 25%

> contribution. For such reasons the pattern of refuges over the country as a whole is very uneven, and we consider this to be an unsatisfactory state of affairs. (SC 1975, §28)

There are still wide variations in the amount of support different refuges receive. In Bristol and Swindon, for example, where the groups have accommodation, they are unable to get any funding from their local authorities, and the Leeds refuge had their request for Urban Aid turned down by the social services department on the grounds that they were not a priority. On the other hand, the Shield refuge at Manchester was granted £10 000 the first year they applied, and a guarantee of £6750 a year for the next 4 years. Similar stories of no, or grudging, co-operation could be told of other areas. Much depends on the attitudes of local politicians. At present, as the National Women's Aid Federation put it,

> the situation is very much like a lottery ... whether or not the woman can actually leave her husband and find alternative housing depends entirely on the various housing authorities and their policies can change with a change in council.

Changes in councils, one might add, due to matters which have absolutely no relation to the needs of battered women.

It is almost impossible to get away from the subject of money with refuges, as it is a constant topic. An April 1976 monthly report of the Canterbury refuge ended:

> On a day-to-day expenditure basis we are getting no financial assistance whatsoever. Social Security are refusing at present to allow a rent allowance to those living here, due to it being a squat and even though we are appealing, this is proving lengthy. We have at present an electricity bill for £252 for the whole winter ... the situation is desperate—we need help now.

At Canterbury, the average expenditure each week from November 1975 to March 1976 was £51.49 and, during that period, the bill for the telephone was £83.78; for rates, £107; for coal, £76.85 (the women contributed £4 a week per family towards electricity and rates).

Very often, the income was way below the expenditure. How is the gap met? In Canterbury's case—as with many other refuges—it is a question of existing on the proceeds of discos, donations, and so on. The National Women's Aid Federation report, *Battered Women Need Refuges*, stresses that raising money is one of the main tasks for Women's Aid groups:

> At first, a relatively small amount will be needed to cover postage, duplicating, etc. Once a house has been secured, much larger

> amounts of money will be needed for furnishings, repairs and workers' salaries. It is possible to operate with voluntary labour alone, but it is certainly not ideal. Some groups have been lucky enough to get substantial urban grants. Most have had to depend upon what they can raise from elsewhere. Jumble sales, raffles, dances and donation schemes are all being used. Applications to local firms, colleges and charitable trusts have had very variable amounts of success, but may have unexpected results, such as donations in kind. One very good source of funds is talks to women's groups of all kinds. Some people have found their local Mother's Union or Townswomen's Guild to be practised fund-raisers and extremely sympathetic. (NWAF, 1975)

Some groups decide to apply for charitable status, which has the advantage of allowing a rate rebate. Would-be donors may also withold their money until the group is an official charity.

LIFE IN REFUGES

Poverty is the first thing that strikes you when you visit refuges: invariably there are peeling walls, patched lino, and a general state of disrepair. Conditions are crowded: small children run in and out of the spartanly furnished rooms, creating minor chaos, and there's little heating. Money is a preoccupation of the women there, too, as they are usually totally dependent on the state. The Women's Aid group not only helps them over claiming various benefits, but also teaches them how to budget and manage their affairs, so that they can cope after they leave the refuge.

There is no such thing as an average routine day at a refuge: emergencies blow up without warning, such as a family wanting to come in when there's no room left, or a husband beating at the door. The day I was at the Canterbury refuge, however, was comparatively quiet. One of the Women's Aid group showed me around the various rooms: most contained two or three women, talking or lying down on the bed. Children sat on the stairs or played in the hall, but were kept firmly out of the small downstairs office. The house, largish and once attractively decorated with painted panels in the main room, was badly in need of repair. Broken glass in some of the windows was papered over. Some of the women were out shopping (they buy their own food), or were taking their children for a walk. From 2 p.m. to 4 p.m., a member of the support group runs a playgroup for the under-5s to give the mothers a break—a chance, perhaps, to go to the solicitor's alone, or the social services, or just to see a friend outside the refuge.

Naturally there are tensions in a refuge full of over-stressed women. The day I was there, a woman was complaining fiercely to one of the support group about another woman at the refuge allowing a boyfriend to come inside. She was asked to bring it up at the meeting to be held that afternoon.

There were, in fact, two meetings a week: one of these had members of the support group present, and dealt mainly with finances. The other was for the women of the refuge only, as they ran things collectively. That afternoon, the meeting was the one which had members of the support group present, but most of the women in the house were there too. There were reports from the secretary of the group on the state of the finances and how the fund-raising activities were going, as well as a general discussion on such things as how to get redecoration going. The woman brought up her complaint, and the matter was thrashed out. Afterwards, most of them went out to the kitchen to make tea. The women mostly spent the evening in their rooms, talking to each other, reading, putting children to bed, listening to the radio.

THE USE MADE OF REFUGES

The statistics kept by the Canterbury group give an insight into the initial intake of women. In the 6 months from the opening of the refuge in November 1975, to the end of April 1976, a total of 140 women came. The main referrals were from the social services, the police, the Samaritans, other refuges, press, and friends. Most of the women were attached to social workers and had been problem cases for the social services department. A typical extract from the list of admissions appears in Table 11.1.

Table 11.1 Extract from list of admissions to the Canterbury refuge

Area	Age	No. of Kids	Duration of stay	Extent of beating
Whitstable	19	1	3 weeks	Internal haemorrhage
Ashford	20	—	1 day	Head injury
Ashford	28	3	1 month	Bitten and internal bleeding
Dover	26	2	2 days	locked up and starved
Canterbury	35	4	1 week	whipped
Herne Bay	21	2	still here	bruised back
Whitstable	50	—	3 days	mental
Gillingham	29	5	4 days	black eyes

The controversial 'open-door' policy—which resulted in serious overcrowding at Chiswick, and is also practised at Canterbury—is a problem which all the refuges face, as there are simply too few of them to meet the need. If a woman who has been badly hurt turns up or phones for help and the refuge is full, what do you do? Different refuges solve it in different ways, always contriving that no crisis cases are turned away. Some refuges have a list of people who will put up a woman and her family during an emergency, though this is not very satisfactory as the emergency might last some time.

Others will put the woman and her family up for the night as an emergency measure and the next day contact other refuges to see which has room available. This may entail the woman travelling some distance, but at least it prevents her from accidentally meeting the husband, which can—and does—happen in the same neighbourhood. Indeed, Leicester refuge is hoping to arrange for wives to 'swap' houses nationwide:

> Wives are too frightened to go back because they know their husband will come after them, especially if they have no phone to ring the police. We say, 'Don't open the door,' but they say, 'He will break it down.' You can replace broken arms on the NHS; no one replaces broken doors.

The phone numbers and addresses of other refuges are kept by the support group, in case they should get into the wrong hands at the refuge—that is, a man's hands. Most refuges would agree with the notice posted on the door of the Canterbury refuge: 'This refuge is run by women for women. Men are only invited in to do a specific job.' Chiswick is one of the exceptions, however, that have men helpers, because it is felt that it is good for the children to see a man around who is gentle rather than violent.

Some refuges keep their presence so secret that, apart from the main referral agencies, who usually have the phone number of one of the support group, few know it exists. The serious disadvantage to this policy is that wives in need must also have difficulty in contacting the refuge. For instance, when I rang the social services department in Hampshire, I was told they could give me no information about refuges in their area. When I telephoned the Bournemouth police, I was transferred to several different police officers and was finally told they did not have the telephone number of a refuge, but would send a constable around if I needed help. A woman who might only be able to make one quick phone call for assistance would have given up long before.

Another disadvantage of secrecy is that the public is largely unaware of the existence of the refuge, so does not support it with donations. One well-wisher sent a large sum to Chiswick Women's Aid, not realizing that there was a local refuge badly in need of funds. On the other hand, publicizing the address and the work of the refuge, and holding whist drives and such like to fund-raise, may result in the husbands turning up at the refuge.

> We have had violent husbands at the door [said Canterbury] and we keep an emergency 2p ready in the phone slot to phone the police—who always come very quickly. Neighbours in this street are also fantastically helpful if there is a rumpus, and phone the police for us. We usually know if there are likely to be husbands coming around, as someone would have seen them drunk in a pub. We then put a chain and four bolts on the door. If the husband is bleating he wants to speak to his wife, it's entirely up to the wife.

THE OUTCOME OF TAKING REFUGE

If the husband does locate his wife, as the Kettering refuge emphasized,

> the pressure they put on their wife to return can be a big factor. They will send bunches of flowers, and promise to do token things like redecorate the house, or make the tenancy over to joint ownership. And the wife says, 'He really has changed, he really is going to try this time.' They get overcome with pity when the husband produces plausible reasons why they should go back, or—which is standard—threatens suicide.

Sometimes, if the wife does go back, the situation is improved as she realizes she can return to the refuge if conditions compel her to. ('I'll give him a chance,' said one woman. 'We had something together once. He's learned his lesson now; he knows I can go.') The stay at the refuge has usually changed the woman too. Few may have questioned their position before, but if they go back, they argue their case—whereas before they accepted it.

If the wives are going to go back, they usually do so within 2 or 3 weeks of arriving at the refuge ('Sometimes within a day you can tell who is going back,' said one refuge.) Although going back may seem incomprehensible to outsiders, there are understandable reasons—quite apart from the pressure and apparent change of character of the hus band. Refuges, for instance, are literally emergency centres: 'My God, it's better at home,' said one new arrival. Community living, with the noise and lack of privacy, can be very hard. The future prospect of living on their own, bringing up the children themselves, worries many of the wives. Many would rather face a beating than loneliness. Some consider, on reflection, that the reasonably happy periods they have with their husbands just about balance out the physical maltreatment. As one said: 'It's like having a baby: straight after, you think, "never again"; then you block it out.' At the refuge, women have each other's companionship, understanding, and support. Many feel, therefore, that although they do not want to stay there indefinitely, and do not want their children to be brought up there, they still prefer it to life at home. Some women just need to come to a refuge for a breathing space, to get time to think things out: it may be for as little as one night.

The following shows what happened to 38 of the early arrivals at the Canterbury refuge:

17 returned home to husband/boyfriend (5 later went back to refuge)
7 went to relatives elsewhere
2 went to other refuges
3 obtained injunctions and went home
1 got rehoused
8 went away to other addresses, but returned to refuge.

Out of the 38, therefore, only 12 returned home for good; after their stay at the refuge, the rest changed their circumstances in some way.

One way in which refuges are of specific help is that the women can compare the demands their husbands have made on them. Until then, some simply do not know if these are reasonable or not. Ever since getting married, they may have accepted that if the dinner was not ready on time, or if they overspent, they would get knocked around. Quite a few of the women complained, too, of the way their husband would keep them up late at night by constant talking. One said her husband would say, 'Get out of bed and make me some tea,' and then, when she had, he would say, 'For goodness' sake get me something to eat.' Once she had, he would say, 'Why did you get this bread? I don't want that.' It was this kind of mental battering that had brought this woman to the refuge. As the Canterbury refuge said: 'Quite a lot of the women who come here have been mentally battered by incredibly petty restrictions on their basic women's liberties in such a way that it makes life unbearable. They feel that staying with their husband has no future and they want to make a different life.'

Mental battering, or abuse, can cause as much, or more, distress as physical battering, and accounts for a high proportion of the women in the refuges. Very often it is constant humiliation by the husband—who is set on ridiculing his wife in public, or proving her wrong, to reinforce his own superiority. Insults and constant criticism can reach intolerable heights—whether sexual taunts or accusations about being a bad wife and mother. When it goes on for hour after hour, the woman is as bemused by it as after physical battering. She loses her confidence in herself, and her general ability to cope.

One woman, who has put up with this for over 25 years, has been to one refuge twice. She returns to the man because he has reduced her to the state where she no longer has the confidence to stand on her own feet. 'To many women, mental battering is the final straw,' said the Hastings refuge. 'They can take the clips round the ears, but not the criticism and the lack of concern when they are ill.' Even those who are physically battered have the mental stress of being under constant threat of cruelty: sitting, knowing that sooner or later they are probably going to get knocked around, and can do nothing about it.

Why *don't* they retaliate? say the sceptics. This, again, raises the wider problem of the way women have been conditioned into playing their accepted, submissive role. 'Little girls don't fight,' is still the maxim: girls can rarely be seen pummelling each other on the ground, like boys. As adults, they are shocked at a blow which a man would automatically counter. Battering can also start insidiously. The first time it happens and the wife, say, gets a black eye, she will think, 'He couldn't have been feeling very well. Something went wrong during the day.' They believe it is a one-off occurrence; and then it happens again. And the man, in turn, having done it once, finds it easier the next time.

Women are also reared to believe that it is *their* job to make a good marriage and that it is therefore their fault if things go wrong. They are ashamed of being seen with bruises or a black eye, as they feel this shows them up, rather than their husband. So they stay in, and will not answer the door. They tell their doctor they have fallen downstairs, and if they do tell the truth the doctor often does not believe it: 'Don't by silly, your husband is such a nice man. I get a dozen neurotic women like you telling me this a week. Are you sure you're giving him enough sex?'

Refuges can be of great help in changing this attitude of guilt which many women have. As one refuge said:

> Several of the women came in at the beginning and used to say, 'I looked after him very well, I always had his dinner ready, and I dressed up and looked nice—where did I go wrong?' Not where did *he* go wrong, but very much blaming themselves. After a few months of exchanging experiences, they begin to realize that they can't all be in the wrong.

One wife at the Kettering refuge said, in a matter of fact manner, 'I have always been beaten up. I thought most women were.' While women continue to accept the frequent male belief that a marriage ring, or cohabitation, reduces a woman to his ownership, to be treated as he wishes, battering will still continue. Changing these indoctrinated attitudes is a problem all the Women's Aid groups are aware of. They avoid any heavy-handed 'big sister' attempt to alter these, however, leaving it to the women to work it out for themselves in conversation with each other.

THE VIOLENT MEN

Violent men themselves need specialized help—as Chiswick Women's Aid has recognized by setting up Men's Aid in a house in North London (briefly described in chapter 12). Such men, however, are often oblivious of anything being wrong with their behaviour. This fact was generally endorsed by the refuges. As Hastings said, 'We see them when they are evicted and they are usually very self-pitying and can't understand what's happened. If their wife has an obvious black eye, they are a little bit more sorry: but if it doesn't show, they can forget it.' Leicester refuge had similar experience: ?'I have met them [the husbands] at court: some say, "It's a complete fabrication, I've never done anything, I love her and want her back. Who else will get my dinner?" Or they are genuinely sorry, and don't know why they did it.' Nevertheless, it's not just uncontrollable anger: there is often a technique to their beating. They are careful to hit the woman where it does not show—punching under her chin, above the hair line, in the stomach and on the thigh.

Kettering refuge thought that much could be attributed to pressures on the husband:

> For instance, too much work or not enough. In a way, it's a show of love, as you always bare your feelings to the person who is nearest to you. I am sure a lot of them do love their wife. They break down and go into a complete decline when the wives move away. It's amazing and terribly pathetic.

The men concerned, however, seem to expect it all ways. The wife is needed for their personal support when the pressures get too much.

The men's attitudes to women, long conditioned by society, are the main root of the problem. The wife is regarded as property; something which the man totally owns, and has the right to treat as he wishes. His behaviour outside the home is often impeccable: people simply do not believe that such an apparently charming man changes once inside the house. The idea of the woman becoming property after marriage is endorsed by many of the women in the refuges. One had her first black eye on her wedding night. ('He was the nicest man you could ever hope to meet.') 'Sometimes a woman has lived with a man for several years,' said the Canterbury refuge, 'and it's been all right; but when they marry, it starts. It's extraordinary.' Other, uninvolved men often tacitly support this attitude. One of the refuge women said that one night her husband had beaten her and she had screamed out, 'God help me.' Her screams could obviously be heard through the wall, as the man nextdoor promptly shouted out, 'Go on, Ben, kill her.' One of the support group at another refuge said she had heard two men laughing in a pub over a woman they had heard screaming, saying she sounded like a child having a tantrum. Wife battering seems to be considered as a sign of strength. Yet it seems to be a weakness in the man's character which results in an attempt to dominate, to show-her-who's-boss.

The domination, possessiveness, and suspicion shown by some of the men involved is certainly abnormal. As the Leicester refuge said:

> Some won't let their wives have any friends: they are suspicious that they have other boyfriends, and never take their wife out with them, but keep her in the house. In one case where the wife was working and the husband was not, he would come every day to the café where she worked as a waitress and sit and watch her and scrounge cups of tea. If she smiled at anyone, he would be suspicious and believe it was a boyfriend. She was both frightened of losing her job and of being beaten up by him.

In another case, a man went to bed with a razor placed under the pillow, which he threatened to use if she did not do sexually what he wanted. Another would go off with other women and when he came in would play a record over and over again, which had words like, 'The leaves are falling on our grave, and the sky is grey; isn't it time you went away.'

The Kettering refuge had come across similar experiences:

> The women can't have a friend, not even talk to the nextdoor neighbour. They can't even go to the shops unless they are back in 5 minutes. It's all right for the husband to go out with others, of course. One woman had a packet of bones from the butcher on top of the fridge, for the dog, and her husband said, 'How does the butcher know you have a dog? You must be having an affair with him.' He then beat her. Another woman said that once, when the television went wrong and the mechanic came to mend it, her husband had gone absolutely berserk because she had made the man a cup of tea. He said she did not care about the kids but cared more about the TV man.

This possessive domination can extend to the most trivial episode. One woman did not have supper ready in time—due to trying to cope with four children—and the man attacked her with a hammer. Another wanted to get the washing done one morning, but her husband was still lying in bed and she needed the sheets. His reply to her request was to damage her spine, kidneys, and break her jaw. In a third case, a husband wanted his trousers, and the wife said, 'I know I should have ironed them, but I had to get the dinner.' The husband went to her purse, saying that she did not deserve any money, and took some out. This particular woman had to tidy the house meticulously before the husband came home each night—making sure no toys were showing, and that there were no crumbs on the carpet—or he would beat her.

FUTURE DEVELOPMENTS

The Women's Aid philosophy of encouraging women to run their own refuges can lead to difficulties. Attitudes of social workers may vary from extremely helpful to antagonistic. Some are worried that the refuge will be unable to cope if, say, a child gets an infectious disease: many also dislike there being no warden in charge. This, however, is fundamental to Women's Aid policy: by giving the women responsibility for the daily running of the refuge, they gain confidence and the ability to face the future as an unsupported mother. A warden would only make them dependent again—as well as taking up space and requiring a salary.

The Women's Aid helpers behind the refuge have been generally unpaid, many holding down other jobs—though some refuge workers do now get a salary. The refuges are immensely time-consuming. One or more of the group—depending on the size and number of the refuges—has to be either at the refuge(s) or available day and night by phone to cope with any emergency decisions or problems. Daily routine work can include: lobbying and liaising with various council departments; arranging legal matters such as helping to get injunctions, contacting solicitors over divorces, and accompanying women to court; helping fund-raising activities; paying bills; keeping records; giving advice asked for by the women; arranging for the children to go to school, or running playgroups; helping with the redecoration of the house; going to weekly support-group meetings and sometimes the weekly meetings of the women in the refuge; and so on. The financial struggle to carry on is probably the most wearing; yet these refuges are plugging an embarrassingly large hole in the country's welfare services. They must be given the financial means to carry on with their work without this constant strain.

Certainly, there are no real alternatives to refuges. The wife can be offered *temporary* accommodation by the housing department, but the husband can walk into this at any time, and remove the children or threaten her. The same thing can happen if she goes to relations—and here there is also the problem of overcrowding. Understandably, relatives are also uneasy at the prospect of their being involved in violent confrontations.

It is essential that there should be enough refuges to house those in need. As well as the refuge itself, however, which acts as a crisis centre, a 'stage-two' house is also needed, where two or three families could stay after moving on from the refuge, while litigation takes place, or a council house is found. Ideally, this would be reasonably near the main refuge so that friendship links could be maintained. Those in the main refuge would be helped by seeing for themselves that there were women who had been through the trauma of leaving, and had succeeded in holding their own and not returning. The main difficulty here is that if there is only a single stage-two house, this may well get blocked by women staying there for months as they wait for housing. Some women from the Chiswick refuge have, in desperation, moved out into any empty house—as squatters—and are sharing the accommodation with one other family, or sometimes two. This gives them the support and companionship they need, particularly over bringing up children. The stage-two house has, in effect, become their permanent house.

CONCLUSIONS

It is very clear from talking to both those who run the refuges and the women who live in them that it is impossible to define the 'typical' battered wife and the 'typical' battering husband. They do not exist. Everyone's circumstances are individual, varying widely over class and income. Certain general patterns do emerge, however.

Drink, for instance, is frequently associated with battering: it leads to fights in pubs and exacerbates underlying aggression. Some of the worst cases of battering have been by husbands who are drunk, or alcoholics, and have lost control—unaware or uncaring of the result. Nevertheless, drink is the catalyst and not the cause.

Battering also tends to increase when there is unemployment: in those circumstances, overspending by as little as 50p can be a major event. The husband's attitude to money often creates problems: sometimes wives are given ridiculously small sums for housekeeping. This naturally creates aggression and matters are sometimes worsened by the husband rocking the financial boat still further by spending the money he saves on drink or other women.

Another important factor in battering relationships is the number of husbands who are obviously disturbed and in need of psychiatric care: their possessiveness or lack of control, for example, is abnormal. Some have already been in psychiatric hospitals, but their outward conduct is rarely extreme enough to result in their committal. As few admit to unbalanced behaviour, it is rare for them to go to hospital voluntarily.

Most women in the refuges come from a relatively poor background. But the main reason for this, according to those running the refuges, is not that only working-class women are involved, but that women with access to money can afford to move out to a place of their own, or have relations who have sufficient room to put them up. Middle-class women are also more confident about organizing solicitors, or legal aid.

A violent background is often claimed to play a distinctive part in battering. Certainly, many of the women in the refuges have married men whose fathers previously beat their mothers, or who have battered a previous wife. But a violent background is not a standard factor: many of the women in refuges say that they and their husbands had a stable background. However, the children of battered wives certainly suffer—even if they do not reproduce the violence in their own marriages. They are not necessarily physically harmed themselves—indeed, it is often only when the man *does* harm them that the wife finally walks out—but having to watch their parents quarrelling and fighting is very traumatic. The mother usually takes the children with her if she leaves home—whether to relations or a refuge—and this may happen several times. The NSPCC report, *Yo-Yo Children* (Moore, 1974), shows the emotional damage resulting from this restless background. And if they are taken into care, it is sometimes difficult for them to form a successful, loving relationship when they marry.

There is a constant call for more research into background causes, so that these, too, can be tackled. There is a danger, however, that too much time and money will be spent on creating a whole research industry around battered wives—supporting, contradicting, or perfecting present findings *ad infinitum*. This time and money would be better spent in improving present refuges, or starting new ones. This is where the real need lies.

The other main need is to re-educate women with regard to their attitude to their husbands or cohabitees. As long as women believe men are the dominant, superior partner, they will be prey to battering. If a man took out his aggression on the first passer-by, he would probably be arrested: women should no longer accept that he has the 'right' to take it out on them.

One of the biggest achievements of the refuges is the change they have brought about in the attitudes of the women who go to them. By comparing experiences, they are beginning to question the man's previously accepted behaviour. If they do return to him, they often do so on a less submissive basis—knowing they can come back to the refuge. They are also making friendships at the refuge with each other, which sometimes leads to families moving out and sharing. This not only solves the problems of loneliness and single-handedly bringing up children; but it is making women question the whole concept of marriage. Many are finding that sharing equally with another woman and her family can be a much less oppressive relationship than they previously had with their husband.

While so many jobs for women remain at factory or secretarial level, obviously marriage appeals as a way out, a successful move on the female-status ladder. Many girls have a romantic ideal about marriage, and the reality is a shock. Members of the support groups behind refuges are doing a particularly important job here by giving talks at schools, pointing out that marriage is not all that rosy: you often have to surrender some of your rights.

The women concerned are not all paragons; and may not be easy to live with. But no man, whatever the real or imagined cause, has a right to inflict the extreme physical injuries and mental abuse that drive women to refuges.

REFERENCES

Dorset Women's Aid (n.d.) *The Sufferings of Battered Women, Battered Mothers and their Children*, Dorset Women's Aid, Central Office, la Harbour View Road, Parkstone, Poole.

Moore, J. G. (1974) *Yo-Yo Children: a Study of 23 Violent Matrimonial Cases*, London: NSPCC.

NWAF (National Women's Aid Federation) (1975) *Battered Women Need Refuges*, National Women's Aid Federation, 51 Chalcot Road, London NW1.

Pizzey, Erin (1974) *Scream Quietly or the Neighbours Will Hear*, Harmondsworth: Penguin Books.

Select Committee on Violence in Marriage (1975) *Report*, session 1974–1975, HC 553—i.

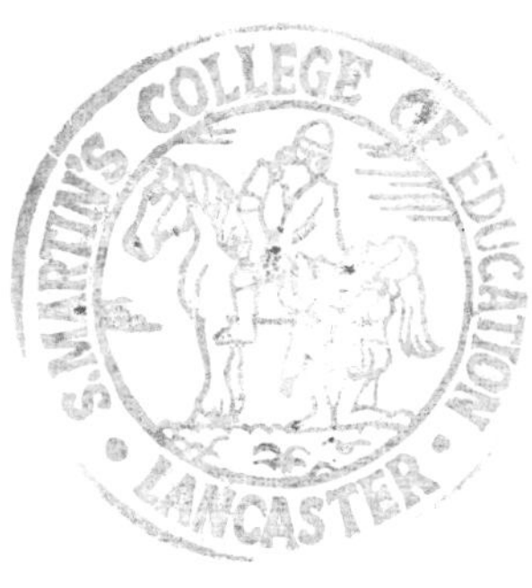

12

A NOTE ON 'MEN'S AID'

Joy Melville

> A lot of men come to Chiswick Women's Aid to try and get their wife back; and inevitably when they see this is not going to happen, they break down and cry and say, 'O.K., where can I go for help?'

The speaker was Ray Lee, who has run 'Men's Aid' from a house in north London since the summer of 1976. As he points out, prison is the only provision for violent people in our society today. 'When people ask me how we see this project, I always say that for alcoholics there is Alcoholics Anonymous; for drugs there are various forms of help; for gamblers there is Gamblers Anonymous—so we have set up the first "Violence Anonymous" in the country.'

Men's Aid provides accommodation for up to six men; a 24-hour service on the phone; a weekly therapy session for both men and for couples; and advice coupled with home visits. It also acts as a 'drop-in for coffee and chat centre' from 9a.m. to 5p.m.,Monday to Friday. In its first three months of operation, the service was used as follows (some men appearing in more than one category):

25 men	telephone service
6 men	drop-in coffee and chat service
4 men	accommodation
32 men	therapy service
10 couples	therapy service
4 men	home-visiting service

Of the above, 46 were self-referrals; five were referred from Chiswick Women's Aid; four from Islington social services; and two from the probation services. The residential accommodation is for men who are left alone after their wife has left, and need to be with people to get over the shock. It is also used by men whose marriages broke down while they were in prison and who have nowhere to go on release.

Many of the men who do go to Men's Aid undoubtedly believe that by this gesture they will succeed in getting their wife back; and indeed in some cases, when the wife feels the husband is making a genuine effort to improve, she does return. But the Men's Aid approach is realistic: it tries to get the men to accept, via group therapy, that their marriage has broken down irreparably—but that having wrecked one relationship, they must now make sure they do not jeopardize the next one in a similar way.

Ray Lee feels the danger is that the scheme is almost too successful; that the men are benefiting so much that they think after 2 or 3 weeks they are cured, and go away. It takes time to build up a man's confidence enough for him to enter into another relationship, in which violence does not play a part. 'They are hitting their wives because it is a necessary communication for them,' says Ray Lee, 'they cannot communicate in any other way, and have never tried to do so. Most of them have parents who were violent to them, and through them learnt to use their fists when they were frustrated. We are trying to make them understand that there are other ways of showing their feelings and desires.'

The men who have inflicted the more brutal and sadistic type of injuries have not contacted Men's Aid for help. 'They feel it is their male right to batter, so they don't see it as a problem,' says Ray Lee. 'The type of man I meet has been battered as a child, has married a very provocative wife and inevitably feels sorry after he has done it.' One such case of provocation he was currently dealing with was where the wife constantly scorned the man's inadequate sexual performance. Sometimes, too, when a woman has had previous relationships where she has been badly hurt, her safety device is to provoke dramas to see how much the man can take to prove that he loves her.

The therapy sessions for couples at Men's Aid is proving of particular use. In one case, for example, a man who used violence towards his very passive wife 2 years previously, lived in fear of it happening again. As he became more and more passive, the wife altered and began to rant and rave at him. During therapy, it was pointed out what games the wife was playing, and the open realization of this helped stop it. Another case involved a talkative, outgoing husband, and an introverted wife, whose favourite response was 'I don't know'. This had caused a great deal of trouble. The husband had hit her several times, and the wife had finally gone to a refuge. Even after joint therapy, the problem still exists; but the husband now sees there is no point in his reacting violently, and both have agreed to see a psychiatrist.

Frequently the men who go to Men's Aid have already seen psychiatrists, without success. Ray Lee thinks that, on the whole, his group therapy is more successful.

> The first thing that I always do when I get a new man coming in is to use the group to work out the problem. I then start off by talking about a problem of my own—such as how I felt when my own marriage broke down—and you can see them thinking, 'God, he's

> got problems of his own, too.' I feel that with psychiatrists, these men see a white coat and a desk in front of them, like a barrier. But they see me as a human being with human problems.

There are cases involving violence which are, however, too deep-rooted for Men's Aid to help. In one of these, a happily-married young soldier was on patrol in Ireland, when his colleague was shot through the head. His control went, he started spraying bullets in all directions, and broke the jaw of the sergeant who tried to restrain him. Since that time, he has been beating his wife.

Men's Aid was initially financed by Chiswick Women's Aid, though the house was given by the Greater London Council. It applied for an Urban Aid grant, but was unsuccessful. Ray Lee, a folk musician himself, helps organize concerts to help finances, and some musical groups have been very generous. Lee hopes to see other Men's Aids start but, as with women's refuges, the financial side is a constant struggle.

The scheme has not been operating for sufficient time to show long-term results. But, as Ray Lee says, it is a least a place 'where someone can come and say, "I am violent," and we don't go, "Ugh" '. There is an obvious need for a place for men to go when they realize that they are violent. There is also a need for the general public to accept that violence in everyday life is on the increase; and that merely condemning it is not enough. We must educate violent people into understanding the nature and patterns of their violence and prepare them, through therapy, for better, non-violent, future relationships.

13

BATTERED WOMEN AND SOCIAL WORK

North West Region of the National Women's Aid Federation

During this century, the scope and involvement of the personal social services in various areas of need has increased enormously. However, the problems faced by battered women have remained largely unrecognized by social work as it is practized within statutory and traditional agencies and it has been left to voluntary organizations to identify the problems faced by battered women and to begin to provide aid for them. Even now, although the awareness of individual social workers has been increased, largely by the work of Women's Aid groups, some agency practices and some social workers' working methods reflect an inability to respond to the needs of a woman who is being beaten by her partner.

Battered women would, however, seem appropriate subjects for social-work involvement. Battered women certainly seem to seek the help of social workers with their problems. Women in refuges have had a great deal of contact with social workers, and a report prepared by the National Women's Aid Federation (NWAF, 1975) suggests that 50% of women coming to refuges have had previous contact with social workers. It also appears that a significant proportion of some types of social-work cases seem to involve marital violence. In South Glamorgan, for example, 39% of applicants for temporary accommodation from social services departments between 1972 and 1974 arose because of marital disputes, and accounted for 47% in 1974 (Select Committee, 1975, *Minutes of Evidence*, p. 147). In an earlier study of six local authorities, Glastonbury (1971) judged that 22% of cases admitted to homeless accommodation between 1963 and 1969 involved 'domestic violence'.

If the evidence exists to support the idea that social workers do encounter the problems of battered women, what quality of help is being offered? Erin Pizzey (1974) attacks all helping agencies, and social services departments in particular. She characterizes the fate of women seeking help as coming 'away through the swish of hands being compassionately washed in all directions with only a babble of conflicting advice and not one jot of practical help'.

The British Association of Social Workers' working party echoes many of Pizzey's criticisms.

> Social Services Departments have shown insufficient concern about this problem. Social Workers may feel they have nothing to offer other than counselling and may feel so helpless that they are driven to deny or trivialise the problem and may therefore appear uncaring or even hostile. (BASW, 1975)

The NWAF also cites examples where women receive little help and where social services departments have obstructed the activities of Women's Aid groups (NWAF, 1975, pp.20–21). It is the experience of other Women's Aid groups that when social workers refer women to refuges they are prone to ignore them once they are resident, or that they use a refuge as a way of overcoming a crisis situation, and afterwards pressurize the women to return home on only the superficial assurance of her partner's sorrow and change of heart.

The National Citizens' Advice Bureaux Council in their report to the DHSS concluded that help provided by social services departments 'was not adequate to meet the needs of these women' (NCABC, 1973). They found that women were rarely given priority and that the most needed forms of help (legal advice and temporary accommodation) were the most inadequate.

In a local study, Hillingdon social services department found that 42% of referrals involving battered women were classified as 'miscellaneous' and requiring no social-work visits (London Borough of Hillingdon, 1974). Nurstein (Nurstein *et al.*, 1972) found that 'marital disharmony' was a very common problem among clients but that in only 22% of such cases was direct help being offered.

These few examples suggest that social workers are either disregarding the problems of battered women or are offering inappropriate help. Admittedly, the demand for all personal social services exceeds the supply and rationing procedures seem inevitable. This requires choices on all levels and these are not necessarily efficient or equitable. They may, as Hall (1974) has shown, be based on prejudices and bias. Society's view is often that battered women are 'undeserving' will 'waste' the services they are offered; and in looking at the social-work services offered to battered women we can plainly see these attitudes reflected in the professional theories and practices of social work. It has been suggested that social work is either ignoring the problems encountered by battered women or is offering inappropriate help. An examination of the ideology of social work suggests why social work has failed to respond effectively to the problems of battered women. Social work as currently 'preached' by the accepted theorists is largely impotent in the area of battered women for two important reasons.

The first is the importance accorded to the institution of the nuclear family both by society generally, and as reflected in social-work ideologies and practices. The family and marriage have been defined by social work, even more than by the general public, as situations of love, growth, and creativity and little recognition has been given to the potentially destructive role of the 'family' as a unit. It is seen almost unquestioningly as a thing to be preserved or, if it is obviously failing, to be improved. Very rarely is it seen as a destructive unit *per se* and even more rarely are the wishes of the individual members of the family acknowledged by social work. In some social-work agencies the seperation of spouses tends to be seen as a failure. The Family Service Unit journal, for example (1974), discussed battered women in 1973 but emphasized 'the F. S. U.'s belief that the marriage must be kept together *at all costs*' (my italics).

Government policy has consistently supported marriage and the family and legislation has created a working atmosphere in which the breakdown of these institutions is seen as disastrous and, even where it is inevitable, all energies should be directed towards making the break a temporary one, reconciliation and rehabilitation being the prime goals. The 1948 and 1963 Children Acts and the 1965 White Paper (Home Office, 1965) all emphasize and support the preservation of the family as the prime purpose of social work and assume that the family will consist of a mother, father, and children. Seebohm (1968), too, maintained and strengthened the tradition of seeing the whole family as the prime target for social-work intervention.

In such a context social workers have found it difficult to work in ways which facilitate the separation of marital partners, or to view marriage and the family negatively. The BASW working party noted:

> to support a wife who seeks separation from her husband has often in the past been seen as undermining the institution of the family grouping. Support and maintenance of the family grouping has always been a major part of the social workers' job (as defined both by social workers themselves and by government directives). Social workers are, therefore, likely to define the problem of wife battering in terms of a marital problem for which therapeutic marital counselling is appropriate.

Social workers tend to see themselves working with a 'marriage' or a 'family' rather than the individuals involved. Pincus (1960) includes in her book a case study involving a violent marriage. Here, despite the fact that the marriage has been unhappy from the start and that Mr Webb had declared at the outset that 'the only problem for her was how to get away', the account blindly sees 'the marriage as the focus of treatment and reconciliation as an inevitable goal'. Mrs Webb's desire to separate is totally ignored and the individuals seem to subjugated to the social institution. Pincus actually emphasises that the caseworker should not accept a client's insistence that she wishes to separate. Apparently some of the most basic principles of social work—acceptance, individualization, self-determination, etc.—have simply to be jettisoned if, by following them, the basic unit of our social system, the family, is threatened. Such is the commitment of social work to the preservation of the family that a request for help in facilitating a separation can even be interpreted as an oblique plea for help in preserving the marriage! This kind of absurdity is built into the 'professionalism' of social work and in fact it merely reflects the prejudices and biases of our social system. It serves to condone and strengthen the trap in which battered women find themselves by supporting the sanctity of the social unit of the nuclear family. With this kind of ideological basis it is small wonder that social workers have been unable to involve themselves effectively in the problems of battered women.

However, even if there is a case to suggest that social work's commitment to the sanctity of the family and marriage is its basic goal and that this fundamental premise has shaped a large part of its professional ethos, social workers are, in their day-to-day work, substantially involved in removing children from families. The profession's reluctance to intervene similarly when women are at risk must be due to an additional influence. Here it is suggested that the second major reason for social work's failure to intervene in the problems of battered women is the profession's attitude towards the woman's role and position in our society. Again, by taking a look at some of the influential social-work theorists, evidence of a sexist basis to social work can easily be identified. So far only a few authors have suggested that social-work texts are characterized by a sexist bias, i.e. 'an ideology which attributes an unchanging set of characteristics to a group of people on the basis of gender ... services to reinforce or justify the inferior position in society of the whole group' (Wilson, 1974), but largely this view has remained unexplored and unrecognized by the profession.

Much discussion of why women suffer violence has focused on the discussion of 'female masochism'. Florence Hollis, an extremely influential theorist, promotes the orthodox Freudian view on this as on other issues. This view was summarized by Karen Horney (1973).

> The specific satisfactions sought and found in female sex life and motherhood are of a masochistic nature ... it follows that, if most women are masochistic in their attitudes towards sex and reproduction, they would indubitably reveal masochistic trends in their non-sexual attitudes towards life.

Such views militate against action aimed at either educating women against the acceptance of violence or removing them from it. The social worker is encouraged to see violence as inevitable and to believe that women who suffer from it may well subconsciously 'provoke', 'need' or even 'enjoy' it.

Hollis cites only one case of physical violence (Hollis, 1949). Mrs Amiral is presented as typical of erotogenic masochism' and is characterized as a woman who, while overtly seeking separation, is 'merely seeking an audience and sympathy for her recital of her husband's cruelty towards her ... ' Hollis stresses the inconsistencies in her story and assumed exaggeration. She also speaks of women characterized by 'moral masochism' which, she says, is an unconscious feeling of guilt and a need for punishment. The worker is clearly encouraged to place a battered woman in one of these two categories and, in either case, if the worker accepts the underlying ideas, an offer of counselling rather than practical help will be deemed appropriate. Again in the same work Hollis illustrates the sexist bias in her perspective. She lays down five criteria against which the caseworker should assess a woman's rejection of her femininity:

> pleasure in tasks involved in making a comfortable, attractive home; enjoyment of some natural skill in caring for children; comfortable preference for staying in the home rather than working; the absence of a marked need to dominate or be aggressive; preference for a masculine type of man.

Hollis sees only the third of these criteria as controversial and sees deviations from them as cues for intervention aimed at better adjustment! Admittedly, the piece quoted was produced in 1949 but Hollis still has high status on some social-work training courses and the views expressed above are still commonly held to be valid both by society in general and by more modern social-work theorists and social-work practitioners. In the context of such ideas, it is easy to see how a social worker may feel justified in encouraging a battered woman to submit to her husband, accept his behaviour, and try harder to please him. Social work should not allow itself to fly the banner of objectivity and professionalism if its ideology condemns a large number of its clients to an oppressed role.

The profession's theorists are thus reinforcing the values widely held by society on two main issues, i.e. women's role within the family, and within society. With this two-pronged influence it is not difficult to see why social workers are commonly heard to express unsympathetic and callous opinions about the plight of battered women. Their profession has an ideological basis which serves to discourage social workers from considering battered women in any other way.

We have attempted above to point out that if battered women are seen by social workers when they are in need of aid, any help offered is usually of an inappropriate counselling nature, and we have looked to the traditional theories of social work and its professional ethos to suggest an explanation of why battered women have been largely ignored by the personal social services. Now an attempt will be made to outline the range of experiences a battered woman may actually encounter when seeking help from social workers. This will obviously involve generalization and will have all the limitations inherent therein. However our experiences as people involved in running refuges, and some of us are also professional social workers, suggests that the following possibilities are not untypical or unrealistic.

A woman who has been battered and presents herself to a social services department will, in the first case, be accorded low priority. If her problem is one of persistent battering over a period of years, during which time she has left her partner on several occasions but has always returned to him, a common social-work response is that this pattern suggests that the woman must get some satisfaction from the violent relationship and that, should she be helped to leave her partner, resources of time and energy will be wasted since she will probably return. In this response the social worker is supported both by the ideological basis of his profession and by society's general attitude towards battered women. However, this totally ignores the reality of that woman's situation. If she has left her partner, where can she go? To relatives, perhaps, where she will be quickly located by the battering man and pressurized by him to 'give it another try'. Alternatively she could seek private accommodation for herself and the children. She may be lucky enough to find a landlord who will accept a woman with children, but how does she secure the income to pay for this accommodation? If the family are in receipt of social security benefits, they will be paid to the man in respect of his family. The woman will not easily be able to make a separate claim for benefit in her own right, especially if she has no independent address. If she looks to the homeless families section of the local council she may well be told that since she has 'chosen' to leave her home she will not be considered eligible for homeless families accommodation.

These are examples of the complexities of the situation which trap a woman into staying with or returning to a battering partner. Social workers are often shamefully unaware of these factors and their analysis of a woman's problem simply reflects the preconceived notions of the general public, i.e. battered women deserve and enjoy the violence inflicted upon them.

If a woman does persist in her intention to leave her violent partner social workers often respond by suggesting that her children be received into care for a while, thus giving her an opportunity to 'sort things out'. Rather than being a solution, this can frighten a woman and prevent her exploring possibilities of further aid; afraid of losing her children, she may terminate contact with the social worker at that point. The offer to receive children into care may be given with sincere and helpful motives and, given available resources, may be an appropriate social-work gesture. It should not be ignored, however, that, after seeking help, a woman would find the social-work response punitive and frightening.

If a social worker does decide that active intervention in the battering problem is necessary, he or she will invariably insist on talking to the battering man before acting. This will be seen as professionally sensible in order to maintain some element of objectivity and fairness. This too often frightens a woman so much that she will terminate contact with the social worker. She suspects that any interview with her partner will probably result in the worker being reassured by a plausible story of contrition and good intentions which will result in the withdrawal of social-work help and her nearly inevitable return home. She may then be attacked for involving outside authorities in the family's 'private affairs' and probably battered for doing so. If a social worker does need a traditional professional basis for his or her actions, then it would seem that the concept of self-determination would be an appropriate one in this situation. If a woman does not wish to return home for fear of being beaten, the social worker could, given available resources such as a local Woman's Aid refuge, respond to this wish and allow the woman to make a decision about her future from a position of safety. Little is lost professionally by this response and one could say that it is the only way of allowing the 'client' to achieve her own solutions, resolve her own problems in a way that is meaningful and appropriate to her.

Assuming that there is a refuge in the woman's locality and that the social worker knows of it and is prepared to put her in touch with the women living in it, has the worker met the 'client's' needs? When a woman does leave home and enter a refuge it is a time of decision, a time when she needs support and reassurances about her decisions and her right and ability to make them. If she chooses to remain away from her partner she faces the future as the head of a one-parent family; an isolated situation where she will probably have to manage on a shamefully low income and without the help of adequate community child-care facilities. To carry through such a decision takes courage and requires support. If her social worker continues to put even 'gentle pressure' on her to return home or enables the man to communicate with her or meet her before she feels she is ready for this, it may make the woman return to him given the bleakness of her alternatives. If a woman makes a decision that she does not want to return to a battering man, then the social worker should be aware of the real difficulties facing her in carrying out this decision, but should see the social-work role in terms of helping her through such difficulties. In many cases social worker's attitudes simply reinforce the woman's feeling that her future alone will be difficult if not impossible to live through. There is help that social workers can offer, to make her future as head of her family more viable, more of a real alternative. Local one-parent family groups can give a woman immense support; help in securing nursery places or day-minding facilities for the children may be appropriate; making sure the woman is receiving her full entitlement to benefits of all kinds is crucially important. Social workers often have a number of one-parent families on their case-loads but rarely feel that they can introduce them to each other although this would enable them to provide mutual support on a casual 'drop-in' basis. Life will still be difficult for a woman, given the lack of alternatives offered in our society to living in a complete nuclear family, but there are these and other ways that a social worker can and should explore to present battered women with a more reasonable alternative to returning home.

The problems that a social worker may have in relating to a 'client' in a refuge are also important. Refuges are likely to challenge most of the worker's known concepts of 'residential care'. They are run by the women who live in them; there are no 'experts' with whom the social worker can relate, and many social workers find this a threatening or confusing experience. A refuge enables and encourages a woman to take power and responsibility for her own life, and to play a responsible part in the group life of the refuge. This experience often has a startling effect on women who have been repeatedly degraded and humiliated by their partners. A social worker can have difficulty in coping with the new strength and confidence which his 'client' displays. One would imagine that such a development would be encouraging and satisfying to the social worker, but in fact many seem to feel discomforted by this equalizing process in the relationship between 'worker' and 'client' and to view it negatively.

It has not been our intention in this chapter to attack social workers as uncaring or callous when faced with the problems of battered women. The comment focused on the ideology and supporting theories of the social-work profession which, it is argued here, are based fundamentally on the notions of the sanctity of the family and marriage and which accept and reinforce the traditional and oppressive attitudes to women in our society. Social workers themselves must be aware of the irrelevance of a large part of their training and professional ethos to their working situation and, to maintain any kind of credibility as helping, caring people, must struggle within their own work situations to expose the myths of professionalism. It is difficult to outline any definitive suggestions of good social-work practice in relation to battered women given that the point of this chapter is to suggest that social work as a professional reinforces the oppression of women within our society by supporting and furthering traditional attitudes to the woman's role and power position within the family. However, as already indicated, there are ways in which social workers can improve their service to battered women even within the traditions of the present system.

First of all, and most fundamentally, social workers must examine their own attitudes to the problems faced by battered women and take care not to fall into the trap of simply reflecting the commonly-held prejudices against battered women. Social workers should not accept violence towards women from men within family situations and should identify this as unacceptable behaviour. Given that many women are still ashamed of being being beaten, and will often make attempts to hide or deny the presence of violence, social workers should be on the alert for signs of physical abuse and transmit to a woman who has shown visible signs of being beaten or has alluded vaguely to this part of her life that they are sympathetic and aware of the problems she faces *and* that she has alternatives to staying at home. In order to do this effectively, social workers should find out about their local refuge, both to know of its existence and of the ways in which refuges operate. As many women are beaten outside office hours, the telephone number of the local Women's Aid group given privately to the woman can provide her with a means of escape and a sense of 'having a way out' if things get too bad at home. A woman arrived at one refuge who had cut the telephone number out of the local newspaper months before. She had read the article about the refuge and had kept the telephone number, knowing that she could use it when she was either too terrified or too injured to stay at home any longer. She had received social-work visits on numerous occasions because one of her children was the subject of a supervision order, but she had never felt able to tell the worker about the beatings she received, in case it would mean that her child was removed from home. The social worker had never explored the possibility of marital violence even though the woman had been bruised on several occasions during his visits. So low was that worker's consciousness of this problem that his work with the family neglected this crucially important area of that family's life and ignored the fact that the violence between the man and the woman was the clue to why the child was in trouble.

If a woman asks a social worker to aid her in finding refuge, that worker should respect the woman's decision and act upon it and not involve the violent man in those actions. A woman should have the right and the means to leave a violent relationship and to decide on her future in a safe place. This means that she should have the choice of deciding when, if at all, to meet or speak to the man. For obvious reasons, the violent man should not be informed of the address or phone number of the refuge, and the woman should be allowed to decide when to initiate contact with him. They key to the whole approach to the problems of battered women is to recognize that in our society the odds are weighted against her. She is in an unequal relationship within the family and this position is reflected in various social institutions which regard her as a domestic appendage of the male 'head of the house'. Her means of escape from a violent man are limited even now since there are not enough Women's Aid refuges to cope with the demand. If she actually escapes from the violence, goes to a refuge, and leaves to take up her own tenancy with her children, her future is difficult and bleak. The maintenance of fairness and 'objectivity' in this situation in fact means that the inequalities within the relationship between husband and wife are perpetuated. In bald terms it means that social work condemns women to remain trapped in extremely violent situations and makes spurious claims of objectivity to forgive itself for doing so.

If the function of social work is simply to ameliorate the conditions in which certain people live, then some suggestions have been made here to illustrate how this can be better achieved in the field of battered women. If social work has a more fundamental role to play in reshaping the inequitable social situation in which people live then it must begin by examining the traditional myth embodied in its ideology, and social workers must challenge the manifestations of these myths in their work. Obviously this has implications for other areas of social work but, hopefully, this chapter has served to present a different perspective with which social workers can achieve a more complete understanding of the situation of battered women and with which they can begin to offer more adequate and appropriate help.

REFERENCES

BASW (British Association of Social Workers) (1975) 'Home violence—is there an answer?', *Social Work Today*, **6**, (13), pp.409–413.

Family Service Unit Quarterly, (1974) No.vi.

Glastonbury, B. (1971) *Homeless, Near a Thousand Homes*, London: National Institute for Social Work Training.

Hall, A. S. (1974) *The Point of Entry: A Study of Client Reception in the Social Services*, London: Allen & Unwin.

Hollis, F. (1949) *Women in Marital Conflict. A Casework Study*, New York: Family Service Association of America.

Home Office (1965) *The Child, the Family and the Young Offender*, Cmnd 2742, London: HMSO.

Horney, K. (1973) 'The problem of female masochism'. In J. B. Miller (ed.), *Psychoanalysis and Women*, Harmondsworth: Penguin Books.

London Borough of Hillingdon Social Services Research (1974) *Marital Violence in Hillingdon.*

NCABC (National Citizens' Advice Bureaux Council) (1973) 'Experience of the Problem of battered women: a memorandum for the DHSS'.

Nurstein, J. P., Pottinger, J., and Anderson, M. (1972) *Social Workers and Their Clients: the Family Composition and Social Characteristics of a Group of Clients Receiving Help from the Social Services*, London: Research Publications Services Ltd.

NWAF (National Women's Aid Federation) (1975) *Battered Women Need Refuges*, London: NWAF, 51 Chalcot Road, London NW1.

Pincus, L. (ed.) (1960) *Marriage: Studies in Emotional Conflict and Growth*, London: Methuen.

Pizzey, Erin (1974) *Scream Quietly or the Neighbours Will Hear*, Harmondsworth: Penguin Books.

Seebohm, F. (chairman) (1968) *Report of the Committee on Local Authority and Allied Personal Social Services*, Cmnd 3703, London: HMSO.

Select Committee on Violence in Marriage (1975) *Report*, HC 553–1; *Minutes of Evidence*, HC 248 i–xv, London: HMSO.

Wilson, E. (1974) 'Sexist ideology of casework', *Case Con.*, 15.

14

TRAINING FOR SOCIAL WORK WITH VIOLENT FAMILIES

Bill Jordan and Jean Packman

Working with family violence raises certain characteristic social-work dilemmas in a particularly acute form. What are social workers' rights to intervene, and what protection do families have against undue interference and invasion of their privacy? How can individual family members be protected from undue suffering and hardship without attracting stigma to themselves and punishment to their persecutors? Is a social worker who gets embroiled in a violent family situation, or in its aftermath, capable of making objective assessments, and of acting decisively yet fairly? Indeed, can an understanding of the emotional dynamics of conflict be effectively employed in modifying its expression and mitigating its effects? Is social work, therefore, a viable form of intervention in such situations, or is it a weak substitute for more traditional approaches or for more thoroughgoing changes in the social order and in social provision?

The training of social workers provides many different perspectives from which these questions can be considered. There would seem to be a number of fairly obviously relevant theoretical contributions from the social sciences which might help the social worker in his attempt to resolve these dilemmas. For instance, a study of social policy since the Second World War suggests an increased number of interventions by social workers into family life (and especially into the lives of poor families with young children). Initially these were largely in the name of support, and for the prevention of receptions into care, but more recently the emphasis has shifted to protecting children alleged to be 'at risk' from cruel or neglectful parents. Familiarity with this legal and administrative background and with the origins of recent shifts in policy, public opinion, and practice, should help the social worker to be aware of the social and political significance both of family violence and of his agency's role in relation to it. At a more general level, the sociology of deviance provides a perspective for the understanding of some of the mechanisms operating in any intervention by an official agent into a family alleged to have transgressed social norms. Like the social policy perspective, it also offers a framework for the critical evaluation of social work's effectiveness as a form of intervention. From the psychological field, a knowledge of normal human development allows a yardstick against which to measure the possible ill-effects of family strife, while a study of mental and physical abnormalities is necessary for the diagnosis of pathological elements in any situation. Finally, both sociological and psychological perspectives can contribute to an understanding of family interaction and the dynamics of interpersonal conflict.

However, the philosophical resolution of these dilemmas provides no automatic recipe for effective social work. Theoretical studies may increase awareness of key factors in social-work interventions, and equally important indications of the inappropriateness of social work for some tasks, but they are not themselves sufficient guarantees of an effective performance in a real-life situation. This, of course, is true of any form of social work; wisdom does not necessarily imply any particular skill, sensitivity, ability to communicate or inspire trust. But this is even more obviously the case in a situation of open conflict. Here what is tested is not the social workers' professional expertise, but also his nerve and his capacity to keep a clear head in a crisis. It often challenges his ability to withstand aggression directed at him or at others in his presence, to handle himself and others in an atmosphere of overt or covert threat, or to act decisively in the midst of actual violence.

These capacities are required of people in many jobs. Policemen, prison officers, teachers, and house-parents in many day and residential schools, mental nurses and others are called upon to demonstrate similar abilities in comparable situations. However, there are differences in roles which are perhaps clearest if we compare the policeman with the social worker. The policeman is quite overtly and unambiguously an agent of social control. His uniform and manner are plainly those of an official who is concerned with law and order and with the suppression of conflict and violence. His presence in connection with an incident of family violence can readily be seen to be dealing with that situation so as to bring about or restore a viable, peaceful atmosphere as quickly as possible, or to inquire about the commission of an offence. His actions can be understood as being governed by law and to consist in the use of whatever measures are necessary to end violence or to remove the threat of it. This single and comprehensible function aids the policeman in a firm and fair performance of his duty—though it should be added the police are sufficiently aware of the complex implications of family violence to be more cautious about any involvement in marital disputes, for instance, than they would be about sorting out a pub brawl.

By contrast, a social worker's role is anything but clear-cut and simple. If he is called into a family situation in which violence is alleged to be taking place he has a number of possible statutory functions. One of the adults may be mentally ill and requiring hospital treatment, in which case he is there to persuade or, failing persuasion, to compel that person to receive treatment. Where a child is being cruelly treated, his role may be that of rescuer—

removing the victim from further harm, on a place-of-safety order. In such circumstances, intervention is immediate, drastic and controlling. Yet, in addition to these statutory obligations, the social worker has a general duty to anticipate and *prevent* such outcomes, and, indeed, many others which may arise directly out of family conflict, such as homelessness, school refusal, delinquency, debt, or family disintegration. Whilst having the power to act *in extremis* he is also required to assess each situation to determine whether such action is desirable, or necessary, or can, in fact, be avoided. To complicate the picture further, the violent family may well require help with other needs additional to or unconnected with the conflict. The social worker carries general responsibilities for promoting 'welfare' (Identifying poverty, isolation, malnutrition, for example) and for the protection of vulnerable individuals such as the very old, the mentally handicapped, or women at the mercy of brutal men. He is also expected to act as an expert referral agent, by putting people in touch with the right professional or the appropriate service—the disturbed to the psychiatrist, the ill to the doctor, and so on. He may well be trying to pursue many or even all of these aims simultaneously. Thus the number and vagueness of his functions (often mirrored in the muddled ideas which families have about social workers are and do) make it much more difficult for him to deal directly and unambiguously with the violent element in the situation. Furthermore, unlike the policeman, the social worker is unlikely to be dealing once and for all with a single incident; he is usually expected to take longer-term responsibility for the family's welfare.

Reinforcing the effect of this multiplicity of roles, the social worker's theoretical perspectives are seldom conducive to a single, simple interpretation of a family situation. It is part of the social worker's characteristic perspective on family violence that it is usually, if not always, a symptom of something else. The violent person is often not simply an angry or hateful person; he is often also very anxious or desperate for affection. The victim's involvement is frequently far from passive, and equally strong and conflicting feelings are often found on the victim's side. Often the act of violence is committed by the 'wrong' person, or on the 'wrong' person, in the sense that the act is displaced so as to be done by or to a 'safe' family member, less destructively. Often it does not arise directly from preceding events, but is the culmination of a period of tension, or a long-term situation in the family.

This kind of interpretation of violence makes a social worker a very inappropriate person to deal directly with many violent situations. Clearly, a psychodynamic approach is not only an ineffective way of stopping a raging punch-up; it also probably leads to misinterpretations of many other violent conflicts. Thus a well-meaning neighbour or doctor might well call upon a social worker to visit a family in which there was a norm of considerable physical aggression yet where no member was truly 'at risk'. Such a well-intentioned intervention could produce justifiably angry reactions from the family. Similarly, the fact that some people, and especially many adolescents, enjoy violence, or find it exciting, is not a point of view that social workers easily encompass, and no doubt for this reason many such clients find it difficult to take social workers' efforts to help them seriously.

Yet there are many situations into which a social worker is called where his intervention (rather than that of a policeman) seems justifiable precisely because it is not clear, or not yet clear, whether an approach based firmly on family counselling may resolve conflict, or whether firmer action is necessary. In such situations, complexity of role and of theoretical perspective cannot be avoided or disclaimed; they are essential features of social-work intervention. Furthermore, without recommending any doctrinaire psychodynamic model, we would consider that sensitivity to emotional interaction, and response to this factor, is the method best suited to most social workers' skills, functions, and physiques in the face of family violence. The point we wish to make about complexities of role and theory is that these may actually make it harder for the social worker to be effective in dealing with really dangerous violence, or the threat of it, in those relatively few cases where they are present. Ambiguity of function and sophistication of analysis can even be used to evade responsibility for decisive action, or to rationalize action which is arbitrary and incomprehensible for the family. In fact, the very vagueness of the social worker's role and expertise can be used as a cloak of mystification, justifying almost any form of action or interaction.

There is no very strong *a priori* reason why social workers should be naturally good at dealing with violence. It generally forms a very small part of their overall work, whatever agency employs them. We suspect that the kind of person motivated to become a social worker is often of a personality type which is not ideally equipped to tackle violent situations. Whereas policemen might reasonably be expected to be rather extraverted, confident, physically large, and physically brave, there are no good reasons why social workers should be any of these things. A training course which selected potential social workers for their promise of resilience in violent situations would be unlikely to recruit those most suited to tasks of helping the more emotionally vulnerable among their clients. So how can courses hope to *train* students to work effectively in such situations?

We are bound to confess that it was not until we were commissioned to write this chapter that we had given specific consideration to this question. We teach in a department running two postgraduate courses for social workers (a 1-year and a 2-year course) which contain not only the theoretical elements mentioned at the start of this chapter, but also a good deal of experimental learning in small groups, in much of which the problem of violence is an important element. Also most of the students do a month's residential work placement, and this issue frequently arises out of that experience. However, we had not previously thought of training for violent situations as a task in its own right, or identified it as a training issue which demanded high priority, nor had we assessed our own success or failure in terms of our capacity to produce social workers with this skill. We have been made to recognize the importance of the very practical and face-to-face problem of work with violent families, and in the rest of this chapter we will concentrate on this aspect of training, rather at the expense of the equally vital issues of social policy and the use of social work in tasks of social control.

For the purposes of writing this chapter we conducted a short practical exercise with a group of second-year students who were just completing the course and with fellow members of staff. We also held discussions with two groups of ex-students attending conferences at the university after a year's experience of social work. The latter groups' comments and some incidents they reported will be used to illustrate some of the points arising from the exercise.

The problem we had in looking at violence in our exercise with the second-year students was essentially the problem of all training for practical tasks done in a university setting. Given that few students meet many incidents of violence in the limited periods of their placements, how can the classroom be used to give any *real* preparation for such experiences? The method we used with our group was of role-play, followed by discussion. This is a method employed a good deal on our courses. It has a number of obvious shortcomings to do with artificiality. However, we believe that generally role-plays exaggerate certain features of real-life situations but do not create very marked features of their own. The artificiality is that of caricature rather than of a mask which obscures reality. The caricature is often a rather cruel one, for the presence of an audience can heighten anxieties and increase self-consciousness in such a way as to make the social worker, in particular, especially vulnerable. Role-play tends, therefore, to highlight difficulties, even if it does not manufacture them. In general, though, we consider it a very useful method of teaching, and several degrees more real for the purposes of practical training than seminars or lectures can ever be.

One of the considerations which we wished to explore was whether the *physical fact* of violence or intimidation was an important factor in the effectiveness of a social-work intervention, and whether the same social worker might be more or less effective according to the nature of this factor. The first role-play was based on a script about a couple who, after 12 years of marriage, were separating and in conflict over the custody of their child. The script involved an argument with a good deal of physical contact (pushing, pulling, hitting with a newspaper) but nothing sufficiently violent to cause as much as a bruise. At the end of the scripted quarrel the social worker arrived on the scene and from then on the cast improvised. His intervention was serious, compassionate, and concerned, and he seemed at once to represent the couple's unexpressed sadness and pain about their relationship, and their unspoken despair about the damage they were doing to each other and the child. He enabled them to stop fighting and to sit down and look at these denied elements. While they continued to make accusations and reproaches against each other, their whole manner towards each other expressed some tacit recognition of a past attachment and of regret at the hurt they had caused. Eventually they agreed to see the social worker again to talk about their future, either in terms of separating or staying together.

In the discussion afterwards, some longer-term dangers of this kind of intervention were identified. By representing the couple's denied feelings to them, the social worker was able to quell their conflict; but if he later came to *embody* this caring and compassion they felt for each other they would increasingly depend on his presence to express these feelings for them. They might fairly soon revert to a cat-and-dog relationship in which they needed him to intervene at each crisis to restore some kind of balance. In the long run, he could become a part of the whole destructive dynamic of their relationship, regarded as and feeling himself to be an indispensable barrier against even more violent conflict, but quite unable to produce a lasting peace or a negotiated separation. Despite these reservations about the future, however, the group felt the social worker had done a most valuable initial piece of work in the interview itself; he had not only dealt with the crisis but laid the ground for further potentially constructive work with the family.

The second role-play was an improvization based loosely on a case previously dealt with by one of the group. A family quarrel flared after a slightly drunken building worker had returned from the pub, having spent his holiday pay there after being made redundant. He had been challenged by his wife and 17-year-old delinquent step-son, and after an argument a fight broke out, the wife extricating herself to telephone her son's probation officer. (The fight was sufficiently realistic to provoke the simultaneous intervention of the social worker—played by the same group member as on the previous occasion—and an innocent and anxious member of the sociology staff, who had not been warned about the exercise, and who had to be reassured by other members of the group.) By then both the protagonists were out of breath, one had lost his shirt buttons, and the other had received several minor injuries to his face and feet.

The social worker found no difficulty in getting the family to sit down and talk, but what ensued was largely a slanging match in which he was unable to make much impression. When this had wound down, he started to discuss the origins of the fight and the underlying emotional conflicts. This seemed to refuel the fire of the quarrel, and though there was no apparent danger of further violence, all the parties simply continued to make accusations and counter-accusations against each other. The social worker took these at face value, and found himself involved in encouraging the three to make long-term decisions about their future, and whether they could stay together as a family unit. Next, he became embroiled in misleading accusations of child abuse, in investigating these (rousing sleeping infants), in listening to counter-claims of criminality, and in turn investigating these in outdoor sheds. His whole intervention began to appear ineffective, inappropriate, and even ridiculous.

The group discussion afterwards suggested that the social worker had quite disastrously tried to explore the emotional dynamics of a situation which should certainly have been put to bed for the night (the participants confirmed they were quite ready for this). Every issue that was raised could much more profitably have been pursued on another occasion. The family gave the social worker many cues which he failed to take up, all of which would have indicated that there was no danger of further violence, and much to be gained by bringing the discussion to an end. One of the participants commented that, while he was relieved at the social worker's arrival, there was no risk of the fight restarting.

> In most levels of family violence the social worker is probably welcomed as a referee. Most fights are looking for an ending, otherwise they would result in the serious injury or death of one of the protagonists. In my experience, the very presence of a social worker to 'hold the ring', as distinct from a policeman in uniform, may calm the situation down.

One possible explanation for the social worker's misguided persistance in the role-play, and his refusal to be satisfied with having quelled the immediate conflict, seemed to be that he was quite thrown by the extent of the physical fight that had taken place, even though this was evidently no unique occurrence in this particular family. His own reaction to the physical fact of violence was such as to switch him off from the messages they were giving him. As one of the family commented, 'He seemed to be in a world of his own'.

The 'worker' himself felt that his reaction was greatly exaggerated by his consciousness of a critical audience, and his expectation that the two protagonists were likely to be extremely unreasonable—whether because of the violence of their previous fighting or because of their known (real-life) characters he was uncertain. As compared with the other role-play, he felt much more anxious, self-conscious, and detached from the family—indeed very much in 'another world', out of touch with the feelings or realities of the other participants. He commented,

> I wasn't being faced with a familiar controllable situation but a very unfamiliar and uncontrollable one. I think it is in these situations that the whole self is exposed—you are facing violence *and* in front of a highly critical audience. I felt totally exposed as a sham or a fraud and defended by isolating and distorting all the messages. Unless we find our real selves and inject into our roles that real naturalness we have no back-up when the mask is stripped away—it's a sham. I injected a truncated, almost rarified, piece of me into an equally rarified piece of a role and ended up with a disembodied imbecile parrotting nonsense.

But he went on to point out that the artificiality which compounded his reactions to the situation was very similar to the artificiality of trying to deal with a violent person in front of the 'audience' of his family. In both situations, the problem is of how to be natural, to reach real touch with people, in the face of one's own fears and their expectations.

This experience tended to suggest that insufficient account is taken in social-work training of what amounts to something like a panic reaction by the social worker in the face of violence or the threat of it, which the worker in the role-play described in terms of 'becoming unreal' and 'losing touch'. This panic may have nothing to do with physical intimidation, or threats made directly against him. It may stem simply from the unfamiliarity of violence itself, in whatever form. Unlike the policeman, the social worker does not expect to have to defend himself, to take physical charge of situations to restore order, or to talk firmly, or authoritatively, to people who are fighting, or have just been doing so. Even so, it is not at all easy for social workers to recognize and acknowledge this panic reaction, with its implications of timidity or cowardice. Consequently, it can be rationalized as something else, or given some kind of objective status as an assessment of a situation. Whether it results in an over-reaction in the form of excessively zealous intervention to prevent unlikely disaster (as in the second role-play), or in under-reaction, as when truly dangerous situations are left severely alone, the cause is probably the same basic panic. We would suggest that this might well have been one of the factors which contributed to the failure of social workers to protect the life of Maria Colwell, whose death drew the British public's attention to the problems of dealing with parental violence. It seems to us no coincidence that the agencies involved showed a marked disinclination to visit Maria's family (in contrast, in at least one case, with a previous conscientious regularity) once her step-father, the menacing Mr Keppel, started to be at home because of sickness. Understandable apprehensiveness about his intimidating presence was apparently allowed to go unrecognized and may well have covertly contributed to the failure of any agency to take direct responsibility for Maria's supervision. A social worker's failure to recognize his *own* fear of violence may also blunt his perception of the *victim's* terror, thus smothering appropriate impulses to protect and rescue, in some extreme circumstaces.

We would suggest that a panic reaction by the social worker may well destroy or cause to be suspended two absolutely crucial tools of effective social-work intervention. The first is the ability to listen to more than one thing at a time, to be able to pick up the consistent and the contradictory notes, so as to get the overall emotional tone of what is happening. The social worker needs to be attuned to several wave-lengths simultaneously in order himself to be able to respond with the right note. If a panic reaction hinders this ability, it will allow the worker to react quite inappropriately, because he will miss certain key messages. One characteristic response will be a tendency to attribute his own anxiety to the family, seeing threats everywhere except where they belong, in himself. Such workers will tend to be over-active and over-protective. The alternative response is for the worker to block off his own anxiety in such a way as to be unable to recognize it in others either. This will result in a tendency to see feelings as something much less intense than they are felt by the family, to refuse to recognize real dangers as such. One indication of this reaction is by the use by the social worker of euphemisms or clichés in descriptions of violence or its consequences.

The second crucial ability of the social worker is his capacity for monitoring his own performance, recognizing both unexpected departures from his normal standards of practice, and characteristic weaknesses or uncertainties. It involves an ability to examine his feelings and fantasies with ruthless honesty, questioning all his motives and decisions. It requires a high degree of self-knowledge and an ability to distinguish the effects of others' subjectivity on his own. It is different from listening techniques, because it often takes place between interviews and can be greatly facilitated by good supervision. If this capacity is impaired by panic, then fears and fantasies, either of his own or transmitted to him by clients, will be taken as the basis of diagnosis, assessments, reports, decisions, and even politics.

In talking of panic and fantasy we do not want to imply that these are simply elements in the social worker's subjectivity. Social work is a process of influence between people in which the worker as well as the client is affected. His diagnostic and therapeutic skills depend not so much on establishing control over his feelings (a sort of emotional impermeability or impregnability) as on having the discipline to use clients' influence on him to their benefit. It is of the very nature of violence that it is frightening, and it is usually intended to intimidate. It follows that, unless the social worker is unnaturally insensitive or phlegmatic, he will feel fear. What he needs in order to be able to help the client is not calmness but courage.

When we talked with ex-students about their experiences in working with violent families they gave many examples demonstrating physical and moral bravery. Some of them are instructive because they illustrate the different kinds of courage which are required by social workers. In one incident, a young woman probabtion officer had arranged to visit a foreign couple in the evening when the wife returned to her husband after leaving him for several days. There had been previous violence between them, and when the probation officer had spoken to the husband earlier in the day he had made a number of threats to kill his wife. When she arrived, no violence had yet taken place, but during the interview the man became very angry and started to hit his wife. The probation officer at once grabbed his arm and told him to stop it. He did so, and from that time there was no further violence. In subsequent weeks they both had a number of discussions with her, eventually deciding to separate. The probation officer described her action as quite instinctive; she did it without thinking, and on reflection it was obvious she had risked injury to herself. Another ex-student described a similar action in coming between two people who were fighting; in his case he felt it was motivated by a mixture of concern to prevent injury and desire to avoid losing control of the situation, though his reaction was likewise instinctive rather than thought out.

Perhaps the outstanding example of bravery was of a young woman who, as a trainee social worker, had been called to the scene of a siege, by policemen and Alsatian dogs, of a house where a man with a shotgun was barricaded with his wife and children. The man had originally threatened an official of the Electricity Board who had come to disconnect their supply. The social worker asked the police to withdraw (which they did under protest), gained access to the house by simply walking up to the door and, after some initial suspicion, found the man very willing to talk to her, and was able eventually to negotiate a settlement with the Electricity Board.

There would seem to be little that a training course could do to *teach* social workers this kind of courage, or indeed the sort of instinctive bravery shown in the previous examples. Perhaps the only credit we as tutors could claim in relation to these products of ours was to have selected students who had the capacity to be courageous in these ways. This was perhaps not entirely fortuitous. We had been conscious of our attempt to choose people with a sort of inner strength, combined with an outer sensitivity, which we had rather unimaginatively described as 'hard at the centre, but soft round the edges'.

The social workers in these examples were risking injury or even death precisely because they were in no position to enforce any kind of physical submission on the participants. Unlike policemen, they had neither the training nor the physique to subjugate an angry man, let alone an armed one. The success of their actions appeared to depend to a great extent on the perception of this fact by the participants, and the recognition of their intervention as an expression of true concern, a genuine attempt to help. It depended on some fairly instantaneous assessment by a violent person of the moral quality of an often clumsy physical intervention. In one of the examples (and in another experienced by one of the authors) a man interrupted in a fight with another actually drew back his fist to hit the social worker, and then, seeming to recognize the inappropriateness of this behaviour, not only restrained himself from doing so, but also ceased the whole attack. It is difficult to specify the cues by which very angry (or even sometimes seemingly uncontrollably drunk and aggressive) clients pick up this quality in the actions of social workers, but these and other incidents suggest that some such a process occurs in many violent situations, which is also paralleled in other kinds of stressful encounters. It may well be that some such perception of the moral quality of social-work interventions has been an important and neglected aspect of the potential influence and effectiveness of social work.

However, these examples of spontaneous, reactive bravery instance only one of the kinds of courage social workers may require. The sudden flaring of violence in a situation where the worker is present is probably much less common than the sense of a growing *threat* of violence before or during an interview. This may take the form of the emergence of an already present covert threat, or of the build-up of a menacing tension, and is usually directed not against the social worker but against another family member. Here both courage and skill are required to find a moment for and a method of drawing attention to the threat. The temptation is for the social worker to ignore it, or to try to defuse the situation without allowing the violent element in it to be recognized or attended to. Such evasion may contribute to tension and to the escalation of fantasy (both by the social worker and the family) about violence and its consequences. It seems a sound principle for social workers to try to draw attention to threats of violence, however covert or veiled these may be. One ex-student pointed out the value of commenting directly on the physical expression of anger and aggression (clenched teeth, clenched fists, etc.) as a means of acknowledging a threat, demonstrating the absence of panic in the worker, and allowing the angry person to become aware of the effects of his feelings on himself and others before they become out of control.

(There is an apparent contradiction here with what we said earlier about the second role-play. However, while as a general rule it is wrong to evade or play down a *threat* of violence, it is equally dangerous to escalate violence once it has been sparked. It seems to us to be bad social work in most cases to pretend not to notice a threat, either ignoring it or accommodating it without acknowledging it. On the other hand, it is good social work to be able to react in such a way as to defuse a situation in which violence has started to flare, and this may sometimes best be done by deflecting attention from it. One ex-student told of how, when suddenly and furiously attacked by a client who was about to spring at her, she had managed, instead of standing up, backing away or flinching—any one of which reactions might have hastened a physical assault—to divert her eyes, reach for her handbag, and offer him a cigarette, which instantly calmed him down. There seem to be a number of very practical 'do's and don'ts' which social workers might learn about how not to escalate conflict—for instance, to sit down whenever possible; where standing is unavoidable, to stand close, to preclude the swing of an arm; and, once withdrawal is deemed necessary, to run like hell.)

Sometimes the most difficult threats to deal with are those made over the telephone, where the worker has no non-verbal clues as to the nature and seriousness of the threat, and no non-verbal means of exerting any influence on the situation. Such threats may also create a fearful reaction in the worker before an interview or may precipitate a visit to a family which is undertaken out of panic. Telephone threats are a very effective means of creating fantasies and fears which are particularly disabling for the worker. Once a fantasy starts to develop, it is much harder for the worker to feel brave enough to draw attention to the potential violence directly. No social worker can expect to be realistic all the time; he is bound on occasions to elaborate on a message and build up a picture of monstrous dangers and frightful disasters looming over families. What is important is that he retains some capacity to recognize fantasy, and the courage to test it out, rather than to retreat or to act as if it was true without proper investigation.

This problem is often present in an interview with one family member who is describing an incident of violence, or the threat of it, by another. Frequently what is being communicated to the social worker is not so much a description of the other or his actions, but the fear the present person feels of his or her *own* anger and violence about some family situation. That fear is then transmitted to the social worker, who in turn becomes intensely anxious about the other, and starts to see him as mad or incurably delinquent. Here the fantasy is not simply the worker's own, but rather a sort of double-dose, incorporating the client's fears as well. Ex-students gave examples of having to screw up considerable courage to visit homes in which one member had been described as uncontrollably angry or violent, and how they had usually found that person much more reasonable and human than the description had suggested. This is particularly important in referrals of people described as needing mental-hospital treatment, or where children are said to be at risk, or adolescents in need of institutional care or training.

In longer-term cases, another disabling fear by social workers is that they are indispensable for the family's safety or survival. Often, when a potentially destructive conflict has been temporarily resolved (as in the first role-play) the family call the worker in to deal with future crises, and he allows himself to take on the function of an ever-available arbitrator who comes to represent all the family's warmth and love and is thus in a sense necessary for their continued life together. Once again, a collusive fantasy develops, fed by the family's fears that without him they would be disastrously violent to each other. There is a special kind of expertise and bravery required to challenge such an expectation as it develops, and to allow the family to take back good parts of themselves from the worker, so that he does not become a perpetual rescuer and they do not perpetuate the need for his protective interventions. Very often this skill involves drawing attention to the role the social worker is coming to play, or even to the consequences of his actions which have been inappropriate. The social worker may share with the family the way he and they are coming to have fantasies about him as a guardian angel, and how absurd and destructive these may be.

Most of the examples we have given have been of first contacts with violent family situations. However, quite a lot of social work consists of long-term work with very deprived or disturbed families where the threat of violence is always present. For instance, when the parents have themselves been neglectfully or cruelly treated as children there may be long periods during which their capacity to care and cohere as a family unit is very fluctuating. The turbulence generated in such families is extremely demanding and exhausting for the social worker. He feels himself torn between the needs and feelings of different members. His own emotional equilibrium is disturbed by daily responsibility for decisions involving risks to health or even to life. Some such families cannot be helped by social work at all; others need authoritative interventions to protect children from harm. Yet there are some who can benefit from a kind of social-work involvement which demands that the worker shares in their most difficult and painful feelings about each other, at considerable cost to himself. It is part of the destructiveness and terror of these families that they can almost physically externalize their feelings, so great is their power to stir up each other, and anyone else who comes into contact with them. So the social worker cannot rely on detached objectivity and expertise; in becoming involved in their problems he is really putting himself at risk. He is often laying himself open to invasion by strong, primitive feelings, which may impel him to thoughts and actions inconsistent with his normal standards. He may find himself in situations of conflict in which he cannot be sure that his ordinary reactions and defences will be adequate to deal with this inner and outer turmoil.

We would suggest that a social worker can only help these families by being brave enough to risk this chaos in himself, and being prepared to act wrongly or foolishly in the short run for the sake of the chance to have some real long-term influence on their pattern of relationships. This is perhaps the hardest kind of courage and judgement to cultivate, the capacity to be honest and self-critical, and to keep faith with such difficult people, without the need to protect himself by professional defences. He needs to be sure enough of himself to enter the chaotic world of the family's nightmare, and yet at the right moment to be able to apply the brake of his own perceptions and standards. It is obviously these most disturbed families who are most likely to induce panic, for they bring the whole problem of violence closest to home, into the very subjectivity of the social worker himself. Only experience (and often learning from mistakes) can teach most social workers the very difficult lessons of work with these families; hence the need for a reservoir of experienced workers in any agency with responsibility for family violence.

Finally, there are occasions when a whole family, or one member, may come to feel intense hostility to the social worker. Obviously this may be the reflection of experiences which well justify the feeling, or simply an expression of personal dislike. But there are also occasions where this hostility is the result of actions which the social worker has taken, and which he feels are justified. One of our ex-students described a case in which she had implemented a place-of-safety order on a child, and had subsequently recommended a care order. There was much evidence of previous neglect and the child had very frequently been in hospital (for 'failure to thrive') for short periods during the previous year. However, the mother in particular was very angry, and any guilt she might have felt about the child's history was expressed in rage against the social worker. She physically attacked her in court, and in an interview immediately afterwards broke a china mug over her head. Quite apart from the injuries sustained, no social worker wants to be seen as an unjust persecutor of a family, and it took a good deal of courage for this worker not only to go on seeing the mother, but also to accept the anger expressed at her, and even to attract it onto herself, in order to free colleagues and fellow professionals to play a more constructive role in the eventual rehabilitation of the family (which has since been successfully achieved). Instead of either retreating or taking a more comfortably supportive stance, she recognized and acted upon a clear need in this case for someone to be firm and consistent about the child's rights to a loving and stable upbringing. In the process she accepted the 'bad' role in the mother's eyes. In other cases, a social worker may need to draw attention to hostile feelings against himself or his department, so these may be directly expressed, and do not distort family relationships by emerging in other more destructive ways.

All these different kinds of courage, and the skills to translate them into effective relationships, will be unevenly distributed in any groups of social-work students, and few will start with all of them. The task of a training course, therefore, is to set up the kinds of experiences in which they can recognize their strengths and weaknesses, and can learn from others. Much of this learning is done on practical-work placements, and good supervision in residential and field work is perhaps the most important factor in this part of training. However, there is also great potential for learning from each other in small groups, and social-work classes may be quite an effective means of doing this, particularly if they can manage to recreate the realities of stress and panic.

It seems possible to suggest a number of stages of learning about how to work with family violence which should occur either in supervised practical work or in the academic part of a social-work course. We doubt whether there is a simple very structured way in which these can be taught or a very tidy division between theory and practice. Rather, these stages are meant to represent an analysis of a complex process of learning which may take place slowly, and develop from theory to practice, or which may stem from certain key experiences on placement, and then be consolidated by reflection and discussion. As a general point, it seems to us that learning on social-work courses is a subtle and many-stranded business, so that a course which imagines it can construct a logical sequence which teaches all its students similar lessons on the same occasions is probably misunderstanding the process. Students appear to us to borrow and adapt ideas, methods, and even aspects of the personalities of other students, staff, and supervisors in ways which do not neatly conform to the logistics of curriculum planning and development. We believe they should be left fairly free to use experiences and classes in their own way, rather than be always presented with logical conclusions and the moral to every social-work tale.

Perhaps the first important stage is the recognition that most social work does involve a certain amount of work with situations which are violent, and that some of these may require that the social worker acts firmly and authoritatively. Social workers' duties do include the use of compulsion to control some individuals, or to rescue others. A clear and honest recognition of this fact and—most vital—the will to communicate it to clients is one important ability for social workers to learn. Without it, clients will feel at the mercy of totally capricious workers with unspecified powers, thinly cloaked by a desire to 'help'—a poor basis for any trust or constructive work. Yet if students are primarily motivated by a desire to help people, or to understand them better, they may find this recognition painful, and may need quite a lot of encouragement to discover ways of acting effectively in such situations. It is hard at first to see that it is not always helpful to families to be a kind, understanding, smiling person ; that in the face of many grim events the only appropriate response is direct and decisive action which, although it is never as simple and clear-cut as a police intervention, nevertheless may temporarily require similar firmness and authority. The importance of neither dodging nor fudging these tasks is something which should surely be conveyed to students at an early stage, either on placements or in the classroom.

A second stage involves the acknowledgement of fear. Violence and the threat of it are frightening and the student needs to learn that his fear is perfectly normal and acceptable. Often students feel that as social workers they should react to abnormal and alarming situations with an equally unnatural calmness. They are disturbed or embarrassed by their real reactions, and try to suppress them, and cultivate a new 'professional' response. We have suggested earlier in this chapter that both suppressing and projecting an inner panic are dangerous reactions by social workers in the face of violence. An open acknowledgement of fear is much healthier and more potentially constructive.

The third stage, therefore, is the development of courage and skill once fear has been acknowledged. There are many ways in which social workers can learn to deal better with situations which initially frighten or immobilize them. Good supervision is particularly helpful in identifying the fantasy elements in reactions to this sort of stress. A supervisor can provide the security in which the student can examine and rehearse difficult interviews, and can test out his fears against the background of his supervisor's experience. A good supervisor will be able to make the student feel that his panic is both understandable and acceptable, and yet hold him to the task of going on facing what frightens him, and of learning more realistic and effective reactions. He will also be able to help the student identify the particular cues which spark off his panic and to analyse ways in which his fantasies are fed by denied feelings from members of the family.

But students can also learn a good deal from each other in groups by discussing cases which raise this issue. Simply hearing a colleague tell of a brave or skilful piece of work can be both inspiring and instructive. Where role-play is used in groups, students can actually model their reactions on those they observe to be appropriate and effective. A current student recently told one of the authors that during a hostile and potentially violent interview with a family on a placement he found himself using words very similar to the ones he had heard in a role-play of a family interview, and that this enabled him to deal with what would otherwise have been a very uncomfortable moment.

Students can also learn, once they acknowledge fear, that there are sometimes very practical ways of reducing it. Joint visits with colleagues are often very reassuring, and even the presence of a colleague in a car outside can allay a terror of violence. Where a physical fight is realistically expected, a request for a policeman or (in a mental-health case) ambulance men to accompany on a visit is good sense and often in the family's interests. A good deal can be learnt by observing these other services dealing with violence. One ex-student said that it was not until she saw how ambulance men dealt with the mentally ill that it really came home to her how much violence springs from fear, and how much it can be minimized by reducing fear, for instance by cuddling a potentially violent person.

But however much learning takes place on a course, it can only be a beginning. The skills and confidence to deal effectively with family violence—indeed, all kinds of social-work skills—need reinforcement and development in the setting in which the new social worker is employed. Individual ability and courage is unlikely to be effective, unless the agency itself has a kind of corporate wisdom and strength to enhance rather than stifle those qualities, which means creating an atmosphere in which uncertainties and vulnerabilities can be shared and mistakes admitted. Thus, the organizational context can help or hinder good social-work practice and we suspect that this is particularly true where extreme and distressing situations are being encountered.

There is probably no blue-print for an 'ideal' social-work organization, just as there is none for an 'ideal' training course, but from our experience the following seem vital elements. First, a team of colleagues who will offer each other tough and honest criticism, within a framework of moral and even physical support. (In frightening situations, two heads and hearts are sometimes better than one.) In an ideal world this means working groups, sufficiently small and stable to build up trust and cohesiveness—a continuation, perhaps, of the kind of experience some students are able to have on their courses.

A second indispensable ingredient, again hopefully carried over from experience in training, is regular and challenging supervision that deals with more than administrative procedures, in the ways we have already described. One ex-student told us of an incident which illustrated both the value of colleagues' support and the potentially disabling effect of bad supervision. He had been threatened by the mother of a runaway teenage girl that if he came to return the girl home the father would be violent. He had been having joint interviews with the family and had been trying to improve communications between father and daughter, and was very reluctant to back down in face of the threat but also frightened by it. He talked with his fellow social workers, who were realistic and helpful, and encouraged him to persist with a planned visit that evening, and offered to accompany him. His senior, having overheard some of this, intervened and suggested that he should not go, and that 'it would not be a cop out' if he postponed the visit. The choice of words confirmed his feelings precisely that it *would* be a 'cop out', yet the unhelpful 'advice' increased his anxiety. He had been offered an unacceptable escape, and felt all the more frightened and alone in consequence. In fact, he made the visit, which was angry but not violent, and which ended constructively, and later was able to point out to his senior just how potentially damaging this comment had been.

A third element in an organization which facilitates good social work would seem to be a clear and predictable definition of roles and responsibilities and a shared understanding of where the social workers' area of discretion begins and ends. Where workers are uncertain of their powers and their limits, and where tasks and decisions may be taken out of their hands at a moment's notice by their superiors, confidence, competence, and even a sense of responsibility are undermined. This kind of unpredictability, which seems not uncommon in some social services departments, creates mistrust and anxiety, rather than allaying it, and may actually contribute to bad practice. It seems obvious to us that this is a pattern which gets passed on to the clients who, like the social workers, feel powerless, inept, and resentful.

A final feature of agencies which enable social workers to do their best work is easier to recognize than to define. It is perhaps best described as sensitivity built on soundness (an organizational complement to the 'hard at the centre, but soft round the edges' quality of the individual social worker?). The whole organization has to be alert to messages of distress and alarm, reacting promptly and sensitively yet not so anxiously and precipitately as to be pushed hither and thither by outside pressures, against its own better judgement. It is in the nature of violence that it creates panic—in agencies, as in individuals—and that quarrels and misunderstandings can flare between those who intervene. In this atmosphere, where 'something must be done'—very frequently by a social worker—an organization strong enough to steer him between the Scylla of clumsy over-activity and the Charybdis of prevarication and passivity is vital. Part of this is the recognition that there are many situations in which social work cannot help, and may hinder, and that it is better to state this clearly to anxious referral agents, rather than to appease them by becoming half-involved with families where other action or no action would be more appropriate.

All this demands a high level of stability and sophistication from any organization, and it is hardly surprising that social services departments sometimes seem to fall far short of the ideal. There is the evidence from the several reported cases in which, in spite of long-term social work involvement, not enough was done to prevent the death of children. The Colwell (DHSS, 1974), Meurs (Norfolk County Council, 1975), and Auckland (DHSS, 1975) reports (cases of children who died as a result of parental violence or neglect) all give examples of bad communications and misperceptions of situations by social workers. We are inclined to believe that because of the very disturbing nature of cruelty to children the combination of a highly-tuned receptivity with organizational steadiness, which we have tried to describe, is specially important. Harassed, anxious departments will not make it easy or sometimes even possible for social workers to record, reflect upon, or make clear decisions about often conflicting evidence of emotionally-charged material. One reaction which was characteristic of these notorious cases was for the social worker, while being anxious about possible dangers, none-the less to evade or fail to notice certain key signs of a very serious situation developing. We have suggested that these under-reactions are often the consequence of unacknowledged fears, which might have emerged and been resolved, given a satisfactory ethos for discussion and supervision.

However, the same anxious and tense atmosphere in social services departments can exaggerate the opposite response to violence—that of over-reaction and an excessive use of official intervention and compulsion. Skinner and Castle have pointed out that anxious but unfocused supervision of families thought to be 'at risk' may actually increase the danger of violence (Skinner and Castle, 1969). In the present climate a wide range of family referrals may be exaggeratedly interpreted as complaints of wife battering or of child abuse. Another ex-student told of a place-of-safety order, taken on a child whose father was reputed to have 'smashed his cot' in a rage. The cot was never seen until long after the event, and proved to have one bar broken. Nor was there any clear evidence that the child had been in it at the time. The case was treated as a 'child at risk' rather than a marital problem; subsequent events suggested that if the couple had been helped with their relationship, removal of the child would not have been necessary. A newly-founded Family Rights Group, based on a Neighbourhood Law Centre in London, has uncovered a number of cases in which departments have taken arbitrary action on insufficient evidence. The group are pressing for the creation of an independent social-work service to safeguard clients' rights in such cases—a vote of no confidence in the statutory social workers.

High-handedness also seems to have emerged in the management styles of some departments. Threats to and coercion of staff are not uncommon. The department which forbids all meetings of social workers unless a senior is present, and another which suspended an area manager for complaining about standards to someone outside the organization, are two examples. It is a style which seems peculiarly incongruous in agencies supposedly based on values of compassion and concern, and it is easy to imagine how this sort of attitude could percolate through to clients and be experienced as very unhelpful. Social workers, in their turn, reacting perhaps in part to this style of leadership, and in part to the panic their violent families create, may themselves do violence of a more far-reaching kind. Increased reliance on court orders giving them extensive powers, is one trend. Another is mounting pressure (supported by many social workers) for more closed and secure residential units for training delinquent adolescents against a background of more children under 17 detained in prisons (on 'unruly certificates') than at any time since 1908.

Reasons for these different kinds of failure are numerous and can only be suggested, not explored, here. Some obvious ones are the continuing effects of massive reorganization; people in management lacking the training or skills for the job; a high proportion of untrained staff, leading to anxious control; failure of training courses to prepare people adequately; unrealistic public expectations of infallibility, and consequent outcry when mistakes are made; policies which have increased departmental responsibilities without providing the resources to match. Less obvious, perhaps, but no less powerful are the effects of working with violence itself—the fears and panics it creates, that can pervade whole organizations from top to bottom, creating vicious circles that are hard to break.

At present, social policy sanctions social-work interventions in many family situations, and social workers' powers are both wide and vague. With social services departments' present defensiveness and lack of confidence, powers which were assumed to increase the possibility of supporting disadvantaged and disturbed families, and preventing their break-up, can instead be used destructively or disrespectfully. Given an atmosphere of fear and tension, social services departments can come to see the threat of violence in families as a pretext for more authoritarian interventions and more anxious controls. Based originally on panic, this reaction can lead to a peculiar sort of despotism, which might be likened to the tyranny of white mice. We have suggested that if social work has something of a 'blind spot' in relation to violence, this might be tackled first as a problem about professional competence in the face of physical threat. However, until social services departments can create an ethos in which both fear and aggression can be recognized for what they are, and dealt with realistically, even the best social workers may be hindered from doing effective work with family violence.

REFERENCES

DHSS (Department of Health and Social Security) (1974) *Report of the Committee of Inquiry into the Care and Supervision Provided in Relation to Maria Colwell*, HMSO.

DHSS (Department of Health and Social Security) (1975) *Report of the Committee of Inquiry into the Provision and Co-ordination of Services to the Family of John George Auckland*, HMSO.

Norfolk County Council (1975) 'Report of the Review Body appointed to enquire into the case of Stephen Meurs', Norfolk County Council.

Skinner, A. E., and Castle, R. L. (1969) *78 Battered Children: a Retrospective Study*, NSPCC.

15

SOME REFLECTIONS ON VIOLENCE AND THE FAMILY

J. P. Martin

This book has examined family violence from a variety of perspectives. Some contributors have been concerned to describe and analyse the forms it takes, while others have considered practical issues of policy, social action, and the training of social workers. Each chapter exists in its own right as a self-contained entity, and conclusions or detailed recommendations will be found there. Taken together, however, a number of themes emerge which are referred to by several authors, or which appear likely to deserve thought in the future. These last few pages, therefore, contain reflections on some, but by no means all, significant topics likely to underly or recur in discussions of the subject.

THE LEGITIMACY OF FORCE IN FAMILY RELATIONSHIPS

The element of power in human relationships is more pervasive in family life than is often recognized. Family members always stand in relationships of power towards each other; the power may be that of adults over children, income earners over those who do not earn, the healthy over the sick and aged, some have legal authority over others. These imbalances are unavoidable, and they are usually counterbalanced by the ties of affection and a common need for the maintenance of a tolerable family life. There is, however, always the possibility that the expectations of the more powerful members may in some way not be satisfied, and one or more may then resort to force in order to get the desired response. The force may take many forms—verbal assault, ostracism, constraint, and physical force. All of these can be subsumed rather loosely under the term 'violence', although its impact and after-effects will vary immensely. The damaging possibilities of violence in the family immediately raise the question of how it is to be regulated.

In considering this question we shall primarily draw on the lessons to be learned from the contributions to this book, rather than attempt an original philosophical and sociological discussion. The regulation of the use of force in family relations depends on two things: first, a statement of principle on what the socially acceptable limits should be; second, some machinery for ensuring that the force actually used is kept within the socially agreed limits.

It is abundantly clear from even the modest amount of comparative and historical material in this book, that the legitimacy of using force in family life is socially determined. This is not just a matter of law, but of social custom. Margaret May's account of violence in the family in nineteenth-century England chronicles changes in both custom and law. She shows how in the eighteenth century 'though the law safeguarded the wife against serious injury the husband might still beat her "for lawful correction" and "to order and rule" ', but after long political struggles the legal position was substantially altered in principle by the Matrimonial Causes Acts which made it possible to grant a judicial separation on grounds of cruelty. Similarly the upbringing of children was the subject of a long campaign both to alter the law and, by persuasion, to influence standards of child care.

At first sight the customs of rural communities in the Latin Mediterranean countries may seem far removed from contemporary life in North America and the countries of Northern Europe, but they are important both because they show how localized social standards may be and because immigrants from these countries have tended to preserve their standards for quite long periods. Britain, too, has had similar experiences of groups maintaining their original cultures and, in the process, creating problems for social workers and law enforcement where there is some hesitation in imposing national standards on close-knit communities. As Banton (1970) has put it,

> In Britain ... problems could arise with respect to Asian communities. If the police were to leave Pakistanis in Bradford to enforce their own laws within their own community Pakistani girls and women might be denied the rights which they have as persons living within the Crown's jurisdiction. Most people in this country would object to some applications of this principle.

Peter Loizos in his chapter indicates how the 'liberal, egalitarian, and reforming assumptions' of many Western societies are turned on their heads in those Mediterranean communities where 'violence between family members may, in local thinking, be necessary and proper to preserve the future integrity of the family itself'. A study of 'honour' crimes in Greece between 1960 and 1963 concluded that

> Male members of the family ... must defend their honour and the family honour in an aggressive, violent manner by assaulting or killing the dishonoured woman and/or those responsible for the dishonour ... killing in defence of family honour was ... a socially expected and approved behaviour. (Safilios-Rothschild, 1969, p.206).

These are not merely picturesque examples of strange customs in distant lands, they take us to the heart of the problem of limiting what elsewhere is seen to be undesirable and even outrageous behaviour. It is that, in the last resort, what matters most is not the individual pathology of violent people—there will always be some deviants from any set of social standards—but the prevailing ethic which, in turn, is linked to the social and economic institutions of a society. The Mediterranean women described by Loizos tend to be valued as symbols of male power, rather than for their own worth. The precise basis of the honour code is open to argument, but to a large extent it seems to result from conditions of economic and social insecurity so acute as to make the family the main source of security. When this is seen to be the case, the task of protection is seen as a masculine activity and its imperative nature justifies the predominant position of men under such conditions.

The Mediterranean case does not, of course, prove that women are more likely to be subordinated in societies where the degree of individual security is low, although to some degree this seems important. More fundamental are the possibilities of economic independence which, in turn, depend on a relatively open job market and a social system which legally and administratively allows for the independent existence of women. Without some such legal and welfare support women, as several contributors have shown, may be trapped into enduring subordination and sometimes violence. This support, furthermore, cannot be merely formal; the staff of public agencies have considerable power to neutralize official policies which are not in fairly close accord with popular sentiment as they see it. Hence the stress in my earlier chapter on the need for the battering of women to be taken seriously, as cause for concern rather than the topic of callous male jokes.

The other main conclusion to be drawn from the comparative and historical material is that there seems to be a fairly close correlation between the level of violence in society as a whole, and that occurring in the family situation. Writing of violence which reached the courts, McClintock concluded that in London, over a 13-year period, 'the increase in domestic disputes resulting in criminal violence follows the general pattern of other forms of criminal violence'. This is not, however, to argue a causal connection between the two; both may be related to other factors, one at least of which might be an increasing sensitivity to violence itself and consequently a greater willingness to complain and report it.

Within a society national standards of behaviour, even within the family, have legal backing in that the criminal law could be applied to many situations of violence, while divorce laws cover a wider range of behaviour. In practice, however, as I have stressed in chapter 9, there are many difficulties facing those who wish to invoke the law. Various measures can be taken to make access to the law easier, and these are discussed both later in this chapter and in chapter 9, but something more fundamental is needed because of the limitations of using the law as a spearhead of social change.

If society's standards are to be altered this is likely to come about from a mixture of direct attack on the prevailing ethic and of economic development. It is not always a matter of ideals being wrong—the principle of loving and cherishing a marriage partner does not easily justify the infliction of harm—but of gaining their genuine acceptance. It may well be a by-product of the concerns about 'battered wives' that the larger issue of the proper nature of marital relationships will be debated and fairer standards affirmed. It seems undesirable that the basic rationalization of much family violence, particularly between spouses, is that wives and children are in a sense a man's property. This can be partially undermined by economic development if it gives women a chance of independence, or at least of gaining their husbands' respect as explicit contributors to the family income. On the other hand, as Richard Gelles has pointed out, this can lead to danger in a traditionally male-dominated society where 'violence is common between husband and wife when men cannot hold down the dominant position that they see society mandating for them'.

In the long run there is probably no substitute for questioning the credibility of the notion of male superiority—now, thanks to the example of innumerable successful women, less thankless a task than that which confronted John Stuart Mill when, as Margaret May describes, in 1867 he initiated a parliamentary debate on female suffrage using 'the battered wife as a central theme of female emancipation'. In most Western countries the political battle has long been won. Women have risen to the top of almost every profession thus fatally undermining the simple notion of inherent male superiority.

The superiority of adults over children is, however, another matter. In all societies it is considered an adult duty to socialize the young, inculcating the standards appropriate for their society, and part at least of this task is usually a parental responsibility. It is probably undertaken with less brutality than in the past, but in the United States and many Western European countries physical punishment is recognized as legitimate—sometimes only as a last resort, but sometimes used much earlier. The problem then is where legitimate force ends and brutality and cruelty begin. Once again, custom plays a large part; the only experience of child upbringing that young parents have had may well have been their own childhood; Letitia Allan for example quotes a parent as saying

> It may seem cruel to you, but as children this is the type of punishment we received, my wife and I, and we were just using the same type of punishment.

Faced with the immense range of what can be regarded as normal there is clearly no absolute standard. There are, however, good grounds for aiming for the lowest possible amount of physical punishment, first, because there is always the danger that punishment will go too far and kill or permanently injure the victim; and, second, experience of violence is likely to make people more callous than they would otherwise have been and, in consequence, the level of violence in society itself might be maintained or even rise. This is not to say that all child abuse is due to legitimate punishment getting out of hand, but undoubtedly the belief that physical methods are justified can be a contributory factor. Margaret May's account of the discussions of how best to punish children, the subject of widespread and detailed attention in 'family magazines in the 1860s and 1870s', suggest what we would surely regard as unhealthily sadistic pleasure for adults and, no doubt, childish suffering disproportionate to the offences for which it was inflicted.

The conclusion about the legitimacy of force in family relationships that would seem to be most justified is that to a very large extent standards are socially determined, and vary from country to country and period to period. They appear to be correlated with the level of violence in society as a whole. As violence implies suffering and harm to individuals, and may also corrupt those who inflict it, every effort should be made to minimize it. Comparative studies show that what is taken for granted in one society may be seen as a local convention, and we should surely aim for the lowest levels that it is possible to attain even if this entails dispensing with hallowed traditions.

PERSONAL FACTORS

The family violence, about which there is so much concern in Britain, the United States, and other countries at the moment, consists of physical assaults on individuals, often accompanied by psychological 'battering' as well. Somewhat apart from this is a different concept, discussed by Dennis Marsden in his chapter, of what is sometimes rather unfortunately called 'structural violence'. This is used particularly to describe the disadvantages facing women (and sometimes children) in their traditional status in the economy and society. It is mainly a matter of inferior status and as such may be seen to entitle men to inflict physical violence, as in the Mediterranean societies described by Loizos, but more direct influences are needed to explain how violence is actually precipitated. For this we have to turn to the more psychological explanations, given in this book by Dr Gayford, Letitia Allan, and Jacquie Roberts.

Several threads run through their accounts. Of these perhaps the most fundamental is the underlying weakness of the violent person. He may feel frustrated and unable to get a desired response from woman or child, stressed, angry at what he cannot control or, deep down, so humiliated by his own position in life that he can only assert himself by abusing those dependent on him. In its extreme form this inadequacy may develop into the paranoid jealousy described by Dr Gayford which may take the form of a long-term, relentless persecution of the victim sometimes ending in her death. Even in more violent societies the weakness of the persistent wife beater is recognized as Loizos has pointed out.

Second, people are not just violent, but violent in particular circumstances, which suggests they are avoiding social controls which they know to exist. Violence occurs above all in private; it may be heard, but is much less frequently seen. Child abusers are particularly anxious to conceal what they have done, and are clearly aware of the norms they have transgressed (even if they also construct rationalizations). Joy Melville and Dennis Marsden both describe the 'Jekyll and Hyde' behaviour of some wife batterers—charming in public and vicious in private—frequently aided and abetted by their victims who feel shamed by what has happened to them, and sometimes ignorant of its abnormal nature.

Third, many violent couples appear to have rushed into marriage with unrealistic expectations of what it will do to solve their personal problems. Some women even have married in spite of having experienced violence from their future husbands. Frequently they have become pregnant and not realized that having a baby creates more problems and stress than it solves. In their anxieties they may become increasingly isolated and suspicious of outsiders, thus increasing their own stresses. To a degree at least they are victims of their own upbringings and of the myth of contented and easy family life so sedulously promoted in romantic fiction.

Fourth, as Dr Gayford has pointed out, violence in marriage is often effective, for a time at least. If the wife puts up with it on more than one occasion there is the situation described by Richard Gelles where 'in most instances marriage licences are viewed as hitting licences'. Only when she both feels she has had enough *and* has somewhere else to go to can she leave; it seems this stage often takes a long while to reach, due mostly to the disadvantages faced by women with children who have to cope on their own.

Finally, many accounts mention the disinhibiting effects of alcohol. It is not a universal influence, but it does seem on many occasions to be a factor which enables latent violence to be expressed.

LIMITING FAMILY VIOLENCE

It should not be thought that family violence can be eliminated. However, it can be limited, and clearly has been in Britain over the past century. This has been the product of a series of social developments—a general improvement in the standard of living, the emancipation of women, particularly their increasingly important role in the economy, new ideas of child care, and a host of legislative and administrative measures designed to improve the position of women and children.

In spite of these improvements there is much concern about both marital violence and child abuse today. Dennis Marsden has described this as an example of what Cohen has called a 'moral panic'. By this is meant a sudden up-surge of public attention towards a phenomenon that had previously attracted little or even no attention. The existence of the mass media has made it possible to concentrate public attention to a degree out of all proportion to any changes that might have taken place in the frequency or nature of the behaviour itself. Clearly family violence was the subject of similar attention intermittently during the nineteenth century and subsequently. Set against a probable decline in the amount of violence, the present concern indicates, if anything, a more sensitive and civilized attitude to the sufferings of some of the weaker members of our society. To describe this as a moral panic is unhappily pejorative, but the usage of the term is undoubtedly consistent with its earlier definition.

So far as battered women are concerned the present interest stems from the specific and highly-publicized development of refuges which introduced a genuinely new possibility into the situation, thus justifying new attention, and from the groundswell of the women's movement which was tackling the fundamental disadvantages facing women in our society. These developments have in turn led to new legislation and an increasingly positive attitude on the part of the judiciary culminating, at the time of writing in the summer of 1977, in the surprising appearance before a London divorce court judge of the Commissioner of the Metropolitan Police who had been required to attend in order to explain why officers in one of his divisions had failed to protect a wife by not executing a warrant for the arrest of her former husband alleged to be molesting her (*The Times*, 4 June 1977). Such an appearance by the Commissioner being unprecedented, the whole incident is likely to have been of considerable symbolic importance, and few of his officers can now be in doubt that such matters are to be taken seriously (in contrast to the passive attitude previously prevailing in some areas and described in chapter 9 of this book).

Although the problem of battered women has only been brought back to public attention within the last 5 years or so the developments, thanks to the publicity and the pressure exerted by the House of Commons Select Committee on Violence in Marriage, have been very rapid in terms of the normal time scale of British social policy. The problems have not by any means been solved, but this issue has been made public in a way that may allow it to be used, as it was by John Stuart Mill in the nineteenth century, to further a broader cause. Mill was concerned with getting women the vote, which took half a century; today's campaigners can use it to tackle the myriad inequalities and discriminations which frustrate so many women from developing their abilities to the full.

While the position of women may well be transformed over the next few decades, children will always be vulnerable and dependent on adult care. Some will always be abused for, as Jacquie Roberts stresses, 'anyone has the potential to harm their child'. Recognizing the problems and strains of child care, particularly for young, inexperienced, and isolated mothers, the most appropriate thought must be 'there but for the grace of God go I'.

Most people, however, manage not to abuse their children, usually because they receive support from friends and relatives and manage to avoid the isolation that is such a common factor in cases of abuse. For the isolated and those in difficulty a fairly elaborate network of services has been organized, following the celebrated cases of child deaths in the early 1970s (see chapter 9). They attempt to co-ordinate a variety of professional workers in supporting parents thought to be 'at risk' of injuring their children. These arrangements are discussed at some length in chapter 9. Here it is important to make three points. First, that these arrangements depend for their effectiveness on establishing genuine, rather than merely formal, co-operation between the professionals concerned. This is obvious in theory but difficult in practice because of the rather narrow specialisms in which each has been trained. Effective co-operation depends on each realizing the limitations of his or her own professional skills, and deducing that one of the most important should be the capacity to work with others.

Second, much effort has been put into devising administrative procedures to prevent serious abuse from occurring. On paper much of it looks sensible but there is also a danger that it will lead to an excessively defensive attitude on the part of the bureaucracies concerned. Given high-calibre leadership there is no reason why this should happen, but without it the services might experience the unhappy restrictiveness so vividly described by Jordan and Packman as the 'tyranny of white mice'.

In the last resort, to intervene in situations of family violence demands a significant degree of moral courage, and the difficulties of locating and strengthening this are sensitively explored by Jordan and Packman. They come to the heart of one of the problems created by the 'moral panic' about child abuse. Although their words refer specifically to social workers, they should be read as applying to all who work in such situations. They should have the last word—'until social services departments can create an ethos in which both fear and aggression can be recognized for what they are, and dealt with realistically, even the best social workers may be hindered from doing effective work with family violence'.

REFERENCES

Banton, Michael (1970) 'Social order and the police', *Advancement of Science*, **27**.

Safilios-Rothschild, Constantina (1969) ' "Honour" crimes in contemporary Greece', *British Journal of Sociology*, xx, 205–218.

INDEX

S. MARTIN'S COLLEGE OF EDUCATION
LANCASTER